Anxious Nation

David Walker grew up in South Australia and graduated from Adelaide University. After gaining his doctorate in history from the Australian National University in Canberra he taught at Auckland University and the University of New South Wales. He is currently Professor of Australian Studies at Deakin University. In 1997-98 he held the Monash Chair of Australian Studies at Georgetown University, Washington, DC. He has extensive experience in the development of Australian Studies programs in Indonesia, PR China and Japan. David Walker has published widely on Australian social and cultural history and edits the journal, *Australian Cultural History*. He is currently researching a further volume on Australian perceptions of Asia for the period 1939 to 1972, provisionally titled, 'Great Neighbours'.

Anxious Nation

Australia and the Rise of Asia 1850-1939

David Walker

University of Queensland Press

First published in 1999 by the University of Queensland Press
Box 42, St Lucia, Queensland 4067, in association with the Australian Studies
Centre, the University of Queensland, and the *Journal of Australian Studies*.

Series Editor: Richard Nile
Typeset and Production: Jason Ensor
Production Crew: Ben Goldsmith, Kerry Kilner, Sandra Brunet,
Michael Peterson, Elizabeth Mitchell, Maele Charlot
Cover: Indonesian mask photographed by Karen Walker

Cataloguing-in-Publication Data
National Library of Australia

Walker, David Robert, 1945–
Anxious Nation: Australia and the Rise of Asia, 1850–1939

Bibliography
Includes index

1. Asians – Australia. 2. Multiculturalism – Australia
3. Pluralism (Social sciences) – Australia
4. Australia – Emigration and immigration
I. Title

305.895094
ISBN 0 7022 3131 2

For my daughters, Zara and Veronica
and my father, Gilbert

Contents

List of Plates, Figures and Tables

Acknowledgements

It has been my good fortune to work with colleagues in the School of Australian and International Studies at Deakin University for whom Australia's relationship with the Asia-Pacific region is a question of major interest. Among my Deakin colleagues in and beyond the School, I thank Joan Beaumont, Allan Johnston, Gordon Forth, Gary Smith, Struan Jacobs, Li Veit Brause, Ed Brumby, David Lowe, Mohan Malik and Ian Weeks for their encouragement and advice. Donna Edwards did clever things to enhance some faded illustrations. Ann Chandler has provided indispensable support in the Centre for Australian Studies. Study leave from Deakin University in 1996 allowed me to begin some uninterrupted writing.

Bruce Clunies Ross, University of Copenhagen, and Angela Smith, Stirling University, concentrated my mind on some of the themes of the book with invitations to address the European Association for Studies on Australia in Copenhagen in 1995 and the British Australian Studies Association in Stirling in 1996. These occasions gave me valuable feedback, particularly from Ruth Brown and Tom Griffiths.

It was a pleasure to work with Ros Pesman and Richard White from Sydney University, ideal collaborators in an ARC funded study which resulted in the *Oxford Book of Australian Travel Writing* and, with Terri McCormack, *An Annotated Bibliography of Australian Overseas Travel Writing*. Both projects added considerably to my knowledge of Australian travellers to Asia.

My interest in Australia's interactions with Asia has been quickened by discussions with colleagues in Indonesia, PR China and Japan. I would like to thank Wardiningsih Soerjohardjo, Reni Winata and Zamira Loebis at Universitas Indonesia for their insights into the workings of Indonesian society. In China, I have always been made to feel at home by the staff of Yangzhou University and by members of the Jiangsu Australian Studies Consortium. In particular I thank Chen Qinglin and Qian Fengqi, now doctoral students at Deakin University, for helping to reveal China to me. Both are valued friends. In Japan, I have benefited from Deakin University's strong ties with Shiga University, particularly in Australian Studies. Hajime Hirai is a mainstay of the program and a good friend and colleague. I would also like to thank Yasue Arimitsu, Doshisha University, Kyoto; Kazue Nakamura, Tezukayama Gakuin University, Osaka; and Michael Jacques, Sophia University, Tokyo, for inviting me to discuss the Australia-Japan relationship with their students.

I am grateful to Monash University for the opportunity to spend a year in the Monash Chair of Australian Studies at Georgetown University, Washington, DC in 1997-1998. In the planning stages and throughout the year I spent there, John Noonan from Monash University was enormously supportive. At the Center for Australian and New Zealand Studies at Georgetown University, Kathy

Burns became a good friend and knowledgable guide to Washington. I owe John Noonan and Kathy Burns debts that are hard to repay. Father Jeff von Arx also smoothed my path as I settled into this impressive institution.

While at Georgetown University I offered a new course on Australian Perceptions of Asia. The students of 303-01, bless them, kept me on my toes and helped me think my way through some of the major themes of the book. In Washington, the Library of Congress with its inspiring Jefferson Reading Room, provided resources and surroundings that could hardly be improved upon. Patricia McCloskey provided skilled research assistance both in the Library of Congress and in the labyrinthine National Archives at College Park, Maryland.

Through the years, my colleagues Stephen Garton and Julia Horne have been the best of friends whose knowledge of Australian history and encouragement have been invaluable. It was a particular pleasure to catch up with them in Oakton, North Virginia, where they were unable to escape a full review of the work in progress. Another great friend and Oakton visitor, David Reeve, made incisive comments on early drafts and maintained a close interest in the progress of the manuscript.

In their various ways John Legge, Graeme and Renate Osborne, Hank Nelson, Ian Bickerton, Nan Albinski, Rodney Mace, Jeanette Hoorn, Richard Nile, David Goodman, Selina Samuels, Miwako Nakamura and Richard Chauvel have clarified my thinking and pointed out useful sources. Wayne Hudson persuaded me to write a chapter for *Creating Australia* which helped provide a framework for the Introduction to this book. Graeme Powell, Manuscripts Librarian at the National Library of Australia and Jim Andrighetti at the Mitchell Library in Sydney were both generous with their time and alerted me to important manuscript holdings.

Juliet Peers has been an astute commentator on this venture whose impressive knowledge of Australian art history has been consistently thought-provoking.

The major research assistant role fell to Genevieve Burnett in Sydney. The book could not have been completed without her. She brought judgement and intelligence of a high order to the many research queries that rained in upon her. I could not have asked for more.

I owe a particular debt to Father John Eddy who did so much to make my Georgetown year a rewarding one. Despite the many calls upon his time as Director of the Center for Australian and New Zealand Studies in the 1998 Spring semester, he read and commented upon the draft manuscript. I was moved by his generosity and benefited from his knowledge and editorial experience.

I was also very fortunate to have Hazel Rowley scrutinise the manuscript. Her editorial suggestions sharpened the prose and clarified the argument. I thank her for the time, intelligence and good humour she brought to the task.

In writing the final drafts of this book, I incurred immense debts to my wife Karen. She commented on every chapter, made valuable suggestions about the structure of the book and helped bring order to the feral footnote. Her incisive comments, practical help, encouragement and companionship were vital.

My daughters Zara and Veronica were patient and civilised throughout this endeavour. Their good humour was a real comfort to me and a great reminder of the world beyond the eternal computer screen. Though I'm sure he was prepared to wait longer, my father was pleased to learn that the book was completed in his ninetieth year.

Finally, through rain and shine, Mrs T Barker and her son, Mr E L F Barker, listened attentively to the various arguments presented to them.

David Walker
Centre for Australian Studies
Deakin University
August 1998

Chapter One

Introduction

One of the remarkable features of Australian history is the periodic rediscovery of our proximity to Asia. It would be possible to chart this phenomenon from the beginnings of European settlement, but this book begins its examination of the rise of Asia from the 1850s when a series of dramatic changes brought Asian nations into greater world prominence. Firstly, in 1857-1858, the assured governance of the British in India was profoundly shaken by the Sepoy Uprisings, a series of events then known as the Indian Mutiny. The violent suppression of the Mutiny was followed by a new determination to instil imperial certitudes into the young. For many Australians of the time, Cawnpore, Lucknow and the other sites of rebellion, became synonymous with heroic deeds of Empire while tales of British pluck were freely contrasted with warnings of the treachery and ingratitude of the 'natives'. The same episodes furnished Indian nationalists with powerful examples of resistance to British rule. It became a central tenet of the late nineteenth century British imperial world view that India displayed the British character at its best. Any case brought by Indians against the Empire was given short shrift.

In the Australia of the 1870s, when Alfred Deakin (later to become Prime Minister on three occasions) was growing into manhood, it was the mark of an educated person to know something of India. The centrality of religion to nineteenth century thought, the discovery that Aryan civilisation had originated in India and the trials and achievements of the British Raj all lent considerable support to the view that India provided the key to knowledge itself. Deakin confessed that in his youth, India, more than any other country, had stirred his imagination, filling him with visions of a splendid, if decaying Antique world. With the publication of his two books on India in 1893 we can stretch things just a little and call Deakin an Orientalist. For a time, Deakin hoped that proximity to India would bring a deepening intellectual engagement between the two societies even to the point where Australia might be able to claim a special knowledge of India. It seemed possible that one of Australia's missions might be to bring knowledge of the Orient to the West.

Secondly, in the 1850s, large numbers of itinerant workers from China came to Australia seeking their fortune on the goldfields, just as they were doing in California. This influx stirred a growing awareness of mobile, migratory Asia and created a sharper realisation of Australia's proximity to great Pacific neighbours: the Celestial Empire, the ancient kingdom of China, and the rising new world democracy, America. Where the 'natives' of the Mutiny were depicted as a defiant subject race, the Chinese were commonly depicted as the forerunners of a subtle invasion. They were seen as a wily and immensely adaptable people, widely credited with unsurpassed survival skills.

In 1893, the year in which Deakin's *Temple and Tomb* and *Irrigated India* were published, Charles Pearson's *National Life and Character: A Forecast* also appeared. Pearson's book won immense critical acclaim. It is doubtful that any book with an Australian inspiration has ever had a greater impact among intellectuals in Britain or the United States than Pearson's. His arresting predictions drew heavily upon his experience both as a resident of the Australian colonies and as a politician and educationist. His book answered the question of how the future of Europe looked to an erudite Englishman resident in Australia. The chapters that attracted some of the most spirited comment were those warning that the 'lower' would overtake the 'higher' races. Pearson predicted that Europe's dominance was endangered by the rise of Asia. He anticipated the progressive asianisation of Europe.

Pearson shifted the locus of interest from India to China, from the Antique Orient to the geo-politics of race and race migration. Pearson thought China would become the dominant world power and on this question his ideas attracted particular attention. Since overflowing China had already been identified as a threat to Australia's future, Pearson felt able to generalise what he recognised as a powerful modern Australian apprehension about the rise of Asia to the European world itself. Australia appeared to be almost surrounded by Pearson's 'lower' races among whom the struggle for survival was said to have reached its most frighteningly intense form.

The conviction that there was an aggressive Asia, bent on conquest, was a challenge too strong for visions of a golden, aestheticised Orient to withstand. Though it did not disappear, least of all perhaps in advertisements for travel to the East, that kind of Orientalism faded from public life to be replaced by a differently configured world of contending races scrambling for opportunity. This was not the Asia of the great religions, but an Asia bent on improving its place in the world, an Asia resentful of European domination.

Though the future forecast by Pearson was very different from Deakin's, there was a similar belief that the likely global impact of developments in Asia could be more clearly discerned from Australia than from Europe. For good or ill, Australia's future seemed directly bound up with developments in Asia and, this being so, both writers anticipated that knowledge of Asia might well emerge as a requirement for thoughtful Australians.

A third pivotal event occurred in 1853-1854 when the United States, seeking a larger role in the Pacific, sent Commodore Perry to Japan. At the point of a gun, Japan opened itself to trade with the West. As Westerners — Australians among them — pushed into Japan, Japanese prints and traditional craft objects flowed into Europe, creating an infatuation with Japanese aesthetics. A new word, 'Japonisme', was invented to describe the incorporation of Japanese influences into European art. While China seemed a pent up dam of uncontrolled human energy, Japan appeared a more courtly and ritualised society, a nation more like Britain with its rich history, manicured landscapes and carefully maintained architecture of social controls. Where China's power and weakness seemed obvious, the power of Japan appeared to be more enigmatically located within the Japanese people themselves and their intricate and elaborately ritualised culture. Well before she was perceived as a threat by Australians, Japan was thought of as a cultivated and enchanted land.

It was not until the 1890s that Japan's military capacities and territorial ambitions began to induce some anxiety over a looming 'yellow peril'. This proved a potent phrase. The first statesman to have used it in public was Germany's Kaiser Wilhelm, who spoke with the Chinese in mind. His remarkably resilient coinage quickly found its way into most European languages. It serves as a powerful reminder of Pearson's influence that the Kaiser's phrase-making was inspired by his reading of *National Life and Character*.[1] Concern at cultural annihilation, of being flooded by migrating hordes, was an important dimension of the 'yellow peril' fear, but so too was the anxiety at being slowly and more subtly infiltrated from Asia. Asia seemed equally adept at sudden attack and an uncanny watchfulness.

Another common phrase increasingly applied to Asia from around the 1870s was 'the awakening East'. An 'awakened East' suggested a people who had gained a new condition of physical and mental alertness where once they had appeared passive, lost in an ancient, unchanging world. Gender identities were central to these transformations. Since the passive, reclining East was more readily figured as female than male, it followed that in speaking of an 'awakening', the West anticipated the emergence of a newly energised, masculinised East. Where the feminine East suggested a recumbent world of sensual pleasures, the masculine East stirred fears of the terrible energies set free by rampaging hordes. It brought to mind flashing scimitars and great warriors like the merciless Genghis Khan.

Shorthand phrases like the 'awakening East' and the 'yellow peril' were often used to transmit a warning to the West that in Asia a new era was in the making. Race war and the unrelenting battle for territory were the keys to this disturbing world of contending masculinities. Many authors turned their hand to accounts of the coming world order. Their titles were stark: *White or Yellow: the Story of the Race War of AD 1908*; *The Yellow Wave; The Coloured Conquest* or, an American title, *The Rising Tide of Color Against White World Supremacy*.[2] These were anxious male narratives foretelling the end of Europe's dominance and the coming destruction of the 'white world'. In these stories Australia appeared as a vulnerable continent subject either to direct attack from the East or to a more gradual loss of its British heritage at the hands of Asian intruders, a betrayal commonly blamed on Australia's elites, who were accused either of colluding with the Asian enemy or of being duped by him.

This book argues that Australia came to nationhood at a time when the growing power of the East was arousing increasing concern. This in turn came to influence how Australians saw themselves as an outpost of Europe facing Asia. Often at this time it seemed possible that Australia's survival as a nation might be at stake. If the East was awakening, the West was enjoined to be ever more vigilant. To many it seemed that the East could no longer be easily controlled. It could no longer be contained. As 'rising tide' or 'flood' the East threatened to overwhelm boundaries and destroy distinctions. Entire peoples and nations might be submerged. This was a vision of drowned cities, lost kingdoms and defeated races tossed aside by forces too powerful to resist. This was the fear of racial annihilation.

In a debate that continued well into the 1930s, it was widely argued that the claim white Australians made for ownership of their continent was unconvincing. When the best way to demonstrate a competent colonising performance was through population growth, it seemed sadly evident that Australia was nowhere near its supposed carrying capacity. In 1888, the Rev James Jefferis believed that 100 million was only a 'moderate' estimate of the optimal population.[3] Before the first world war, the pugnacious W M Hughes, later Labor Prime Minister, similarly argued that Australia should endeavour to reach a population of at least 100 million by the end of the twentieth century.[4] In 1912, *Australia To-Day*, a strenuously patriotic and handsomely produced journal, its pages graced with beautiful photographs of stately gum trees, published a map of Australia bearing the sign: 'Room for 50,000,000 Energetic White Settlers. The Centre of the World's Coming Markets'. The journal wanted millions of hopeful immigrants to enter Australia in a matter of years.[5] Such projections were not scaled down until the 1920s; even then wildly optimistic forecasts continued to win widespread support. This was the heroic age of 'big country' talk.

After its first century of white settlement Australia held a population of four million people. Not only was this number of white settlers considered indefensibly low but, even worse, these people were congregating in the coastal cities. Cities were frequently blamed for encouraging luxurious, even decadent life-styles and their inhabitants were routinely judged incapable of defending the nation; they were said to lack the virile energy and patriotism of rural folk. In the invasion narratives, it was the bushmen from the rough interior who inevitably formed the core of a guerrilla resistance to Asiatic armies. City people seemed to have lost the will to breed. In another sign that many commentators found disquieting, by the early twentieth century the Australian birth-rate was in decline. Critics complained that 'Young Australia' had become far too contented with the narrowing comforts of the suburban home. The question arose: how could these self-satisfied people hope to hold and develop an entire continent? If

Australians were to be thought of as a vigorous new nation, they needed a more substantial, heroised national portrait. There needed to be fewer signs of comfort, ease and relaxed modernity, less evidence of pipe, slippers and the suburban home and more indications of strenuous endeavour, race pride and willingness to confront and overcome danger. This need increased the cultural pressure to single out and laud the distinctive qualities of the sturdy bushman as race hero.

This book will argue that powerful masculinising and racialising impulse in Australian nationalism would have been a good deal less intense, had it not been for the geo-political threat attributed to awakening Asia from the 1880s. In popular fiction, speculative encounters with an Asian enemy put a premium on bush skills and horsemanship. Asia, when figured as an enemy, helped sharpen the sense of national purpose, provoking an analysis of the skills and capacities that would serve Australia best in the event of race conflict. A fascination with the bush as the breeding ground of a new type is apparent in all the stories of Asian invasion. Even 'Parabellum', a German author with no apparent link to Australia, sang the praises of the sturdy bushman.[6] The invasion narratives also reinforced a litany of complaint about the deficiencies of city populations. By the 1890s, the bushman had acquired a special value as the quintessential Australian. He was increasingly seen as the person best equipped to keep Australia safe from Asia. Grouped at the opposite end of the spectrum, often frustrating the bushman's attempts to warn the nation that it was in danger, was an increasingly predictable list of suspect moderns: feminists, urban dwellers, intellectual males and equivocating politicians. These were people whose 'bush content', according to invasion narratives, was considered dangerously low. It seems obvious that the city should come to mind when we look for the opposite of the bush, but it might be also be instructive to see Parliament and the institutions of government in this role, where Parliament was commonly accused of being only a weak expression of national longings and national fears.

Although Australians optimistically predicted that their country could support a massive future population, commentators remained divided over whether a flourishing white Australia was really possible. One major concern was the long-term effects the Australian climate might have on people of Anglo-Saxon stock. The answer one gave to this question mattered a good deal. If the climate was seen as invigorating then it could be argued that Australia could play a valuable role in restoring enervated Europeans to a state of virile health. Viscount James Bryce willingly indulged this antipodean hope. In the 1920s, he described Australians as 'a virile and high-spirited race, energetic and resourceful' and believed that they would ultimately 'increase and spread out' to fill their vast continent. Judgements of this kind conferred the special status a people small in number required if they were to be noticed and their race potential appreciated. To many Australians, Bryce, in calling them 'an asset precious to the world', had struck exactly the right note. There was a clear message here that the 'higher' races, commonly represented as Nordics through the 1920s, needed more space to develop their distinctive attributes than lesser races among whom crowding was to be expected.[7]

Yet how would matters stand if the Australian climate caused racial deterioration? How could four million heat-impaired Europeans hope to retain a continent so prized and yet so empty? Even worse, how could these climatically maladapted types settle northern Australia whose tropical regions seemed manifestly better suited to Asian populations? In excluding coloured workers, were Australians justified in holding back the development of tropical regions which might contain some of the richest territories in the continent and perhaps the world?

Speculations about what Asian nations would make of Australian opportunities were quite persistent. In 1909, *Australia To-Day* invited the prominent journalist, Alex M Nicol of the *London Daily Chronicle*, to contribute his thoughts on Australia's future.[8] Nicol wrote of a British colleague, possibly an apocryphal figure, who had addressed this exact topic in a recent public lecture in Sydney. This man tells the capacity crowd about a dream in which he sees Australia in the year 1960. It has become a populous continent, dotted with prosperous villages and linked by an extensive railway system. An appreciative murmur runs through the hall. The audience is pleased to hear that the population which has seemed so resolutely urban, so inclined to cling to the south-east corner of the continent, had moved out to develop its hinterland.

The speaker has more to reveal. In his dream he has seen numerous ports crowded with shipping from all quarters of the globe, undeniable evidence that Australia has become a global force in world trade. Prosperous rural industries are supported by the advanced skills and technologies of a sophisticated manufacturing sector. His audience is again delighted. It is a rare pleasure to hear unequivocally good news from such a prominent visitor. Once again, the speaker holds up his hand to quell an excited audience. He has one final revelation: at no point in his dream has he seen a white face. The populous Australia of 1960, with its efficient trains, busy shipping lines and remarkable prosperity, is Asian. The act of transformation has been an entirely Asian accomplishment. At this, his audience explodes with anger, their hopes cruelly betrayed. To the implied question: which race would own Australia, Nicol suggested that a strand of British opinion believed that ownership would pass to Asia. Australia would become Asian.

This story, brief and to the point, gave one account of Australia's Asian future: Australians would fail to develop the continent and it would become an Asian land. It was a generalised threat made to enforce an unmistakable command: develop the continent or surrender it.

Nicol's story provides one example of how 'Asia' could be used as a rhetorical device to force Australians to behave responsibly on matters of population growth. Invidious comparisons were often made between the energetic, land-hungry spirit of Asia and Australia's comfortable suburbanites, apparently unwilling to defend their continent with arms or with ideas. In this context, the invocation of an Asian future required Australians to consider what dispossession might mean. It also encouraged them to reflect upon the qualities of mind and spirit, the nation-building strategies, needed to make Australia a developed and therefore, secure nation.

The idea that Australia might have an Asian future, even to those who considered this highly unpalatable, nevertheless promised exciting copy. The prospect of a disrupted future, of racial conflict and the possible disappearance of a promising young culture provided thrilling narrative possibilities. Narrative loves danger. If British Australia had a tame and rather short past, its location on the edge of Asia seemed to ensure an eventful future. An Asian threat could make Australia appear interestingly vulnerable in much the same way that the maiden in distress was at once a cause for concern and a godsend for fiction. What line would these stories of an endangered people then take? Would Australians join forces to keep Asians out? Who would fight and who would collaborate? Would the end come swiftly or would there be a slow conquest of the continent, with remnant tribes of white settlers heroically holding out against the invaders in a protracted guerrilla action? How would the invaders conduct themselves? What would become of Australian women and children? There were endless possibilities.

By the 1880s it was a commonplace to depict Asia as a world of huge populations 'teeming' with a terrible energy. Asia was a force about to engulf the world's underpopulated zones. Added to these powerful stereotypes was the theme of a malign Oriental intelligence, patiently manoeuvring for advantage. These attributes of formidable Asia were sometimes contradicted by patronising representations of diseased, immoral, superstitious, badly governed or child-like peoples. But from the late nineteenth century, Australians were regularly reminded that the Asia on their doorstep harboured clever, unscrupulous and resourceful opponents; none more so than the brilliant but deadly Dr Fu Manchu.

The fictional Doctor was sent before the reading public for the first time in 1913 and was an immediate publishing success. He represented, not so much the villainous, leering Orient of melodrama, craven, cunning and cowardly at heart, but the new, educated Asia, constantly testing itself against Europe, growing more and more confident of its power. Fu Manchu was no grovelling Oriental, but a profound thinker, deeply learned in Western science. He was a man who never slept, a man who seemed to have cheated death itself. He was a man on a quest: the overthrow of the white world. The Doctor infiltrated Chapter 13 of this book one dark, mist-shrouded morning, enjoying, no doubt, the superstitious dread his presence there would cause.

Imagined encounters with Asia were deeply implicated in the gendering process. Would the female or male principle determine the course of Australian life? While the question would not have been posed in quite such an explicit way, it was often implied in the many battles over the 'new woman' or the relative merits of suburban as against rural masculinity. It was also a familiar literary convention to configure Australia both as 'Woman' and the 'Future'. This is evident in a poem by Roderic Quinn published in 1910. Quinn, a once respected, but now forgotten poet, ponders the grounds on which Australia might be included among the nations of the world. 'She' appears to meet none of the old-world criteria for nationhood, predicated on strong monarchs, ancient conquests and military glory:

> Where came she, the new young nation?
> What title deeds had she
> To a throne-ship with the kinglands?
> What claim to majesty?
> What desperate deathless glories
> Achieved by land and sea?

But Australia has a ready answer for these difficult questions:

> She spoke: "I am the Future,
> The Force, the Power new-born;
> I am the Dream, the Promise,
> The destined Land of Morn,
> The Pilot-Star, the Beacon
> To a world war-scarred and worn".[9]

Australia would act as mother and nurse to a sick world mired in conflict. Australia's justification for nationhood, her 'title deed', rested on the belief that she might show war-torn Europe the path to peace and a hopeful future. But in other writings Quinn expressed his concern that Europe might lose Australia. Australia's 'paramount danger', he wrote in 1907, was 'invasion by an Asiatic force'.[10] He saw Australia standing in the path of a coming conflict between Europe and Asia for world supremacy. 'She' was in imminent danger of becoming a prisoner of Asia's territorial ambitions. In the process, Europe would lose the last great continental space available for race renewal. If Europe surrendered Australia, it would lose, so Quinn argued, one of its major sources of future strength and regeneration.

One further characteristic cultural response invoked by 'Asia' can be found in a cartoon which appeared in 1923 in the pro-immigration journal, *Millions Magazine* (Plate 1). In this cartoon, India, Java, Indo-China, China and Japan are represented by glowering men of colour, population figures for their crowded countries written at their feet.[11] Each stares down at the map of Australia, in the centre of which lies a lone male figure, propped against a tree. He is asleep in the sun, hat over the eyes and legs folded, without a worry in the world. This indolent figure seems quite unaware of the resentment his behaviour arouses among the figures to his North. The cartoon suggested that proximity to Asia required Australians to work and behave differently from other European peoples. To do otherwise was to put Australia at risk since Australia was a country monitored and shadowed by Asia. The cartoon's corollary was that those who put Australia first would be those most aware of Asia's proximity. It followed that Australia was a country whose best citizens were concerned at how Asian nations would judge a country with such a small population. There were constant warnings about the dangers of sleep and repose.

A further theme of this book is the apprehension that in some way rampant 'Asia' might 'Aboriginalise' the Australian people. Invasion narratives frequently drew close analogies between the fate of the Australian Aborigines and the fate of white Australia. The Aborigines were commonly depicted as a timorous, unprepared people who had been displaced and humiliated by the more powerful and determined British. Would the newly awakened East brush aside white Australia's small city-based populations with the same contemptuous ease? It seemed possible that the British occupation of Australia would prove a relatively short interregnum between the extended Aboriginal past and a successful Asian future. Nicol's story had suggested as much. A letter published in the *Sydney Morning Herald* in July 1905 made the analogy even more explicit: 'If we cannot people our Commonwealth ... our race will wane, and eventually be extinguished even as the aboriginals have disappeared before the might and numbers of their white foes'.[12] An English visitor, writing in 1910, judged Australia harshly: 'You claim as justification for taking Australia from the blackfellows, the aborigines, that they were not utilising it for the benefit of mankind. Neither are you'.[13] Similarly, in the 1920s, the Rev T E Ruth warned his flock at the Congregational Church, Pitt Street, Sydney, that in the face of the 'intelligence and genius of Japan' they were 'as much asleep to the problems of possession and the responsibilities attaching to patriotism as the aboriginals were to the significance of the coming of the British'.[14] Ruth turned European Australians into the 'white Aborigines' of the Empire. Against powerful and populous Asia, Australia seemed all the more sparsely settled, diminutively tribal and fibreless. To Ruth, patriotism seemed a weak growth in Australia.

Because population growth and the art of peopling a continent became such a high priority for the new Commonwealth, this book must also consider some of the attempts to define the nature of the Australian continent. From the beginnings of European settlement, the British suspected that they may have settled an Asian rather than a European landmass. The question arose: could it be developed more productively by Asian settlers? As early as 1829, Edward Gibbon Wakefield, famous exponent of systematic colonisation, pointed out Australia's proximity to Asia. He predicted that Asia's immense populations would present Australia with undreamt of trading opportunities. Wakefield also believed that Chinese settlers could turn the Australian wilderness into a productive garden. In Wakefield's eyes, Asian markets and Asian immigrants would make Australia blossom.[15]

These ideas persisted. In 1910, John Foster Fraser, the English author of *Australia: The Making of a Nation* and a possible model for Nicol's critical English visitor, claimed that Australia was 'an eastern country inhabited by men from the west'.[16] Politician and immigration enthusiast Richard Arthur later made the same point: Australia was an Eastern country accidentally occupied by Europeans.[17] Later the idea emerged that Australians might have to understand Asia better before they could hope to develop a culture suited to their geographical location. For the architect Hardy Wilson, writing in the 1920s, Australia was an 'Oriental' country whose climatically impaired inhabitants would remain shallow beings until they learnt to draw upon the philosophical wisdom and the architectural traditions of the Chinese.[18] A supporter later wrote of the need to 'Orientalise' Australian thought.[19]

Co-existing with the suspicion that Australia might be an Asian landmass, a part of Asia, was the argument that proximity to Asia might bring considerable trade benefits, another of this book's major themes. In 1895, the year following the signing of the Anglo-Japanese treaty, Mr E Jerome Dyer addressed a Melbourne audience on 'Australia and the Asian-Pacific'.[20] His talk was sponsored by an impressive cross-section of organisations: the Melbourne Chamber of Commerce, the Chamber of Manufactures, the Royal Agricultural Society, the Royal Geographical Society, the Melbourne Employers' Union, the Reform Club and the Trades Hall Council. His message was that huge markets were opening up in the Asia-Pacific region and that Australia enjoyed a favourable, even providential, geographical proximity to a world of great trading opportunities.

As interest in Asian trade grew, some commercial figures began to see that Australians stood to gain from a closer knowledge of Asian cultures. The teaching of Asian languages in Australian universities was mooted. Ninety years ago, at a prestigious public lecture at Adelaide University, J Currie Elles, Founding Chairman of the Stock Exchange of New South Wales, recommended the closer integration of commercial education with the study of Asian languages and cultures in order that young Australians might better understand their Asia-Pacific future.[21] While Elles's sentiments sound modern, from the little we know of him it seems clear that he was a staunch Empire man, a British gentleman of the old school who lavished high praise on the 'Orient' as the source of world civilisation.

Nicol's colleague, who dreamt of an Asian Australia in the year 1960, and Elles, who spoke of an Australia which valued and understood Asia offered two diametrically opposed visions of the Australian future. One imagined the elimination of the white race from the Australian continent, the other the development of a powerful nation with strong trading and cultural links with Asia. Asia was sufficiently protean to promise both elimination and greatness and almost every shade of possibility in between. While there were regular calls to find a stable, knowable 'Asia' it was nonetheless apparent that Asia contained multiple and often sharply contradictory identities. Put simply, there were a lot of stories coming out of Asia. That Asia was a highly mobile entity was itself a source both of fascination and anxiety. In what form would 'Asia' manifest itself next? The fluidity of its representations, the difficulties presented by Asian languages, its complex and tangled histories, the uncertainty of the sources of information and the notion that any story emanating from Asia was inherently believable made the injunction to know and understand Asia almost impossible to fulfil. Asia seemed no more knowable than Dr Fu Manchu himself.

From 1901, Australia became known internationally for its White Australia Policy.[22] This book does not deal directly with the origins and development of the White Australia Policy, a subject that has already received considerable attention elsewhere.[23] Likewise, the administration of the policy has attracted sufficient analysis not to require another survey of its workings.[24] Even so, white Australia mentalities inform a number of the central themes of this book: the relationship between climate and settlement, particularly in the 'empty north'; the transfer of the Northern Territory to the Commonwealth; the question of Australia's optimum population; the debate over 'race mixing' and miscegenation; the prospects for expanded trade with the East and Australia's role as a Pacific nation. Moreover, arguments had to be made for keeping Australia white, which inevitably kept alive the question of what it meant to be non-white. White Australia, by placing race at the centre of national life, helped maintain a pre-occupation with Asia, including a belief that Australian actions were under intense Asian scrutiny. For well over a century, Australians have had 'Asia' on their mind, nervously aware that their 'title deed' to the last continent available for mass migration was not impregnable.

While white Australia has attracted a considerable literature, some of the more wide-ranging studies of Australia's interactions with Asia deserve immediate notice. Two of the most effective studies, a collection of essays edited by Ian Clunies Ross, published in 1935, and Jack Shepherd's lucid history of the Australia-Asia relationship, published in 1939, fall within the period of this study and are examined in Chapter 16.[25] Werner Levi, an American Fulbright scholar, wrote a fine general history of Australia's interactions with Asia in the 1950s which has attracted less attention than it deserved.[26] All of those who have worked on the Australia-Japan relationship are aware of David Sissons's substantial body of published and unpublished writings on this subject, extending over a period of forty years, beginning with his much cited MA thesis on Australian responses to Japan between 1890 and 1923.[27] Showing a similar enthusiasm for his subject, Eric Rolls has written two encyclopedic histories of the Chinese in Australia.[28] There are no similar histories for the Australian relationship with India or with the Netherlands East Indies for the period to 1939, although Jill

Roe's study of Theosophy illuminates the turn-of-the-century fascination with Indian thought.[29] The early stirrings of Asia-Pacific consciousness were elegantly laid out a number of years ago by Neville Meaney whose interests in the Australia-Japan relationship have been carried forward in a study of Edmund Piesse, one of Australia's leading Asia-Pacific intellectuals from the Great War to the 1930s.[30] The relationship with the Philippines, which receives relatively little attention in this book has been explored by Reynaldo C Ileto and Rodney Sullivan, while Australian contacts with Siam [Thailand] until the 1950s have been covered by Paul Battersby.[31] The wider cultural history of Australian responses to Asia is the subject of a special issue of *Australian Cultural History*, published in 1990 and is the focus of major recent studies by Alison Broinowski, Robin Gerster and Maryanne Dever.[32]

Informing many recent studies of the West's understanding of Asia, certainly since the publication in the late 1970s of Edward Said's immensely influential analysis of 'Orientalism', is the fascination with 'otherness'. What conditions produced 'Asianness' and what constituted 'Asia'? For much of the period covered in this study, a good deal of energy was invested in the task of establishing that Australia was neither Aboriginal nor Asian. Yet the business of creating a boundary which divided Australia from its 'other' created a heightened unease over invasion and violation. There was also a growing fear that the will to maintain distinctiveness might weaken to the point of collapse. Viewed in this light, Australia was simultaneously threatened with disappearance at the hands of aggressive outsiders and from decadent forces at work within the nation.

This book explores some of the many points at which 'Asia' was introduced into speculations about Australia's future. It examines the cultural meanings that have attached to Asia through a formative period in our history and it documents a culturally rich, often contradictory, demonology of the 'East' along with an extensive and varied discourse on each of the major societies of the region: India, China and Japan and, to a lesser extent, what was once the Netherlands East Indies and is now Indonesia. It proposes that a range of Asia-related discourses, many of which sought to reveal the truth or essence of Asia, were disseminated through Australian society from the 1850s. It argues that from the late nineteenth century there was a growing belief that developments in Asia would have an increasing impact upon Australia. By the 1930s, despite the already familiar complaint that Australians knew too little of the outside world, there was, nonetheless, a sustained commentary on Asia-Pacific themes, not least the merits of forming closer political, economic and cultural ties with the region.

Chapter Two

The Antique Orient

From the earliest days of the British settlement of Australia, India and the crown colony of Ceylon were a familiar part of the colonists' world. As Margaret Steven has noted the first links made by the new colony were with India.[1] When supplies ran short, as they often did, ships from Calcutta brought grain, foodstuffs, spirits, clothing and live animals. India provided a lifeline for the new settlement. Many trading and shipping connections then developed creating an increasing flow of administrators, merchants, army personnel, clergy and tourists between the Indian subcontinent and Australia. Australians constantly heard about the conditions of life in India along with its scenic marvels, architecture, philosophies, mysteries and climate. Australia's Indian connection was to remain strong for much of the nineteenth century.

From the beginnings of settlement, the diverse traffic in people, ideas and products between Australia and India was largely supported by the imperial connection. Robert Campbell, the first independent merchant operating in Sydney Cove provides an excellent illustration.[2] He was born in Scotland in 1769 and went to India at the age of 27 to join his elder brother in the family export business, which by the 1790s had become a regular supplier to the new colony in New South Wales. Robert later emigrated to Australia, where he built Campbell's wharf, an agency house to facilitate the Indian trade and a private home that was the first Australian house built in the 'whole-hearted Indian bungalow form', a building style that was to become something of a fashion in colonial Australia.[3] Campbell went on to become a leading public figure and a wealthy pastoralist. Many other early colonists had Indian experience. At the highest level of early colonial society there is the example of Lachlan Macquarie who served in India before arriving at Sydney Cove late in 1809 to become Governor of New South Wales. He brought with him an Indian slave who worked as his manservant. There were regional identities like Foster Fyans who spent some years with the British army in India before becoming first police magistrate in Geelong in the 1830s or the medical practitioner, John Coverdale, who was born in Bengal in 1814 and practised in India before moving, in the 1830s, to Tasmania's more manageable climate. There are household names, like Caroline Chisholm, the famous philanthropist, who founded the Female School of Industry for the Daughters of European Soldiers in Madras, where she lived for six years before moving to Australia in 1838. Such links nourished an awareness of India in colonial society from the beginnings of European settlement.[4]

What motivated these various Anglo-Indians to come to Australia? Land grants to ex-army personnel and growing commercial opportunities made a new beginning in the Australian colonies an attractive proposition. There were, no doubt, less flattering reasons for thinking that Australia might be the place to go after India: legal trouble, money trouble, family trouble, drink trouble. Many early settlement choices were influenced by considerations of climate and health. In the nineteenth century, when the sources of disease were poorly understood, climate was thought to have a much greater impact on health than is now considered to be the case. Firm distinctions were drawn between demanding and healthy climates. Australia, it was hoped, offered a compromise between the extremes of cold in Britain and the tropical heat and associated diseases of India. Tropical heat was thought to coarsen white men and to ruin the health of white women and children. Writing as an intending settler in 1828, James Henty contrasted temperate New South Wales with India's 'pestilential climate under a burning sun'.[5] Climate was one factor which influenced Henty to emigrate to Australia and by 1830, when he had taken up land on the Swan River in Western Australia, he believed his settlement might serve as a health resort for British officers and their families serving in India.[6]

Later in the nineteenth century, the effects of climate became the subject of serious medical study. Terms like 'tropical neurasthenia' were coined to characterise the state of settlers in tropical climates who appeared nervous and fearful, yet incapable of action or effort. The growing linkage between tropical climates and debilitating disease states in turn raised difficult questions about whether Europeans could ever successfully settle in tropical countries. In contrast to India, Anglo-Saxons were expected to flourish in Australia. This certainly was the opinion of Phillip Muskett, the respected author of *The Illustrated Australian Medical Guide*, an influential text which appeared around 1890. Muskett based many of his reflections upon the relationship between climate and health on the British experience in India with particular reference to Sir William Moore's earlier work, *Family Medicine in India*.[7]

Once having chosen to settle in Australia, colonists would be given chances to reflect on the benefits of their choice. All too often in the nineteenth century Australians read in their newspapers dreadful accounts of outbreaks of disease or famine in India. In October 1877, the *Town and Country Journal* publicised a call from the Lord Mayor of London for aid from cities throughout the Empire for a major famine in India. The paper, noting how 'wisely directed beneficence is better than artillery' urged its readers to give generously and so strengthen imperial ties.[8] By November, at least £6,000 had been collected for the Indian Famine Relief Fund. At a meeting in the Town Hall in Sydney, donors were to see an exhibition of photographs from the famine areas and to hear disturbing accounts read from a letter by a Madras Native Infantry Captain of how 'children were being killed and eaten by their parents'.[9] After such searing tales, Australian life seemed rather benign.

Trade provided even stronger links with India than did charitable aid. As early as the mid-1820s, the potential of eastern and particularly Indian trade formed one important reason for Lieutenant-Governor James Stirling's settlement of the Swan River district in Western Australia. Stirling anticipated that the export of horses and wheat to India would prove especially profitable. In the case of horses, these predictions proved correct as the export of Australian horses for use by the British in India expanded into a promising colonial trade from the 1830s. Remounts and sporting horses, soon called 'walers' by reference to New South Wales, were sent in increasing numbers until the 1870s when the once flourishing trade fell into disrepute after dealers allegedly supplied too many animals 'of wretched sorts'.[10] By the 1890s most of these problems appeared to have been resolved and the Australian colonies were able to export 50,000 horses to India over the decade.[11] Many were sent from Victoria, particularly from the Western District where the squatter, Francis Henty, one of James Henty's younger brothers, was one of the more successful exporters.

Australia also imported many goods from India. From the eighteenth century, India supplied the West with a range of new textiles, textile designs and loosely fitting garments, which were quickly appropriated into European style. The Indian banyan gave rise to the male lounging robe and dressing gown while the Kashmir shawl with its vivid patterns became an important item of fashionable dress for nineteenth century women.[12] In addition, there were a wide range of culinary links traceable to India. Beverley Kingston has provided an extensive list of these items which included many herbs and spices, pickles, chutneys, curry powders and, not least, tea.[13]

The habit of tea drinking, which colonial Australians seized upon with particular avidity, generated substantial imports. For decades, tea was routinely included in the staple provisions meted out to Australian shearers. Yet tea drinking was also a habit which had always been closely associated with British life in the tropics, particularly in India. That fortunes could be made in the Indian tea trade can be seen in the commercial success of James 'Rajah' Inglis, creator of 'Billy Tea' (Plate 2). Inglis, rather a colorful character who liked to sport an Indian turban, was an active member of the New South Wales Legislative Assembly and an outspoken advocate of free trade. He gave public lectures in Australia on Indian subjects and also wrote books on India with rousing titles, including the alliterative *Tent Life in Tigerland*. In the early 1880s, James Inglis and Co., won the lucrative Sydney agency of the Indian Tea Association of Calcutta. Inglis consistently promoted Indian and Ceylonese teas, which he insisted were ahead of the rival Chinese product because they were made under British supervision. By 1897 Ceylon and India had come to dominate the Australian tea market.[14]

Even for Australian settlers without direct family or trading links, India was a country of great interest. India was seen as the glittering jewel in the imperial crown, a country of great strategic importance and one that also magnificently exhibited the benefits of British rule. In the 1830s the leading British historian, Thomas Macaulay, marvelled how Britain managed to govern this distant country, whose people differed from us 'in race, colour, language, manners, morals, religion'. He concluded that these were 'prodigies' without precedent in world history.[15] Most nineteenth century accounts of Empire propounded the belief that the British exhibited a unique capacity for governance. To these writers, the British presence in India only confirmed the overwhelming importance of the British. No other race seemed able to retain so much territory and rule over such huge populations. Australian colonists, however, had another satisfaction from secure British rule in India. They perceived it as a substantial barrier to Russian imperial ambitions. For many years, Russia was believed to be the major enemy to British and therefore Australian interests in the Indian and Pacific Oceans.

But it soon became apparent that the British presence in India was under threat. Between May 1857 and late 1858 a series of Sepoy uprisings, collectively known at this time as the Indian Mutiny, although now interpreted by Indian historians as the early stirrings of the Independence Movement, challenged British rule. In response to the rebellion of native Sepoy troops in the Indian army, British troops and their families and dependents were driven into fortified positions at Agra, Cawnpore and the British residency at Lucknow. After fierce fighting, many British positions were eventually captured with heavy casualties. Women and children were prominent among the casualties. These actions swiftly generated severe retaliatory massacres of both Indian troops and Indian civilians by British units sent in to relieve the conditions of siege, which then sparked further Indian retribution.[16] News of these events soon reached Australia where most newspapers covered the Mutiny in considerable detail and an Indian Mutiny Relief Fund to aid the British survivors was quickly established.

At the time, imperialist accounts saw the Mutiny as an event where the heroic British male gallantly defended vulnerable women and children against murderous 'natives' guilty of 'unreclaimed barbarism'. One example is the response of the Melbourne *Argus* to the Cawnpore massacre:

> Fiendish malignity and ferocious cruelty could not well devise any forms of torture more ingeniously horrible, repulsive, and appalling, than have been re-sorted to by the brutal ruffians of the Bengal Native army for the maiming, mangling, and murdering of the inoffensive women and innocent children who have fallen into the hands of these remorseless wretches.[17]

Although there has been no detailed study of Australian responses to the Indian Mutiny, the evidence of the major newspapers suggests strong contemporary support for British policies.

The tale of the Indian Mutiny quickly entered the complex mythology of Empire. Its story was to be told many times over in histories, popular fiction and biography and its resonances reached deep into the British psyche. There was a prolific flow of stories about the events of '57, usually featuring the genus, 'Mutinous Native'. Stories about frontier life on the borders of Empire become popular as the Empire burgeoned into a strident, red occupation of the globe. There were moves to ensure that children learnt correct Imperial sentiments. The history of the British Empire became an important school subject and from 1905, the celebration of Empire Day was an annual ritual in all Australian schools.[18]

India, with its wealth, size and diversity, its architectural splendours and mighty traditions, was the great collector's piece of Empire. Given the maritime links between Australia and India in the nineteenth century, India attracted many curious and enthusiastic Australian travellers. India was a natural stopping point for British immigrants on their way out to Australia and for Australians returning for a visit to the Old Country. For help in planning their tour, these travellers could consult James Hingston's *The Australian Abroad on Branches From the Main Routes Round the World* (Plate 3). When Hingston's book first appeared in 1880 in two handsome volumes, it quickly attracted enthusiastic reviews. Hingston was acclaimed as a travel writer and compared to Mark Twain, often to the latter's disadvantage. In 1885, *The Australian Abroad* was made more affordable and convenient, when it was re-issued in a single volume by the Melbourne publisher, William Inglis and Company.[19] It was one of the major travel books to emerge from Australia before the first world war and remains one of the most comprehensive and engaging accounts of travel through Asia to have appeared in our literature.

Already well-known for his journalism, James Hingston became something of a literary celebrity. His tone and jaunty manner marked him out as a distinctive voice. Hingston was a philosopher at large, for whom travel provided an opportunity to reflect upon human diversity. While not as circular and digressive as Laurence Sterne's famous creation, Tristram Shandy, Hingston nevertheless displayed a Shandean wit and a gift for story-telling. He was drawn to the strangeness and intractable difference of the mysterious East. He saw India as 'the land of the wonderful', home of 'all that is imaginative, fantastic, sensuous, and extravagant'.[20] Like many of his contemporaries, he found in India the appeal of the Arabian Nights, that 'famous entertainer of our youth'. Hingston was fascinated by India's sharp contrasts, by all the glory and shame, splendour and decay, grandeur and ruins, to be found in 'this gorgeous Eastern Land!'.[21] India was a site for cultural feasting. Hingston was keen to see Delhi, the setting for *Lalla Rookh*, Thomas Moore's series of Oriental tales in verse. Here he found fascinating historical remains indicating how successive invasions had shaped this ancient city. It was a vivid reminder of that considerable nineteenth century theme, the mutability of civilisations, captured in Shelley's 'Ozymandias' by the description of the ancient tyrant's statue, broken and abandoned in the desert sand.

Admittedly, Hingston travelled through India as a confirmed imperialist. He retained his robust enthusiasm for British rule. Like Macaulay, he marvelled at the way little Britain had come to 'own' a country with a population of 250 million people.[22] He recognised the importance of British trade and the vitality of the great 'producing powers' of India.[23] But he was also aware that at times Britain had been guilty of commercial excess, particularly in relation to the opium trade, a commerce which he believed to be as sinister in its impact as slavery. Hingston believed that the greed of the East India Company had been a major precipitating cause of the Indian Mutiny. He blamed the annexation of the Kingdom of Oudh in 1856, of which Lucknow was the capital, for quickening the tempo of resentment towards the British. While acknowledging that the British were not beyond criticism, Hingston supported their rule, believing the loss of India would quickly reduce Britain to a second-rate power.

In Delhi, Lucknow and Cawnpore, Hingston was presented with potent reminders of the comparatively recent Indian Mutiny. As he visited massacre sites and memorials, he copied inscriptions into his notebook and recorded his impressions as an Australian who felt himself still very much a member of the British family. As he noted in Cawnpore:

> The dark blue sky of India has been terribly clouded for humanity, at many times, ancient and modern; but, for Great Britain and her family, never more so than in '57.[24]

Characteristically, Hingston used European literary associations when describing events. 'We go to see Cawnpore', he wrote, 'as we would see Hamlet or Macbeth'. He found Cawnpore one of the great tragedies of the British Empire, as integral to the story of the British people as Shakespeare's greatest dramas. He knew that the names he read on the monuments at Lucknow would be 'familiar to all readers' — even those who read 'nothing beyond the daily press'.[25] Yet as an Australian democrat he noted that although the monuments listed the names of fallen officers, the rank and file were 'lumped together in death' with only a number.[26]

Hingston took a keen interest in many aspects of Indian culture and threw himself into the life of the Indian cities, making a point of visiting and describing the bazaars and living conditions of ordinary Indians. In Benares he bathed in the Ganges and drank from the Well of Knowledge and the Well of Purification.

He attended a cremation which he described as one of the most moving and memorable things he had ever seen.[27] Yet he honestly admitted there were some times when he would have gladly sacrificed time amidst the 'gilded' grandeur around him for a cold beer. Travel through India was thirsty work.

As he left India, Hingston was conscious of how much still remained for him to see and reflect on; it would take years to thoroughly explore this vast country and a lifetime then to fully understand what had been seen.[28] He was convinced that India was a profoundly important culture from 'the oldest of peopled countries'.[29] No-one, he argued, was really fully educated without a knowledge of India. To see India was to learn 'there is an object in life'.[30] Hingston was also deeply interested in India's great religions and the spiritual links between India and the West. He often alluded to the common Aryan origins linking the British Anglo-Saxon and the Hindu. At the same time, he had little difficulty in reconciling his interest in India's glorious past with a robust enthusiasm for British rule. He welcomed the British presence in India on defence and security grounds and also appreciated the potential cultural enrichment that might flow from a continued interaction between these two countries.

In later years, the antiquity and spiritual wealth of India noted by Hingston were to become regular themes in Western travel writing and an attraction for those fascinated by the ancient world and its treasures. But it is equally the case that many Australian visitors to India were powerfully struck by the specifically biblical nature of the scenes they encountered in Indian village life. The South Australian parliamentarian, Thomas Playford, sent by his government to investigate the suitability of Indian labour to develop the 'Empty North', was reminded of the Bible when he saw two women grinding corn not far from Delhi.[31] Others felt similarly when they saw women gathering water at wells. In the 1870s the *Town and Country Journal* identified the theme of 'Women at the Well' as a sign of the 'unchanging' nature of 'Asiatic peoples'. It noted that the well formed a focal point for many biblical stories: Jacob first met Rachel at the well, Christ talked with the woman of Samaria at the well; the Scriptures were full of references to wells and the drawing of water.[32] Later, T B Fischer, an Australian missionary visiting India in 1912, found the sight of oxen in the fields and women grinding corn or drawing water from wells was a constant reminder of the people 'among whom our Saviour walked'.[33]

Fischer travelled with a camera in one hand and his Bible in the other. Like many Australians of the time, he was convinced that in India there was missionary work to be done. The 'millions of India' had to be saved from the 'darkness of heathenism and the blackness of sin'. Fischer appealed to young Australians to help him in this grand Christian endeavour:

God's word is a lamp — it guides in difficult places — it marks the rocks and
shoals of the ocean — it is the lamp to light us through the valley of the shadow
of death ... Will you do your best to send that light to brighten dark India?[34]

Readers could follow the progress of missionary work in India in papers like the
Murray Independent, including extracts from letters sent home by Eleanor Rivett,
the first Australian to join the London Missionary Society in North India.[35]

Alfred Deakin, one of the towering figures of Australian public life, was
another to be struck by the biblical nature of Indian rural life. Born in Melbourne
in 1856, Deakin grew to be an avid reader, fascinated by India. He quickly rose
in public office, attaining the office of Prime Minister in 1903, when he was still
an energetic figure in his forties. By his own assessment, India had been an
enormous influence. He wrote:

Some words are enriched with historic memories and the reflection of early
enthusiasms so that they present themselves before us with a glamour greater
than that of romance. Such a magic name is India, before which the throng of
unimpressive words falls back as if outshone by a regal presence, clothed "with
barbaric pearl and gold".[36]

Deakin was first drawn to India for its inexhaustible stories, legends and
mythologies. He then began to appreciate its human knowledge and spiritual
depth and he began to study the great religions of Islam, Hinduism and Buddhism.
During the 1870s and 1880s, he found in India many answers to pressing questions
of his day, particularly on the origins of humanity and the nature of religious
belief. It was only from the 1890s, when his interest turned towards nation
building, that he became less concerned with India. Fascination with India then
seemed somewhat beside the point, a little disreputable, even a forbidden luxury.
India now seemed to demand a sensibility hardly permitted in modern, early
twentieth century Australian public life. Although the older Deakin wrote of
India as a powerful, but awkward memory, India always remained one of the
'impressive' words in his vocabulary.

Deakin's chance to visit India had come in 1890 when the proprietor of the
Age, David Syme, invited him to inspect India's irrigation program. Deakin
accepted with alacrity; irrigation was one of his many enthusiasms. Walter
Murdoch, Deakin's friend and first biographer, described the trip as only a 'two
month dash', but noted: 'the preparation for it had been spread over many
years of study; he knew the history of the country as few Englishmen knew
it'.[37] Deakin's two books on India, *Irrigated India* and *Temple and Tomb in
India* were published in 1893 and confirmed his reputation as a keen student
both of Indian religions and the British Raj, interests that have sometimes been
overlooked. Murdoch had stressed Deakin's Indian enthusiasms, but his next
biographer, J A La Nauze, researching his subject in the 1960s, clearly considered

Deakin's religious interests and his fascination with India subjects best passed over as briskly as possible. These seemed regrettable lapses in an otherwise impressive career. In a recent study, Al Gabay has given Deakin's religious quests the centrality they deserve.[38]

For his part Deakin wrote of India, its architecture, history, religions and stories without any sense that these were inappropriate subjects for an Australian politician. Interestingly, Deakin also could readily blur the boundaries between northern Australia and southern India to locate Australia firmly within an Indian sphere of influence. Deakin was convinced that Australian developments would be directly influenced by the course of events in India and that distances between the countries would soon decrease with rapidly improving transport and communications. He liked to describe Australians as a new people of Western background 'settled under the shadow of an antique Orient'.[39] Moreover, Deakin reminded his readers that people of Hindu background 'were not without kinship' to people in Australia. This was an acknowledgment of shared Aryan origins, the appreciation of which was sharpened by the new scholarship then emerging which marked Sanskrit as the source of all Indo-European languages. 'The study of Sanscrit', Deakin believed, had 'given a new tone and turn to nineteenth century thought'.[40]

This is not the place to test Murdoch's assertion that Deakin knew the history of India as few 'Englishmen knew it', though the claim, an interesting one, merits closer scrutiny. But what is clear is that Deakin had looked to India to furnish answers to some of the great questions of his day. He understood the growth of civilisation as an 'unceasing struggle for supremacy between East and West'. He felt Indian history confirmed this proposition, just as the British presence in India would help determine the outcome of the struggle. Deakin believed that anyone wanting to understand the modern world must understand the struggle for supremacy between East and West and so had a responsibility to learn about India. In *Temple and Tomb* he predicted that India and Australia would show a growing convergence of interests, arguing that the two countries were allied already 'politically and intellectually as well as geographically'. It was evident that Australia should be well informed also about other nearby 'Asiatic empires' whose future, Deakin believed, would be bound up with the future of 'our own tropical lands'.[41]

Deakin returned to the theme of the close community of interests between Australia and India in *Irrigated India*, citing shared concerns over 'trade and invasion, peace and war'.[42] He saw considerable mutual benefit in closer trading links and believed that free trade policies created export opportunities for Australian products in India, while Indian products were likely to find a growing market in Australia. These trade links would then draw the two countries closer 'year by year'. In addition, although Deakin was cautious about the future labour needs of northern Australia, he was prepared to make a case for the importation of

Hindu workers, if 'coloured' labour should prove indispensable to northern development.

Deakin also turned briefly and rather tantalisingly to the intellectual implications of Australia's proximity to India. He anticipated growing occasions for cultural interaction. 'That intellectual give and take', he wrote, 'which is everywhere a stimulus to thought should be especially quick and prolific between Australasia, or Southern Asia, and its northern continent [India]'. Since travellers already flowed freely between the two countries, Deakin thought it reasonable to suppose that Indian students might be attracted to Australian universities and that Australian intellectuals might become authorities on India and its people. Since geography had brought Australia and India 'face to face' Deakin supposed that it might yet 'bring them hand to hand, and mind to mind. They have much to teach each other'. Yet at the same time Deakin noted that many Australian colonists:

> in their pride of descent and haughtiness of national feeling, seem apt to for-
> get that they have made their homes neither in Europe nor America, but in
> Austral-Asia — Southern Asia — and that their fortunes may by this means be
> linked in the closest manner, in trade and in strife.[43]

Deakin's use of the term 'Southern Asia' is of particular interest here, for it was a coinage that he hoped would encourage Australians to develop a more systematic awareness of how close they were to India. While Deakin acknowledged that Australians had made their homes on the edge of Asia, from his vantage point in 1890, this provided a golden opportunity to get to know India. He was ready to predict that India would have a growing and increasingly positive impact upon the cultural, spiritual and economic development of twentieth century Australia. Events, however, proved him wrong.

Deakin always remained deeply interested in Indian religions. He quoted the views of Sanskrit scholar and Oxford Professor, Max Müller on how ancient India had been fundamental to the development of Western thought:

> we know that all the most vital elements of our knowledge and civilization, our
> languages, our alphabets, our figures, our weights and measures, our art, our
> religion, our traditions, our very nursery stories, come to us from the East.[44]

But Deakin drew a sharp distinction between ancient thought and the 'motley mass of degenerate and degraded beliefs' which he believed constituted modern Hinduism.[45] In this, he also followed Müller's opinions since Müller venerated the India of village communities two thousand years earlier but could argue in his private correspondence that degenerate modern India should be Christianised.[46] Ancient India was readily celebrated while modern India and Indians were routinely disparaged.

Deakin also subscribed to Müller's view that ancient Indian literature could assist Europeans to develop a fuller, more perfectly realised inner life. At this time, Deakin was hardly alone in drawing a sharp contrast between the spiritual wisdom of the East and the material wealth of the West; between other-worldly and this-worldly approaches to life and its meaning. He pictured an ideally balanced civilisation as one which displayed Anglo-Saxon energies, which he greatly valued, but which could be deepened and enriched by the spiritual traditions of India. A century later, this distinction between the spiritual East and the material West has been repeated to the point of cliché.

India not only had its own great religions, it also provided a fertile environment in which Western people in search of spiritual truths could develop new religious beliefs. One of the most important of these, emerging in the nineteenth century, was Theosophy. Jill Roe has shown how closely the rise of Theosophy in Australia can be related to the growing interest in Eastern religions in the late nineteenth century. Edwin Arnold's celebration of Buddhism, *The Light of Asia*, first published in 1879, enjoyed great popularity. Its Australian readership is difficult to establish, though a character in Joseph Furphy's *Rigby's Romance* cites Arnold's book as an indispensable spiritual guide.[47] Deakin soon noted how Theosophy, the 'latest doctrine' from India was finding converts among 'modern-minded men and women'.[48] He joined the movement himself, albeit briefly, in February 1895. The imperial connection, which guaranteed a regular shipping service, aided those seeking this type of spiritual connection with India. A stopover on the way to England in 1882 allowed Professor John Smith of Sydney University to visit Bombay where he joined the Indian chapter of the Theosophical Society.[49]

Those attracted to Theosophy were typically dissatisfied with the teachings and practices of institutional Christianity, yet were unable to do without some form of religious faith. The appeal of Theosophical thought to Australians at this time can be evidenced by an unpublished sketch of Wilton Hack, written for his children in 1907, to record his life and spiritual struggles. He outlines how his search for spiritual wisdom led him from Christianity to Freethought to Spiritualism and then to Theosophy. 'I went through the most terrible misery when I gave up the Xtian platform', he wrote. 'I saw that the old dogmas were bad & untrue, but I had nothing to put in its place; & that state of mind is wretched indeed'. Hack journeyed to India and Ceylon 'in search of wisdom & spiritual knowledge'. In the East he was sure he would find men of 'great intellectual power' with a 'wonderful knowledge of Philosophy'.[50] He visited Adyar, the Theosophical headquarters in India, where he worked as a librarian. Returning to Ceylon, his attempt to initiate a mining venture ended in betrayal and bitterness. Only Theosophy with its emphasis upon Brotherhood provided a stable point in his life. In the depths of despair and racked by illness, Hack turned to the Masters, the Mahatmas, the spiritually perfected ones, asking them to grant him a new beginning or put a swift end to his miserable existence. 'During that night', he wrote, 'I awoke & there was a bright golden light about me'.[51] Signs and occult messages persuaded him that the Masters had cured his physical and mental afflictions. On his return to Australia, Hack enjoyed the company of the 'ladies and gentlemen of intellectual & mental prominence' at the Adelaide branch of the Theosophical Society.[52] Yet, as will be seen later, for others in the community, these small gatherings signalled the growth of a troubling pro-Eastern presence in Australia, a force to be counteracted.

As Roe reminds us, Theosophy spoke to its moment in history, to the 'collapse of old prescriptions' in the 1880s and the social turmoil that came with increasing industrialisation and urbanisation, both in Britain and her Australian colonies. It was one of a number of movements which 'promised a new unity amid the bewildering changes of modern life'.[53] The aim was to create a bridge between East and West. Using teachings from ancient Indian texts, Theosophy stressed the perfected inner life and the pursuit of a radiant spirituality. Its adherents believed Australia provided the ideal setting for spiritual awakening. They hoped the 'light of Asia' would shine brightly on Australia, a land whose providential purpose seemed to be to create a new race of beings of great spiritual sensitivity. Bernard O'Dowd, Melbourne poet, intellectual and parliamentary draughtsman, hoped for a new beginning in the Antipodes, among a race of 'sun gods'.[54] He had studied Eastern wisdom throughout the 1880s.

Climatic affinities between tropical Queensland and India particularly encouraged the belief that Theosophy would flourish in Australia's tropical regions. Indeed by 1896, the Theosophical Society in Queensland had eighty members, a promising beginning in a new colony. Theosophists' interest in Queensland stemmed from the belief that it provided the conditions suitable for the emergence of a new race. Madam Blavatsky, in her great tome, *The Secret Doctrine*, held that Mankind was divided into a number of root-races, each made up of various sub-races. Higher races supplanted lower races in an evolutionary cycle. She predicted that the Aryans, the fifth root-race, were, at the end of the nineteenth century, poised to evolve into a more spiritually perfected sixth root-race. The great event was expected to occur in California. But it quite possibly might also take place in Queensland which, Theosophists argued, had the right climate and a very promising population mix of British peoples augmented by Germans, Italians and Chinese. This was exactly the racial combination predicted for the emerging sixth root-race.[55] In these ideas, supported by its pursuit of spiritual truth and universal brotherhood, Theosophy challenged many concepts of racial exclusivity that had become so pervasive as themes in the intellectual debate at the end of the nineteenth century. Mainstream Australian opinion exhibited no enthusiasm for racial mixing under any pretext, and was much more inclined to the view that Queensland's future lay in the development of a climatically adapted white race, protected against tropical diseases and alert to the dangers of a tropical climate.

While Australians learned about India through many different channels, the most persistent conception of India was of an ancient land which had long been a source of deep spiritual truths. Fakirs, bearded prophets and philosophers seemed to spring from the soil. In 1924, the *Pacific* saluted antique India:

> India is old. Before Egypt flourished India was. She saw Babylon rise and fall. Greece and Rome were but fragments of a passing dream beside the misty antiquity of this ancient Aryan land. That wisdom which she treasured through the ages she would give to the world were she but free and happy. She knows wonderful secrets of life.[56]

While the appeal of antique India persisted, the relevance of turbulent modern India as a guide to human conduct, with its complexities of caste, its crowded cities, dreadful diseases and awful poverty, was to fade for Australians as the twentieth century wore on, not to be revived until the 1960s.

Chapter Three

Blood, Race and the Raj

In the latter half of the nineteenth century, the greatest threat to the mighty British Empire was thought to come from Russia. If one assumed this to be the case, then India became central to most strategic conceptualisations of Australia's future. Australia was seen as a vulnerable, under-populated nation, positioned at a point of great strategic risk between the Indian and Pacific Oceans. In the 1890s, Alfred Deakin articulated many of the prevalent concerns. Russia, he claimed, had every reason to occupy India in order to obtain access to strategic territories, resources and deep water ports. As any Russian presence in India would pose a direct threat to Australia, Australians had an important interest in the continued survival of the British Raj. Australians, Deakin believed, had to learn to think of Australia as part of 'Southern Asia' in order to develop more systematic responses to the region in which they lived and the defence strategies this imposed.[1]

Yet from the mid-1890s, Australian fears of Russia were in decline. China's huge population was a potent concern, soon to be matched and then surpassed by anxieties about Japan. As the geo-political significance of India to Australia began to decrease, interest in India, its spiritual traditions, its myths and legends, even the pomp and circumstance of the Raj, slowly weakened. Australian interest in India began to focus more narrowly upon explicitly martial and imperial concerns. In the 1890s and 1900s, India was often reduced to little more than a colourful backdrop for stirring yarns about Anglo-Saxon fighting prowess. Through such accounts of British bravery, Anglo-Australian authors sought to maintain sturdy, imperial disciplines among a people who, in their view, seemed too attracted to the luxurious vices which were so often identified as the root cause of imperial decline.

In the late 1890s when the British-born Australian historian, A W Jose, wrote of the Indian Mutiny in *The Growth of Empire*, he described the main episodes as though they were real and immediate events, still fresh in the memory, not as events which had occurred more than thirty years earlier, before he was born: 'For three months we hung there, immovable against attack, gathering our forces for a decisive blow ...'.[2] Jose's rhetoric conveyed the pride of race that many of his generation felt so keenly. In his view, Australia was part of the British story of Empire. Jose's study of Empire was not a tale of personal travel like Hingston's, nor was it a repository of philosophical and spiritual truths as it was for Deakin. It was a school text book, prescribed reading, telling a tale of martial disciplines and racial vigour. For Jose, the events of 1857 gave important assurances, first that 'the breed had not failed' and second that the British had once again shown their capacity for 'fine government'.[3]

Jose's *The Growth of Empire* was crammed with battle dates ready for rote learning. It sounded the sonorous notes of all the Mutiny's core mythologies and shared some 'essential' truths: 'the east breeds tigers as well as elephants ...'.[4] For Jose, the East was inevitably violent, inhabited by 'natives' who were treacherous and given to superstition. His narrative was carried forward by descriptions of plots, conspiracies and intrigues. When he referred to certain Indian acts of brutality, the underlying meaning was all too clear. The British women and children captured at Cawnpore 'were imprisoned and kept for a worse fate'.[5] Here was the ultimate horror. The Indian Mutiny, more than any other event in the nineteenth century, generated a widespread belief that any insurrection or rebellion in the East led to the sexual violation of white women. As Jenny Sharpe has argued in *Allegories of Empire*, no case of Indian rape of white women can be substantiated throughout the entire period of the Mutiny, but this hardly mattered.[6] Stories of rape and mutilation became an invocation and a rallying cry. These were culturally powerful stories which helped confirm the cause of Britishness and were used to rationalise the brutalities of Empire.

The Tale of the Great Mutiny by the Rev W H Fitchett, published in 1902, provided a further account of the bloody events of the Indian Mutiny in a popular history designed to instruct the young. The book was reissued in a popular edition for Australian readers by E W Cole, proprietor of the famous Melbourne Book Arcade.[7] Fitchett was a formidable public figure, a devastating debater and as President of Methodist Ladies' College, one of Victoria's leading educators. He had gained an international reputation through his best-selling book *Deeds that Won the Empire*, which had appeared in 1897.[8] For his attachment to battle in the name of Empire, the *Bulletin* had dubbed him 'Bleeds' Fitchett.[9] Through his account of the Mutiny, Fitchett attempted to rekindle the ardours of the imperial spirit in a new generation.

To Fitchett, the sources of Indian revolt were too trifling to deserve serious attention. He referred slightingly to the 'mind of the East', the treachery of the 'natives' and the urgings of the 'bazaar rabble'. Few Indians were even named. Those who were, not least Nana Sahib, one of the major Indian military commanders, were represented as embodiments of treachery and cunning. Nana Sahib was a 'man behind a mask'; an 'epicure in cruelty, who was inclined to take his murders in dainty and lingering installments'.[10] Fitchett saw the Mutiny as an heroic story of badly outnumbered Britishers, helped by a few 'good natives' bravely holding off swirling tides of noisy fanatics. When order was eventually restored, the Empire emerged strengthened, reassured that justice had been done. Fitchett was a great believer in British justice.

Throughout his story Fitchett contrasted the 'iron-nerved' with those suffering 'failure of nerve'. A nervous temperament in a soldier of Empire was a danger;

it could encourage a spirit of mutiny. Fitchett knew how imperative it was for the British to retain their controlling will, permitting lone individuals to stare down and master the more numerous and excitable 'natives'. This was a world of the unflinching gaze and the imperious gesture. Fitchett continually emphasised how the influence of 'one brave man' might shape the fortunes of war. He argued that the Sepoys had only attacked once they saw they had the numbers: 'it was the sense of power that induced them to rebel. The balance of numbers, and of visible strength, seemed to be overwhelmingly with them'.[11] Fitchett's tale was one of authoritative masculinity, fashioned, hardened and perfected by the requirements of Empire.

Fitchett wrote that the news that Indian troops had violated white women was a critical factor in spurring the British to new heights of revenge. He explained and excused the wholesale hangings committed by Colonel Neill, one of the most brutal of the British officers, as the understandable result of manly emotions aroused by this fearful news. The Mutiny was presented as a tableau of oppositions between 'Saxon courage' and 'Hindu cruelty', between British chivalry and Eastern misogyny. The war heroes were all found on the British side. Fitchett even seems to suggest that one of India's major contributions to the world was the development of heroic British imperialists: 'steady of nerve, quick of eye, deadly of aim, proud of their blood and race'.[12] Yet the stridency of his tone reveals how far he thought the imperial cause was in need of resuscitation.

The need for a restoration of a powerful, imperially-minded manhood was a common theme in the decade or so before the Great War and is much in evidence in the writings and actions of Baden Powell, founder of the Boy Scout Movement.[13] Even the sophisticated Alfred Deakin interpreted the Mutiny as yet another vindication of the Anglo-Saxon qualities of 'dauntless courage and inexhaustible endurance'.[14] But in the 1890s, the fear was growing that these qualities were under threat. As Gail Bederman has noted, there was 'a widespread cultural concern about effeminacy, overcivilization, and racial decadence'.[15] Anxiety about imperial decline pervades Fitchett's narrative.

Fitchett's Mutiny was not a sanitised tale: limbs were torn from bodies, heads were blown off, blood ran copiously from ghastly wounds. When compared to the majestic sweep of Hingston's or Deakin's interests, Fitchett's India was a narrowly imperial and distinctly blood-splattered offering. By the turn of the century, this gory tale may well have acquired some new and uncomfortable meanings for Australians. Could Australia itself become an embattled community seeking to repulse surrounding Asiatic nations? Wasn't Australia surrounded by teeming Asia in much the same way as the Residency at Lucknow had been surrounded and outnumbered? Was a tenacious identification with an Empire that had forced itself on Asia the best strategy for Australia?

Fitchett derived his ideas of the beneficial effects of military combat from widespread beliefs, reaching cult status, that had been prevalent in the late nineteenth century. Consider gentle John Ruskin, one of Britain's most influential literary critics at a time when the 'man of letters' was a force in the land. In *Crown of Wild Olive*, published in 1866, Ruskin recorded his discovery that war was the foundation of 'all the high virtues and faculties of men'. He found that war 'nourished' great nations while peace 'wasted' them. Great nations learnt their greatness through war, but were deceived through peace; they were 'born in war and expired in peace'.[16] Fitchett subscribed to these views and hoped, with many others, that Australia would achieve nationhood by the discovery of a worthy enemy and a nourishing war.

Jose and Fitchett who had done so much to ensure that the heroic deeds of the Mutiny were widely known, would have been proud to hear how two athletic supporters of 'the Grand Old Empire', G W Burston and H R Stokes, from the Melbourne Bicycle Club, pedalled around the great imperial sites of British India in the late 1880s. Starting out from Lee's Hotel in Cawnpore, they visited all the massacre scenes: the Memorial Church, the nearby well, the Barracks, the Memorial Gardens with their adjoining cemeteries and the Suttre Choura Ghat, where a desperate party of doomed British escapees took to their boats. At Lucknow they were shown over the Residency by an old soldier 'who fought in it, sir', and they visited the graves of Henry Havelock and Sir Henry Lawrence, two of the greatest heroes of the Mutiny. Every memorial, stone and cannon shot that spoke of British valour interested them intensely. They hung on the words of the veterans who recalled the events of '57. They loved imperial Lucknow, but abruptly dismissed the native quarters and bazaars, which 'don't interest us'. They knew of the events enacted at Cawnpore and Lucknow down to the smallest detail. This was their Empire and their story.[17]

For Australians unable to visit India, the compelling stories of Rudyard Kipling brought the scenes of the British Raj vividly to life. By the 1890s, no Australian with any literary pretensions could claim ignorance of Kipling. Martyn Lyons and Lucy Taksa, in their study of Australian reading habits between the 1890s and 1920s, found that Kipling was one of seven authors remembered by over one third of their respondents.[18] Moreover, he was the only author from these top seven whose writings were set in 'the East'. Men were found to have a keener response to his writings than women, perhaps because they were more strongly drawn to his barrack room themes and tales of army life. In November 1891, some Australians had the good fortune to meet the famous author. Despite the brevity of his visit, most Australian newspapers carried interviews with Kipling, affirming his high literary standing and popularity. 'His books are inquired for at the booksellers', the *Sydney Mail* reported, 'and are in constant demand at the circulating libraries and their titles are as familiar in the mouths of our reading public as household words'.[19] His major titles including *Plain Tales from the*

Hills (1888), *The Jungle Book* (1894), *Kim* (1901) and *The Just So Stories* (1902) reached huge audiences throughout the British Empire. Kipling's prominence and popularity helped confirm India's reputation as a magical land of story and legend.

Kipling was an outstanding recorder of the lives of the British imperial elite. Among this ruling class, Australians of a certain background were most welcome. The India of the Raj is documented in the letters Ruby Madden sent home to her family and friends.[20] Ruby was the daughter of Gertrude Stephen and Sir John Madden. Gertrude Stephen came from a distinguished New South Wales legal family with direct connections to Robert Campbell, a gentleman we have already encountered as Sydney Cove's first merchant. The Madden family was similarly eminent. Sir John Madden was appointed Chief Justice of Victoria in 1893 and later became Lieutenant-Governor. Ruby was twenty-six years old and a veteran socialite when she received an invitation through family friends to visit India for the Great Coronation Durbar in Delhi in January 1903.[21]

At the Durbar, Ruby stayed with Lord Kitchener's entourage, enjoying the splendid spectacle of this lavish occasion (Plate 4). Her stay in India seems to have been one protracted whirl of parties, balls, dinners, ceremonies, visits to the races, tea on the lawn, even an elephant ride. At the grander homes, peacocks practised ballet steps and toe points on the lawns. In her prolific letters home, Ruby Madden described her dresses, complained of the Indian heat and noted the difficulties she had in dealing with her Indian servants. There were brief glimpses of 'native' India, which Ruby Madden generally encountered at its most exotic and bejewelled. Socially, she met only Indians of the 'better sort', people such as an old Indian Colonel, renowned for his bravery: 'Everybody loves him and the men all say that he is a real white man except for his skin which seems to be the greatest complement a white man can pay anybody!!'.[22] After her Indian sojourn, Ruby Madden married into Australia's pastoral elite, continuing a family tradition of imperial loyalty and staunch political conservatism.

Lindon Brown, who described his time in India in *Letters from an Australian Abroad*, published in 1910, also conveys the life of frivolity and amusement that characterised the British elite. In Calcutta he visited the Tollygunge Recreation Club. 'We have nothing like it in Australia', he noted. 'There is a racecourse, golf links, croquet and tennis lawns, to say nothing of a bowling alley, [and] two fine club houses, two and three storeys high'.[23] Sir James Penn Boucault, Australian judge and former State Premier, also commented on the lavish lifestyle of the British when he described his visit to India and Ceylon in *Letters to My Boys*, published in 1906. Despite his lofty social standing, he disliked the grand and formal meals: 'At Watson's in Bombay, and at the Grand Oriental in Ceylon, there are often over two hundred at dinner, which is served, *à la Russe*, in the most pretentious style'.[24]

Pretentious Anglo-Indian lifestyles were supported, as many visiting Australians noted, by the ubiquity of the 'native' servant. H Chalmers Miles deplored the socially harmful effects of this practice in a lecture given in 1860 to officers and men of the Royal Artillery and Royal Engineers. 'The life of the European in the East is widely different from that followed in any other part of the world', he noted. The soldier quickly learns 'never to do anything for himself that a native can do for him'.[25] When Judge Boucault visited India he was not altogether impressed by the throng of servants awaiting their master's every command.[26] Lindon Brown also noted the numerous servants but was very much taken by their ornate liveries: crimson at the Governor's Residence, plum at the Bishop's, dark green at the Bengal Club.[27] Burston and Stokes, however, bicycling through India, suggested that the practice of keeping any kind of servant was inappropriate for independently-minded Australians:

> We have done without a servant, for they are a nuisance, and if two able-bodied Australians cannot get on without a darkey at their heels there must be something wrong somewhere.[28]

The ready availability of so many servants profoundly affected British attitudes to Indians. As H Chalmers Miles noted:

> The whole course of existence in India — from boy to manhood, from the lowly condition of the private soldier to the gorgeous state of the Viceroy — leads the European to plume himself on the superiority of the white over the coloured race.[29]

Deakin certainly disliked the frosty spirit of command that pervaded British conduct towards Indians. He both revealed and courted colonial sensibilities by condemning 'the cold and haughty character' of the British administration. He condemned its failure to understand the aspirations of ordinary Indians and its 'almost contemptuous indifference' to their needs. To treat ordinary Indians in this way betrayed what Deakin understood to be one of the primary justifications for British rule: the provision of stable government that returned some benefit to the common people.[30] British India confirmed Deakin's belief that the creation of a racially separate 'servant class' could not be tolerated in Australia. Such a class of people gave too much encouragement to bullying and snobbery and the determined cultivation of superior airs. He wanted Australian democracy to develop warmer and more human qualities than were on display among the British in India.

Deakin, however, approved some aspects of the British Raj. Apart from applauding the Anglo-Saxon spirit in India, Deakin praised British engineering feats. Railways, roads, telegraph lines and irrigation schemes were high on his list of imperial accomplishments. They were liberally distributed, useful and

destined to foster prosperity and the public good. But they were too often
overlooked by writers on India in Deakin's view, and deserved fuller
acknowledgment.[31] Yet others questioned whether Indians would ever be able
to maintain this great engineering tradition. Sir James Penn Boucault did not
think they would survive ten years without English supervision. If Indians were
not governed by 'English foresight they would become careless; they would let
the works rust ... and the whole establishment would go bung'.[32]

In the late nineteenth century, when the importance of India was fading for
many Australians, a few continued to stress its continuing importance both to
the integrity of the British Empire and to Australian security. Such strategic
considerations greatly concerned Dr Richard Arthur, an outspoken critic of
Australia's defences. He argued that the British presence in India remained
critical, an essential bulwark against the dangerous Russians. He was seriously
worried that Russia, China and Japan might conspire to allow China and Japan
to invade Australia while Russia swept into India.[33] 'The more ties and
relationships Australia has with India', Arthur argued, 'the more she will be
interested in helping maintain it [India] as part of the Empire'.[34] Every effort
had to be made to strengthen Australian ties and relationships with the British in
India, not because they were already strong, but because Arthur feared they
were rapidly weakening.

Arthur wanted to do all he possibly could to persuade Anglo-Indians to settle
in Australia. He sent a regular flow of letters to the Indian press extolling the
benefits of the Australian climate and the marvellous economic prospects facing
the Anglo-Indian immigrant. In a letter published in the *Madras Times*, Arthur
promoted Australia as the land of 'sunshine and gold', a land of promise.[35] In
1907 Arthur visited four Anglo-Indians then attending Hawkesbury Agricultural
College in New South Wales. He had great hopes for them, immediately imagining
they were 'the forerunners of hundreds, even thousands of settlers with capital
from India'.[36] More letters went off to the Indian press. The *Eastern Bengal
and Assam Era* carried an article by Arthur that again painted Australia in the
most glowing of terms. 'This is a land of pleasure-seeking,' he wrote, 'of
constant holidays, of strenuous searching after the joy of living'.[37] A hedonistic
lifestyle was presented as Australia's great attraction for intending immigrants,
but it was hardly a convincing story coming from a fellow who, when at home,
strongly condemned holidays and mere pleasure.

Arthur's convictions about the importance of India were considerably
strengthened by the publication of *The Day of the Saxon* in 1912, written by an
American military strategist, Homer Lea. Arthur insisted 'every man in authority
in Australia should be compelled to read this book'.[38] Arthur had also read and
approved Lea's earlier publication, *The Valor of Ignorance*, which warned that
Japanese power in the Pacific had reached the point where the United States
was vulnerable to invasion. Lea was fond of contrasting the military capacity of

the determined Japanese with the supposed decadence of the United States.[39] Already weakened, he believed, by their susceptibility to 'the contamination of feminism and commercialism' the Americans would inevitably succumb.[40] It has been claimed that the Japanese edition of *The Valor of Ignorance* went through twenty-four editions in one month, while in Germany Adolf Hitler would later insert several paragraphs from the German edition into *Mein Kampf*.[41]

The Day of the Saxon addressed similar military themes. The 'Saxon' of the title typically inhabited the white, English-speaking world and his days, Lea believed, were certainly numbered. Decadence had eaten out the heart of the British Empire and its future was in serious doubt. The key to the continuance of the Empire was India:

> With the loss of India through revolt or conquest the Empire is shattered and Saxon Australasia will at that time ... pass under the tenure of another race. The first principle of Australasian defence is the defence of India.[42]

Arthur's infatuation with Homer Lea's ideas was not shared by George Morrison, well-known Australian correspondent for the *Times* in Peking. Morrison scoffed when Lea styled himself 'General'. This appellation, Morrison declared in a letter to a colleague, was merely based 'on the fact that when resident in Los Angeles he taught the goosestep to some Chinese laundrymen'.[43] Morrison's caustic comment was based on some knowledge of Lea, who was a hunchback, just five feet tall, with a long-standing interest in military strategy. He had successfully drilled a force of anti-Manchu Chinese in California and went on to become chief military advisor to Dr Sun Yat-Sen, first President of the new Chinese Republic. In 1933 *The Dictionary of American Biography* considered Lea 'perhaps the most gifted American who ever joined a foreign legion'.[44] He was certainly one of the most unusual.

By the turn of the century, some younger Australian writers began to reject the British imperial theme and with it the idea that India had to have a special meaning for Australians (Plate 5). Louis Esson, writer and dramatist, who turned twenty-one in 1900 was left cold by imperial loyalty of the kind represented by the Madden family. Esson was anti-imperial in his views, a stance he shared with his friend and fellow writer, Vance Palmer who hated Fitchett and all that he stood for. Although Esson was a foundation member of the Victorian Socialist Party, formed in 1906, his socialism was mainly literary. He was more concerned with the liberation of creative energies than with the grubby business of improving working conditions at the local boot factory. Esson was in his late twenties when he visited India, Japan and China in 1908. His responses throw an interesting light on changing Australian perceptions of Asia.[45]

The circumstances in which Esson made his trip are not at all clear. It appears likely that he was encouraged to go by Frank Fox and perhaps also received Fox's financial support. Fox was the editor of the *Lone Hand*, which published Esson's articles from his Eastern trip. Publication in this journal ensured widespread exposure of Esson's views. The first issue of the *Lone Hand* appeared in May 1907 and had an astonishing print run of 50,000 copies. This had been achieved through the close links cultivated by Fox with the Commonwealth Government, which showed its approval of his journal by purchasing 10,000 copies for distribution throughout Britain and America.[46] From the outset, the *Lone Hand* stressed Australia's vulnerability to attack from Asia, especially from Japan. The dangers said to flow from Australia's small population, particularly in the Northern Territory, were another regular concern. Protection for local industries, increased funding for defence, unswerving commitment to a White Australia and a critical stance towards British policies in Asia were all *Lone Hand* priorities. Esson certainly shared these views. He did not go to India with an imperialist interest in the British Raj or in the Indian Mutiny. Though interested in India, Esson was much less convinced that it was central to Australia's future than Deakin had been almost twenty years before, nor did he in any way share Fitchett's imperial enthusiasms.

Esson's first series of articles from his trip was collectively entitled 'From The Oldest World'.[47] Like Australian travellers before him, he was drawn to images which spoke of human activities carried on in the same manner, and probably in the same place, for centuries. He too was much taken by the spectacle of Indian women drawing water from wells. The extraordinary diversity of India certainly appealed to him. In Jaipur he experienced a 'constant excitement of the senses, a feast of the eyes, a stimulus to the imagination'.[48] The voluptuous disorder bore in upon him: the elephants, beggars, minstrels, tiger-tamers, the jumble of rich and poor, human and animal, rags and finery. It was all too real and all too improbable: 'It is surely an Oriental extravaganza, a fairy tale, a caprice of some poor poet drugged with opium and flowers'.[49] This was unique, vast, poetic India. As for the Maharaja of Jaipur, Esson was strangely attracted by his attachment to the old ways, his indifference to the people and his sumptuous lifestyle. As far as Esson could judge, Jaipur had escaped both the baleful influence of the British and of modern Western life and was fortunate to have done so. Esson feared the British would kill the razzle-dazzle and sheer energy of cities like Jaipur, substituting 'toil and sweat' and the dreary laws of the production line. He accused Britain and apologists for Empire of standing only for an undignified scramble for trade, an attitude for which the *Bulletin* used the generic term, 'shoddy'. Esson wrote:

> India is wealthy and the white man is there to sell Brummagen goods. In pursuit of this worthy object he acquires an especially enlarged liver, plumps for cheap labour, and reckons our coloured fellow-subjects, whom he kicks whenever he can, are eminently desirable immigrants for Australia.[50]

Esson also made further irreverent comments about the Anglo-Indian fears of the *Swadeshi* movement, a nationalist initiative that encouraged the purchase of local rather than foreign goods and was seen by many Anglo-Indians as yet another sign of sedition. Esson was more sympathetic, seeing the movement as an explicable, although not very efficient attempt to apply the principles of economic protection to Indian affairs. He mocked the Anglo-Indian for seeing 'sedition' everywhere: 'if his table "boy" comes around three minutes late with the green peas, or undercooks the vegetable curry, such conduct he regards as downright insurrection'.[51]

For Esson, the British in India presented an unedifying mix of racial arrogance, venality and bureaucracy. He was repelled by the intricate snobberies and heartless cruelty that permeated the imperial enterprise and he deplored the 'ultra-Conservative type of Anglo-Indian' who all too often kicked and abused his servants.[52] Esson experienced no enthusiasm for the British imperial mission and had no pride in a shared Britishness. Esson advised Australian to dissociate themselves from the British in India and their Anglo-Australian supporters, not least the Rev W H Fitchett. It was a message the *Lone Hand* supported fully.

In Esson's articles there is no sense that India might have a special bearing on Australia's future and no enthusiasm for trade links or strategic connections designed to keep the Russians at bay. The Russian menace had faded from view following their defeat in the Russo-Japanese war of 1904-1905. There were no claims that Esson's boyhood imagination had been fired by tales from India. Interested though he was in India, its people and their religions, Esson believed that it represented the past not the future and would play a diminishing role in Australian affairs. In any event, Esson suspected that India's future would increasingly lie in Indian hands. China and Japan were a very different matter. Both fitted comfortably enough within the rubric of the 'awakening East'. Esson believed the awakening of China would be slower and more problematic than that of Japan, though with consequences of enormous moment for world politics and the future of Australia. When he turned to Japan, Esson was no longer dealing with the 'Oldest World' but with 'The Asiatic Menace'.[53] Japan was the country to watch. Its policy could be summed up in one word: 'expansion'. Where Japan had taken its place among the 'Great Powers', India was 'stagnant' even after 'centuries of the blessings of British rule'.[54]

Chapter Four

One Hundred Work as One

In the 1850s, the widely publicised discovery of gold in Victoria and New South Wales attracted immigrants to the Australian colonies in unprecedented numbers. Many Chinese were among these hopeful migrants. By 1859, there were around 50,000 Chinese in Australia. Indeed, on some Victorian gold fields, one in four miners was Chinese. At this point, the colonies passed strict legislation restricting further Chinese entry. Although this had an effect, the legislation was again strengthened in the 1880s amid fears of a further increase in Chinese immigration. By 1887, it had become very difficult for any Chinese to enter Australia.[1] Their numbers had fallen below 30,000 in 1901 and continued to decline. Even so, there remained many more Chinese in Australia than Indians. Estimates of the Indian population in 1901 range from 7,000 to a mere 800.[2] The Chinese were the major focus of concern about the possible impacts of non-Europeans on the development of Australian society.

The appearance of the Chinese in the 1850s and their movement into gold and tin mining ventures in Queensland and the Northern Territory through the 1870s and 1880s gave Australians some lasting impressions of the East. The Chinese, 'stirred some of the volcanic sub-texts' of everyday life.[3] Most of the known vices were attributed to them: they were represented as gamblers, drug addicts and sexual deviants. They lusted after white women. They were diseased. They carried leprosy and all the poxes: small, chicken and other. Others stressed their disciplined work habits, arguing that Chinese were the most adaptable of all settlers. They were methodical. Their powers of working together in disciplined units were uncanny and unnerving. They were frugal and would eke out a livelihood in circumstances no European could endure. No climate deterred them, no circumstance defeated them, no soil was too poor for them to cultivate. In a highly regarded study, *The Races of Europe*, published in 1899, William Z. Ripley of Columbia University described the 'great Mongol horde' as 'perhaps the most gifted race of all in its power of accommodation to new climatic conditions'.[4] They were the most numerous and enduring race on earth and they had reached Australia.

The manner of their arrival was prosaic enough. They had come by ship like everyone else, though often in conditions so crowded as to enhance impressions of their unnatural powers of endurance (Plate 6). Early descriptions of their arrival quickly began to indicate deeper Anglo-Saxon anxieties. The Chinese were presented as a vast mass of humanity as indistinguishable from each other 'as the grains of yellow sand on the seashore'. Their movements were described as tidal. They 'flooded' into the colonies.[5] China was described as a great dam, soon to burst, sending inundating rivers and flows of migrants into neighbouring countries. Floods and tides obliterate boundaries and destroy recognised landmarks. They carry all before them. If the Chinese were a flood bearing down from the North, the future of the British race in the Australian colonies was clearly under direct threat. Australia's tiny British communities might go under. The inundation of an entire community was a potent theme, well suited to the nineteenth century European imagination; the decline and fall of civilisations and the impacts of barbarian hordes upon vulnerable civilisations were then popular topics. It was a powerful narrative, wreathed in pathos and full of dramatic possibilities.[6]

The Chinese presence in the colonies stirred many Australian anxieties. Australian colonists liked to think of themselves as British, but they began to see they were British in strange geo-political surroundings. They suspected Australia might be on a great Chinese flood plain. It was clearly well within reach of Chinese influence. California, another gold rush society, had also experienced a substantial influx of Chinese.[7] The realisation grew that Australia should not look just to Britain. It shared strategic interests with other white communities in the Pacific, especially with America. But the Pacific was a contested ocean. From the 1880s, it was increasingly apparent that China and Japan were also nearby Pacific nations.

The presence of so many Chinese intensified debate on the potential character of Australian society. Potent concerns had developed about civic values in gold rush communities, concerns aggravated by Australia's convict origins. Gold was a seductive, richly mythologised substance. Its discovery in the Australian colonies publicised their potential more than anything else had yet done. Gold attracted a young, cosmopolitan, ambitious, predominantly white male population, often imbued with advanced democratic views. Yet as David Goodman has shown, this influx stirred anxieties about the moral stability of these gold-seeking communities. A gold-obsessed society appeared a poor foundation for a stable, cultured society.[8] Many social commentators found the prospect that working men could gain sudden wealth in this way very disturbing. Would people still value achievements wrought by steady labour and industrious habits? What would happen to moral values? There was another more disturbing thought. If Australia could produce only these rough, uncivilised communities, might it not lose the moral authority by which Australians, claiming the rights of a superior culture, sought exclusive access to the continent? Were Australians still worthy of their immense opportunities?

Questions of tenure and entitlement were intensified by the dispossession of the Australian Aborigines. One of the main justifications used at that time for taking over Aboriginal lands came from the belief that they were a primitive, nomadic people with no fixed settlements or habits of agriculture. It was thought that they did not value their land and had no capacity to develop it. One of the troubling paradoxes of gold seeking populations was that they also were a highly mobile wandering tribe, in some ways similar to the Aborigines they sought to displace. Anxieties about the continuity of white settlement in Australia intensified impulses to vilify Aborigines and to keep Asians out. The major question revolved around entitlement to the land. In the blunt language of the late nineteenth century, if white had replaced black because black was not developing the continent, why should yellow not replace white on precisely the same grounds? If European communities in Australia were not seen to be civilised and productive, the case for sole tenure of Australia by whites might be seriously weakened.

The Chinese threat was seen more in terms of sheer numbers of settlers rather than in terms of direct military action by China. Australian colonists were more inclined to fear possible war with the Russians, at least until their defeat in the Russo-Japanese war of 1904-5. Russia, backed by considerable naval and military power, posed a persistent threat to the British Empire especially in India. The British Consul in Fukien explained to George Morrison, the *Times* correspondent in Peking in 1898, that Russia could well mount a successful attack upon India which might lead on to Britain's withdrawal from Asia and if that occurred 'our story wd. be done'.[9] In contrast, nineteenth century China was an Empire in sharp decline, facing enormous threats, both external and internal. At the end of the Opium war in 1842, Britain imposed severe and humiliating terms on China. The Treaty of Nanking opened five Treaty Ports to foreign trade, ceded Hong Kong to Britain and provided payment of millions of dollars in indemnity. Further humiliating settlements were made in the 1859 Treaty of Tientsin after the 'Arrow War'.[10] As Immanuel Hseu has written: 'By 1860 the ancient civilisation that was China had been thoroughly defeated and humiliated by the West'.[11] Within China seismic social disturbance and rebellion continued over thirty years from 1850. The Taiping Rebellion lasted sixteen years, raged across sixteen of the eighteen provinces, destroyed over 600 cities and killed millions. At that time, the disintegration of the Chinese state seemed a real possibility.

After visiting China in 1879, James Hingston, author of *The Australian Abroad*, doubted China's capacity ever to become a cohesive, modern society. Having explored Shanghai, he concluded: 'The Chinese are not to be feared. As a nation they are the weakest of warriors, and incapable alike of aggression or defence'.[12] Neither did they appear to be interested in new technologies. Hingston had heard the sorry story of the British-built railway line running to Woosung. Local mandarins had forced the local governor to buy the line from the British and destroy it as a most unwelcome symbol of the modern world. Hingston saw the main problem facing China as the difficulty of holding the country together. It was crucial, he felt, that this was somehow achieved, for if it was not, Chinese labourers would 'flood' the world's labour markets.[13]

While Hingston saw nothing to fear militarily from China, the Chinese capacity for hard labour and their intelligent adaptation to varied circumstances was another matter altogether. The 'superior civilisation' of the Chinese gave them 'powers of combination' unknown in any other society: 'one hundred work as one'.[14] But might this not make the Chinese a remarkably successful colonist? Hingston asked:

> What is to stop his progress and his dispersal over the world, now that the Chinese Empire, mainly through the shaking of English assaults, is tumbling to pieces? As the Goths and Huns overran the Old World, so it seems probable that the hundreds of millions of Chinese will flood the present one, and that at no very distant date.[15]

Hingston anticipated many themes later developed by other Australian commentators. He was convinced the world would become increasingly Chinese, not through military invasion, but by 'dispersal'. Yet Hingston's observations were largely free of hostile prejudice. He found much to admire in the Chinese and believed their successes both hard-won and well-merited. Hingston also saw lessons in history. He warned that domination of one group by another had occurred often in the past and would do so again. Tidal population movements across the globe were possible. It was China's turn to shake the world.

Hingston believed that destabilisation of China, largely through British actions, now meant that the dispersal of her immense population was inevitable. Yet the 'East' had posed no significant threat to the 'West' until European powers had forced themselves upon Asia for their own benefit. The *Bulletin* expressed similar views. It noted that the Chinese had been happy to keep to themselves until 'England came along with a bayonet, and a keg of opium, and a Bible' determined to interfere in Chinese affairs.[16] Moreover, it argued, Britain, dominated by tawdry trade motives, had given the Chinese access to the Australian colonies merely so 'that she might have Free Trade in cutlery and shoddy at Shanghai and Canton'.[17]

Hingston's *The Australian Abroad* was published in 1880. This was a volatile year in colonial politics when the presence of the Chinese was a major concern. From the late 1870s there had been a growing anti-Chinese movement, sparked by the increasing concentration of Chinese in the major cities and their growing prominence in the furniture trades. A monster petition protesting the Chinese presence was presented to the New South Wales Parliament in 1878. In that year the Australasian Steam Navigation Company exacerbated the situation by announcing the replacement of European seamen by Chinese. Public reaction was swift. The labour movement was quickly mobilised around the threat that Chinese labour was said to pose to working conditions and wages. The Chinese presence had become a labour issue. The Seaman's Union went on strike and the Company was forced to change its policy. In Sydney's Hyde Park, 10,000 protesters, mainly working men, made their opposition to the Chinese very plain. Throughout this period, physical attacks upon Chinese increased in number and severity. In 1880, increased numbers of Chinese entering New South Wales and Victoria helped keep the agitation alive. The Premier of New South Wales, Sir Henry Parkes, suggested that the time had come for an inter-colonial conference on the Chinese question. The industrious Chinese seemed poised to take over the labour markets of the world. Each Australian colony then introduced tougher legislation to restrict Chinese entry. But even as numbers of Chinese began to decline, the centenary year of 1888 was marked by protracted anti-Chinese protests and strained relations between the colonies and the British Government.[18]

In 1888, the Governor of New South Wales, Lord Carrington, summarised under seven headings the case against continued Chinese immigration into Australia, for the Imperial government:

> firstly, the Australian ports are within easy sail of the ports of China; secondly, the climate as well as certain branches of trade and industry ... are peculiarly attractive to the Chinese; thirdly, the working classes of the British people in all the affinities of race are directly opposed to their Chinese competitors; fourthly, there can be ... no peace between the races; fifthly, the enormous number of the Chinese intensifies every consideration ... sixthly, the ... determination ... to preserve the British type in the population; seventhly, there can be no interchange of ideas of religion or citizenship, nor can there be inter-marriage or social communion between the British and the Chinese.[19]

Francis Adams, a bright young radical journalist, who wrote extensively for the labour paper, the *Boomerang*, was keenly interested in the Chinese question. Adams, like Hingston, felt Australia had more to fear from Chinese capacities than Chinese vices. As they could 'beat us in the struggle for existence', he argued that Europeans and Chinese could not co-exist. To Adams it was a simple law of nature: 'The Asiatic and the Turanian must either conquer or be conquered by, must either wipe out or be wiped out by the Aryan and the European'; just as nations had been 'wiped out' in the past, they could be 'wiped out' again in the battle for racial supremacy.[20] Adams drew upon familiar late nineteenth century social darwinist rhetoric. In this schema, competition between races was deemed the oldest and most enduring of all competitive forces at work in the world. There had been great struggles in the past, followed by a long period of relative calm in which Europe had imposed her authority on the world. Now, Adams believed, the long age of European dominance was coming to an end. The East was set to explode with accumulated resentments, population pressures and an awakened sense of national purpose. Adams saw Australia placed near the centre of the ensuing struggle.

Adams' article, 'What the Chinese can teach us?' published in the *Boomerang* in 1888, summarised much of his thinking.[21] Surprisingly, he opened with consideration of the history of Java. There, a thousand years earlier, Hindus, who were 'Aryans as well as we', had introduced a 'complex and stupendous civilization'. Their greatness was still evident in the majestic ruins of Borobudur and Prambanum. But this mighty civilisation had been defeated: 'an extirpation more complete than even that of the Britons by the Angles and Saxons'. Although the Chinese could not be directly blamed, Adams argued that Malays, whom he considered racially similar to the Chinese, were responsible. It might seem that an account of the fall of Borobodur was an unlikely way to inflame anti-Chinese sentiment among Queensland workers. Hadn't the issue lost some of its urgent topicality in the intervening millennium? Yet Adams clearly felt he had made a strong case for lasting incompatability between Aryan and Chinese races. If it had happened once at Borobodur, there was no reason to believe that it might not also happen at Bundaberg or even Ipswich.

Adams did not want to appear prejudiced against the Chinese. He scorned arguments for Chinese exclusion on the grounds that they were a vicious or filthy people. Historical precedent and the laws of nature persuaded him that Chinese efficiency, not Chinese vice, was the real issue. Given a foothold in Australia, the Chinese, he was convinced, would inevitably come to dominate. They might even develop a more egalitarian, republican and efficient civilisation. Even their dietary practices were superior. Adams believed the white labourer drank too much, ate too much and wasted too much energy, whereas the Chinese had achieved a near-perfect balance between food intake and energy requirements.[22] Their civilisation was so tenacious and enduring that even its lowest, least regarded workers could work with remarkable discipline. The European 'title deed' to Australia was quite insecure, a mere accident of history. Yet now the colonising was done, Adams felt there was no option but the complete exclusion of the competitive Chinese.

Another writer deeply concerned about the Chinese presence in Australia was William Lane, the moving force behind the *Boomerang* and a powerful figure in the Australian labour movement. In 1888, William Lane was in his late twenties and, though born in England, was a recent immigrant from America, where he had spent almost ten years, acquiring in the process many of his views on the conflict between capital and labour and, possibly, many of his anti-Chinese sentiments as well. In Australia he quickly established his name as a labour activist and radical intellectual. He exhibited intense admiration for Queensland bushworkers perhaps sharpened by his own delicate health, short-sightedness and limping gait.[23] Lane's views on the relations between capital and labour reached a national audience with the publication in 1892 of his novel, *The Working Man's Paradise*.[24] Lane was not given to compromise and was frequently prey to obsessions. He left Australia in 1893 with over two hundred supporters to found a utopian community in Paraguay, a famous experiment that soon ran into difficulties, many of them aggravated by his autocratic conduct.[25]

Lane travelled a different path from Francis Adams, but reached similar conclusions. Writing for the *Boomerang* under the pseudonym, 'Sketcher', he described himself as a student of 'the history of race movements' whereby 'mighty nations and great States' had been submerged by 'advancing tides of antagonistic races'. Like Adams, he relied on distant epochs to sustain his case, citing the Cymric swept aside by the Saxons, the Celts overtaken by the Teutons and again, the fate of Aryan civilisation in Java. He asked: 'If race movements changed the constitution of States in the past as they undoubtedly did, why should they have ceased to be similarly influential now?'[26]

Lane and Adams differed, however, on the question of the moral character of the Chinese. Lane insisted that the Chinese were a morally degenerate race whose vices would inevitably weaken and corrupt the entire community. He had visited an opium den near Brisbane's Queen St, in order, he claimed, to get a clearer sense of what the Chinese were up to. This was a border crossing, an episode where racial boundaries blur and where the European enters the world of 'the other' and for a moment submerges his identity. Lane's expedition found him in a cramped, foul smelling room filled by a bed on which smokers reclined. On the wall, in his direct line of sight, was a print of a half-naked woman. Lane tried some opium:

> I noticed mostly that I began to hate less these calm faced impassive invaders
> of our civilisation and to feel less intensely against their abominable habits
> and vices and to take less notice of the stifling air and overpowering odours.[27]

The world around him grew softer, more alluring. His hostility began to fade. But then his gaze travelled to the picture of the half-naked woman. He remembered a white girl ruined by opium, seen living with Chinese. Angry again, he now wanted to destroy every opium den he could find, and drive out Chinese who threatened to 'bury our nationality in a deadly slough of sloth and deceit and filth and immoralities'.[28] Lane clearly distinguishes between a pure white civilisation and the inescapably impure Chinese, between good and bad vice. He defended European vices; drinking, tobacco smoking and betting on horses were the pastimes of a virile, manly race. They were proof of vitality, the best antidote to the corrupting practices of the sensuous, opium smoking Chinese (Plate 7).

Lane believed that the Chinese differed from the Aryan in the ways they expressed their sexuality. He thought Chinese expended excessive sexual energy. Lane's description of the warm, stuffy opium den suggested intense, unhealthy preoccupations. It was a place of lingering, enervating sensuality, of emasculating introspection. Although Lane did not refer directly to masturbation, that great nineteenth century vice, he conjures its presence through his references to the semi-naked woman on the wall, the heated room, his obsessive concern with filth and moral pollution.[29] Lane's idealised Aryan would not allow any such expression of open sexuality; his vigour was the high-spirited expression of youthful vitality. Robust manhood was the active agent in the creation of a wholesome civilisation.

Unlike Adams, Lane considered Aryans more than a match for the Chinese on an individual level. The problem was there was so very many Chinese. Lane revealed his calculations for different 'swarming populations', in other words, the surplus population ready for emigration. China, he figured, had an annual 'swarming population' of 65 millions. They could go nowhere but Australia: 'There is no land so convenient and so promising, so unoccupied yet so hospitable'.[30] The problems would be intensified by Chinese industrialisation. Lane pictured millions thrown out of work, swelling the vast tides leaving China. Again China was a dam about to burst. Lane was convinced the Chinese had their eyes on Australia. He thought the four Chinese Commissioners, who had visited Australia the previous year, had come as spies on the look out for underpopulated regions.[31] In fact, these Commissioners had come to report to the Chinese government on the treatment of overseas Chinese.[32]

The visit of the Chinese Commissioners certainly had aroused considerable interest. In Sydney, fashionable society turned out in large numbers to greet them at a function hosted by the Lady Mayoress.[33] The Commissioners, sumptuously attired in official costume, caused a sensation. The Sydney Chamber of Commerce ferried them around the harbour on the Government steamer. There was much talk of closer trade ties with China.[34] Lane's sensitive nostrils quickly smelt a conspiracy among the Anglo-Australian elite to hand fair Australia over to the Chinese.

Lane believed that the only way to avert this new threat was to fill Australia up as quickly as possible with white immigrants. But they could not be found in Europe, which had a 'swarming population' of only 16 millions. North America was the only hope. When he got to work with his abacus, Lane found that America would fill up within a generation. Then it could direct its surplus population, 'the brain and sinew of the Pacific slope,' to Australia. If Australia could hold on for two more generations it might become a relatively safe destination for surplus Americans. And until that time? Australia was in 'appalling' danger.[35]

Another critical issue for Lane was the role of Britain. Lane thought that England was largely to blame for provoking the Chinese dragon: 'It was England, with her disgusting cant and hideous passion for trade, who blew open the gates of China to let the opium merchants in and the Chinese hordes out ...'.[36]

Moreover, in Lane's view England was entirely unrepentant. Lane believed Britain would always put its commercial interests far ahead of any needs of distant, yet vulnerable Australia. To Lane, John Bull stood for little more than tawdry profit and commerce.

At the time Lane wrote, throughout the Western world there were growing concerns that a battle for racial supremacy was unfolding in the Pacific. While Australian commentators tended to see Asia as the primary threat to Australia's national survival, British and American opinion was much more inclined to fear the growing dominance of Russia. In 1898 the Russians forced the Chinese into ceding control of Port Arthur. Two years later, during the Boxer rebellion, they made massive troop commitments to Manchuria, a development revealed to the world by George Morrison. Russian military pressure seemed intense and was designed to expand military and commercial access to the tottering Chinese Empire and to threaten British interests in the lucrative China trade. These developments naturally caused profound unease in London and Washington. By 1900, British trade and investment in China had already reached staggering dimensions: one sixth of British exports went to China and three quarters of China's trade was carried in British ships.[37]

The American interest was less immediate, but the prospect of profitable trade with China had not escaped Washington. Moreover, as Stuart Anderson has argued, there was a shared Anglo-Saxonism operating at the highest levels in Britain and America which construed the contest with Russia as a battle for racial supremacy between Anglo-Saxons and Slavs. Events in China were viewed as the setting for another great racial struggle between these conflicting interests. Six months before the outbreak of the Russo-Japanese war, President Theodore Roosevelt, speaking in California, identified the Pacific basin as the region most likely to determine which race would come to dominate the globe. At that time, his greatest concern was Russia. The defeat of Russia by Japan, a nation Roosevelt greatly admired, saw the collapse of the 'Slavic Peril', but it did nothing to relieve Australian anxieties which had focused more strongly on China and Japan. When Britain forcefully pursued its economic and imperial interests, further destabilising and exploiting China, it appeared to be putting Australia's security at risk, without any real appreciation of Australian vulnerabilities. Lane was convinced that one way or another Australia would become a hapless casualty of British policy in China.[38]

In discussing the Chinese, Lane developed a global view of history in which antagonistic races struggled to achieve and maintain world dominance. While the European races had enjoyed a period of dominance, he was convinced that in the late nineteenth century a new phase in world history was beginning to unfold. The stirring of the great Chinese Empire would inevitably change the balance of world power and present new challenges to Europe. It is a comment on the thinking of the 1880s that Lane gave little thought to the emergence of

Japan, a nation still largely identified, as we shall see, with refined artistic traditions, exquisite landscapes and polite behaviour.[39] Very similar comments apply to Charles H Pearson's *National Life and Character: A Forecast*, first published in 1893.[40] Pearson, described as 'the outstanding intellectual of the Australian colonies', took as his subject world history.[41] He maintained that what he termed 'the higher races' would soon lose their position of dominance in world affairs to encroaching 'lower' races. Once again, China was seen as the major engine of change. Pearson's book was to have a powerful influence on predictions about the racial character of the twentieth century many years after it was first published, not least because the rise of Japan as a world power threatening Anglo-Saxon dominance seemed to confirm his view that the 'higher' races were in decline. Though Pearson barely mentioned Japan, much of what he had to say about the role that China would play in the distribution of world power was readily transposed to Japan. For Pearson it seemed inevitable that in certain parts of the world the 'black and yellow' races would soon 'swamp' the white races.

Pearson drew a sharp distinction between what he called 'evanescent races', like the Australian Aborigines, the Kanakas and the American Indians, and other more enduring races like the Chinese, the Hindu and the Negro. The 'evanescent races' would disappear, no matter what efforts were made to preserve them, while the remaining 'lower' races were beyond extermination. There were too many of them and extermination was no longer 'sanctified by religion'.[42] Of the many historical examples that Pearson drew upon to illustrate his views, he found the case of Natal, in South Africa, particularly significant, both as a colony of mixed race and as an indication of what could be expected to happen in Africa generally. Natal also provided Pearson with some telling comparisons with developments in the Australian colonies.

Natal, which was seized by the British in 1842, offered rich lands and a range of favourable climates to British settlers. Assisted immigration programs and the presence of the British army in the late 1870s provided extensive opportunities for the sale of farm products and contract labour. Nearby diamond and gold fields added to Natal's attractions. Yet Pearson noted that after fifty years there were not more than 36,000 white settlers in a total population nearing half a million. By the late nineteenth century, European settlers had become dependent upon abundant supplies of African labour, which in turn reinforced the view that certain kinds of labour were beneath the white man. Pearson argued, 'from the moment that a white population will not work in the fields, on the roads, in the mines ... its doom is practically sealed'.[43] Such a population would contract to a narrow elite, while the increasingly prosperous black population would gain access to education and ultimately demand a share in running and governing the colony. The remaining whites would then either leave or be absorbed into a mixed-race community of 'mulattoes or quadroons'.[44]

This was both a warning about dangers to be avoided in Australia and a recognition that whites would not find a permanent place in Africa. Pearson also ruled out the tropical world, including most of South America, as potential 'Aryan' homelands, largely on the grounds that tropical climates precluded white settlement.

The most dynamic factor in Pearson's account of race developments was his views on the likely impact of the Chinese throughout South East Asia. After reviewing a range of possibilities he concluded that a great people like the Chinese, backed by enormous natural resources, 'will sooner or later overflow their borders, and spread over new territory, and submerge weaker races'.[44] Pearson was convinced that world-wide, the 'lower races' were increasing faster than the 'higher races'.[45] He believed that one day members of the Aryan race would be 'elbowed and hustled, and perhaps even thrust aside' by peoples they were accustomed to regard as inferior. In this mixed and turbulent world, the citizens of 'lesser' societies would claim admission to the 'social relations of the white races'. Pearson imagined them patronising the hallowed race tracks of old England, infiltrating the salons of Paris and finding acceptance as marriage partners. Ill, despondent and not far from death as he wrote *National Life and Character*, Pearson hinted that he was among those in whom the feeling of 'caste' was so strong that it might be better to die than live to see the birth of such a world.[46]

Pearson's global view reserved an important place for Australia as a continent largely free from the disabling problems that had bedevilled British settlement in Natal. In Australia, cheap labour was not available in such abundance that white society ran the risk of becoming a narrow elite. In addition, since Pearson classified Australian Aborigines as an 'evanescent race', he thought they were unlikely to pose a sustained challenge to European settlement. Not so the Chinese. Drawing on official statistics, Pearson observed that in 1857 Chinese gold miners represented as much as 13 percent of the adult male population of Victoria. To Pearson, this indicated that Chinese could readily settle in Australia in substantial numbers. As they faced no natural barriers, exclusive legislation was the only available strategy Australian colonists could use to prevent Chinese entry. As Pearson believed Australia's climate was well suited to European settlement, he concluded that Australia was the last remaining part of the globe still available for the 'higher races'. He saw Australia as the last Aryan homeland, a land where white races could breed, regenerate and marshall their forces. By this positioning, Pearson turned Australia from an outpost of Empire to a nation with a vital role to play in a global racial struggle. Pearson had moved Australia from the margins of world history to a position close to centre stage.

Pearson's book attracted an immense amount of comment in England and America that continued well into the 1920s. In May 1894 the *Sewanee Review* published a 26 page review article on *National Life and Character* by Theodore

Roosevelt, who was already a major figure in American political life and soon to become America's 26th President.[47] Roosevelt shared Pearson's conviction that Australia had a crucial role to play in the development of the British race and that 'the peopling of the island continent with men of the English stock is a thousand fold more important than the holding of Hindoostan for a few centuries'.[48] Roosevelt believed that Australia had the potential to become a permanent homeland for the white races, an outcome that he agreed was unlikely to occur in Africa or India. Roosevelt reached into the distant past to cite the process by which the Greek rulers of Bactria had been absorbed by local tribes, eventually to disappear. He then speculated that a similar fate might await the British in India. The theme of the disappearing race served as a constant reminder that fragility and 'evanesence' were central to the human condition. Evidence of peoples, nations and races disappearing in the past was taken as a sure sign that unprepared peoples who ignored the lessons of history would themselves disappear. Roosevelt shared Pearson's conviction that history, no matter how remote, furnished directly applicable lessons about the conditions for race survival.

Even so, Roosevelt could not accept Pearson's melancholy conviction that the 'higher' races would inevitably lose substantial ground to the 'lower' races. He was also quite unconvinced by Pearson's contention that populous China would come to exert an immense influence throughout Asia. Moreover, he believed that it was highly unlikely that Chinese would ever displace an entrenched European population. Where Pearson was willing to attribute military capacities to the Chinese, Roosevelt was not. He maintained that the Chinese had never been a great military power and doubted that they would become one. Even if they did, Roosevelt saw no reason to believe that the rise of China need 'stunt and dwarf the peoples of the higher races'.[49] He looked back to Elizabethan England and argued that while Turkey had then been a major power, this had not inhibited Elizabethan achievement. Pearson had locked his 'higher' and 'lower' races into fixed positions, whereas Roosevelt maintained that if a 'lower' race attained impressive industrial and military capacity, this would mean that they were civilised: 'We should then simply be dealing with another civilised nation of non-aryan blood'.[50] Roosevelt saw a much brighter future for what he called the 'dominant races' than could be inferred from *National Life and Character*.

The Right Honorable George F Curzon's *Problems of the Far East*, published in 1896, also devoted considerable space to a detailed refutation of Pearson's concerns about the Chinese.[51] Curzon had travelled widely in India, Persia and the Far East and was the author of *Persia and the Persian Question*, published a year earlier than *National Life and Character*. A famous orientalist, Curzon was soon to become Viceroy of India.[52] The formal, aloof and witheringly superior Curzon maintained that the widespread apprehension that another 'invasion of the hordes of Jinghis Khan' might soon occur, had received a 'fresh and formidable impetus' from Pearson's 'remarkable work'. Like Roosevelt, Curzon was unable to accept Pearson's 'melancholy' forecast which was so 'complimentary to China and so lugubrious for ourselves'.[53] Curzon doubted that the existence of Chinese settlements in countries around the Pacific was a sign of impending 'commercial and political domination'. Rather, he attributed Chinese emigration to the formidable difficulties Chinese workers faced in attaining adequate employment in their own badly governed and troubled country. For Curzon, the fact the Chinese were forced into expatriation did not mean the Chinese were determined to colonise the world. As for Chinese military prowess Curzon would have none of it: 'There is no country in the world where the military profession is of smaller account, or where the science of warfare is less intelligently studied...'.[54] Curzon maintained it was 'the wildest freak of fancy to suppose' that the Chinese could create an all-conquering army. Such a possibility lay so far into the future that it resisted speculation. When Curzon came to Pearson's reflections upon possible Chinese infiltration of the salons of Europe and the race tracks of England, he could not have been more dismissive. He was adamant that China was a 'stationary' society. Chinese people, despite their strengths, seemed content to 'stagnate'. Curzon dismissed Pearson's fears as nothing more than a 'brilliant extravaganza of the imagination'.[55] His objection to any references to British Imperial decline became very apparent at the great Durbar celebrations of 1903 when he forbade the singing of the hymn 'Onward Christian Soldiers' because it contained references to crowns perishing and kingdoms waning. Curzon believed the British Empire would never fail.[56]

Others were less confident. Some of Pearson's central concerns were developed by H A Strong, Professor of Latin at University College, Liverpool, who in 1896 set out his opinions in a lengthy preface to Pearson's *Reviews and Critical Essays*.[57] Strong was a measured and scholarly man. Like Francis Adams, he was impressed by Chinese perseverance and their ability to maintain 'bodily vigour' on a scanty diet in many extremes of climate. He thought they would be able to establish flourishing settlements in parts of Australia that Europeans found intolerable. He also thought Chinese made impressive soldiers.[58] Strong believed that Australia's future was threatened if Chinese immigration continued, not least because Australians, in becoming rapidly urbanised, were losing their physical strength and martial disciplines. Strong observed:

> our population is more and more displaying a tendency to settle in large towns where the physique of the nation deteriorates, so that in process of time it may be assumed that our qualities as a fighting race will not increase with our numbers.[59]

For Strong, this was an issue of grave concern and he exhorted Australians to fight urban degeneracy. If the Chinese could flourish in climatic extremes, maintaining 'bodily vigour' in adverse circumstances, Australians needed a similar adaptability. If the Chinese had notable fighting qualities, Australians must develop these too. If Asia had large populations, then Australia needed a population in the scores of millions.

In his biographical sketch of Pearson, Strong drew attention to the views of his friend and former pupil, George Morrison. Morrison considered the industrial capacities of the Chinese unimpaired, despite the disordered state of their country. Morrison spoke from direct experience. His book, *An Australian in China*, published in 1895, was based upon his extraordinary journey from Shanghai to Burma on foot, the previous year. Though he spoke no Chinese, Morrison was an acute observer and he had seen parts of China that few Westerners had visited. Morrison admitted that when he had begun his journey he had harboured 'the strong racial antipathy to the Chinese common to my countrymen'.[60] But by his journey's end he held a high opinion of the Chinese who, with rare exceptions, treated him with courtesy and respect. The men contracted to him for each stage of his journey invariably proved honest, disciplined and skilful. Morrison was convinced that the missionary endeavor in China was largely futile and held out no hope that China would be converted to Christianity. Converts were pitifully few and their motives could be questioned. But failure to convert the Chinese to Christianity did not mean they then became a military threat. In his extensive travels, Morrison saw a bizarre array of weaponry, but little was in working order and ammunition was rarely available. In addition, much of the country through which he passed was in a dire condition, rampant with disease, poverty and civil disorder.

Although Morrison challenged the key anti-Chinese prejudices of his countrymen, he was utterly opposed to the idea that they should be permitted to enter Australia. Morrison, who was medically trained, believed that the Chinese were differently constituted from Europeans. The Chinese 'sensory nervous system' was either 'blunted' or undeveloped.[61] This explained their cruel punishments and their capacity to endure the unendurable. Morrison considered the Chinese formidable competitors and tenacious colonists. 'Admitted freely into Australia', Morrison maintained, 'the Chinese would starve out the Englishman, in accordance with the law of currency — that of two currencies in a country the baser will always supplant the better'.[62] The Englishman, with his more complex and fully developed sensory organisation, might be superior to the Chinese, but he could not withstand direct competition. Morrison lent the authority of direct experience, which Pearson was unable to do, to the view that the Chinese would prove invincible colonists if admitted to Australia in any numbers. This admission contained a reproach. For all their sterling qualities, Australian settlers appeared to lack the discipline, determination and inexhaustible vitality of the Chinese.

Chapter Five

The Enchanted Island

No country presented a more enigmatic or beguiling face to young Australia than nineteenth century Japan. To Europeans, the Japanese appeared a remarkably self-contained people. They had no history of emigration. Indeed, before the Meiji restoration in 1868, it had been a capital offence to leave the country. Japan had been largely closed to the world until America's Commodore Perry appeared in Yokohama with his famous Black Ships in 1853-54, forcing a reluctant Japan to open treaty ports and begin trade with the West. But after the Meiji restoration, Japan opened to the West increasingly on its own terms and in pursuit of new technologies and new ideas. Japan soon became famous for its receptivity to Western influence. It was admired for the beauty of its natural scenery and the discipline and cleanliness of its people. Japanese art was collected, admired and studied throughout Europe. Japan appeared at once charmingly Eastern yet thoroughly progressive. As the American orientalist, William Elliot Griffis, observed in 1905 in his introduction to *Bushido: The Soul of Japan*, Japan was 'working with resistless power' to cut a middle way between the antique wisdom of Asia and 'the energy and individualism of Europe and America'.[1] Japan was the newly emerged and vigorous East.

Inazo Nitobe, author of *Bushido* professed that he was discouraged from writing more about Japan in English when dazzling accounts were already available in the writings of Lafcadio Hearn, Mrs Hugh Fraser, Sir Ernest Satow and Professor Chamberlain. Satow's comprehensive *Handbook for Travellers in Central and Northern Japan* had first appeared in 1881 and was then revised and updated by Professor Chamberlain. Hearn's *Glimpses of Unfamiliar Japan* was published in 1894 and quickly won a wide readership. By the time Mrs Fraser's *A Diplomat's Wife in Japan* was published in 1899, there were numerous handbooks, including the widely used *Murray's Handbook for Travellers in Japan* and other foreign accounts available to Australian travellers. Relative to the number of books published on France, a comparable European centre of culture, the number of books published in English about Japan rose sharply between 1850 and 1880 (Figure 5.1).

The processes by which nineteenth century Australians formed their views of Japan deserve separate study, but among educated Anglo-Australians there were undoubtedly direct influences, even if hard to measure, from the depictions of Japanese life which appeared in nineteenth century British and American literature. For the author Hal Porter, Japan stole into his life through wind-chimes and other manifestations of his mother's 'Austral-*japonoiserie*' domestic

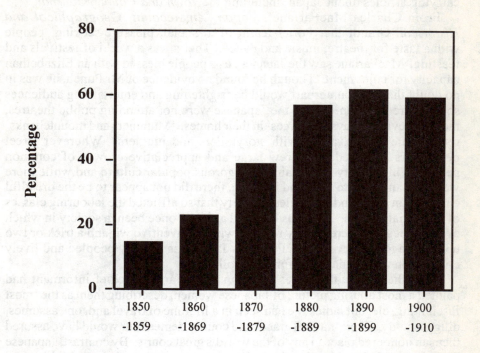

Figure 5.1: Publications on Japan presented as a percentage of publications about France, 1850-1910 as catalogued by the United States Library of Congress.

tastes.[2] Then when his grandfather died in 1920, young Hal was given his books on Japan, including Charles MacFarlane's *Japan*, published in 1852, A B Mitford's *Tales of Old Japan*, published in 1871, and Isabella Bird's *Unbeaten Tracks in Japan*, published in 1880. His grandfather, Porter recalled, had lived for years on 'little more than reading, port wine, cigar smoke and imperial behaviour'. His gift to his grandson revealed that he had also 'loved Japan'.[3] Porter's intriguing comments unfortunately reveal little about the cultural tastes and intellectual interests that nourished Grandfather Porter's fascination with Japan, though we can see he was a gentleman of taste, something of a connoisseur. Much must have been learnt from periodicals. British magazines like the *Edinburgh Review*, the *Westminister Gazette* and the *Fortnightly Review*, which enjoyed a wide readership in the colonies, maintained a steady interest in Japan. Indeed, some of Mitford's tales had first appeared in the *Fortnightly Review* and *Cornhill Magazine*. There were also informative Australian sources carrying articles about Japan, including the *Town and Country Journal*.

From Charles MacFarlane's *Japan: An Account, Geographical and Historical*, Grandfather Porter learnt of a 'social, pleasure-seeking' people with a taste for theatre, music and dance. Theirs was a world of festivals and feasting. MacFarlane saw the Japanese as a people blessed with an Elizabethan capacity for enjoyment. Though he found no evidence of Mr Punch, he was in no doubt that his counterpart would be frightening and entertaining audiences somewhere in Japan. When the Japanese were not attending public theatres, they improvised 'plays and farces' in their homes. 'Mummers and mountebanks' roamed the streets, along with storytellers and jugglers. Wherever street performers appeared they drew large and appreciative crowds of common people. This society had retained a vigorous popular culture and while there were rich and poor to be found in Japan, there did not appear to be the dreadful emiseration and grinding, joyless poverty that so afflicted the labouring classes of industrial Britain. This was England as it had once been, a society in which even the beggers were 'merry rogues' with an inventive wit and a trick or two up their ragged sleeves. MacFarlane's Japan was a richly peopled and lively civilisation with a talent for 'fun and drollery'.[4]

Then there were the ladies of Japan. MacFarlane's chief informant had painted a most alluring picture of Japanese women, describing them as the 'most fascinating, elegant ladies' he had seen in a lifetime of travel and, one assumes, diligent study. Their 'natural grace' and courtly demeanour would have assured them an honoured place in any of the world's great courts. By contrast, Japanese men, despite their evident loyalty and patriotism, were too given to drinking and immorality to be considered entirely worthy partners of these estimable women. MacFarlane confessed, with thinly veiled eroticism, that it was the descriptions of Japanese women 'that first excited me to a deep and lively interest in the subject of Japan'.[5] To their many other virtues, MacFarlane also drew attention to the cleanliness of the Japanese, who were widely known to be much given to the rituals of the bath. Public bathing was universal among them and provided opportunities for European males to covertly appraise these graceful and shamelessly naked Asian ladies. MacFarlane's generously illustrated *Japan* was a pleasing confection; a thought-provoking accompaniment to a Victorian gentleman's after-dinner port and cigars (Plate 8).

As MacFarlane's account makes clear, certain understandings of Japan were already well-established as early as the 1850s. In his instructive study of the stereotypes of Japan found in British literary magazines and periodicals, Toshio Yokoyama, author of *Japan in the Victorian Mind*, notes that the politeness and formality of the Japanese and the singularity and immutability of their culture were constant themes, certainly from the 1860s.[6] Yet there was also a narcissistic impulse to establish analogies between Japan and Britain. Many British observers admired in the Japanese the qualities they most admired in themselves. There was a frequent appeal to the idea that the Japanese, as another enterprising island people, had something in common with the British and that, of all nations, Britain was the best equipped intellectually, diplomatically and even climatically to develop a sympathetic bond with the Japanese. It was almost as if the Japanese had emerged as ideal foreigners. They could certainly be thought of and treated as worthy partners. The Japanese had a similar enthusiasm for Great Britain and began to call their country *Dai Nippon*, Great Japan.

Japan was routinely regarded more highly than China in the periodical literature, despite the high commercial value that the British placed upon the lucrative China trade. Belief in a sympathetic bond between the British and the Japanese was strengthened by speculations that the Japanese had allegedly sprung from similar racial stock. Yokoyama found a 'rosy' image of Japan in British periodicals, which increasingly stressed the cultivation and sophistication of the Japanese, qualities supported by the beauty of the scenery. One measure of the high approval rating was the willingness to see the Japanese, particularly Japanese women, as impressively cultivated and refined. Yokoyama noticed an element of friendly competition over which of the two nations had the best manners. Even so, there were some tensions in the presentation of Japan to British readers. As the process of westernisation increased in the 1870s, there was a growing fascination with 'old Japan' and a more critical response to the Japanese as an imitative people. At the same time, more commentators expressed their astonishment at a nation that could leap from feudalism to modernity in a matter of years. It was commonly described as a revolution like no other in world history. Travellers tried to pursue 'old Japan' in regions beyond the increasingly europeanised Treaty Ports. From the mid-1870s, restrictions on travel eased and more foreigners found their way to the great cultural centres like Kyoto, Nikko and Nara. Yokoyama discerned in the commentaries of the 1870s a growing unease over the impact of British civilisation on Japan. As more writers became convinced of the classical harmonies and refinement of Japanese civilisation, there was a corresponding anxiety about the coarsening influences of western civilisation.

In the familiar contrast with China, Japan invariably appeared cleaner, less crowded, more cohesive, more artistic and more civilised. The West's discovery of Japan came at a time when the enthusiasm for *chinoiserie* had long since declined into a weary and rather decadent attachment to the exotically gaudy and ornate. Interest in *chinoiserie* had been supplanted by amusement at the 'Chinaman', a debased and immoral figure who made regular appearances in Britain's premier satiric journal, *Punch*.[7] By contrast, artistic Japan's impact on the West was immediate, profound and enduring. It reached into every corner of modern taste and shaped the cultural sensibilities of some of Europe's most important and innovative creative artists. One of the first and most influential collectors was Sir Rutherford Alcock, British Minister to Japan from 1859 to 1864 and a key figure in introducing the enthusiasm for Japanese art to British audiences.[8]

Alcock assembled a major collection of Japanese art objects and crafts for the International Exhibition held in London in 1862. To obtain these choice items he had scoured some of the less well known quarters of Tokyo, where Europeans rarely ventured. He was always on the lookout for new discoveries and was rarely disappointed: 'Every day brought some new and interesting fabric to light, some original application of Art to industrial purposes, or examples of artistic work of unrivalled beauty'.[9] The display of Japanese arts and crafts at the 1862 Exhibition which created such interest throughout England, was visited by some Australians, including Henry Austin and James and William Macarthur.[10] Eager buyers quickly snapped up all that was on offer. The collection inspired a lecture by John Leighton on Japanese Art at the Royal Institution in 1863 during which he commented on the Japanese Court at the Exhibition. It was 'divided by a distance of six feet from China, which it immeasurably distanced — an enchanted island of great beauty around which visitors were never tired of travelling'.[11] As soon as the Exhibition was over Alcock was invited to address the Philosophical Society at Leeds on Japanese art and its industrial applications. The interest in things Japanese was considerable and remained so for decades. 'Within a very few years', Alcock later wrote, 'I found Japanese fabrics, silks, and embroideries, Japanese lacquer, china, faience, bronzes, and enamels exhibited for sale in the shops of every capital in Europe'.[12]

By the early 1860s, William Rosetti, a key figure in the pre-Raphaelite movement, had recognised the technical and aesthetic contribution that an understanding of Japanese art would have upon British and European artists. He wrote of Japanese art as a revelation. The *Art Journal*, a widely read and influential British publication carried enthusiastic and informative articles on Japanese art.[13] The English architect and designer, Edward William Godwin, fell under the Japanese spell. His homes and wallpaper designs were directly influenced by Japanese artistic practices and motifs, while 'successive wives and daughters wore kimonos to harmonize with the settings'. Arthur Lasenby Liberty, creator of Liberty prints, was another influential arbiter of modern taste who found in Japanese art and design an opportunity to make a striking aesthetic statement. By the 1870s he had persuaded mills in the English Midlands to produce fabrics carrying Indian and also Japanese designs and he later visited Japan.[14] These various influences had an impact; one authority on the British aesthetic movement has noted that from the mid-1860s until the turn of the century, 'Japan was the strongest design influence' operating in England.[15] English enthusiasts interested in Japanese art were able to consult two handsomely produced, generously illustrated and informative books on Japanese arts and crafts, *The Keramic Art of Japan*, which was favourably reviewed in the

Australasian Sketcher in 1881, and Alcock's *Art and Industries of Japan*. Americans, who by the 1880s had also become enthusiastic collectors of Japanese prints and art in general could consult Christopher Dresser's *Japan: Its Architecture and Art Manufactures*, published in 1882.[16]

The new taste for Japanese art had also become widespread in France. In 1856, the etcher Félix Braquemond had stumbled upon a volume of *Manga* or sketches by the Japanese print-maker Hokusai that had been included as packing material around a shipment of porcelain.[17] Other artists soon shared his early enthusiasm for these striking prints and many similar books were soon sent on their way to Paris. Each new shipment brought 'fever-pitch excitement'. The American expatriate artist James McNeill Whistler and the French art critic, Zaccharie Astruc, came to blows over who had the right to purchase a prized Japanese fan.[18]

Appreciation of all things Japanese was further stimulated by the extensive *Exposition Universelle*, held in Paris in 1867. After the International Exhibition in London in 1862, the Japanese government had become more receptive to the idea of exhibiting its products and made a substantial commitment to the Paris Exhibition. The Japanese Court reinforced the impression that Japan was a society in which an appreciation of art shaped every aspect of daily life, an ideal with considerable appeal to intellectuals increasingly alienated by the ugliness of industrialisation. The Paris Exhibition fed the rapidly growing interest in things Japanese that was already apparent in France. One commentator remarked that 'Japanese prints were everywhere' at the time of the Exhibition, so much so that some of the earliest enthusiasts for Japanese art were now disgusted by its growing popularity. In 1868 the Goncourt brothers complained: 'We were the first to have this taste. It is now spreading to everything and everyone, even to idiots and middle-class women'.[19] The great modern department stores, for which Paris was famous, responded to the demand for Japanese items with a multitude of print albums and other affordable art objects.[20] Also from Paris came the lavishly illustrated periodical *Artistic Japan*, the English version of *Le Japon Artistique*, published in monthly installments from mid-1888 to 1891, by the celebrated French dealer in Eastern art, Siegfried Bing. This publication reached a wide and influential audience throughout Europe and the United States. The Arts and Crafts Society of New South Wales, founded in 1906, acquired a complete set of *Le Japon Artistique*. The expatriate Australian painter, Charles Conder, came into close contact with European enthusiasm for Japanese art when Siegfried Bing commissioned him to decorate a boudoir in a group of display rooms prepared for his shop *l'Art Nouveau* at 22 Rue de Provence. Conder was deeply impressed by this 'Paris of Verlaine and the Japanese Club'.[21]

The triumphant advance of Japanese art was so complete that by 1872 the French collector and art critic Phillippe Burty had coined the term '*japonisme*' to describe the impacts of Japanese aesthetics on the practice of Western art.[22]

The influence of Japanese prints was so strong that 'virtually every major artist in late nineteenth century France benefited' from contact with this new art form.[23] James McNeill Whistler was one of the first to incorporate elements of Japanese art into his painting. By 1864, his painting 'The Little White Girl' introduced many elements from Japanese prints including 'a linear quality, asymmetrical composition, flat colour patterns and blossoms peeking in along the edge of the frame'. His subject, a girl in a 'fluffy white dress', holds an Eastern fan.[24] In 'Caprice in Purple and Gold No 2: The Golden Screen', a young woman is seen 'seated on an oriental rug contemplating Japanese prints'. Behind her stands 'a *yamotoe* screen'.[25] In a similar manner, Edouard Manet's 1869 portrait of Emile Zola placed the famous writer in a studio decorated with Japanese screens and block prints, thereby linking the European avant garde with Japanese aesthetics.[26] Such effects could be overdone by lesser artists as is the case in Girolamo Nerli's, 'The Sitting', painted in Australia around 1888, where a woman poses against a background cluttered with Japanese fans and eastern artifacts. Then again, might this have been a satiric comment on the fashionable *japonisme* of the wealthy woman who was the subject of the painting?[27]

Claude Monet was another enthusiastic collector of Japanese prints. He had over two hundred on display in his home at Giverny, while his famous garden was planted with Japanese plum trees and willows. Having enlarged the pond, he installed a Japanese footbridge and planted wisteria on surrounding trellises.[28] In 1876, his painting 'La Japonaise', showed his wife 'wrapped in a spectacular Japanese-appliqued cloth with fans on the wall behind her'.[29] Japanese influences, particularly the Japanese use of colour, have now been recorded and studied in the art of many other impressionist painters including Degas, Pissaro, Sisley and the Americans Whistler and Mary Cassat. Japanese art also affected many post-impressionist painters including Gauguin, another devoted collector of Japanese prints, Bonnard, Vuillard, Seurat, Van Gogh and Toulouse-Lautrec.[30] In the Paris of the 1880s, Toulouse-Lautrec designed brilliant posters for the fashionable *Divan Japonais* cabaret which was exquisitely decorated with fans, silks, and served by waitresses in gorgeous kimonos. A photograph from the early 1890s shows the artist wearing a kimono and Japanese hat, a fan in one hand, a doll in the other.[31] Likewise, Van Gogh made an extensive exploration of Japanese art and its influence can be seen in his many paintings of flowering fruit trees, bridges, butterflies and other Japanese-inspired subjects. The non-Western qualities of Japanese art generated continuing interest and analysis. Degas was particularly attracted by the Japanese use of asymmetry, sharply foregrounded figures, exaggeration and inventive use of spatial effects.[32] French applied and decorative arts also benefited from the new Japanese influence. These arts gained a 'new appreciation of nature' which was soon registered in many diverse areas including 'media-ceramics, glass, jewellery and metalware, furniture, textiles, wallpapers, and bookbindings'.[33]   Interior designers, in particular, frequently turned to exotic Eastern settings with 'fans applied to the wall in asymmetrical patterns, parasols, screens, a profusion of Oriental porcelain [and] ... hanging paper lanterns'.[34]

The influence became so pervasive that it drew a sharp criticism from Victor de Luynes, one of the judges of the 1878 World Fair: 'Japonisme! Attraction of the age, disordinate rage which has invaded everything, taken command of everything, disorganized everything in our art, our customs, our taste, even our reason'.[35] Yet the influence continued unabated, proving so diversified and adaptable that it not only served to nourish the romantic ideals of late nineteenth century artists but also acted as 'catalyst in the exploration of modernist aesthetics' to many artists in the early twentieth century. *Japonisme* influenced both the 'whiplash line' of *Art Nouveau* while also contributing to the formal aesthetics of Art Deco.[36] While Japan continued to impress the modernist art world, Japan as the 'attraction of the age' was near its height in the 1880s and 1890s.

Australian commentaries on Japan in the nineteenth century suggest that a fascination with this newly revealed culture soon travelled to Australia. Much of this influence came indirectly via Europe. Before the turn of the century, few Australian artists had visited Japan. Those who did, included the etchers E L Montefiore and Mortimer Menpes, the water-colour painter John Peter Russell and the architect John Smedley. Travellers suggested that Australians could learn a good deal from the culture and customs of the Japanese. In *Travelling About Over New and Old Ground*, the spirited Australasian traveller, Lady Barker, observed the Japanese to be 'a generous and brave people, frugal, thrifty, scrupulous, clean ... wonderfully ingenious, and full of patriotism and devotion to their institutions'. Refinement, good manners, discipline and patriotism were among the most frequently noted Japanese virtues.[37]

Early in 1871 the well-known Australian publication, the *Town and Country Journal*, carried several striking Japanese woodblock prints showing Japanese women, attired in handsome kimonos, preparing silk. Sliding doors, tatami matting and a pleasing air of industry and order are much in evidence. The art had been supplied by Dr George Bennett and had evidently been displayed at an Exhibition hosted by the Acclimatization Society. It would seem probable that by the late 1860s Japanese prints had found their way into the hands of some private collectors in Australia, while others were exposed both to Japanese art and the enthusiasm it had generated in their travels through Britain and the Continent.[38]

In 1874 the *Town and Country Journal*, now alerted to Japan, noted that it had received an unsolicited copy of the *Japan Mail*, a 44 page newspaper from Yokohama. The *Journal* was quite adulatory, judging the *Japan Mail* to be one of the largest and best-produced papers in the world. It noted an astonishing 'proficiency in reasoning' and knowledge of 'the writings of political

economists'. It also remarked upon the volume of trade transacted by the
Japanese and the efficiency of their railways. The *Town and Country Journal*
sounded a note that would be heard frequently over the next half century. The
rapid transformation of Japan, virtually a closed book to the West just a generation
earlier, was now one of the greatest wonders of a 'wonder-achieving age'.
This was practical Japan, quickly acquiring an impressive array of technical
skills.[39]

The *Town and Country Journal* was perhaps unaware that another wonder
was the influence of the Australian expatriates John R Black and J H Brooke on
the development of the modern Japanese newspaper industry. John Black had
emigrated from Scotland to South Australia where he lived for a number of
years before setting out for Japan. Here he emerged as a notable innovator. In
1926 the *Osaka Mainichi* included Black among its ten 'great pioneers' of
Japanese journalism. In 1871 he established the *Nisshin Shinjishi* which quickly
developed a reputation for reflective and informative comment. For this paper,
Black achieved the extraordinary coup of exclusive publication rights for key
government edicts. This made his paper an indispensable source for serious
students of Japanese affairs. Black was the first to introduce the editorial along
with letters to the editor, both features becoming standard practice in Japanese
newspapers. Black's great labour of love, his two volume history of contemporary
Japan, titled *Young Japan*, was published posthumously in 1881. It was
considered one of the more informative accounts of recent events in Japan and
served as an important reference for many years. Black was also renowned for
his 'fine vocal powers', a talent evident in one of his sons, Ishii Black. Ishii, in
a career no less extraordinary than his father's, went on to become a professional
reciter and storyteller. He lived, worked and dressed as a Japanese, though he
inflected his stories with narratives and motifs drawn from Western folk tales.[40]

In 1871, J H Brooke, another Australian, became the editor and proprietor of
the *Japanese Herald*, a position he retained until his death in 1902. Brooke was
born in England but had emigrated to Victoria during the goldrushes. He entered
Victorian politics and achieved a meteoric rise to Cabinet status. He fell from
favour just as swiftly and retired from office in 1864. Brooke left for Yokohama
in 1867 with his wife and daughter, the elegant and accomplished Gertie Brooke,
and an unprecedented volume of baggage. His 'Impressions of Japan' were
published in a six-part series in the *Argus* late in 1867, perhaps the first extended
account of Japan in an Australian newspaper. Brooke described a society that
was still uneasy about foreigners and where encounters with sword-wielding
daimyos were not uncommon. Yet he was impressed by what he saw. He
particularly admired Japanese elegance and artistry. As for the people, he
considered them alert, intelligent and exquisitely well-mannered. Like many
other Australian travellers who followed him, Brooke was also greatly impressed

by their cleanliness. 'A gayer, more light-hearted people than the Japanese I cannot imagine under the sun', Brooke wrote, 'and they have also an amount of natural and easy politeness that I believe to be nowhere excelled'.[41]

By 1869 the *Japan Times Overland Mail* had become concerned at the influx of Australians into Japan. In a sub-leader, it noted the arrival of the 'Albion' bearing even more fortune hunters and inquisitive travellers. The *Mail*, rather implausibly, blamed Brooke's approving *Argus* articles on Japan for their arrival. It is reasonable to conclude, however, that by 1870 Japan had become a country that adventurous Australians considered well worth visiting. Japan had become a destination offering an enchanting new world to the traveller.[42]

Prominent among the early Australian visitors was our dear friend, James Hingston. Hingston advised Australians wanting to return home from San Francisco to visit Japan rather than travel via Honolulu and Fiji. While many Australians had looked to the Pacific islands as a tourist destination, Hingston was confident that Japan had much more to offer. Visitors would see an astonishing country, newly opened to the world, with three prosperous and well-established European settlements where there were already many Australians. 'Scarcely an Australian but can remember some one from some part of Australasia', Hingston noted, 'who has made Japan a home'.[43] Japan was the only country in the East which Hingston believed Australians might consider calling home.

Hingston referred to the Japanese as both the 'French' and 'British' of the East. They were 'French' in their cultivation and unwillingness to allow religion to interfere with pleasure. They were 'British' in their spirit of enterprise and pragmatism. In these sentiments he was echoed by a leading Melbourne business figure who declared that the Japanese had 'the common sense of the Briton, the sprightliness of the French and the logic of the German'.[44] This was a formidable combination. The purpose of the statement, however, is clear enough. The speaker wanted his audience to realise that the Japanese possessed a civilisation of a very high order and one that showed every sign of adapting to the modern world of new technologies and progressive social philosophies.

The conviction that Japan remained unspoilt by industrial civilisation was central to Hingston's travel narrative. He felt that they had not yet been corrupted by the commercial spirit. For all its macadamised streets and signs of modernity, there was every sign of a rich traditional culture. Wherever he travelled, Hingston was fascinated by the range of popular entertainments available to the people and the pleasure they derived from them. Though he didn't speak a word of Japanese, Hingston loved the itinerant story tellers and the laughing crowds they invariably gathered around them. Whenever the hat came round, Hingston made his contribution. A late nineteenth century literary man, proud of his Britishness, could hardly pay a more generous compliment than to compare Japan to Elizabethan England:

If one would know how the people of Britain lived in the days of old, when there were maypoles and morris-dancers, and caps with bells to them ... when folks were educated to excel in sports and manliness ... to tilt at the quintain, and go hawking and hunting and fishing, as the chief occupation of a Joyous Life, we may go to Japan, look at the Japanese, and learn all.[45]

These sentiments suggest that for Hingston, the Elizabethan achievement was culturally, not racially determined. That Japan might have carried the essential features of the Elizabethan age into the modern world was something to write home about. Hingston nominated 'the Joyous Life' as the highest ideal to which a nation could aspire, an ideal he had observed in 'Elizabethan' Japan. Where Hingston found 'Joy', Brooke, a decade earlier, had found 'Gaiety'. These were sunny, outdoor qualities. The Japanese appeared to be a people who had not allowed themselves to be dominated by religion, least of all the moral severity and gloom that Hingston attributed to Christianity. He admired the fact that the Japanese had kept on dancing and took that to be a sure sign of a country in which religion served the interests of the people, not one in which religion had crushed their spirit. Moreover, in Hingston's view, industrialisation had not yet caste its dark pall over the Japanese.

Japan came closer to providing the greatest happiness for the greatest number than any country Hingston could think of. He described the Japanese as a capable, polite and talented people who had brought the art of living to a very high pitch. He approved of their diet, dress and frugal habits, their honesty and manners, their religion, architecture and gardens and their story-tellers and ceremonies. Hingston also bestowed paeans on praise to the climate. He knew none more perfect and believed that this greatly contributed to the felicitous condition of the people. Hingston stressed the artistic prowess of the Japanese and the formal beauty of their culture. Japan enchanted him.

When the Australian scientist, Julian Tenison Woods, set out for Japan in the mid-1880s he was pleased to find that there was a good deal of 'new and valuable information' available to the traveller, although he was unimpressed by one of these 'authorities' (clearly Hingston) who had 'boasted of having ... read nothing about the country, so as to be unbiased!' Hingston's wily ironies had obviously gone unappreciated. Tenison Woods claimed that he could not agree with Hingston's flattering account of Japan as a country of 'Arcadian simplicity', especially in matters relating to diet. He was unimpressed by raw foods and believed they gave the Japanese dyspepsia. Yet, as much as he seemed to disagree with Hingston's enthusiasm for Japan, Tenison Woods was hardly less enthusiastic. Delayed in Kobe, he found himself living very well in a traditional house of paper and wood. Though deep snow lay all around him, he was snug and contented: 'I could not be more comfortably lodged or better taken care of in any country in the world', he wrote to his sister-in-law. To his brother, he wrote from Hong Kong that 'he was quite disenchanted about China and liked the people less and less'. But Japan was another matter: 'I never liked any country so much as I liked Japan, and would go there tomorrow if I could'.[46] The contrast with China was a commonplace of the period. Hingston felt similarly and so did Rudyard Kipling, that most influential commentator on the East.[47] Kipling loved the scenery of Japan, the elegant houses and the glimpses they offered of 'perfect cleanliness, rare taste, and perfect subordination of the thing made to the needs of the maker', but he loathed China and disliked the Chinese.[48]

Hingston's trip to Japan coincided with the 1879 International Exhibition in Sydney, which introduced its many visitors to Japanese arts and manufactures. The 'Japanese Court' at the Exhibition carried an impressive range of exhibits from industrial and agricultural products to the art works and delicately wrought crafts for which Japan had become famous. Sydney audiences clearly responded warmly to the Japanese Exhibition, with the *Sydney Morning Herald* declaring after the first day that the Japanese Court was the most popular of all the international displays.[49] Japanese exhibits featured prominently among the prize-winning entries: porcelain, china, cloisonné ware, earthenware, silk garments, fans and 'fancy articles', paper products and photography along with bronze, iron and copper castings all won first prizes. The 'Ladies Court', featuring folding screens, lacquer ware and wooden furniture, was a particular success with the judges, winning three first and two second prizes. In a gracious gesture, the Japanese government bequeathed the entire exhibition to the people of New South Wales.[50]

Some of these objects entered the collection of the Sydney Museum. The museum catalogue lists an impressive collection of Japanese materials acquired before 1900. These include many specimens of food and plant products typical of Japan such as saki, soybeans and eight types of edible seaweeds; a range of Japanese furniture and artifacts including cabinets, screens, fans, porcelain, swords, a shansen, a rickshaw and a collection of thirty domestic and agricultural utensils. There were also drawings and small models of a Japanese house and a Japanese ship. A collection of skeins of raw silk, presented to the Agricultural Society of New South Wales by the Emperor of Japan was also displayed by the Museum for some time but was withdrawn in July 1933.[51]

When the International Exhibition moved to Melbourne in 1880, the Japanese Court attracted the attention of James Smith, one of Victoria's leading art critics and a regular contributor to the *Argus*. Smith readily acknowledged that one of the remarkable developments flowing from the comparatively recent opening of Japan to Western influence was the profound impact of Japanese art in Europe and America. The embrace of Japanese art had been so swift and comprehensive that art critics the world over had been taken by surprise. Though Smith wondered if Japanese influences would maintain their original intensity, he nonetheless acknowledged that Japan's impact on the West was considerable. He admired the 'exuberant fancy' and 'richness of invention' in Japan's craft traditions and had the highest regard for Japanese portrayals of the natural world which he considered as fresh, ingenious and skillfully crafted as anything created in the West. There was about Japanese art, 'a delicacy and precision of touch which testify that the Japanese is not only an artist by instinct, but has inherited the culture, experience, and practice of centuries'. Smith maintained that any lingering doubts in the West about the quality of Japanese crafts had been effectively dispelled by the breathtaking Japanese exhibition at the *Exposition Universelle* held in Paris in 1867.

Smith was fascinated by the relationship between physiology and art production. He believed that the nervous organisation of individuals and races shaped artistic sensibilities and aptitudes and that among the Japanese, motor skills and optic nerves had been developed to a remarkable degree. Smith observed that in Japan the strong hereditary traditions of craft-work ensured that 'the organs and faculties of each generation, improved and developed by habit and experience, would be inherited by its successor in a condition of higher efficiency'. Smith believed that this conditioning explained the highly developed artistic sensibility evident in Japanese art and in crafts such as metalwork, pottery and porcelain.

To the physiology of art production, Smith added a series of cultural arguments which affirmed the high standing of the artist in Japanese society. Like Charles MacFarlane, Rutherford Alcock, James Hingston and a host of other commentators on Japan, Smith celebrated in the Japanese the qualities that he believed were most endangered by rapid industrialisation in the West. Smith believed that the best and most fulfilling societies were those that venerated art and craft traditions. Japan seemed to be just such a society: 'Instead of being a mere cog or wheel in a vast and complicated piece of human mechanism ... and feeling no interest whatever in his occupation ... the Japanese artificer works in the spirit of the medieval artisan'.[52]

In 1885, Australian audiences were delighted by the first performances of Gilbert and Sullivan's, the *Mikado*.[53] Explaining the opera's appeal, the *Sydney Morning Herald* noted that Australia's enchantment with Japan had dated from the 1879 Exhibition which had shown Australia that Japan had a 'civilisation as thorough in its own way as it was distinct from any preconceived notions of our own'.[54] The *Mikado*'s scenery was reported to be based on faithful reproductions of Japanese domestic architecture and the Japanese-made costumes were placed on display in the windows of a department store in Sydney where they attracted large crowds.[55] Later, another opportunity to survey aspects of Japanese life was presented by 'a Japanese village' in Sydney, which reproduced houses and featured Japanese demonstrating traditional arts and crafts. These exposures to Japanese culture all contributed to the view that Japan had developed a remarkably refined and original civilisation.

At least one Australian of that time who was sufficiently entranced by the Japanese house to have one built for himself. It was built for Judge Paul in the Brisbane suburb of New Farm in 1887. Every care was taken to ensure authenticity. The house was designed, built and decorated by Japanese using materials especially imported from Japan. In an enthusiastic illustrated article on the house, the *Boomerang* suggested that Japanese architectural practices might help 'solve the problem of semi-tropical architecture' in Australia. In its design, furnishings and use of screens, ceramics and art, the house struck the *Boomerang* author as a perfect realisation of Japan in an Australian setting. He noted how the tonings of the house and its furnishings were more subdued and carefully integrated into a satisfying whole than most Australians might have suspected, given their exposure to the brightly coloured objects typical of the local trade in Japanese curios. Taken altogether 'the harmony of decoration and the perfection of colour and outline is as perfect in its way as was that of the Greeks in theirs'. The meticulous care taken over the building of this house suggest that residence in Japan had converted Judge Paul into another considerable enthusiast for Japanese culture.[56]

While it was impossible for most Japan enthusiasts in Australia to go to the lengths taken by Judge Paul, many nevertheless exhibited Japanese artifacts in their houses. Mount House, for example, in Strangways Terrace, North Adelaide, the home of solicitor William Pope, was 'filled with souvenirs of visits to the Middle East and Asia' and featured, in the entry hall, a large Japanese embroidered hanging of two peacocks. Similarly, the drawing room in the home of John Brodie Spence, brother of Catherine Spence, at Glenelg, Adelaide, displayed a collection of Japanese fans and other objects, a cushion covered with a Liberty print and an E W Godwin coffee table. Other examples of E W Godwin's ebonized Anglo-Japanese furniture were advertised for sale in 1885 by Cullis Hill & Co., Melbourne. The firm's manager, Morde Cullis William Hill, had his home, Tudor House, hung with large Japanese embroideries and adorned with Japanese vases and screens. For a touch of colour in a room he advised the inclusion of a Japanese screen.[57] If they did not purchase from Cullis Hill & Co., collectors could often purchase Japanese items at auction. In May 1889, John Willard, auctioneer, advertised the sale of Japanese curios, including 600 walking sticks, pictures, vases, screens, fans and furniture. These had been collected by James Murdoch, educator, journalist and historian, on his 'recent tramp of 3000 miles through the previously unknown parts of Japan' (Plate 9).[58]

On 17 August 1889, an exhibition opened in Brixton's Gallery, Swanston Street, Melbourne. Called the '9 x 5 Impressions' Exhibition', it took its name from the fact that the artists, who included such luminaries as Tom Roberts, Arthur Streeton and Charles Conder, had painted their 'impressions' on 9 x 5 inch cigar box lids. These were Australian paintings, yet like work of French Impressionists, they had been influenced by the East, especially Japan. This influence was evident in the cherry blossom drawn on the cover of the catalogue by Charles Conder and in the environment created to display the paintings. The artists 'looped and knotted "Whistler draperies" and Liberty silk' around the gallery and distributed 'Japanese umbrellas, screens and fans' through its rooms. The *Sydney Mail* noted how these, together with 'great Japanese vases of japonica and daphne ... gave the room that "quite Japanese" appearance that is considered so desirable nowadays' (Plate 10). These decorations had been supplied by Cullis Hill & Co.[59] The studio of A E Aldis, the English painter who boarded with Rose and Percy Grainger in Hawthorn, Melbourne, revealed a similar Japanese influence with a profusion of fans, as recorded by the artist in a painting completed in 1891.[60]

One of the most prominent popularisers of Japan from the 1890s to the outbreak of the Great War was Douglas Sladen, a graduate of Oxford and Melbourne Universities, who came to Victoria in 1879. In 1880 he married a squatter's daughter from the prosperous Western District of Victoria and wondered at the benefit he might extract from having a former Premier as a member of the family. While in Victoria, Sladen developed a lasting friendship with George Ernest Morrison, a fellow student at Melbourne University. Sladen took credit for the publication of Morrison's only book, *An Australian In China*.[61] Sladen moved comfortably in Anglo-Australian circles, where interest in Japan was particularly apparent. After graduating in law from the University of Melbourne, he immersed himself in the local literary world. He had a brief period as a lecturer in modern history at Sydney University, then left Australia in 1884, although he maintained his Australian connections. Sladen produced three anthologies of Australian poetry in 1888 and continued until the 1930s to bring out books on Australia. While attracting some favourable comment, they hardly set the world alight. By 1890, Sladen had developed a more lucrative enthusiasm: Japan.[62]

It is hardly conceivable that Sladen, a regular in Melbourne literary circles in the early 1880s, did not know Victoria's celebrated traveller, James Hingston. Whether the triumphant reception of *The Australian Abroad* influenced Sladen is impossible to say, though writing in the late 1930s, Sladen confessed that the East had called him all his life. He had lit upon 'the shores of fanciful and mysterious' Japan, brimming over with the highest expectations. The encounter changed his life. He had now come upon a really popular subject. He called his first book on Japan, *The Japs at Home* and claimed the dubious honour of being the first author to use 'Japs' in a book title.[63] He shed his label as the 'Australian poet' and became known as an authority on Japan. When an American colleague commented that Sladen had developed into a more imposing literary figure, Sladen responded: 'I am glad you've shifted me to the main division for I have gradually drifted away from Australia and am now always talked of in connexion with Japan'.[64] *The Japs at Home* sold 150,000 copies 'laying the foundation of my career as a travel-book writer'. In the preface to the fifth edition, published in 1895, Sladen recorded the recent Japanese victory over China. He now regretted that 'I did not devote my book to an advocate's presentment of the greatness of Japan instead of treating the country from the viewpoint of the pleasure-pilgrim'.[65] Sladen wrote at least six more books about Japan, including *A Japanese Wedding* and *Japan in Pictures*, all of them effusive and laudatory.

Entries on Sladen in the *Oxford Companion to Australian Literature* and the *Australian Dictionary of Biography* make no reference to his outpourings on Japan, yet it was Japanese subject matter that established his popularity and helped secure his income as a writer. Sladen found that Japan was an object of curiosity among the reading public in a way that Australia was not.[66] The infatuated Sladen wanted one of his books, *Lester the Loyalist*, to be published in Japan. Though it was a mere twenty pages in length, it took two months and infinite patience to print. Sladen was overwhelmed by the result. He admired the type, the block printings, the 'silky ivory-tinted' paper, the covers of 'steel-grey paper crepe' and the cover with its elegant white silk label: 'The good taste, the elegance, the colours ... fairly amazed me'.[67]

For Sladen, Japan was a land of 'fairy-tales'. In Tokyo's Shiba Park, he was overcome by the beauty of the Temples and the courtyards with their stone lanterns, fountains and limpid streams stocked with leisurely golden carp. He gushed over fluttering geishas and elegant teahouses. He enthused over terraced mountain sides and shaded walks. He was dazzled by scarlet azaleas and groves of wild wisteria, their gnarled trunks deepening the air of profound antiquity which clothed so much of what he saw and admired. He considered Lake Biwa one of the most 'exquisite' lakes in the world and was enchanted by nearby *Ishiyama-dera*, a beautiful temple complex on a pine-covered hillside overlooking the lake. It was hard not to be impressed. A thousand years before, Lady Murasaki had written *The Tale of Genji*, the world's first novel, within the Temple grounds. Sladen also loved Nikko with its 'sky-blue river, running beneath the sacred scarlet bridge'.[68] Typically, there was always an Australian visitor who was not quite so impressed. George Meudell, reflecting on his many journeys, thought Nikko was overrated. He knew 'a spot on a hill near Kangaroo Flat in Victoria, Australia, infinitely to be preferred to Nikko'.[69] Nevertheless, by 1912, the idea of taking a holiday in Japan, perhaps to see the beauty of the Cherry Blossom Season was well established. Burns, Philp and Company ran a regular tourist service to Japan.[70]

Consistent with the enthusiasm for Japan, the first Australian novel to be set in Japan, A M's *From Australia and Japan*, was published in 1892. The author, A M, was James Murdoch, also a likely candidate for authorship of the article on Judge Paul's house in the *Boomerang*. Murdoch was born and educated in Scotland. A graduate of the universities of Aberdeen and Oxford, he moved to Queensland in the 1880s. His career appears no less extraordinary than those already narrated of John Black and J H Brooke. While in Australia, Murdoch wrote a number of articles for the *Boomerang* and then fleetingly joined Lane's New Australia experiment in Paraguay. He left rather quickly, realising that he was highly unlikely ever to agree with Lane's ideas on how to run a utopia. He would later discover that Japan came much closer to his idea of utopia than Paraguay ever could.[71]

From Australia and Japan, Murdoch's first novel of Japan, told the tale of two fellows with socialist sympathies who had sought to escape various Australian entanglements by travelling to Japan. One became involved in the world of journalism while the other became an English teacher. This tale provided a sympathetic portrait of Japanese life, although the superior masculinity displayed by the two tall foreigners invariably enabled them to outwit their Japanese rivals. The illustrations depicted the Japanese as a rather diminutive people.[72] In the same year the prolific Murdoch also had another novel published in Yokohama; *Ayame-san, A Japanese Romance or the 23rd Year of Meiji (1890)*. Here the hero is Phelan O'Rafferty, the Japanese-speaking son of an Irish father and a Japanese mother. The unlikely O'Rafferty had made his fortune at Broken Hill but, being in his own estimation, neither good enough for the priesthood nor bad enough for the New South Wales parliament, he had returned to Japan. Murdoch plots an intricate romance between O'Rafferty's friend, an American artist, and the beautiful *Ayame-san*, interspersed with commentaries on old and new Japan. The book was illustrated with striking photographs of Japanese landscapes, street scenes and portraits taken by Professor W K Burton from the Imperial University of Japan.[73]

At the end of 1889, Murdoch had written a report, possibly for the Japanese government, on conditions in Australia. Here he claimed that 'Australian popular opinion is wonderfully favourably inclined towards Japan and the Japanese'.[74] As with commentators previously mentioned such as Tenison Woods and Rudyard Kipling, Murdoch would never have made the same enthusiastic observation about the Chinese. At this time Murdoch's comments on Japan were no doubt coloured by his own enthusiasms. He was already developing an extensive knowledge of the Japanese people, their language and their history. Even so, there is no question that in the 1890s Japan had become the object of considerable sympathetic interest in Australia.

Murdoch became proficient in both modern and ancient Japanese and went on to become one of the great historians of Japan. He was appointed to the foundation lectureship in Japanese at the Royal Military College, Duntroon, in 1917, a position soon upgraded to a chair. Murdoch was then thoroughly immersed in his three volume history of Japan, an important text in this field for decades. Although never well known in Australia and ignored in Australian historiographical surveys, the history remains in print.[75] The first volume, *A History of Japan During the Century of Early Foreign Intercourse (1542-1651)*, was written in collaboration with Isoh Yamagata and appeared in 1903 to enthusiastic reviews. William Elliot Griffis, writing in the *American Historical Review*, acclaimed it as a 'great work' written by a scholar 'using a half-dozen languages' and based on 'years of research and critical comparison of native and foreign authorities'.[76]

A subsequent volume outlined the mighty sweep of Japanese history from its ancient origins to the arrival of the Portuguese in 1542. Murdoch wrote a substantial and fascinating introduction to this work, in which he sought to explain Japan's more recent 'meteor-like' rise to world prominence. He noted how this phenomenon had continued to baffle many Westerners unable to overcome their narrow understanding of history. 'Many very worthy people', he wrote, 'seem to think that anything that is not strictly synonymous with European, or so-called Christian culture, cannot be regarded as civilisation'.[77] Murdoch believed this approach could hardly be considered adequate for, at a stroke, it removed the towering attainments of Mohammedan culture which had flourished at a time when the West was steeped in 'mental stagnation'. Japanese attainments had suffered a similar fate, though Murdoch noted that it had been clear to the Jesuits at the end of the sixteenth century that 'the Island Empire was fully abreast, if not positively in advance, of contemporary Europe in all the essentials of cultured and civilised life'.[78] Murdoch knew Europe had no monopoly on civilisation.

In the two centuries that followed Japan's rejection of Catholic Europe in 1637, the military, scientific and industrial power of the West expanded dramatically, leaving the Japan that Commodore Perry encountered in 1853 well behind, particularly in industry and science. It had been all too easy for Europeans to dismiss the Japanese as 'barbarians', albeit 'picturesque and exceedingly polite barbarians'. Murdoch disputed this facile view and sought to assess in convincing detail the 'actual assets' of the Japanese at the time of Perry's visit. He quickly dismissed the idea that there had been a long period of mental stagnation when the Japanese were wholly isolated from outside influences. He documented the influence of Sung philosophies, adapted from multiple contacts with China, which had helped discipline and sharpen the Japanese intellect, though not advancing the country economically. The contact with China was quite substantial enough to dispel any sweeping generalisations about Japanese isolation. Murdoch also doubted that the isolationist argument was sustainable in relation to Europe. He pointed to continuing contacts with the Dutch and through them an 'acquaintance with the developments of contemporary European science' among the Shogun's officers.[79] These contacts had continued into the nineteenth century and extended up to the time of Perry's visit.

After the opening of Japan to the West, Murdoch argued, it had taken only two generations for the Japanese to demonstrate a brilliant mastery of three hundred years of Western knowledge. This was surely evidence of a highly developed 'national intellect'. Murdoch had no time for those who argued that the Japanese were mere imitators, incapable of originality. All the evidence suggested that the Japanese were highly cultured and as capable of innovation as any Western nation. Murdoch had made a powerful case for the Japanese as a polished, highly civilised and intellectually gifted people whose long and impressive history pointed to an equally impressive future.

Chapter Six

Trade with the East

The need to reach a decision about the importance of trade with the East was first impressed upon the Australian colonies by the signing by Britain and Japan of the Anglo-Japanese Treaty of 1894.[1] In the decade or so following this agreement, there emerged a clear case for a closer commercial and cultural orientation of Australia towards Asia, supported by calls for the study of Asian languages in Australian universities and by warnings that the repeated expression of anti-Asian sentiments would poison Australia's reputation in the region and damage Australian interests. These observations were backed by calls for the development of a marketing culture in Australia, sensitive to the changing tastes and requirements of Asian consumers. In the same period, the emerging case for closer commercial ties and greater knowledge of Asia was met by increasingly determined efforts by some Australian nationalists to have these commercial aims represented as imperialist cant and crude self-interest. These nationalists sought a far nobler national calling for young Australia. They called for the establishment of a community in the Pacific that would serve as a model white democracy. It was as this debate unfolded that white Australia emerged as a profounder and more important ideal than the promotion of world commerce. Locality and race won out over cosmopolitanism and free trade.

In October 1895, a select sample of Melbourne's business and political community gathered in the supper-room of the Town Hall to hear Mr E Jerome Dyer speak on the implications of the Anglo-Japanese Treaty for Australian trade. Dyer was a commercial agent who had visited Japan earlier that year on a trade mission supported by the Victorian Government.[2] He explained to his Melbourne audience that the terms of the Treaty gave the Australian colonies two years in which to decide whether to become signatories. The advantages included improved access to Japanese markets, but among the political difficulties was the need to agree to the unrestricted entry of Japanese into Australia. Dyer was convinced that the potential benefits of the Treaty far outweighed the possible disadvantages.[3]

The *Age* described the audience for Dyer's address as 'moderate' in number, but noted that it included 'representative and influential persons'.[4] In pressing his case, Dyer spoke of the huge markets emerging in the Asia-Pacific region, commenting that a 'wise Providence' had not only placed Australia near Asia but had also given her a climate able to produce the products that Asia required. He predicted: 'the time may not be far distant when the importance we attach to European markets will be more than evenly shared by those Eastern countries'.[5]

Dyer sought to overcome his audience's possible fears about Japanese immigration. He agreed that Japan could hardly be described as sparsely settled, but argued that its population density did not mean inevitable territorial expansion. The diligent Japanese were not prone to migration and their population could readily double without causing undue population pressure. In Dyer's view, concerns about uncontrolled Japanese migration were ill-informed and it concerned him that such baseless fears might play a determining role in shaping colonial opinion.

Dyer was impressed by Japan's rapid emergence from obscurity to world prominence. This subject, he knew, had already attracted so much attention that he would not need to reiterate the story. But he wanted to make the point that Japan's triumphant emergence as a modern, industrialising nation would create important trading opportunities for Australia. Dyer described Asian markets as 'immeasurable' and saw 'illimitable possibilities for Australian enterprise'.[6] While traditional Japanese tastes might not, he admitted, provide much scope for market penetration by European products, the new Japan was quickly discovering new needs and requiring new products. Dyer wanted Australians to appreciate the pace of cultural change in Japan and the new markets this created. For example, the Japanese could be encouraged to forsake their traditional reliance on silk and cotton to take up the use of wool. Development of a wool trade between Australia and Japan was, Dyer argued, a great example of the possible complementarity of trade between the two countries.

Yet to develop these possibilities Australia had to learn to look after her own interests. During his recent trip to Japan, Dyer had discovered that the existing trade was largely controlled by agents acting for European or American firms. These players, he found, had no desire to promote Australian trade or to encourage new competitors. Dyer wanted Australia to establish its own agents and by implication develop its own marketing strategies. He might have used extravagant language, but his enthusiasm for trade with Japan was well grounded in the commercial realities of his time. The meeting chair, Mr W Madden, supported Dyer's position, urging Australians to 'open up trade with half the population of the globe who were not at present customers of ours'. Was it sensible, he wondered, to put so much effort into highly competitive European markets, while 'neglecting altogether an immense field where all the conditions were in our favour'?[7]

Not all who heard this message accepted it uncritically. David Syme, editor of the *Age*, had also visited Japan to acquaint himself with the country and its commercial future. On his return, no doubt with Dyer in mind, he was sharply critical of the 'sanguine ideas' of 'commercial emissaries'. His own conclusion was that Japan would be much more likely to undersell Australian manufactured products than welcome them in their own markets.[8]

By the 1880s, it was clear that the Japanese had been unable to establish a pastoral industry of their own.[9] Yet there was a growing demand in Japan for woollen goods, a change accelerating from the 1870s when official uniforms, including army uniforms, began to be made from wool rather than from the traditional cotton.[10] In 1878, Monckton Synnot, a Melbourne wool merchant, arranged a shipment of high quality wool from the Western District of Victoria to a trading company in Yokohama.[11] Soon afterwards, a Japanese Commission of Inquiry visited Australia with a view to furthering the export trade in wool. Negotiations were stalled by the indifference of colonial Governments and then by the death of Monckton Synnot.[12] Yet in the mid-1880s, when wool prices fell, Synnot's son, R N Synnot, organised a Woolgrower's Association with prominent industry backing to once again pursue trade with Japan. But history repeated itself. Prices for wool rose and woolgrowers became 'indifferent or lethargic in their attitude' towards a trade which they felt would only expand 'in the dim and distant future'.[13] Meanwhile there was a response from the Japanese side when, in 1890, Kanematsu Fusajiro opened a Sydney office of the Fusajiro Kanematsu Japan-Australia Trading Company, to export Australian wool and cowhides and to import Japanese rice and traditional crafts.[14]

As it happened, the hopes of those who supported the Treaty were not to be realised. The colonies, with the exception of Queensland which extracted special concessions, were too concerned by the prospect of increased Japanese immigration, and did not sign. Despite this setback, R N Synnot, now working through the National Wool Company, based in Melbourne, remained keen to develop the wool trade. He continually sought to place it on a more secure footing by involving the various colonial Governments in the promotion of Australian wool and in the negotiation of wool contracts with Japan. But the establishment of the trade was not aided by British diplomats or businessmen residing in Japan who feared that the development of a Japanese textile industry supplied with wool from Australia would threaten British wool manufactures. So for over twenty years, wool exports into Asia were an on-again, off-again proposition. Yet throughout that time, as Synnot noted, there always remained a core of committed Australian producers willing to back this new trading venture. By 1895, New South Wales was able to export wool to the value of £43,110 to Japan.[15] The Fusajiro Kanematsu Japan-Australia Trading Company also reflected and encouraged hopes for stronger trading links. By 1898, and despite the Treaty setback, it employed 36 people, all Japanese; 27 in Kobe, five in Tokyo and four in Sydney. Five years later, the Russo-Japanese war greatly increased Japanese demand for Australian wool; raw wool sales increased almost fourfold from £71,582 in 1903 to £332,602 in 1904.[16]

The potential was also explored for a horse export trade from Australia to Japan. By the 1890s, the horse trade with other parts of Asia and particularly with India, already represented a profitable industry of some standing.[17] There were also exports to Java. Horses to the value of £19,046 were exported from Australia to the Netherlands East Indies in 1906.[18] By the turn of the century,

S B Salter, a commercial agent with pastoral interests, reported that Japanese officials, anxious to improve the quality of their cavalry horses, planned to send an expert to visit Australia to investigate the purchase of breeding stock.[19] In 1904, horses to the value of £9,892 were exported to Japan. This trade link, however, unlike the wool trade, failed to develop further.[20]

The 1894 Treaty presented the Australian colonies with a moment of choice. Some argued that Australia should embrace its trading future in Asia, expand its Asian connections and permit limited Japanese immigration. Others firmly rejected this path, believing Australia should try to become a model community based on racial purity, developing its primary ties with other like-minded communities, notably the United States. This view, which contributed to Australia's ultimate rejection of the 1894 Treaty, was supported by a powerful labour movement which feared competition with the Japanese, and by powerful protectionist interests seeking to prevent an influx of cheap Japanese goods. Concerns were also raised at this time over British interests and priorities. The fact that Britain had signed the treaty with Japan indicated to some that Britain was now abandoning support for Australia as a white homeland and putting trade before any other consideration.

Nevertheless, there were moves by the colonies and later by the states to establish trading relationships with Japan through the use of commercial agents. The Hungarian-born Alexander Marks who was trading as a merchant in Yokohama as early as 1859, acted as Honorary Consul for Japan in Australia from 1879 to 1896 and then as Honorary Consul in Victoria from 1896 to 1902. Fluent in Japanese, Marks became one of the best known advocates of trade with Japan.[21] In addition, in 1896, the Victorian Government sent two public servants, S H Rowe and J L Kelly, to Japan to examine possibilities for trade, while the South Australian Government dispatched J L Parsons on a similar mission. S B Salter, a commercial agent who had interests in the horse trade, also developed links with Japan at this time. The commercial agent, Ernest A P Whiteley, appointed by the New South Wales Government in 1902 to develop trade connections with Japan proved a popular choice among the Sydney business community, including its Chinese community. But his fate was an unhappy one. Just seven months into his service, he was to die of smallpox in Fuzhou. His successor, appointed in 1903 was J B Suttor who was to become an influential figure in the development of the trading relationship with Japan.[22]

Other journalists, prominent business figures and parliamentarians urged development of trade ties with Japan. One important figure was John Plummer, whose lively and engaging commentaries on Japan appeared regularly in the *Japan Daily Mail* from 1895 to 1898, an indispensable source for historians.[23] James Currie Elles, founding Chairman of the Stock Exchange of New South Wales strongly advocated trading links with Japan and was supported by Mr J Barre Johnston, President of the Sydney Chamber of Commerce and William

McMillan, a prominent New South Wales politician. Another influential figure who joined the debate was the ardent Japanophile, Colonel George W Bell, the United States Consul in Sydney from the mid-1890s until 1900. Bell remained a prominent public speaker and Sydney identity until his death in 1907.[24]

J B Salter, like Dyer before him, was impressed by the trading opportunities opening up in Japan. He too argued for independent commercial representation, realising that it was crucial to have Australian agents serving Australian interests. He was concerned that Australia's long-term reputation had been damaged when companies had filled exploratory Japanese orders with shoddy products. Salter remained confident that there was a big market for Australian products in Japan, but maintained that they had to be 'first class' and effectively marketed.[25]

William Sowden, an outspoken South Australian newspaperman, traveller and free trader, provided another indication of the growing interest in Australia over trade with Japan, when he published in 1897, *Children of the Rising Sun: Commercial and Political Japan*. He described the growing links as 'direct and indirect, immediate and prospective, geographical and commercial'. But like many Australians of his time he still could not get over his tendency to see the 'little Japanese' as a rather comic people.[26] Impressions of this type should have been counteracted by the latest opinions on Japan, brought to Australia by the war artist, Frederic Villiers (Plate 11). Billed as 'the Hero Artist of Nine Campaigns', Villiers began a national tour in Sydney, where his illustrated lectures drew large audiences.[27] Appearing in campaign costume, with knickerbocker pants, a shooting jacket and all the appurtenances of a war correspondent, he applauded the 'strategy and dogged pluck' of the Japanese in the recent Sino-Japanese war.[28] He described the ordinary Japanese soldier as a natural fighter, while the officers, often trained in Europe, were 'excessively brainy, clever men'.[29] (There was a continued interest in Japanese brains and their capabilities were regularly upgraded.) Villiers also turned, none too subtly, to matters of trade. He had no doubt that Japan would become a great manufacturing country. 'The Japanese are patriotic, industrious, and thrifty, and will eventually become excessively rich', he predicted, 'and are therefore worth looking after'. He suggested it was high time that the Australian colonies 'had agents over there, hustling about, and paving the way for the development of trade'.[30]

John Plummer commented at length on the trade debate and closely followed the discussion generated by the 1894 Treaty. In 1896 he quoted the views of two New South Welshmen, Dr Bell and Mr Picker, who had spoken to the press on their return from a trip to Japan. They had been impressed by the Japanese people and believed that their agricultural system was among the best in the world.[31] Favorable views also reported by Plummer, appeared in the *Launceston Examiner* which went so far as to compare Australia unfavourably with Japan. The paper maintained that while modern, enterprising Japan was now poised to attain a prosperous future, cautious Australia was retreating to an isolationism found only in old Japan.[32]

For proponents of an expanded trading relationship between Australia and Japan, the attempts to develop Australia as a white enclave in the Pacific seemed not a bold advance to a bright future, but a dogged retreat to walled seclusion. These commentators wondered if Australia had really understood the essential message behind Japan's achievement. Here was a nation that had repudiated its isolationist past in order to avail itself of the best examples of modern practice in almost every sphere of life. In making themselves more receptive to the world, in their thirst for knowledge and willingness to innovate, the Japanese pointed the way for Australia's future. They seemed to have captured the very essence of progressivism and modernity.

Implicit in Australian celebration of Asian markets was an appreciation of Asia's potential power to transform Australian cities into trading giants. Australia might have its own Venice, London or New York. This was a recurring dream of size, power and influence; a dream of being centrally placed within a populous and economically expanding region rather than in a remote and readily forgotten backwater. There was a touch of magic in stories of an insignificant nation swept to the forefront of the world's attention through proximity to Asian markets.

Predictions of a great trading future between Australia and Japan soon became entangled in intercolonial rivalries. When the Premier of New South Wales, George Reid, acted to restore free trade principles, Plummer was ecstatic, predicting that 'the ancient glories of Venice may become revived in the Southern Hemisphere', and that 'a greater future than even Sir Henry Parkes has dreamed of ' would be achieved by the 'Britain of the South'.[33] Protectionist Victoria would miss out. The *Argus*, a Melbourne newspaper with free trade opinions, warned that unless Victorian policies changed, Sydney would take the lead as the 'great commercial centre of the South Pacific'. Melbourne would be 'outstripped'.[34] Alexander Marks declared that although he was a Melburnian, he had advised the Japanese to focus future development on Sydney rather than protectionist Melbourne.[35] Local Sydney opinion, as evidenced in the *Daily Telegraph*, felt sure the future lay with their city, 'the London of the Southern Seas'.[36]

While those supporting Asian trade developed these images of a glowing future, commentators in many major Australian newspapers were fanning fears of unwarranted Asian influence and strongly urging an Anglo-Celtic future. The *Sydney Morning Herald* uncompromisingly supported 'Anglo-Saxon rule in the Southern Hemisphere', which in its view, was a more important and far-sighted objective than closer commercial ties with the East. It warned of the dangers of Asian immigration that could follow trade ties:

no commercial benefits that we can conceive would be commensurate with the evils that might come upon Australia from an unrestricted influx of Asiatics, such as would be rendered possible by the acceptance of the Treaty as it stands.[37]

Similar thoughts were expressed by the Queensland Attorney General, Mr Byrnes, as reported in both the *Sydney Morning Herald* and the *Age*: 'The manifest destiny of Australia is to be a country for the Anglo-Celtic race. We are to be dominant in the South Pacific'.[38] The *Sydney Morning Herald* justified its views on the grounds that the Japanese were 'an actively migratory race'.[39] While trade treaties might be appropriate for a densely populated country like Britain, geographically remote from the East, Australia was both sparsely populated and on Asia's doorstep. To the *Sydney Morning Herald*, the threat was obvious. Plummer, who believed Australia was definitely low on Japan's list of desirable destinations, considered this an 'absurd' argument. Other Australian newspapers lined up with the *Sydney Morning Herald*. The Melbourne *Age* suggested 'mere traders' might take an essentially commercial view of the Treaty, but colonial Governments had to ask themselves whether 'the design of making Australasia a permanent home for the Anglo-Saxon race is to be maintained or abandoned'.[40]

Concerns were also raised about British priorities. It was felt in many quarters that Britain put trade considerations before any concern for Australia's future as a racially cohesive community. This view, prevalent in rural Australia, was expressed in the *Maitland Daily Mercury* of November 1896. If Britain refused to help the colonies retain their racial character, the paper observed, 'she is no mother at all, but only a cruel step-dame'.[41]

Many feared economic harm from closer links with the East, as evident in the great boot controversy of 1896. 'For several days,' Plummer wrote, 'nothing was talked of save the anticipated heavy imports of boots and shoes from Japanese factories'. This great scare appeared to have begun at some election speeches given in Sydney, and then spread far and wide. Rumours of a great boot invasion appeared impossible to refute. Enoch Taylor and Sons, one of Australia's biggest boot and shoe manufacturing and importing firms, even issued a statement denying that Japanese imports posed any problem for local manufacturers. It had little impact. After careful investigation, Plummer claimed that in the eighteen months from January 1895 there had been only two modest orders by Grace Brothers in Sydney for Japanese boots. Alexander Marks, then Consul-General for Japan, felt that the boot scare revealed Australia's lack of confidence in its own products and indicated the inability of Australian businesses to respond creatively to export opportunities in Asia.[42]

In December 1896, Plummer's column in the *Japan Daily Mail* brought together the two contradictory tendencies in colonial responses to the trade treaty: the case for closer engagement with Asia and a brilliant trading future versus the development of an Anglo-Saxon bastion removed from Asian influences. Hence Plummer welcomed the arrival in Sydney of the *Yamashiro Maru* of the Nippon Yusen Kaisha line, the first steamer in what was to become a monthly service between Australia and Japan. There was a considerable press response to the visit. The *Sydney Mail* commented approvingly on the benefits to trade that the new line would generate, noting that it would also create splendid opportunities for tourism: 'The scenery in many parts is extremely beautiful, while the modes of Japanese life are so different from that of Europeans that much novelty and interest attach to a visit to Japan'. There were a number of press interviews with Captain Jones of the *Yamashiro Maru*, who had a high opinion of the Japanese and their commercial capabilities. He anticipated growing trading opportunities with Japan in the export of live stock, wool and horses. Yet, even as the *Yamashiro Maru* docked in Sydney harbour, the New South Wales government was doing all it could to pass the Alien Restriction Bill into law before the Christmas break.[43]

The Alien Restriction Bill included all non-Europeans within its provisions, even although this was known to offend the Japanese.[44] Plummer noted that the Bill did not pass without public criticism. He cited one correspondent who said it was absurd to exclude the Japanese, when Australia's north was left unpopulated and undeveloped. This correspondent was appalled to think that a people from a 'progressive and highly cultured nation' were not welcome in Australia. Was it wise to offend Asian nations whose understandable reaction might be to break off commercial relations? Moreover, what right had Australians to exclude anyone, when they claimed their own title only from an act of violence against its original inhabitants?[45]

The Alien Restriction Bill proved to have a complicated and troubled history. After considerable negotiation between the Foreign Office, the Japanese government and the government of New South Wales, the Bill was passed in November 1897 as the Coloured Races Restriction and Regulation Bill. This version, while no less severe than the original, now based its grounds for exclusion on the Natal formula (a European language test). The Japanese considered this somewhat less offensive, given that the grounds for exclusion could be thought of as educational rather than overtly racial. It was clear that the Japanese took an active interest in Australian legislation that touched upon race relations.[46]

In February 1902, Britain and Japan signed another important strategic treaty, the Anglo-Japanese Alliance. Australian politicians were not made party to the negotiations and only became aware of the new position by the cable service. Nevertheless, both the Federal and State governments approved the new Alliance. The Prime Minister, Edmund Barton, tried to allay possible Australian fears maintaining it is 'impossible to suppose that anything in the treaty increases any risk of any attack upon Australia'.[47] On a more positive note, the Barton government suggested, in a view shared by the state governments, that the

Alliance offered substantial commercial benefits to Australia. The *Sydney Morning Herald* summarised these benefits in terms echoed throughout the Australian press and on all sides of politics:

> an offensive and defensive alliance with Japan will, it is contended, not only protect the northern portions of the Commonwealth, but will secure the trading interests of Australia in the Far East.[48]

As one of the major purposes of the Alliance was to provide a check on Russian territorial ambitions, there was also a widespread conviction that with the signing of the Alliance, one important potential threat to Australian security was now removed. The region was now even safer for trade.

Once the Alliance was signed, the main focus for developing trade in Asia was now clearly Japan. William McMillan, prominent New South Wales politician and proponent of free trade glowed at the possibilities: 'In the East, with their teeming millions of consumers', he declared, 'the opportunity was waiting for us open armed'. He saw a growing market for Australian food products in the East in general and urged the immediate appointment of an agent to develop trade links with Japan.[49]

In 1903, the President of the NSW Chamber of Commerce, Mr J Barre Johnston, also pointed to Japan as a 'positively marvellous object lesson in development' and urged that every effort should be made to encourage Japanese interest in the Australian wool trade. He considered the Japanese an impressive, commercially astute people with whom Australians should develop a secure and profitable trading relationship. Johnson dismissed as 'intolerable nonsense' the idea that slight differences in skin colour should constitute any barrier to trade.[50]

The appointment of J B Suttor in 1903 as New South Wales Trade Commissioner to Japan was no doubt influenced by his solid grounding in the pastoral industry and the political influence that the well-connected and politically active Suttor family was able to mobilise. At the time of his appointment, he appears to have had no experience or connections in Japan, having spent 25 years as an engineer with the New South Wales Railways Commission. As he settled into the utterly strange environment of Kobe in December, unable to speak the language and with a sharp winter drawing on, the prospect of making a lasting success of the position must have appeared remote. Yet Suttor dug himself in and began learning Japanese. He developed links with the local business community, kept his ear to the ground, studied the markets and soon became a model Trade Commissioner, whose reports were widely circulated within and beyond government. Suttor's responsibilities were not confined to Japan. His reports also covered China, Korea, Manchuria, Hong Kong, the Philippines, Singapore, Burma, India as well as the Netherlands East Indies for which he entertained high hopes for future trade. Yet he always regarded Japan as the key to Australia's trading future in Asia. Suttor found much that was gracious and charming about Japan and soon developed a deep attachment to the country and its people.[51]

Isami Takeda makes the persuasive case that relations between Australia and Japan were so cordial in 1904 and the prospects for increased trade so bright that Prime Minister Alfred Deakin felt able to conclude a liberalised Passport Agreement with Japan. Japanese merchants, students and tourists could now visit Australia more freely. This was the Commonwealth Government's first act of independent diplomacy. Suttor played an important mediating role throughout the negotiations and was delighted to see one of the obstacles to trade removed. The new arrangements not only made entry to Australia much simpler for business visits, but also suggested to the Japanese that Australia might be prepared to reconsider some of its previous discriminatory practices.[52]

Unfortunately, Suttor's initial optimism was soon to fade. It quickly became apparent that the White Australia Policy and opposition to Japanese migration still presented a major obstacle to the development of trade. In his reports to the New South Wales government, Suttor noted that Japanese newspapers often carried articles on anti-Asian sentiments in Australia. He claimed that Australian policies and attitudes played directly into the hands of her trade competitors. Discriminatory policies not only caused offence to the Japanese; they were 'skilfully utilised' by other countries wanting a share of Australia's trade.[53] To these obstacles were also added high tariff barriers. Much to Suttor's annoyance, Canada, unlike Australia, became an unconditional signatory to a commercial treaty in 1906, thereby placing Australian exports at a further disadvantage.[54] For many at that time, Australia's proximity to Asia was a mixed blessing. While it created the prospect of close and alluring markets, these 'teeming millions of consumers' could all too easily be pictured as millions of potential invaders. Canada, further from its Asian markets, was evidently less vulnerable to these fears of being overrun by Asian hordes.

Suttor consistently advocated the direct representation of Australian commercial interests and close study of the tastes, requirements and cultural practices of Asian societies, particularly Japan, China and the Netherlands East Indies. All too often he learnt of trading opportunities lost through reliance on intermediaries. He reminded the New South Wales authorities that these were competitive markets and if Australians wanted to succeed in Asia they would have to learn how to promote and market their own goods, rather than hope that others might do it for them. The need for Australia to promote its interests more effectively in Asia could not be limited to questions of commercial representation and marketing, though both were important. Suttor was equally insistent that Australians must learn that their anti-Asian sentiments were reported in the Asian media and would have adverse impacts both upon trade and the wider relationship between Australia and Japan. Though he saw the East as Australia's 'great and natural trading centre of the future', Suttor was afraid that a combination of neglect, cultural ignorance and active prejudice would continue to inhibit Australia's Asian trade.[55] He had previously identified adverse comments in the Australian press as:

> a serious impediment to commercial expansion as well as a handicap to the endeavours being made to improve the commercial relationship between the Orient and Australia .... If we are anxious to build up a great commerce with the Orient, we cannot expect to do so on such lines.[56]

Suttor linked what he saw as a careless disregard for Asian sensibilities to haphazard, often contemptuous approaches to marketing. His reports list a host of ignorant, lazy and dishonest practices. The packaging of Australian goods, particularly tinned products, was a constant source of complaint, along with unreliable supplies. In 1910 Suttor visited Batavia, but was disappointed to see no Australian products on display. He could not cite a single instance of 'a business house conspicuously displaying Australian goods'. On enquiry he heard tales of bad packaging and products so inferior that they could not be sold. Complaints to Australian suppliers invariably went unanswered. In a market that Australia was in an excellent position to control given its proximity, Suttor found that Australian products were considered inferior to those of its competitors.[57]

Suttor was especially appalled by what he learnt about the market for tinned butter. He became 'sick and tired of hearing complaints from prominent persons' about Australian butter. Butter was a product in considerable demand. Yet after some initial interest in the Australian product, suppliers bought European butters, which were competitively priced, more appropriately labelled and arrived in better condition. Australian butters were frequently 'so much slush', presented in rusty, damaged tins. Not a good look.[58] Even worse, some unscrupulous Australian traders cheated Asian importers. In 1906, the *Worker* reported that an Australian firm had tried to supply a Chinese merchant with 50 lb sacks of flour that actually contained only 19 lb. For a 500 ton consignment, the deficit would be around 20,000 lbs of flour. The *Worker* noted that while this shortfall might have been due to carelessness, it nevertheless left an impression of dishonesty which was detrimental to Australia-China trade.[59]

Despite all the difficulties, Australian trade with East and South-East Asia did begin to improve. Between 1903 and 1910, exports to this area increased almost threefold from £791 million to £2362 million (Figure 6.1). The proportion of total trade with East and South-East Asia going to individual countries by 1910 is shown in Figure 6.2. By 1910 exports to Japan led other countries in the region but without yet having established a clear dominance.[60] Some commentators believed Australia should be exporting a great deal more. In May 1908, Mr William Baldwin, a prominent commercial figure from Sydney, returned from a fourteen month tour of the East including China, Japan, Eastern

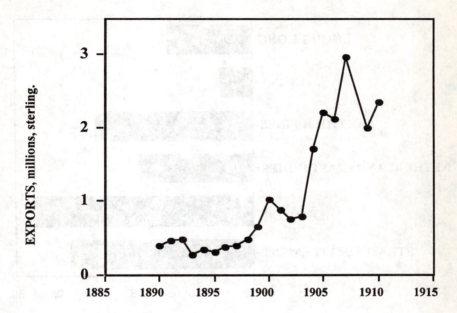

Figure 6.1: Exports from Australia to East Asia and South-East Asia, 1890-1910. Source for data: Sandra Tweedie, *Trading Partners: Australia & Asia 1790-1993*, op. cit., Appendix, pp 224-5.

Siberia, the Philippines and Singapore, and reported unrivalled trade opportunities for Australians in the East, now being wasted. 'Capitalists and big merchants here in Sydney', he asserted, 'are sound asleep and their snores can be heard in Vladivostock'. Baldwin saw splendid opportunities in the East for the sale of Australian butter, cheese, jams, wine, frozen meat and tinned meat, milk and biscuits. This business, he believed, could make Sydney a great southern trading city.[61]

Colonel George W Bell, former United States Consul, believed there were particularly promising prospects for Australian trade with Japan. Bell was the author of two topical books on Japan, *The Little Giants of the East or Our New Allies*, published by the New South Wales Bookstall Company in 1905, and *The Empire of Business! or How to People Australia*, published the following year. *The Empire of Business!* was based on a public address that Bell had given to the New South Wales Chamber of Manufacturers.[62] In fact, Colonel Bell, a well known advocate of the blessings of trade, had given versions of this talk to

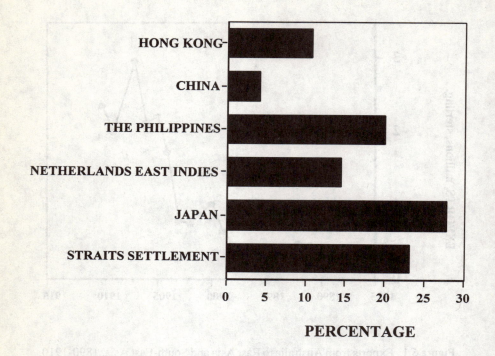

PERCENTAGE

Figure 6.2: Exports from Australia to Asian countries as a percentage of total trade to East and South East Asia, 1910. Source for data: as for Figure 6.1.

audiences throughout New South Wales. In November 1896, at a jovial gathering held in his honour at the Sydney Town Hall, Colonel Bell declared:

> I hold that commerce is the basis of civilization; that all nations are civilized in proportion as they are commercial ... As the ideal of the race is the higher civilization, and as commerce is the chief factor in progress, I hold that he who does most to promote commerce, does most for the age in which he lives and the race to which he belongs.[63]

A decade later, Bell brought his enthusiasm for commerce to bear on the question of Australia's Asian future. By this time Bell had become a popular identity in New South Wales, certainly among the commercial and political elite, and was regarded as one of the foremost orators of the day. In describing modern Japan he became a torrent of superlatives. Brandishing a globe, he told his audience at the Chamber of Manufacturers that the emergence of Japan from relative obscurity to world prominence in little more than a generation was a 'momentous' event, 'the most picturesque volume in all the history of nations'.[64] This was achieved, Bell stated, by a talented people of unsurpassed discipline. He could not understand why Australians would want to keep such people out of their country. In the empty north, in particular, he was sure the Japanese would achieve wonders. Bell, of course, knew the prejudices of his audience well enough. He took a dim view of Australian exclusivity. Having spelt out Japanese capabilities, he went on to ask: 'Might we not regard them even as worthy to cut scrub in the Australian bush, or to raise cane, cotton or coffee on the Queensland plains?'[65]

Although Bell understood that Australians might not accept Japanese immigrants, he implored them to keep an open mind about the prospects of trade with Japan. He flourished the globe again. There was Japan, here was Australia. Was it possible to imagine a nation placed in a more favourable position to take advantage of the economic transformation of the East, than Australia? He did not think so. He forecast a great trading future for Australia and huge growth in her coastal cities. He pictured Sydney leaping forward in wealth and power to rival New York, while the Australian Commonwealth would come to surpass Britain in the extent of its trade. Japan was so central to these predicted developments that it would surely become 'Australia's largest and most profitable customer'.[66]

Bell's pamphlet attracted the attention of *Truth*, the principal vehicle for John Norton's wild and intemperate anti-Imperial and erratically pro-labour views. Calling the former Consul 'bumptious, blatherskite Bell', *Truth* poured scorn on his claim that business had a civilising mission. 'When Bell bawls about "business", he tells his hearers, with much rhetorical rhodomontade, that "business" is not only "business", but that it is the light of the world and the basis of civilisation'.[67] There followed a long discourse on the evils of capitalism, supplemented with an extensive reading list, which included Marx on Political Economy. Bell's comments on the impossibility of whites settling the tropics, the capabilities of the Japanese and on the virtues of the Chinese all came in for a savaging. *Truth* warned Australians not to be put off their guard by Bell's 'baneful bunkum'. If his views were accepted Australia would soon be filled 'not with the sturdy, highly civilised people of Europe, but with half-castes possessing all the vices of the whites, and none of the virtues'.

James Currie Elles was another who, like Bell, tried to encourage trade with Japan. An historically elusive figure, Elles was born in Sydney in 1853, son of Andrew Jamieson Elles, a master mariner and his wife Clementina. He spent his early years in Dunedin, New Zealand, where he attended Otago Boys' High School. This was followed by two years (1869-71) at Glasgow University, which he left without completing a degree. A relative, Jamieson Elles, born 1828, was a Glaswegian Merchant and Banking Agent based in London and Amoy.[68] It is probable that James Currie Elles developed his first Asian experience and banking expertise through this connection. Later, James Currie Elles would claim extensive experience in the East and reportedly had contacts with some of Britain's leading figures in Asia, including Sir Ernest Satow, Sir Harry Parkes and Sir Robert Hart. In addition, he appeared to know several Asian languages.

In 1908 Elles delivered the prestigious 'Joseph Fisher' lecture at the University of Adelaide. His topic, 'The Influence of Commerce on Civilisation' was characteristically sweeping and his presentation was sprinkled with his normal range of quotations in several languages, including Latin, Greek, French, German and Mandarin.[69] He described how the growth of commerce multiplied contacts between cultures, helping the spread of knowledge and fostering energy, enterprise and inventiveness. Elles suggested that Australia's 'predominant position on the shores of the Pacific' gave it similar opportunities for culturally invigorating commercial contacts. Elles could see Australia developing into a great trading nation. Yet these possibilities would only be realised if Australia's youth was educated to take advantage of the new world emerging in the Pacific. Elles therefore called for the creation of Chairs of Oriental languages in all Australian universities with links to Chairs of Commerce. Then:

> when our Australian commercial community is educated thoroughly to under-
> stand, appreciate and respect the great civilised nations of Asia, from whom
> most, if not all, of our civilisation has been derived, then may commerce and
> civilisation, go hand in hand and may it be said about Australia that she has
> derived "Ex Oriente lux".[70]

For all his pomposity, Elles had some views ahead of his time. Integral to his message about the riches of the Orient was the need for Australians to develop a much broader awareness of the major cultures to their north, particularly those of China, Japan and India. Elles may have been unusual in proposing an educational strategy that would permit Australians to develop robust trade and cultural exchanges within the Asia-Pacific region, but he was not alone. Similar ideas had been in circulation for several years. In 1905, the New South Wales Chamber of Manufacturers considered a recommendation from the New South Wales Department of Mines and Agriculture that the teaching of Asian languages would improve the State's trade performance in the East. Germany's trading success was attributed to its having encouraged close study of Asian languages and customs. In its report of these deliberations, the *Sydney Morning Herald* noted that J B Suttor wanted to see a greater emphasis upon Asian languages and cultures in the New South Wales education system and had recommended the creation of a Chair of Oriental Languages at Sydney university. Over a decade later, James Murdoch was the first to hold this newly created position.[71]

Several years later, in a report of the annual dinner of the Chamber of Commerce in July 1910, the *Sydney Morning Herald* observed that the Governor, Lord Chelmsford, had given a speech of 'vital interest' to all Australians. Chelmsford predicted that the Pacific would become an increasingly important focus of world trade. In order for Australia to make the most of its favoured position, Chelmsford argued that the acquisition of Asian languages should become part of the curriculum in all commercially oriented courses. If Australians were to develop their trade with the East, there could be no escaping the need to learn the major languages of the region. 'How many Australians in Sydney to-day', Chelmsford asked his audience, 'would be capable of going into Eastern parts and pressing their wares in the language of the country which they visited?'[72]

Endorsements of the civilising effects of trade did not go unchallenged. A recurrent motif in the debate over the future of the Anglo-Japanese Treaty was the way tawdry Britain had sold her soul for profit. Britain, it was argued, would do a deal with anyone. Randolph Bedford, the ebullient, entrepreneurial Australian patriot was among those prepared to lambast Britain.[73] For Bedford racially compromising trade contacts were to be avoided wherever possible. He urged Australians to look to America rather than rely on Britain. Bedford claimed America took a keen interest in the White Australia Policy, a policy he described as 'the finest attempt ever made by a nation to rule itself by sentiment and belief rather than by mere commercialism alone'. Any idea that trade with the East could act as an agent of civilisation and regeneration was anathema to Bedford. He wanted Australia to be quarantined from Asia and Asian markets, not inter-related with them. He hoped to see a racially 'clean', radiant Australia rise above the shabby temptations of 'mere commercialism'.

Bedford was also a noted member of the literary community. At this time it was common for those of literary bent to draw a sharp opposition between Art and Commerce. White Australia was an ideal belonging to Art: something clean and dignified. Bedford maintained that if ever a country had 'allotted to it by civilisation some duty whose performance would benefit all the world — some idea which would better civilisation', then that country was Australia. The mission ahead was clear: 'Australia has been given to it as a sacred duty the breeding of a pure race in a clean continent'.[74] Commerce, on the other hand, was something unclean, the province of greed and opportunism leading, in Bedford's view, to racial contamination. Commerce put profits ahead of racial purity. It allowed mixing, promiscuity, hybridity. Bedford was convinced that developing trade with the East formed no part of Australia's providential purpose.

'England,' Bedford declared in 1911, 'has not played the white man's game in the Pacific'.[75] He argued that in the event of war, Australia would be better off under the racially compatible Germans than under the rule of the Japanese. He welcomed the German and Dutch presence in the Pacific, while maintaining the hope that the United States would eventually become Australia's major political partner. Bedford's derogatory references to non-Europeans, his dismissive account of Britain's motives and his promotion of a white brotherhood in the Pacific can be contrasted with Elles's promotion of a trading future with Asia. Elles, however, conveyed his message in mannered, obscure prose, peppered with untranslated quotations, while Bedford wrote for ordinary readers in journals with a wide circulation.

Understandably the case for Australia's trading future in Asia could fall on deaf ears if presented to the public with condescending erudition, or if it seemed a slavish attempt to placate British commercial interests in Asia. Even Dyer tended to have the air of a man casting pearls before swine. Likewise Alexander Marks could grow irritable in the face of those who automatically assumed superiority to the Japanese. Plummer tried to remain even-handed in his commentaries, but still became annoyed that boorishness and misconceptions played such a prominent part in discussions of Australia's role in Asia. The sympathetic 'Asianist' was so often exasperated by people who seemed unaware of the momentous changes sweeping through Asia. As Australia was a country likely to be strongly affected by these changes, such ignorance and complacency seemed uniquely ill-conceived.

Chapter Seven

Pacific Visitors

Australians had their first opportunity to see significant numbers of the remarkable Japanese at close quarters in May and June of 1903 when a Training Japanese Squadron, numbering an impressive 600 officers and men, visited Australian ports under the command of Admiral Kamimura. After a brief visit to Perth where it was enthusiastically received, the squadron enjoyed a public welcome at the Adelaide Town Hall early in May. The *Advertiser* reported that the approaches to the Town Hall were crowded with spectators as the Premier welcomed the visitors. Throughout the entire time they had been in the city, the Japanese had been 'feted and toasted incessantly'.[1] On the Saturday, a large crowd greeted the squadron as it paraded through the streets of Adelaide. On the Sunday and the following Tuesday, thousands gathered to inspect the visiting vessels, packing out all the trains to Largs Bay and throwing the timetable into confusion. The *Advertiser* was impressed by the 'intelligence and manners' of the Japanese officers: 'They were eager to understand, anxious to learn, and delighted to oblige'.[2] For South Australians the visit had been 'a wonderful eye-opener', revealing as never before the 'intelligence, progress, and resources' of the Japanese.[3]

When the squadron visited Melbourne, the *Hashidate* was opened for inspection and a steady stream of people went out by boat and launch to investigate the new marvel, while others gathered on the piers. The squadron enjoyed a range of official visitors, including the Prime Minister Sir Edmund Barton, his minister for defence Sir John Forrest and the Victorian premier Mr Irvine. The *Age* estimated that upwards of a thousand of Melbourne's best people attended 'an Anglo-Oriental temple of life and color, of fashion and felicity'.[4] The *Argus* reported a brilliant reception during which the Japanese band played 'lively dance music with admirable taste and finish'.[5] Sailors performed athletic feats for the assembled guests. On their departure, the ladies were presented with miniaturised decorations featuring the Japanese and British flags. Twenty thousand people later braved high winds and driving rain to view a military parade in Albert Park.[6]

The *Argus*' coverage of the visit included a detailed account of the squadron's naval capabilities, along with a description of the mighty turret gun mounted on the *Hashidate*'s foredeck. This weapon was capable of launching an 800 lb projectile over a distance of ten miles. The comments addressed Japanese capacities and technical aptitudes, rather than the threat their weaponry might pose to Australia. On all sides, the *Argus* found evidence of order, efficiency and considerable technical competence. The sailors impressed as 'powerful, determined, thick-set men' who went about their shipboard duties with great vigour. As they did so 'a first class brass band, equipped with the best modern instruments, was playing a waltz by Strauss on the quarter-deck'.[7] Astute observers noticed that the *Hashidate* was equipped with 'the latest wonder of wireless telegraphy'. This was the first time that Melbourne, which prided itself on its receptivity to modern inventions, saw wireless set up for daily operation.[8] Similar approving comments were made by the *Age* which had been particularly impressed by the 'alert, keenly intelligent and progressive' spirit of the Japanese officers.[9]

When the Japanese squadron docked in Sydney, a large crowd began to gather around the sea wall near the Botanic gardens, extending as far as Lady Macquarie's Chair. The *Sydney Mail* covered the squadron's visit in detail, noting that close to 50,000 people had gathered in Centennial Park to catch a glimpse of the squadron and local troops.[10] And the events continued. Tens of thousands of people had also crowded Sydney harbour at night, to see the illuminated British and Japanese naval vessels.[11]

The *Sydney Morning Herald* invited the people of Sydney to do all they could to make the Japanese feel welcome. In an editorial welcoming 'Our Japanese Guests' the paper approved Japan's rapid emergence as a world power. It noted that Japan and Australia had interests in common, particularly the future of the Pacific. 'Japan is not only Britain's ally but Australia's near neighbour', the paper stated. The *Herald* pointed out that both countries had developed as modern states with a Pacific presence only in the last thirty years or so. In the future there were likely to be closer interactions between Australia and Japan.[12] For its part, the *Sydney Mail* showed some caution when summarising the impression created by the Japanese:

> Clean-limbed and nattily dressed they created an openly and warmly expressed feeling of admiration in the minds of many who have not yet been able to realise that Japan is well up in the front of the great naval powers of the world.[13]

We might stop to consider here exactly what this journalist had in mind. The statement certainly acknowledges 'openly and warmly expressed feelings of admiration' for the Japanese. That was not in question. But it hints at something more, that feelings of open admiration were most readily expressed by people who did not yet appreciate Japan's new role as a great naval power. It implies that there was a certain innocence about the welcome. Perhaps these glad responses were more suited to the 1880s and 1890s than to the coming century? Had Australian crowds gone too far?

While the *Sydney Morning Herald* welcomed the Japanese as allies and Pacific neighbours, the *Bulletin* as far as possible, ignored their visit. After a desultory comment or two, it noted that the Japanese 'yearned to watch the girls, especially the blond ones'.[14] Likewise the Sydney *Worker* seemed to feel that it was best not to mention the visit.

Three years later, in 1906, the Japanese squadron made another visit. Once again enthusiastic crowds of ordinary citizens were much in evidence. When the Japanese Consulate announced that it would issue tickets to intending visitors, 'a great rush of persons anxious to make the inspection took place'.[15] The Melbourne *Argus* estimated that over one weekend at least thirty thousand people visited the training ships. 'Every train and every tram running to Port Melbourne was crowded with passengers', the paper reported, 'many persons drove down, and thousands from the nearer suburbs walked'.[16] The *Age* noted that 'crowds of suburban residents thronged the streets of the city' to view a naval parade which again numbered 600 Japanese officers and men. In the area around upper Collins street there were at least 50,000 spectators.[17] The glittering State Government reception held at Parliament House also drew an immense crowd of invited guests.[18] Wherever the Japanese appeared in any numbers, a crowd seemed assured. On the day the squadron left Melbourne, trams leaving to farewell the squadron were packed with people, many of them young women, carrying chrysanthemums.[19]

In Melbourne, at the Lord Mayor's Dinner held in their honour, the Victorian Governor showered paeans of praise upon Admiral Shimamura (Plate 12): 'We admired those great successes which your armies achieved; we admired the spirit which inspired your nation; we admired your patriotism; we admired your courage ...'. He equated Admiral Togo's achievements with those of Lord Nelson and the naval victory of the Japanese over the Russian fleet with the Battle of Trafalgar.[20] Japanese achievements in the Russo-Japanese war had been widely reported in the Australian press and occasioned some glowing accounts of Japanese capabilities. In the *Sydney Morning Herald*, F A A Russell observed that Japan was experiencing a 'great heroic epoch'; Japan's achievements would 'remain among the permanent records of the world'. Once again there was a comparison with Elizabethan achievements: 'Can we claim that England, in her heroic Elizabethan age, was more splendid? She was certainly not more enlightened'.[21] Nevertheless a shift was taking place in such commentaries from an appreciation of enchanting, aesthetic Japan to a greater awareness of its sterner, more disciplined, soldierly qualities.

In Edwardian England soldierly Japan was also attracting notice. Inazo Nitobe's *Bushido: The Soul of Japan*, an exposition of the Japanese national character, joined the best seller lists.[22] At the height of his fame in 1918, the British war correspondent E Ashmead Bartlett contributed an article to the *Town and Country Journal* on 'Some Famous Men I Have Met'. This included a portrait of General Baron Noji, a figure one can assume Ashmead Bartlett discussed often over port and cigars.[23] Ashmead Bartlett had won fame and enduring respect in Australia for his reports of the Gallipoli landing. He had also served as a war correspondent during the Russo-Japanese war and had been present when Port Arthur fell to Japanese troops under Noji's command.[24] Of all the military figures he had met, Ashmead Bartlett confessed that Noji surpassed them all: 'there is no man of whom I cherish more pleasing memories'. The Baron was represented as the embodiment of *bushido*. In 1912, Nogi and his wife committed suicide in the samurai manner on learning of the death of Emperor Meiji. Their extraordinary deaths pushed interest in *bushido* and respect for Japanese discipline and loyalty to new heights. In fact, Noji's record as a military strategist was not as impressive as Ashmead Bartlett's account suggests. Noji hurled troops at the enemy and sustained such huge losses that Tokyo had to send in a more adroit strategist to rescue the campaign.[25]

When the Japanese squadron visited Sydney in 1906, the foreshores of the harbour were again crowded with tens of thousands of citizens who greeted the fleet with prolonged cheering. In the course of this visit 1,500 invited guests enjoyed an at home held on board the *Hashidate* and her sister ships. The *Sydney Morning Herald* commented:

> The heartiness of the welcome extended by the citizens to the officers and men of the Japanese training squadron ... could not have been exceeded, and the friendly — almost brotherly feeling — everywhere exhibited was fully reciprocated by our worthy allies.[26]

When a large party of Japanese visited Parramatta they were received by huge crowds who endured miserable weather to greet the visitors.[27] In his welcoming speech, the acting Japanese Consul General, Mr Iwasaki, insisted that the warmth of the reception shown by the Australian people was a natural expression of the sympathies which united Britain and Japan. He conceded that although in some quarters there were antipathies to the Japanese, these feelings were not natural: 'They are manufactured by misrepresentations, appealing to ignorance, and thus arousing prejudices which blind the judgement and awaken distrust, hatred and fear'. This speech was received with 'great applause'.[28]

The *Sydney Mail* gave the squadron's 1906 visit extensive coverage. Under a banner headline titled 'The Return of Our Allies' it presented a photo-essay confirming many of the impressions made elsewhere in the press. A photograph of Admiral Shimamura in full naval uniform revealed a man of considerable dignity and strength of character. A group portrait with his staff showed the Japanese officers radiating an unmistakable air of command.[29] At the end of the visit, the paper summarised the events:

> the Japanese have been feasted and honoured, and the national cry of triumph and rejoicing "banzai" has been heard at all public functions at which they have participated.[30]

The *Australasian* was no less impressed. It ran a full-page story on Admiral Shimamura, stressing his standing as a hero of the recent Russo-Japanese war. This man possessed 'a tremendous force of mind and resoluteness of purpose'.[31]

In its editorial 'The Japanese Visit', the *Sydney Mail* repeated the theme that despite the evident differences between Australia and Japan, the two countries had much in common. In the week of the Japanese visit Australians had also been celebrating the 50th Jubilee of their parliamentary system of government. The *Mail* noted that during the same period, the Japanese had emancipated themselves from feudalism and laid the foundations for a modern and efficient new nation. Australia and Japan could both be thought of as new nations, with modern histories dating back not much more than fifty years. Moreover, 'both are situated in the Pacific — that new arena of commercial and national competition, as it has been called, where to be weak will presently mean to be defenceless, and a tempting prey to the competing powers'.[32] Whereas the *Mail* was convinced that the Japanese had passed all the tests of nationhood thrust upon them over the preceding half century, it did not believe the same could be said for Australians. The *Mail* thought Japan had set an example that Australia had so far failed to match.

In short, the training squadron visits of 1903 and 1906 aroused immense public interest in all Australian cities visited. In 1906, a strong air of 'romance' surrounded the Japanese squadron, so recently victorious on the field of battle. In both visits, the Japanese appeared constantly on the move from venue to venue. In New South Wales small contingents went as far afield as Lithgow and Newcastle. Elaborate decorations, illuminations and street displays marked the visits. There were bands and athletic events. Every potted palm was recruited to the cause. Barely a chrysanthemum was left standing when the fleet left town.

The *Bulletin* was concerned by the Australian response to the visit of the Japanese squadrons. After its silence in 1903, it finally published an editorial on 'The Japanese Welcome' in May 1906. It promoted racial arguments against the Japanese, though there was a patronising admission: 'The little brown man has done marvellous things'. But the *Bulletin* believed that the time had come for some home truths:

> That slant, narrow brow of the Jap marks him as a man who has obeyed for thousands of years, obeyed implicitly, automatically, Asiatically ... They can imitate the present results of Caucasian thought; by their blind faculty of obe- dience seem to surpass in results their teachers ... But ultimately the higher brain and the loftier type must prevail. The Caucasian is not "played out" and the way to future advancement is not by patterning our religion and our civil organisa- tion on the Asiatic.[33]

Beneath the truculence that was a *Bulletin* trademark, there were some profound anxieties on display. In dismissing the idea that the Caucasian was 'played out', the journal nevertheless affirmed that it was a heresy that demanded correction. Why would the *Bulletin* deny the need to pattern Australian culture on Japanese models, if such an idea was thought to have no currency and no support? Fears of the decline of the Caucasian were closely related to growing unease about racial degeneration. Between 1903 and 1906, the state of New South Wales embarked upon a major inquiry into the decline of the birth-rate. This was commonly interpreted as an indicator of national decline and widely viewed as yet another sign that women had given themselves up to luxury and self-indulgence. But if the European race was in decline was this Australia's opportunity? Perhaps it made the need to establish the conditions for race renewal in Australia more urgent. It gave Australia an important role. Maintaining imperilled European blood lines could be interpreted as a substantial new world, race-building mission.

The *Bulletin* nevertheless conceded that Japan presented important lessons for Australia in the transformative power of patriotic effort. It noted that in not much more than a generation the Japanese had turned themselves from a nation with a comic opera reputation into a considerable power; a country to be taken seriously. Indeed, the *Bulletin* now found fewer opportunities for thigh-slapping laughter over the Japanese than had been the case a decade earlier. How, in no time at all, had the Japanese turned themselves (as the *Bulletin* would have it) from one of the lowest of nations into one of the highest? The *Bulletin* maintained that the Japanese leadership had adopted a policy of Japan for the Japanese, backed by highly protected industries, intensive cultivation of the land and the creation of a citizen army. As the *Bulletin* saw it, this was its own policy for Australia! If Japan could succeed so well with limited resources and mechanical brains, what might Australia achieve 'with its greater area of better land, its vast mineral resources, its civilised hands and Caucasian brains'? It was a clear case of anything they could do, we could do better: if only Australia could match the Japanese in the quality of their leadership and the unyielding intensity of their patriotism. There was every reason to believe that the Japanese had brought both qualities to a higher pitch than any other nation. But the *Bulletin* clung to the belief that Australia's greatest hope lay with its large-brained innovators. On this issue, there was no reassurance to be had from Douglas Sladen's immensely popular commentaries on Japan. In *Queer Things About Japan*, published to celebrate the end of the war with Russia, he noted that while the Japanese had once been dismissed as imitative and intellectually limited, their 'wonderful brain-power' had been 'universally recognised' after the Russo-Japanese war.[34]

Still in search of an explanation for the welcome, the *Bulletin* wondered if official Australia had resolved to leave nothing to chance by making the reception the best thing that money could buy. But although the *Bulletin* wanted to believe that boot-licking, imperial Australia had foisted the festivities upon a reluctant nation, the evidence was overwhelmingly against this explanation. Even so, the *Bulletin* was unwilling to dismiss altogether an official, British contribution to the Japanese welcome. The argument went as follows: the Anglo-Japanese Alliance was designed to destroy Russia's power in Asia and particularly any threat to India. When the Japanese defeated Russia, the check upon German power in Europe was removed. The *Bulletin* maintained that by 1906 the Anglo-Japanese Alliance was regretted in Britain because it had unwittingly contributed to the sudden growth of German power. Rather than admit this mistake, official Britain put the best possible face on the Alliance; hence, according to the *Bulletin*, 'the frantic praise showered on the Japanese in London and in all places where London influence stretches', including Australia. There was still room to blame Britain for Australia's problems with Japan.

The *Bulletin* nursed other grievances. As we have seen, commentators had noted that the achievements of contemporary Japan matched, perhaps surpassed, the incandescent achievements of Elizabethan England. This was particularly offensive. The *Bulletin* had hoped that Australia itself might inherit the Elizabethan spirit. It wanted the declining energies of the Anglo-Saxon race to flower again in the unique conditions of a new continent. Literary and artistic circles around the *Bulletin* were particularly attracted to the prospect of Australia as the home of a brilliant new race, a new breed of adventurers; even, in O'Dowd's phrase, 'sun-gods'.[35] The *Bulletin* wanted Australia to be the setting for the renewal of Caucasian energies and the full flowering of the Caucasian mind or brain. It was an affront that the Japanese were now promoted as the new Elizabethans at just the time when the Australians were pressing their own claims to that title. This rankled. Here were the 'Asiatic' and imitative Japanese, showered with adulation, at just the moment when the eyes of the world should have been upon the newly created Commonwealth of Australia. Upstart Japan occupied centre stage. And there was plump John Bull, installed in the front row of the admiring audience, his broad back turned against young Australia.

In its coverage of the 1906 Squadron visit, the *Worker*, official organ of the Trade Unions and Labor organisations, echoed many of the *Bulletin*'s grievances. It condemned a group in the community called the 'pro-colour fanatics' and called upon all good Australians to examine the squadron visit more critically.[36] The *Worker* was astonished at the reception which the Australians had given the Japanese, believing that Japanese intentions in the Pacific could only be regarded as hostile. It was particularly irritated by the 'leading shopkeepers [who] decorated their windows with Japanese designs and legends, prominent amongst them being Old King Cole of the Book Arcade'.[37] As for the British, the *Worker* knew they would be quite willing at any time to give the Northern Territory to the Japanese in return for an unsavoury trade deal. Moreover, if Russia and Japan patched up their differences and embarked on a war of conquest, Russia might attack India, leaving Japan free to attack Australia. The *Worker* insisted that Australia was in urgent need of white immigrants. These could be supported by the introduction of a graduated land tax. It also argued for the immediate development of munitions factories to ensure that in the event of an invasion, the population might have something serious to fire at the enemy.

In its opposition to the Japanese, the *Truth*, always recklessly outspoken, saw the visit as a mixture of imperialist orgy, Jewish betrayal and female weakness. 'It seems incredible that a presumably sane people should go mad over a visit of three warships from the land of Geisha', the *Truth* remarked in one of its more lucid sentences, 'and that our authorities should spend large sums of money in their honour'. The *Truth* also noted that many Japanese soldiers had gone to the theatre where they saw 'The Country Girl', a performance that involved a good deal of 'show-leg business', evidently enjoyed by the sailors. That was disquieting. However, the *Truth* was distinctly unimpressed by other incidents. It derided 'Mrs Hilma Parkes and her band of incompetent meddling petticoats' who welcomed the Japanese at a gathering in a city cafe, praising their bravery and heroism. Worse was in store outside the *Bulletin* office, where the *Truth* reporter claimed to have seen some 'white degenerates waving Japanese flags' introduce a group of Japanese sailors to a number of 'white women unfortunates, who received them with all outward expressions of good-will and affection'. The paper dubbed these women 'George Street Geishas', remarking that incidents like that made criticism of prostitution and the debasement of women in Japan that much harder to sustain.[38]

The Japanese were not the only visitors in port. The *Baltimore*, a United States cruiser, had also visited Sydney, but the *Bulletin* felt that the Americans had been vitually overlooked in the mad scramble to fawn upon the Japanese.[39] The US Consul in Sydney, Orlando H Baker, would not have agreed with that assessment, but the contrast with the Japanese visit nevertheless concerned him. He reported that during its four week stay in Sydney, the *Baltimore* had attracted many visitors, while the officers had been treated to a number of fine parties from highly placed citizens. It was a successful visit and one that he thought should be repeated. 'Although we have no complaint as to the attention paid to the *Baltimore*', Baker continued, 'that given the Japanese Squadron was far greater and more enthusiastic'.[40] The US Consul reported that the Japanese had orchestrated and publicised their visit expertly. They had been very thorough. There were other contrasts. Hardly a day passed when Baker was not called upon to bail out an American sailor who had got into trouble with the law. There were attempts to desert and two crew members could not be located when the *Baltimore* left Sydney. In contrast, while hundreds of Japanese sailors were on leave in the city each day, there had not been a single arrest: 'If they had been in battle they could not have been more obedient to orders'.[41]

The Japanese visit was not only a brilliantly executed affair, but was also well funded. Money seemed no object. Baker had been particularly impressed, not to say envious. He singled out a splendid harbour excursion on board a special steamer when more than 500 leading citizens were entertained by Sydney's best band. There was sufficient food for Baker to describe the event as a 'feast'. As the steamer criss-crossed the harbour, the best people mingled with the immaculate Japanese officers. It had not only been a dazzling social success, but had provided the perfect vehicle for optimistic speeches about the opportunities for growing trade between Australia and Japan. There was no doubt in Baker's mind that the Japanese had left no stone unturned in their effort to make the squadron visit a resounding success. As far as making in an impact in Australia went, Orlando Baker was quite convinced that the Americans had more than met their match in the Japanese.[42]

The American response provides further confirmation, though it is hardly needed, that the visit of the Japanese squadron was a major event to which the Australian public had responded with considerable enthusiasm. In his attempt to explain the welcome, Baker emphasised the formidable organising talents of the Japanese, their careful planning and skilful publicity. Not only had they attracted the interest of ordinary citizens, they had also appealed to the sensibilities of the elite. Fine food, delightful music, an imposing and educated officer class, the latest technologies, working seamen of exemplary discipline along with ostentatious displays of spit and polish came together in a powerful cultural display. Australians had not simply encountered a battle ship, as had been the case with the *Baltimore*. The Japanese had shown Australians that they were the bearers of a new and impressive civilisation. Australian crowds had been given a glimpse of the new Japan. Baker could see that onlookers had every right to be impressed by what they had seen and that the US would need to mount a fuller, richer and more deeply considered naval display of its own if it wanted to make a comparable impact as a Pacific neighbour. Australians did not have long to wait for such an event.

The visit in 1908 of the US Atlantic Fleet, dubbed 'The Great White Fleet', quickly overshadowed the scale and impact of the Japanese squadron visits.[43] Australia had not been included on the Fleet's original Pacific itinerary. Alfred Deakin, realising the impact that such a visit would have, not to mention its favourable political auguries, set out to ensure that the Fleet visited Australia.[44] This was to prove a diplomatically complex procedure, for the invitation had to be extended to the United States from Britain. It could not come directly from Australia because on international issues, Australia at that time still had to operate through the Colonial Office. Yet the British were exhibiting growing unease about the mounting pressure within Australia for the Commonwealth to have its own navy, a pressure largely orchestrated by Deakin.[45] By 1907, and in the aftermath of Japan's striking victory over Russia, Britain's decision to leave

Australia's naval defence increasingly to its new ally, Japan, caused growing unease among Australians. As much as Australians might have admired Japan, it was another thing altogether to have the Japanese fleet act as Australia's guardian. For its part, the Colonial Office did not want anti-Japanese sentiment in Australia interfering with their alliance with Japan. To refuse an invitation to the US Fleet might antagonise Australian opinion, but to have the Fleet visit might occasion passionate displays of racial unity that could be interpreted as both anti-British, in so far as the British had not made a similar display of naval power in the region, and anti-Japanese on the grounds that Australians increasingly saw competent Japan as a threat to Australian security. Throughout the decade there continued to be unease over British naval policy in the Pacific. James Edmond, writer for the *Bulletin*, asked: 'If it becomes a question of risking war both inside and outside the Empire to keep Australia white, or arousing war inside the Empire in order to make Australia brown or black, which side will Britain take?'[46]

While in London for the Premier's conference in 1907, Deakin had lobbied the American Ambassador to Britain on Australia's behalf.[47] He had also made two in-person calls on the Consul-General in Melbourne, which the Americans interpreted as a clear sign of Deakin's determination to have the Fleet visit Australia.[48] In a letter to the US Consul-General in Melbourne, Deakin pointed to the similarities in political philosophy and sentiment between the United States and Australia and doubted if 'any two peoples could be found who are in nearer touch with each other'.[49] He had sent a similar message to the American Ambassador in London in which he had stressed that America and Australia shared an 'oceanic neighbourhood'.[50] If the Americans, in effect President Roosevelt, could be persuaded to consider changing the itinerary to include Australia, Deakin believed it would be difficult for the British to withhold a formal invitation. The Americans were also in favour of the idea. Writing to President Roosevelt, Elihu Root, Secretary of State, stated that he had been impressed by Deakin's letter and believed that the day would come 'when it will be important for the United States to have all ports friendly and all causes of sympathy alive in the Pacific'.[51] The Americans agreed to include Australia and New Zealand on their Pacific itinerary. The British Government was far from pleased, but issued the formal invitation that Deakin had sought. The Fleet was on its way.

Coverage of the event in the Australian press was extraordinarily intensive, beginning well before the Fleet arrived in Sydney harbour, its first port of call in Australia. British and American newspaper coverage was also extensive. The response to the 'Great White Fleet' far exceeded the welcome given to the Japanese squadrons; indeed it was generally conceded that the event drew bigger and more enthusiastic crowds than anything in Australian history, including the ceremonies that ushered in the inauguration of the Commonwealth in January

1901. Country towns were virtually empty and all available rooms in Sydney and Melbourne were booked out. Visitors were accommodated in private homes. Many slept in parks. Australia gave the visiting Americans a welcome like no other they had seen. In greeting the American Fleet as 'cousins' it was clear that Australians sought to lessen the isolation they felt in the Pacific, an arena that was increasingly seen as a potential centre of world conflict. Discerning the meaning behind the extraordinary reception accorded to the 'Great White Fleet' became a familiar journalistic endeavour.

The American Franklin Matthews, was one of the shrewdest and most thorough commentators. An officially accredited journalist, his account of the tour, *Back to Hampton Roads*, was published in 1909. He was ideally placed to comment on what was said in the host of official speeches that accompanied the visit, but he was no less interested in what took place behind the scenes. Matthews believed that fear of the 'yellow peril' was the most frequently expressed sentiment throughout the tour and was bound up with a new resolve to 'make and keep this a white man's country'. While he found that these references were nearly always made in 'the nature of asides', they nonetheless expressed both a profound sense of vulnerability and a determination to ensure that Australia should become a 'white' continent.[52] While bunting, speeches, crowded streets and elaborately choreographed displays of massed school children were to be found at every point of the tour, Matthews also measured the emotional intensity of these sentiments by the avalanche of poetry that the visiting Fleet occasioned. American correspondents accompanying the Fleet were often kept busy late into the night opening endless mail bags of verse.[53] There were enough poems to give the galley fires a roaring start. Roderic Quinn, penned one of the better known effusions, an ode entitled, 'Hail! Men of America, Hail!' which was sung by 500 school children at Sydney's St Mary's Cathedral. Quinn's ode included the lines:

> The powers of the earth are as lions
> That scent afar feast on the gale;
> For the sake of our race of the future
> Hail! men of America, Hail![54]

But Matthews felt that the great Western Australian people's poet, 'Dryblower' Murphy, had come closest to expressing the national mood in a poem which told how the visit of the 'Big Brother' to 'the lonely kangaroo' had quickened the resolve to keep the Pacific 'clean and free'. The visiting Americans had lessened the sense of loneliness Australians felt (Plate 13). Matthews believed that Australia saw itself as a nation engaged upon 'an Anglo-Saxon fight all by itself with little attention from the mother country and the rest of the world'. He found a people who, in the words of a Western Australian newspaper, longed 'for community of thought and aspiration with the white races'. Dryblower's 'Big Brother' poem caught the mood and when set to music became an instant success. Matthews heard it everywhere: 'in barrooms, in clubs, in drawing rooms, at public meetings, at formal dinners, at garden parties'. Whenever someone started singing it, people leapt to their feet with a mighty shout and started singing along, dancing, stamping their feet, waving handkerchiefs, drawing others in, roaring out the defiant words:

> We'll all stand together, boys,
> If the foe wants a flutter or a fuss;
> And we are hanging out the sign
> From the Leeuwin to the Line:
> This bit o' the world belongs to us.[55]

For Charles S Sperry, Admiral of the Atlantic Fleet, it soon became apparent that the Asian shadow was an ever-present reality in Australia, and an issue that required delicate handling. As the Fleet left Sydney he confided to his wife that he had to word his speeches very carefully 'as the Asiatic question causes great excitement here'.[56] Wherever the Fleet had travelled, from Chile to Australia, Sperry encountered the view that the Atlantic fleet was the one force that might prevent Japan from embarking upon a 'career of adventure' in the Pacific. Though Sperry insisted in official speeches upon blood ties and the cause of Anglo-Saxon unity, he informed his wife that 'the imperial English' did not seem to 'altogether enjoy' the attention that had been showered upon the Americans.[57] The welcome could all too easily be construed as a criticism of the Anglo-Japanese alliance and a comment on the failure of the British to recognise Australian vulnerabilities. The democratic Americans seemed more understanding and more willing to help their Pacific cousins than the remote British.

The American coverage of the Fleet visit was at once extensive and uninhibited about drawing attention to the anti-Japanese sentiment that was said to lie behind the welcome. In a full survey of the visit in October 1908, *Current Literature*, a prominent journal of opinion, commented that concern about Japan was intensely felt in Australia and that the Governor-General, Lord Northcliffe, whose official support for the Anglo-Japanese Alliance was undiminished, had suffered a decline in his popularity. At the same time it noted that support for Prime Minister Deakin had never been greater. *Current Literature* thought there was no question that Deakin had used the Fleet visit to further the idea that 'strategically vulnerable Australia' needed a navy of its own.[58] For the *New York Times*, the Fleet visit was a demonstration of 'white supremacy in the Pacific' and a vindication of Australia's need to develop its own navy, a theme that it pursued throughout the visit.[59] *Harper's Weekly* also took the view that Australians had every reason to fear Asian immigration and doubted that Australian interests coincided with those of Britain.[60] The *New York Herald* noted bluntly that the American Fleet was welcomed by a people protesting the 'withdrawal of British battle ships from the Pacific'.[61]

The London *Times*, which gave the Anglo-Japanese Alliance its unwavering support, was critical of sections of the American press that encouraged the view that British policy towards Japan and the Pacific was opposed to Australia's interests. The *Times* thought that when it came to expressing unease about Japan's territorial ambitions Australians needed no encouraging.[62] Well before the Fleet had reached Australia, V Chirol, editor of the *Times* wrote an angry letter to his colleague George Morrison complaining that Australia had dared to go ahead with 'a demonstrative invitation to the American Fleet to visit Australia, at a time when the voyage ... was being described all over the States as a "warning" to Japan'.[63] Morrison, who had grown very suspicious of Japanese actions in Manchuria, had come to regard Chirol and the *Times* as uncritically pro-Japanese and blind to the limitations of the Anglo-Japanese Alliance.[64] For all the talk of blood ties and Anglo-Saxon unity, there were sharp divisions of opinion over how best to secure the future of the Pacific.

Regular reports of the progress of the American Fleet also appeared in the Japanese press, which quickly drew attention to the *New York Herald*'s lurid warnings about the 'yellow peril' and the common racial bond that united the Australian and the American people.[65] As the Fleet left Sydney for Melbourne, with Admiral Sperry convinced of the delicacy of the Asiatic question in Australia, the *Japan Times* carried a report on 'Anti-Japanese Sentiment' in Australia which tied the enthusiasm for the visit to a growing insistence upon a 'white' Pacific policy backed by an Anglo-American Alliance.[66] The paper reported that the Japanese Consul in Sydney was hard at work endeavouring to convince the Australian public that Japan was not a threat to peace in the Pacific. These assurances came at a time when the Japanese nation celebrated the 50th anniversary of its first Treaty with Britain, an event which occasioned a very flattering account of Japanese achievements in the London *Times*. The *Japan Times* acknowledged the glowing tribute from its powerful namesake, but feared that it would simply encourage Japanophobes to entertain new 'misgivings about our national destiny'.[67] There followed, right on cue, a summary of news items in the Japanese press, including a report from the Tokyo *Asahi* which, according to the *Japan Times*, 'almost despairs of the possibility of removing the deep-rooted prejudice entertained in the Australian breasts in regard to this country'.[68]

Chapter Eight

The Invasion Narrative

In the late 1880s, at a time of stringent curtailment of Chinese immigration, the first fictional representations of an Asian invasion of Australia began to appear. By this time, the invasion story had already become an established genre in British literature. It served a number of expository, analytical interests and can be placed into the yet wider field of European war literature. Invasion narratives sought to condition ways in which international conflict and patriotic disciplines were understood and validated. The invasion narrative was commonly a discourse upon vulnerability at a time of growing anxiety about the decline of British power against a background of intensifying European rivalries. How would the British, who had created the world's most powerful and extensive Empire, maintain their place at the pinnacle of world power? While nations and races rose to positions of dominance, it was understood that they also declined and grew decadent. Australian invasion writing forms part of this much broader discourse on the relationship between national strength, military capacity and the patriotic spirit. It was a period in which decadence and the suspect masculinities it generated seemed sharply at odds with the intensifying demands of national survival.

I F Clarke's *Voices Prophesying War* demonstrates that British invasion writing was a substantial genre, a point also made by Patrick Brantlinger in his critically acclaimed study of the literature of empire.[1] David Trotter suggests that the 'political agenda' of the spy-thriller and the invasion novel distinguished the genre from other forms of sensational fiction, though their forms of politics may simply have been less explicit.[2] Certainly the identity of the imagined invader or the secret spy varied with current political circumstances. The stories also readily swapped one enemy for another.[3] In most British invasion stories, it was the European Powers, especially France, Germany and Russia, that sought the destruction of Britain. Uncertainty following the Franco-Prussian War saw the serialisation in *Blackwood's Magazine* in 1871 of the invasion story 'The Battle of Dorking'. This serial aroused great public interest, boosting sales to record levels, much to the delight of author, Sir George Tomkyns Chesney, whom Clarke regards as the originator of the invasion story as popular fiction.[4] Chesney's story inspired the Australian journalist George Rankin to try his hand at an account of a Russian attack on Sydney. His book, *The Invasion*, was published under the pseudonym W H Walker in 1877. Many similar fictions were to appear before the turn of the century.[5]

One of the leading exponents of the new genre was William Le Queux, who had learned something of military conflict through his service as a newspaper correspondent during the Balkans War and who later worked closely with the fledgling British Secret Service.[6] In *The Great War in England in 1897*, published in 1894, the Russians join the French in invading England. Le Queux apparently found the inspiration for this Franco-Russian attack in the visit of the Russian Fleet to Toulon in 1893.[7] *The Great War in England in 1897* emphasised how a militarily unprepared nation like Britain provided a powerful incitement for the resentment and contempt of more martial peoples. In such a world, the strong had every right, perhaps even a duty, to prey upon and eliminate the weak. The idea that Britain was an imperilled island grew in the 1880s and 1890s as she faced economic competition from newly industrialised nations, as her free trade policies met increasing protectionism and as her social consensus was fragmented by the Irish Question, growing unionism, labour militancy and agitation over women's rights.[8] The invasion novel sought to direct attention to external threats, while highlighting the costs of disunity. Revelations of Britain's vulnerability to attack, however, can hardly have reassured empire loyalists, who placed their faith in a resolute British navy shielding the sparsely settled Australian continent from Asian invasion.

Apart from detailing the mechanics of an invasion, the invasion narrative drew upon and developed the theme of international espionage and with it the figure of the spy. What is commonly regarded as the first modern spy novel, Erskine Childers, *The Riddle of the Sands*, was published in 1903.[9] The book caused a sensation and has never been out of print. Childers' Britain was pictured as a country weakened by the dispersal of her Empire and undermined at home by disloyal foreigners, not least the Jews, a common target of hostility. *The Riddle of the Sands* brought together exciting detective work, robust action-adventure and nautical tales drawn from Childers extensive experience sailing along the English and northwest German coast.[10] Experts from the Military Intelligence Department, however, found very little basis for Childers' suggestion that the Germans might prepare an invasion of Britain from the Friesian coast.[11]

Two years later, William Le Queux again took up the espionage theme in *The Invasion of 1910*. Le Queux imagined a German invasion of Britain, predicting, some claimed, the outbreak of the Great War.[12] Le Queux described how the German Army had planted 'hundreds of spies' amongst Germans working in London. These undercover agents sabotaged British defences as soon as the invasion flotilla set sail. In his next book, *Spies of the Kaiser*, published in 1909, Le Queux pictured Britain infiltrated by an army of German spies; 'fixed agents' who were busy conducting an extensive intelligence survey of the entire country and 'travelling agents' who collected all the reports and paid the necessary remuneration.[13] Le Queux's breathless style and overwrought suspicions were parodied by A A Milne in *Punch*. Undeterred, Le Queux insisted that *Spies of the Kaiser* was founded on real people and actual events.[14] He had drawn on some analyses made by Lieutenant-Colonel James Edmonds of the new Military

Counter Intelligence Section MO5 when constructing his plots, but his estimate of the numbers of German spies in Britain was wildly exaggerated. The Germans had only a few naval agents employed at British dockyards.[15]

Another body of invasion writing grew out of nineteenth century proposals to link Britain and France by tunnel. This genre has been deftly analysed by Daniel Pick, who concludes that the tunnel proposal, which was put before the British Parliament in the 1880s to widespread consternation, 'evoked the dread not only of war and conquest, but also more subtly of miscegenation, degeneration, sexual violation and the loss of cultural identity'.[16] Invasion writing inevitably dwelt upon anxieties generated by the rapid inflow of hostile populations with all that implied about the mixing of blood, violation and lost sovereignty. In each case, the idea of invasion appeared to have the full backing of history. Indeed, there were those for whom history was not much more than the story of successive waves of invaders sweeping all before them. The most terrifying of all invaders, the classic horde, came from the East. Even Britain might feel this fear, according to F V White's *The Decline and Fall of the British Empire*, published in 1881. Purportedly written by a Chinese Professor of History, it told the story of the Chinese conquest of Britain. Thereafter, through the 1880s, British invasion stories concentrated on more immediate European threats, at least until the publication in 1907 of H G Wells' futurist novel, *The War in the Air* which described the formation of an Asiatic Federation between China, Japan and India which waged war on Europe and America.[17] Stories of Asian invasion soon became Californian and later, Australian specialties.

Before the Chinese even set foot on American soil, the accounts of traders and missionaries to China had presented a negative view of the Chinese to the American public. In early debates over the use of 'coolie' labour, the Chinese were included together with Blacks and American Indians, but from 1865 an anti-Oriental discourse began to develop.[18] Anti-Chinese fears became a recurrent feature of American popular writing, particularly in the last two decades of the nineteenth century. In 1880, 'Lorelle' published 'The Battle of the Warbash', an account of a future 'Amero-Mongolian' conflict in which the Chinese, having exterminated the American army, come to dominate America itself. By the year 2078 at the new capital of St Louis, there are 'pigtails everywhere'. There are three Chinese to every white; Chinese freely marry white women and white men have been reduced to 'Asiatic slavery'. California has been 'celestialised'.[19] Robert Wolter's *A Short and Truthful History of the Taking of California and Oregon by the Chinese in the Year AD 1899*, published in 1882, the year the first Chinese Exclusion act was passed in California, told a similar story. From 1880 there has been an unobtrusive movement of Chinese into California. By 1885, few white families are without a Chinese cook, a Chinese laundryman or a Chinese youth to mind the baby and a 'heathen temple' stands alongside Grace Church in San Francisco. Californians are reconciled to the Chinese presence. China then begins developing its naval power. In 1898, Prince Tsa Fungyang Tung Tai sails his fleet through the Golden Gate to the welcome of an admiring populace. Lovely women are entranced by the Chinese Prince. But a plot is underway, the ubiquitous Chinese are forming a secret organisation. When Prince Tsa returns in 1899, the signal for action is given. The ubiquitous Chinese cooks poison all the food they prepare for the white population and roving bands of Chinese slaughter anyone still left alive. The Chinese then take over California and Oregon. As 'the Europeans displaced Red Indians by driving them into the West' the 'alien Mongolian' now deals with the Caucasian race.[20] Other American invasion novels include Pierton W Dooner's *The Last Days of the Republic,* published in 1880 and Otto Mundo's *The Recovered Continent: A Tale of Chinese Invasion,* published in 1898.[21] As William F Wu has suggested, such nineteenth century American fantasies of Chinese invasion are notable for their portrayal of the invaders as 'masses of mindless automata', a stereotyping that carries echoes of much older fears of the endless hordes of Mongols invading Europe.[22]

Australian invasion writing has many parallels with its Californian counterparts. Both drew upon themes also evident in the British genre, although with an enemy reconfigured as Asian. Fears of weakness, decline and moral pollution along with anxieties over the decay of patriotism and the untrustworthy nature of women, often figured as betrayers of national promise, recur. In Australia, invasion narratives drew upon contemporary commentaries on the damaging impacts of Australia's high rates of urbanisation, her relatively small population and, from the late 1890s, the decline in the birth-rate. The key literature in which the Chinese feature as invaders includes the anonymous *The Battle of Mordialloc, or How We Lost Australia* published in 1888 and clearly indebted to 'The Battle of Dorking'. More detailed and more culturally revealing is an invasion novel by William Lane, serialised the same year in the *Boomerang*, and Kenneth Mackay's, *The Yellow Wave: A Romance of the Asiatic Invasion of Australia,* published in 1895. There was also Raymond Longford's film, *Australia Calls,* produced in 1913. Now apparently lost, this film described an attempt by Chinese invaders to conquer Australia.[23] In these narratives, unlike their British and American equivalents, the fear expressed is not loss of cultural identity so much as a fear that Australia's historically shallow and remote colonies might not be given long enough to establish coherent identities at all. Australia was not much more than an idea and there was some doubt as to whether it was even a good one.

The Australian invasion narrative provided a fine opportunity to gauge the nation's capabilities. The invasion story was always there to say at least as much about 'us' as about 'them'. Both Lane and Mackay noted particularly weak links in Australia's defence chain. Both saw danger in the tendency to underestimate Asia's fighting prowess. Mackay considered the Chinese to be formidable opponents and Lane also warned that they were an intelligent enemy. Both saw further dangers in the Australian people themselves. Australians could become fanatical over horse racing or cricket, but remain calmly indifferent to matters of defence. They talked of the great open spaces, but were addicted to urban pleasures. Moreover, some were too well disposed towards Asia. This was not merely the product of capitalist greed and the pursuit of illimitable markets. Mackay and Lane detected a fatal Asian power to fascinate and charm. They feared the power of the beguiling, mysterious East.

In his elaborate narrative *White or Yellow?*, William Lane developed and fictionalised themes of violation and moral decay which he invariably associated with the Chinese. The serial is set twenty years into the future, in Queensland in the year 1908. Lane estimates the state now has a population of 42 million: 30 million whites and 12 million Asians. Only the migration of 15 million white Americans has saved Australia from complete Asian domination. This multi-racial community is presided over by a corrupted Anglo-Australian elite which favours British policies of racial appeasement not Australian policies of racial exclusion. Moreover, the Chinese, whom the British Government has ruled must be given civil rights, quickly cease to be hewers of wood and drawers of water: they dominate key industries, sit in Parliament, occupy leading positions in the public service and take their place in the judiciary. Prominent among them is the wealthy Sir Wong Hung Foo, scheming to marry into the rich Anglo-Australian Stibbins family. Lord Stibbins is premier of Queensland. His title, commercial instincts and slavishly pro-British policies are sufficient, Lane insinuates, to allow him to accept a Eurasian future both for his grand-children and for Queensland.

The Stibbins' breakfast table, where Lord and Lady Stibbins and their daughter Stella are joined by Sir Wong adds some telling detail to the big picture. The fact that Stella is their only daughter provides a palpable sign that as well as decorating their breakfast room in the French style, the Stibbins have adopted the Parisian fashion of race suicide. One child was simply not good enough. There they sit, the suave Lord, his lady, their perfect daughter and 'unctious' Sir Wong. Stibbins is an athletic looking man who might have been handsome but for a hooked nose and calculating eyes, features suggesting Jewishness. Wong is the Australian-born son of a Chinese merchant. While he is a fabulously wealthy man of great intellect, his 'heavy lips and drooping eye-lids' are unmistakable signs of his gross sensuality. Over breakfast, Stibbins and Wong plan to conquer the white trash of Australia, creating a Chinese Australia with Wong as Emperor and Stella his Empress. Miscegenation is to be Australia's fate.[24]

But Stibbins and Wong are not unopposed. They have to contend with John Saxby, farmer, Australian patriot, doting father of Cissie and secretary of the Anti-Chinese League. He is also a leading player in a secret army organised among miners, labourers and farmers. Saxby is assisted by the sturdy Bob Flynn, Cissie's sweetheart. Both are decidedly manly men in the Caucasian mould. Throughout his serial, Lane contrasts rural and working class white Australian manhood with its Chinese counterpart. Australian manhood was described as having the sturdiness of the oak. In comparing men to trees in this way, Lane evokes powerful images of strength, while avoiding any suggestion of sexual feeling, let alone lust or sensuality. For him, Australian manhood was a forest. It prospered out of doors, drawing nourishment from the soil and needing space to develop. Its mature growth was strong and protective. Chinese men were presented in a very different light. They were pictured as typically complex, sensual and calculating. Theirs was an interiorised world of debasement and moral pollution, where lusts were nourished by fantasies of racial domination and fuelled by never to be forgotten humiliations at the hands of Europeans. They were by turns indolent and unpredictably violent. Even worse, Lane insisted, their terrible passions always lay cunningly hidden behind a mask of impassivity. They were at once calculating and closed to all scrutiny.

Both Saxby and Flynn are vehemently anti-Chinese and ready to die for the cause of a White Australia. What of the heroine, Cissie, if this were to happen? Flynn is adamant: 'Cissie can die as well. She is Australian too. And I'd sooner kill her with my own hands than have her live to raise a brood of coloured curs'.[25] This proves unnecessary. Saxby and Flynn discover Cissie's body in a nearby paddock. She has died defending her honour in an attack by the lascivious Sir Wong. News of her death so angers the white community that they rise up against the Chinese and their supporters.

In Lane's 'White or Yellow?', women were shown as largely unresponsive to the anti-Chinese message. It took Cissie Saxby's ugly death to win the women over to the cause of race war. But once the women are converted they willingly fan the fires of hatred which their past 'indifference had mainly held back for so long'. The emergence of a republican, anti-Chinese movement is directly linked to Wong's attempted sexual assault. Cissie becomes the murdered virgin whose death lent inspiration to the cause. When the fighting is over, the victorious republicans gather around her open coffin:

> She lay there like the virgin Nationality which had found its life in her death ... lay there typical of the faith and purity and holiness of thought which had lent strength to the upheaval.[26]

The violation of young Australian womanhood by the Chinese allows white men at large to emerge as principled defenders of female honour. Living women might impede, if not actually subvert the task of national defence, but dead ones, especially sacrificial virgins, displayed like Cissie Saxby, become potent symbols for the cause of racial unification.[27]

Lane's writings argued that Australian women should be grateful for their status in Australia. In 'White or Yellow?' he clearly implied that in an Australia dominated by Asia they would fare much worse. At that time, many such contrasts were made between European and Asian women. Contemporary accounts frequently endeavored to show that European women were much better situated than their Asian sisters. An example is George Morrison's *An Australian in China*. Although the book was intended as a tribute to Chinese civilisation, Morrison nevertheless provides a harrowing account of young girls sold into slavery. With his characteristic attention to detail and price, Morrison recorded that upwards of 3,000 children had been sold to dealers in one of the districts through which he had passed. His account of them carried and sold like poultry was hardly calculated to give a favourable impression of the status of women in China. Indeed he concluded: 'the lot of the average Chinese woman is certainly not one that a Western woman need envy'.[28] At the same time, his story gave no support for the view that Chinese men could be expected to rape and violate white women.

One of the arguments in favour of the Chinese and one advanced by Francis Adams was that their tenacity and skill would turn Australia into a miracle of productivity. Lane disbelieved this claim. In 'White or Yellow?' he described how the fine Western architecture of Queen Street, Brisbane is 'tainted' by gilding and gaudy painting. The fine building, once home to the Brisbane *Courier Mail*, is now a seedy restaurant serving rat and rice. Young 'unformed' girls are leading sordid lives in neighbourhoods 'drenched in all the infamy of Chinese vice and shame'. The smell of opium wafts from every doorway.[29] This is a hopelessly miscegenated and degenerate community, riddled with drug abuse and moral infamy.

In 'White or Yellow?', although the white forces led by John Saxby are victorious, Lane's story runs into difficulty with the fate of over 12 million Chinese survivors. The plan is to move them to North Queensland and ship them, presumably without objection, to the Netherlands East Indies. Did Lane or his readers consider practicalities? Assuming adequate port facilities in North Queensland and the co-operation of Dutch authorities, it would have required 24,000 ships, each carrying 500 passengers to rid North Queensland of the defeated Chinese. At a notional $400 per ship, the venture would cost $9,600,000, a solid sum. This, of course, imposes an inappropriately literal reading on Lane's text, yet his treatment of the population issue also points to a persistent unwillingness among invasion writers to explain how the mighty 'swarming populations' of the world were to be transported.

The Battle of Mordialloc, was perhaps a response to Lane's account of race war in Queensland (Plate 14). Its purpose was to warn readers that in rejecting the British connection, as Lane advocated, Australian colonists only made themselves more vulnerable to invasion. *The Battle of Mordialloc* told the story of a people cut adrift from Britain, easy prey to a combined force of Russian and Chinese invaders. It narrates 'the closing scenes in our national history'.[30] As in *White or Yellow?*, *The Battle of Mordialloc* was the story of a fragile, vulnerable nationality seeking the conditions that might ensure permanence.

Lane had also stressed Australia's geo-political vulnerability. So too did Kenneth Mackay's, *The Yellow Wave: A Romance of the Asiatic Invasion of Australia*. Mackay was born in 1859, the son of Scottish-born pastoralists in Wallendbeen, New South Wales. He was a versatile fellow, strongly attached to the bush, horse-riding, soldiering and writing. His novel, the work of a comparatively young man, was published in 1895, the year Mackay was elected as a Protectionist to the Legislative Assembly. He was soon busy raising a volunteer cavalry force in New South Wales and was promoted to Lieutenant-Colonel for his efforts. After service in South Africa during the Boer War, he maintained his military connections until his death in 1935.[31]

Mackay's story is set in 1954, the year of the Eureka centenary. The century may have changed, but not the technology. Australia's defence still depends on horsemanship, bush virtues and fortifications reminiscent of the Eureka Stockade. In Mackay's story, Australia's governing classes are again so enslaved by the commercial spirit that they are blind to Australia's vulnerability. Unlike Lane, Mackay saw little of value in the labour movement. The capitalist classes, 'exposed alike to climatic influences and the iron law of environment' have 'similarly degenerated'.[32] The allusion to degenerationist anxieties was a characteristic 1890s touch, quickened by the recent debate over Pearson's *National Life and Character*, published in 1893. In Mackay's story, only those independent producers who stand between capital and labour have retained their 'full vitality'. The rest can be dismissed. When the attack comes, the defence of Australia lies in the hands of an independent force of bushmen of mainly Scottish background, helped out by a crusty squatter or two.

Mackay sets his story at Fort Mallarraway, a co-operative settlement based on democratic principles and the cornerstone for the moral and physical defence of northern Australia. Mackay makes few references to the 'ladies' of the co-operative. We learn that without servants, the women contribute their own labour to the general good, but only in a domestic sphere. Fort Mallarraway is a community of bush thinkers, independent of the banks, the government and the labour unions. Their task is to create a fair and equitable society. To these sturdy bushmen, the unionist, the capitalist and the Chinese labourer are little better than slaves, all are seen as enemies of Australian democracy.

In *The Yellow Wave* the invasion is a joint Russian-Chinese effort, involving a simultaneous attack on British India and northern Australia, considered two of the more vulnerable points of Empire. Mackay emphasises that the pleasure-loving capitals did not take news of the attack seriously, especially when they know the enemy is Chinese. They advance upon the invading Mongol armies 'not only without fear, but with positive contempt'.[33] This is a grave mistake. The better disciplined Chinese cut the disorganised southern army to ribbons. Significant resistance came only from 'Hatten's ringers', named for their leader, 'one of those self-reliant, dare devil guerrilla leaders of which the Australian Bushman is the ideal prototype' and perhaps modelled on Mackay himself. Hatten's troop is an irregular force of stout-hearted men, 'splendid in physique and courage'.[34] These are the racially fit, a class of men who, not for the first or last time in these speculative encounters with an Asian enemy, are assigned a vital role in the anticipated struggle for racial survival in the Pacific.

Lane and Mackay both speak to a powerful utopian impulse in late nineteenth century Australian political culture. Anti-Chinese sentiment was strengthened by the conviction that coloured labour was no better than slave labour which might well contribute to the growth of capitalism and the accumulation of wealth, but would contribute little to the creation of a new and better society. Lane was particularly influenced by the hope that Australia would become the home of a distinctive Aryan community, drawing migrants from racially similar peoples, particularly from North America, but standing well apart from the corrupt British Empire and its compromising Asian entanglements.

While both Lane and Mackay presented themselves as democrats, neither felt that parliamentary democracy was either democratic or worth defending. In 'White or Yellow?' the Parliament of the future is manipulated by unprincipled men greedy for titles. By 1908, parliamentary democracy in Queensland is little more than a tool for British interests. Similarly, in *The Yellow Wave*, southern Parliaments merely squabble and posture while matters of grave national importance, like defence and the growing hold of foreign ownership go undiscussed.

There was a powerful juxtaposition in Lane and Mackay between the shining purity of a white Australia and the dirty compromises of British capitalism, between symbols of youth, cleanliness and purity and those of age, decay and exhaustion. One of the most stigmatised figures in Australian invasion literature was the business man, often pictured as a figure deficient in both manliness and patriotism. Soft goods and drapery, businesses easily characterised as feminine, were singled out as especially demeaning. Many encounters, such as that between Hatten and the Minister for War were contests over the nature and meaning of manhood. The Minister is pictured as a man of many words and little substance. Neither his ministerial rank, nor his background in commerce have made him a man. His British sympathies confirm him as credulous fellow with little understanding of the powerful forces governing the modern world. Wordy and rather dandified, he is clearly an effeminate modern. In contrast, Hatten, the silent man from the dry interior, without title or position, is the proper embodiment of racial fitness. It is the sturdy Australian bushman, not the city businessman, turned politician, who will be called upon to save Australia in her hour of need.

While Lane set his story in 1908 and Mackay's took place in 1954, both harked back to the glory days of the Eureka uprising on the Ballarat gold field in 1854. Lane's race patriots rally around the Southern Cross flag first used at Eureka. Mothers hold their babies aloft to glimpse it. The sick drag themselves from hospital beds to get a better view. One illustration in 'White or Yellow?' shows a band of heavily bearded males, rifles in hand, gathering to meet the enemy. In another, a band of horsemen attacks retreating Chinese with sabres.[35] Sabres in 1908? Both text and illustrations celebrate earlier, mid-nineteenth century forms of warfare. This is particularly evident in *The Yellow Wave*. To one observer, Fort Mallarraway with its iron bark and box log fortifications has the appearance of a Maori pa. It is not that Mackay failed to anticipate that a box log fortification was unlikely to be state of the art defence in 1954, but rather that his purpose was to depict a stout guerrilla action mounted by a troop of race patriots true to their bush inheritance. He was making the case for the continuance of bush values. In both novels, the Asian enemy at the gate provided a powerful pretext for an unequivocal rejection of the moral and physical degeneration associated with the city. This was a rejection of cosmopolitanism, a mixed form, born out of big cities and blurred identities, but proudly modern.

The Yellow Wave was published in London where it may have been read by British popular writer, M P Shiel.[36] Shiel had been asked to write a war-serial based around Chinese concerns.[37] His response was 'The Empress of the Earth', re-issued in 1898 as *The Yellow Danger*.[38] It was the story of Yen How who swoops down from the East at the head of a 'yellow horde' and proceeds to devastate Europe.[39] The novel was sweeping in its condemnation of the Chinese, revealing the principle points of their character as 'immeasurable greed, an absolute contempt for the world outside China, and a fiendish love of cruelty'.[40] The shrill screams of the invading Mongols spread sheer panic, a 'yellow terror' among the Europeans.[41] Finally a devastating plague checks the Chinese advance and allows the Empire troops, aided by the Americans, to achieve final victory.[42] The British Prime Minister is able to announce that the destiny of the European races is now 'to renew and administer the earth'.[43] This was unapologetically a white supremacist message and more triumphalist in tone than the Australian literature which carried a simpler message about the need to defend Australia from a Chinese attack .

The Yellow Danger was followed in 1900 by another invasion novel, *Queen of the World*, set in AD 2174, when the Chinese use air power to rule the world. However, from around the turn of the century invasion writers began to see Japan as the coming danger.[44] In 1897, J H Palmer predicted a future Japanese attack on Honolulu and San Francisco in *The Invasion of New York, or, How Hawaii was Annexed* and in 1898, the British novel, *What Will Japan Do?*

narrated events which anticipated aspects of the Russo-Japanese War of 1904-5.[45] For Australians, the Japanese victory over Russia signalled that Japan was likely to soon play a more important role in the Pacific. That there was a good deal of iron, steel and muscle in the new Japan was becoming increasingly apparent. Japan was emerging as a strong, martial nation, not just a chain of exquisite but remote islands, the source of dainty gifts, delicately wrought crafts and colourful silks. In the decade after 1905, boyhood conscription was introduced, a military academy was established at Duntroon, the Australian Navy was formed and the 'empty' Northern Territory became a national rather than a South Australian responsibility. Spending on defence increased five-fold between 1901 and 1914. Despite any assurances from proffered Anglo-Japanese Alliances, it seemed to many Australians that Japan had emerged as a tenacious adversary.[46]

In this atmosphere, concerns were soon expressed over forces thought to be subverting the nation's preparedness. Prominent among them were anxieties about Australia's very high levels of urbanisation and the growing numbers of unfit and possibly effeminate city-born men, the emancipation of women and the appreciable decline in the national birth-rate.[47] While these concerns soon surfaced in the later Australian invasion literature which dealt with Japan, Mrs Rosa Campbell Praed was one Australian writer who went against the trend. She dismissed any concerns over the rise of Japan and in a subversive rebuttal of the invasion literature made the figure of the sturdy Australian bushman heroically repelling the Asiatic invader, an object of satire. In *Madame Izàn: A Tourist Story*, published in 1899 and set in Japan, Praed was clearly unconvinced by the dismissive characterisation of Australian women evident in invasion novels and was amused by the large claims made on behalf of rural manliness.[48] She reversed the accustomed roles. Praed's courteous, intellectually curious women approach Japan in a spirit of open-minded enquiry. Her ill-read men, despite their excellent bush credentials, are by turns bewildered and hostile in the face of sophisticated Japanese difference.

Madame Izàn opens in a large Hong Kong hotel, where guests include 'sallow and tired-looking' ladies who nevertheless exhibit that 'indefinable self-conscious smartness acquired by English women quartered in the East ...'. Moving silently among this company are the Chinese 'boys', tending the tables, working the fans, 'always imperturbably remote'.[49] Among the guests is John Windeatt, a Queensland squatter, bound for Japan with his sister, a travel writer. Also staying at the hotel is the alluring Madame Izàn with her travelling companion, Mrs Bax. As soon as he sets eyes on Madame Izàn, poor Windeatt is smitten. He is most disappointed to learn she is married, but cheers up on hearing that she too is bound for Japan.

Madame Izàn and Mrs Bax soon guess that Windeatt was Australian; they 'recognised the type', considering him a 'magnificent' specimen of manhood.[50] Indeed, Windeatt is tall and powerfully built, an embodiment of the manly qualities that would, it was commonly supposed, protect Australia against assault from the north. For her part, Madame Izàn is a beautiful, reflective and Australian-born example of the 'new woman'; modern, independent, cultivated and with a mind of her own.[51] The intricate requirements of the plot necessitate that she has been blind from birth. Caught up in a match of convenience, she can't recognise her Japanese husband, Mr Izàn. This most unlikely plot nevertheless permits a contest for Madame Izàn's affections between Windeatt, the 'splendid Australian Apollo', and Mr Izàn, his Japanese rival. With her sight restored, which of the two men, each representing sharply opposed understandings of masculinity, would the new woman choose?

Unknown to the travellers, Mr Izàn has disguised himself as their guide, assuming the name 'Mr Kencho'. Madame Izàn quickly appreciates his qualities. Though he is physically unprepossessing, she finds Mr Kencho a cultivated, well-read and interesting gentleman who believed that a new civilization would be created from the fusion of Eastern and Western cultures.[52] Ernest F Fenollosa, in an article published in 1899, the year *Madame Izàn* appeared, had similarly expressed the view that East and West shall 'aim at a new world-type', rich in a 'million possibilities of thought and achievement'.[53] Mr Kencho's ideas impress Madame Izàn. She sees that Japan and its people should be taken seriously, confiding: 'here in Japan there is a reality, a dignity about men ... a depth and a knowledge which one had never thought of before'.[54] This is bad news for Windeatt in whom these qualities are not at all apparent. When it comes to her moment of choice, Madame Izàn opts for 'the learned and courteous' Mr Kencho, not the Queensland squatter.

Praed's witty novel was a lively satire of Australian manhood: its material obsessions, its patronising attitudes to Eastern cultures, its superior attitudes to women, its intellectual limitations and self-important warnings of the threat from the North. Windeatt was seen to harbour the standard apprehensions of his sex and class: he believed that the Japanese were masters of espionage and that their every move concealed 'some hideous plot against Australian life and liberty'.[55] He was at one with those who warned of invasion. Likewise he was convinced of his sacred duty to defend white women against the terrible threat from the East. Yet the idea that the role of the Australian male was to protect Australian women from the lecherous advances of oriental villains was confounded. If Madame Izàn was endangered by the predatory male, the threat came from Windeatt. Praed made much of Mr Kencho's strict adherence to rigorous codes of gentlemanly conduct, particularly in relation to women.

Although Praed's story was both witty and amusing, not all shared her joke at the expense of Australian manhood. Dark warnings of a Japanese invasion of Australia soon began to emerge. 1903 saw the publication of T R Roydhouse's *The Coloured Conquest*, a topical novel which capitalised on the recently signed Anglo-Japanese Alliance and incorporated some very up-to-the-minute references to the visit of the Japanese Training Squadron earlier that year.[56] The book was published by the New South Wales Bookstall Company, which specialised in take-away fiction with large print runs and arresting covers, designed to catch the eye of suburban commuters wanting an engrossing story (Plate 15).[57] Over the next decade Japanese invasion was a major theme in three other novels, A G Hales' *The Little Blue Pigeon*, published in 1906, Ambrose Pratt's *The Big Five*, serialised in the *Lone Hand* from December 1907, and C H Kirmess's *The Commonwealth Crisis*, which appeared in the *Lone Hand* in 1908. Japanese invasion also featured in three plays: Randolph Bedford's unpublished, indeed unpublishable, 'White Australia, or The Empty North', Frances Hopkins's *Reaping the Whirlwind: An Australian Patriotic Drama for Australian People* and Jo Smith's 'The Girl of the Never Never'. There were also many articles and short stories.[58]

In Britain, the flurry of invasion novels, spy scares and lurid warnings prompted P G Wodehouse's irresistible parody, *The Swoop ... A Tale of the Great Invasion*, in which 'Britain is overwhelmed by simultaneous onslaughts of Germans, Russians, Chinese, Young Turks, the Swiss Navy, Moroccan brigands, cannibals in war canoes, the Prince of Monaco, and the Mad Mullah' until a brave boy scout saves the day.[59] One of the few nations missing was the Japanese. The British invasion writers, perhaps due to Britain's treaty arrangements and to geographical remoteness, did not appear to have the same anxious concern about Japanese intentions as the Australians. In 1907 R W Cole published *The Death Trap*, a story in which Britain, once again invaded by Germany, is saved when the Japanese allies land veterans of the Manchurian Campaign in Liverpool. Not a plot likely to appeal to Australian readers of that time.

For British writers, conflict between Japan and America seemed more likely than between Japan and Britain. Both J Crabapple's *The War of 1908 for the Supremacy of the Pacific* and A W Kipling's *The New Dominion*, described an American-Japanese War in the Pacific. At the same time, American invasion writers expressed lively concerns about the Japanese. In 1907, Marsden Mason's *The Yellow Peril in Action* predicted that the Japanese and Chinese would destroy American ships at Pearl Harbor. In 1909, Ernest Hugh Fitzpatrick wrote *The Coming Conflict of Nations, or, The Japanese-American War*, where the Japanese wipe out the American Fleet with a darkness bomb. In the same year Japanese war with America was the theme of a book by M J Phillips, *In Our Country's Service* and it also was the theme of a number of short stories. No doubt much of this publishing activity had been inspired by the immense publicity surrounding the voyage of the Great White Fleet in 1908.[60]

The Great White Fleet is directly mentioned in the preface to the English translation of *Banzai!*, an invasion novel by the German author Ferdinand H Grautoff, writing as 'Parabellum'. The book was published in America in 1908.

It displayed intense distrust of the Japanese.[61] Multitudes of spies were pictured at work in America, preparing the way for Japanese invasion. Meticulous intelligence work ensures that Tokyo possesses precise details of all American fortifications.[62] Once the war begins, Europe is complacent, but Australia at once recognises the appalling danger to America. Australians stage tremendous public demonstrations and mass-meetings when they hear the terrible news of the destruction of America's Pacific Fleet.[63] In Sydney, the windows of the Japanese Consulate are smashed and Japanese settlers are forced to leave the country along with the remaining Chinese; 'the yellow man's day in Australia was ended'.[64] Meanwhile England offers the hand of friendship to the Japanese. She is more interested in her commercial interests than in Japanese actions in the distant Pacific. The dastardly British even try to prevent Australian volunteers fighting for 'their big brother', America.[65] It was a story that could well have been serialised in the *Lone Hand*.

'Parabellum' expressed an obvious appreciation of the fighting characteristics of those 'splendid fellows of the Australian bush', a nice touch in a German author.[66] Within Australia the sturdy bushman, despite Praed's ironic characterisations, was widely presented as the figure on whom Australia would have to rely in the event of attack. For Frank Fox, editor of the *Lone Hand*, the bushman or yeoman farmer was 'the backbone of the resistance which the White Man will make to any Flow of Asia along the Pacific littoral'.[67] In sharp contrast, urban manhood, supposedly unfit and hedonistic, was thought to present a vulnerable target. By 1900 the American social scientist Adna Weber had identified Australia as exemplifying the modern trend towards urbanisation with almost a third of its population living in or near the capital cities.[68] The implications of urbanisation for national character were a common preoccupation. The city, with its increasingly mixed populations, its varied transactions with the world at large, its more flexible approach to questions of gender, its spirit of cultural and commercial experiment, was depicted as a corrosive force. The more complex, commercially oriented and progressive the city became, the more removed it seemed from the iron laws of national survival in the competitive world of invasion literature and racial struggle. The application of these laws in the Australian context brought competition down to the raw levels of military threat and territorial conquest. This was the Big Battle, looming over the horizon, a contest that might well push the softened, modern city-dweller to the wall. But the bush would hold firm.

Cities were seen as breeding grounds for decadent cultures and effeminate manhood. By their very weakness they were thought to provide an obvious incitement to invasion. Professor Macmillan Brown, the distinguished anthropologist and Pacific historian, was convinced that decadence was a powerful force eating away at Western civilisation. In a series of articles to the *Sydney Morning Herald* in 1913 he warned that 'leisure and pleasure' had already eroded the stabilising disciplines underpinning British civilisation in Australia. He condemned 'the sluicing of Western populations into city life', describing the city as 'the yawning abyss into which nations and races vanish'. The notion of the vanishing race was central to the invasion narrative, just as it was a recurrent discourse in late nineteenth century accounts of the rise and decline of nations. Brown urged Australians wanting to avoid decay from within and external attack to 'de-urbanise'. This, he reasoned, would prove to be Australia's best defence against militant Japan.[69] According to Brown's logic, the bush and its disciplines would be the making of Australia and the only force capable of withstanding Japan's *bushido*.

The developing hostility to urban manhood was articulated by Arthur Adams in a short story first published in the *Bulletin* and then reprinted in 1909 in the *Call*, a journal with a direct interest in strengthening Australian defences. The main character is a despicable and timorous clerk, the employee of a large Sydney importing firm. His anti-Labor views and low opinions of Australian naval, military and manufacturing capacities show him as the very model of an anglophile and suburbanised masculinity. The clerk turns out to be no match for the clever, disciplined Japanese, bent on invasion. The story ends with the clerk lying dead, 'half of his bowels trailing on the lawn in front of him', a much more loathsome object than his tough Japanese assailant who quickly sheds his identity as a businessman at the first signal to invade.[70] The Japanese businessman/spy, unlike the Australian clerk, is depicted as a considerable patriot and a figure to be admired. The clerk, tending his tiny patch of lawn, is another reminder of the suspect masculinities supposedly proliferating in Australian cities. With Japan as a possible enemy, the Australian male was reminded that he might need to be a bigger, more assertive man than the average city clerk. In this encounter, the Japanese invader was clearly portrayed as a finer specimen of manhood than the clerk. Was Japanese manhood stronger and finer than Australian manhood?

Chapter Nine

Beware the Empty North

In January 1911 the Commonwealth Government assumed responsibility for the Northern Territory after the passage of the Northern Territory Acceptance Bill.[1] The Commonwealth was taking over a perplexing political problem and one that was attracting increasing international attention. Since 1863 when it first came under South Australian control, European settlement in the north had been miserably slow. There had been no sign of the great population influx anticipated by enthusiasts for development. By the late nineteenth century, accusations of inertia, ineptitude or downright incompetence were routinely levelled at the politicians and bureaucrats responsible for the Territory. But there were also deeper anxieties at play. The transfer of the Northern Territory to the Commonwealth pointed to a growing realisation that Australia could not hold on indefinitely to territories it did not use. Australia could not afford to run the risk of appearing indifferent to the mounting population pressures and restless energies of emerging Asian nations in its immediate neighbourhood. A nation that seemed content to leave its Northern Territory so empty for so long ran the risk of being considered irresponsible or, worse again, as posing a menace to world peace. The idea emerged that it might be necessary to transfer all or part of the Northern Territory to nations better able to develop its potential.

United States President, Theodore Roosevelt, spoke for many Anglo-Saxonists of his generation when he warned his countrymen that failure to actively colonise newly acquired territories would mean:

> Some stronger, manlier power would have to step in and do the work, and we would have shown ourselves weaklings, unable to carry to successful completion the labours that great and high-spirited nations are eager to undertake.[2]

President Roosevelt had made it quite clear that his concerns about the failure to colonise empty territories applied to Australia. In January 1906 he met the Australian, Octavius Beale, President of the Associated Chambers of Manufacturers. Beale, a pro-Natalist zealot and leading force on the New South Wales Inquiry into the decline of the birth-rate in 1903-4, was touring the world in search of evidence that declining birth-rates threatened the future of the white race.[3] Roosevelt, who more than anybody had popularised the phrase 'race suicide', shared a number of Beale's enthusiasms and concerns. Roosevelt declared:

Next to my own nation, I am interested in the progress, success, and safety of your great democratic island continent. Beware of keeping the far north empty.[4]

Back in Australia, Alfred Deakin, then Prime Minister, responded in Parliament to Roosevelt's message:

Next to our own nation we place our kindred in America. I agree with him, too, that we should populate the far north, and, while preferring those of our own nation for that purpose, I am willing to look elsewhere if they are unable to accomplish the task.[5]

During the visit of the 'Great White Fleet', President Roosevelt's name was often invoked and almost always with shouts of approval. Franklin Matthews, an American journalist who accompanied the Fleet, found that Australians were well acquainted with Roosevelt's warnings of 'race suicide' and took a good natured interest in the great cause of population growth. Americans during the Fleet visit had been particularly amused by a skit appearing in a local newspaper on the population theme:

> Mr Teddy, rough and ready,
> To the crowd doth cry:
> "See the rabbit!
> Get the habit;
> Go and multiply!"[6]

Roosevelt's concern had helped turn the 'Empty North' into a matter for international comment. Others soon took up these concerns. In Britain, in 1905, the influential magazine, *The Nineteenth Century and After*, addressed the morality of a situation where four million Europeans refused entry to nearby nations 'teeming with a virile population just awakening to the first expanding wants of civilisation forced upon them by the white races'. The author warned that Australian attempts to maintain exclusive possession of an empty continent were morally indefensible and might spark a terrible racial conflagration.[7] In July 1910, the *Times*, commenting on the responsibilities to be undertaken by Andrew Fisher's new Labor Government, also noted how the 'Empty North' was becoming an issue of international concern:

The overshadowing Australian problem relates to the huge rich unpeopled northern territories. There is need for a rapid awakening of Australian opinion on this vital issue, and Australian politicians should realise that they are merely stewards for the rest of the world.[8]

Domestically, concerns about Australia's reputation and colonising performance had been building through the 1890s. In 1897, William Sowden, then one of South Australia's leading journalists, had ruefully summed up the Northern Territory as an 'unoccupied and distressful' region.[9] No government seemed able either to generate workable settlement proposals or put the plans of others into practice. Indeed by 1911 there were only 1,698 Europeans settled in the Territory. At this date, a large proportion of the non-Aboriginal population was still Chinese (Figure 9.1), even although Chinese numbers were declining following very restrictive immigration legislation. More 'acceptable' migrants were desperately needed. Sowden urged the settlement of 50,000 Japanese or Hindus to get the Territory moving, a comment that reveals not only Sowden's optimistic estimate of the Territory's carrying capacity but also his view that 'coloured labour' was a commodity that could be shifted around the globe at will.[10]

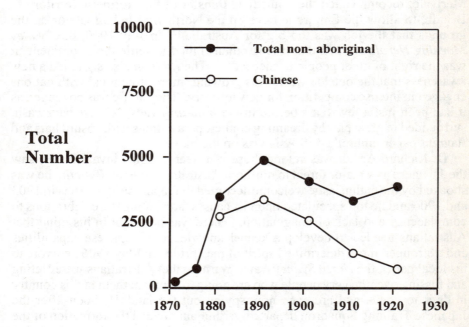

Figure 9.1: Change in the total population and in the Chinese population of the Northern Territory 1871-1920 according to figures in the South Australian Census 1871-1901, and the Commonwealth Census 1911-1920.

A report tabled in the South Australian Parliament in 1901 by J Langdon Parsons, a former Government Resident in the Territory agreed with Sowden's assessment that non-white settlers were essential to northern development. He dismissed as unscientific the idea that 'white Australia' principles could be applied, pointing out that the Northern Territory was a tropical country 'in the same latitude as Mozambique, Samoa, Abysinnia and Senegambia' and could only be developed by 'tropical races'.[11] Parsons agreed with his fellow South Australian parliamentarian, Thomas Playford, that Indian labour was perhaps best suited to Territorian development. That was not to say that the Territory did not have marvellous potential. Parsons was in no doubt that its proximity to 'South Asia and the Netherlands-India Archipelago' guaranteed a great commercial future, particularly if it could develop profitable trade links with nearby Singapore.

In 1907 the President of the Sydney Chamber of Commerce, George Merivale, recommended the immediate transfer of the Northern Territory to Britain, to allow the Empire to develop the North with Indian labour on the grounds that the job was too big for Australia.[12] In July 1910, the *Sydney Morning Herald* warned that if Australians failed to settle their continent 'it was the right of other people to succeed'.[13] The *Bulletin* also signalled a new awareness that the outside world was growing 'more strenuous' with nations engaged in intense competition for new territory. The Pacific was no longer, as it had been just a few years before in the *Bulletin's* view, 'a mere backwash, surrounded in great part by dreaming comic-opera nations with absurd hats and flagrant paper umbrellas'.[14] Asia was on the move.

Dr Richard Arthur was among those who feared Asian invasion. He saw the Japanese as a major threat to northern Australia. Like the *Bulletin*, he was shocked by the enthusiastic welcome accorded the Japanese squadrons in 1903 and 1906 and he too speculated upon its causes, attributing the celebrations to complacency and lack of imagination. There was no doubt in his mind that Australians needed to develop a keener knowledge of Japanese capabilities and a stronger, more determined spirit of race pride. In May 1906 he wrote to his local paper, the *North Sydney News*, warning that Australians were 'feting and fussing over the very people who are going to supplant them in this country in days to come, and are even now spying out the land'.[15] Soon after the Japanese Training Squadron departed, Arthur announced the formation of the Immigration League, created to aid the immigration of white people into Australia. Arthur saw this as a matter of dire urgency: 'The question of questions in Australia to-day' is how best 'we may fill up this empty continent, before it is too late, with people of our own choosing'.[16] Arthur believed that the formidable Japanese 'with their patriotism, their efficiency, and their powers of organisation', could soon be 'undisputed masters of the Northern Pacific'. While there was time, Arthur wanted to see a Northern Australia Commission scour the 'white world' for suitable settlers. Otherwise, Arthur warned of 'a fate more hideous than any that has ever before befallen a white race'.[17]

Arthur's first preference for his millions of white immigrants was for British settlers. But he doubted that there were sufficient to meet Australia's needs and he also took thought of the consequences of Britain losing too many of her people. If pure Anglo-Saxons were unavailable, then perhaps Jewish or Southern European immigrants could be encouraged to settle in northern Australia?[18] Such a prospect alarmed many members of the Immigration League, who defected to form a breakaway group, the British Immigration League.

In 1909, Herbert Easton, Honorary Secretary of this new group, assured the editor of the *British Australasian*: 'our policy is Anglo-Saxon first'. His British Immigration League was quite opposed to the creation of non-English speaking migrant communities. Easton argued:

> our breed will not be improved by being crossed with those of Spain, Italy, Greece, Southern Russia and Roumania [*sic*]; and common sense tells us that these men cannot be relied upon to fight for Australia in case of invasion, the danger of which is our principal raison d'etre.[19]

The British Immigration League believed Australia's only hope lay in developing a cohesive Anglo-Saxon population, a stout community of yeoman farmers. The crucial task of improving the breed was always seen as a rural not an urban endeavour.

Meanwhile Arthur was sharply criticised by the British Immigration League for denigrating Australia at home, while celebrating its boundless possibilities abroad. One could understand his problem. He wanted to attract masses of immigrants to a country that he also believed might be invaded within ten to fifteen years. This was not a strong selling point. Arthur tried to keep the nightmare prospects of invasion for domestic consumption only. Tales of impending invasion might smarten up the locals, getting them to think about more than Victor Trumper's glorious cover drives and graceful leg glances. Describing Australia abroad, Arthur adopted very different tactics. In 1907 he asked the League's London Secretary to ensure that promotional material contained nothing 'to the detriment of Australia'.[20] At the same time he urged the London editor of *Australian World* to 'Let Australia be "God's own Country"', and the 'climate and the people and the politicians perfection'. This was rather a whopper from a fellow who routinely criticised Australia's climate, people and politicians. He added: 'never a word about the Yellow Peril, or Socialism or Strikes. And print everything you can lay your hands on to the detriment of Canada'.[21]

Soon after Federation, South Australians had began to tire of the seemingly insurmountable problem of the Northern Territory and began moves to make the Territory a Commonwealth responsibility, an action Parsons had recommended in his report of 1901. But how was such a massive transaction to be valued? Was South Australia merely divesting itself of a white elephant or would the Commonwealth acquire an asset of considerable significance to the new nation? Was the Territory an inhospitable wilderness or was this a rich prize urgently coveted by more enterprising and perhaps more deserving nations? The idea that the Northern Territory was keenly sought after by the populous nations to Australia's north encouraged the view that the Territory was a valuable acquisition, with the capacity to carry a population numbered in millions. Yet the resources of the Territory were very poorly understood, leaving commentators free to imagine any kind of development that suited their interests. High hopes and even higher population figures were the order of the day, particularly as there was a growing imperative to quickly fill one of the world's empty spaces.

Many of the themes explored in public debates about the future of the Northern Territory were also developed in fiction. Take Frances Hopkins' *Reaping the Whirlwind: An Australian Patriotic Drama for Australian People*, published in 1909.[22] The play opens in the office of a high ranking Japanese official, Baron Kokura. The Baron often looks admiringly at his map of 'Austral Asia', a land of magnificent distances and incalculable wealth. He is particularly fond of its Northern Territory which he imagines will readily support 500 million people. His intense love for this country is indicative of the imagined natural affinity of Asian peoples for northern Australia. Given half a chance, they will turn the region into a miracle of productivity and a passionately defended homeland.

Ambrose Pratt, *Age* journalist and popular novelist, developed his thoughts on northern development and the Asian menace in *The Big Five*, a novel discussed further in Chapter 10. *The Big Five* was first serialised in the strenuously pro-development *Lone Hand*.[23] It tells the story of a scientific expedition into the Northern Territory, conducted for Sir Phillip Trevor, a British capitalist who has purchased a huge slab of Arnhem Land. The expedition is made up of Sir Phillip and his wife, the young, wilful and wonderfully statuesque Lady Trevor, five robust adventurers, and several scientists. The five adventurers, the 'Big Five' of the title, all have the adventuring spirit thought to characterise 'Aryan' manhood at its most muscular. The very first page presents the reader with their precise height and their impressive chest measurements. Their cranial capacity is omitted but undoubtedly they measure up in this respect as well. They are the embodiment of racial fitness, living proof that Australian conditions do not cause the withering away of Anglo-Saxon racial attributes. These were the big men Australia would need in its battle with Asia. The novel's themes are plotted against the background of exotic Arnhem Land, replete with crocodiles, wild buffalo, 'hostile blacks', ominous diseases and suffocating heat. The final test is capture and imprisonment at the hands of a dangerous band of Asian settlers.

When the expedition reaches Palmerston (not renamed as Darwin until March 1911) McLean, the reflective leader of the party, is appalled by the way the Territory has been neglected. The harbour is virtually empty:

> its tremendous potentialities ignored, its inexhaustible resources undeveloped — yet calling, calling, calling — a curse upon such infamous inertia and ineptitude at the instance of the Asiatic hordes so perilously near.[24]

Again, there is a disturbing contrast between the relentless energies of the awakening East and the indolence and foolhardiness of the Australians.

McLean finds that Palmerston is becoming an 'Asiatic settlement'. It is full of Chinese and Japanese acting as if they owned the country. Although the few whites look out of place, McLean admires them 'gamely striving to do Australia's duty for her, to hold this lonely outpost for the apathetic thankless nation'. Asia ('five days steam away') is certainly ready 'to take this land so shamefully neglected by the whites, and hold it and develop it'.[25] Big Jim McLean is certain there is no richer country on the face of the globe nor one more worth fighting for.[26] A decade later, George Morrison, in Australia on a short visit, was to make a very similar speech at Melbourne's Wesley Church.[27] McLean's views were part of the common language of the day.

As Pratt's expedition slowly journeys into Arnhem Land they encounter a group of warlike Aborigines. Although McLean kills three, he does not blame them for their aggression, admitting that they 'were only defending their country, and ethically were right in attacking us'.[28] Many more ethically-correct Aborigines will die as the expedition proceeds. Examining the country around them, the scientists report that Sir Phillip owns 'a region capable of supporting as dense an agricultural population as the Yang-tse-Kiang valley'. In addition, there are great forests comparable 'to the richest jungle lands of Ceylon or Hindostan'.[29] The Northern Territory is revealing itself as China one moment, India and Ceylon the next. The apparent reluctance of white Australians to settle in such abundant territory seemed as baffling as it was morally inexcusable. Yet it was ominous that northern Australia was so reminiscent of Asian regions. The exploratory party has already had the experience of being in an Asian setting in Palmerston and they had not liked what they had seen.

Their apprehensions are soon realised as they burst upon a substantial, permanent Asian settlement with gardens under intensive cultivation and native boats or praus lining the river. McLean suggests they should quietly withdraw, advising Commonwealth authorities that 'while the Australian nation had been sleepily considering the advisability of peopling and developing the Northern Territory with whites, the Chinese had quietly and stealthily stepped in and actually founded a thriving little colony'.[30]

But the party are quickly discovered and attacked. Sir Phillip and most of the others are killed, but Molly Trevor and Jim McLean survive, taken into captivity by a Malay prince. McLean admits the prince has some dignity, but he also notices that he wears the shrivelled and mummified hand of an infant as a magic charm. McLean finds such gross superstition 'lowering' in a man of such noble blood and assumes it reveals the Prince's 'savage' makeup.[31] Later, McLean has an opportunity to observe the degenerate society of the new settlements. He is made to observe the slow drowning of a coolie thief by a Chinese torturer. A 'blood mist' swims before McLean's eyes at the thought of northern Australia peopled by such a race.

McLean is disorientated to be within his own country, yet to see such evidence of other cultures and other races. The Northern Territory clearly is only nominally a white possession. The Aborigines are its true owners, certainly until such time as the whites chose to develop the country. Yet if development is taken as the criterion of ownership, will the Asian nations have a stronger claim than the somnolent whites to a territory with which they have so many affinities?

At the end of the novel, Molly Trevor and the vast territories Sir Phillip had owned pass to the eugenically superior McLean; an affirmation of strenuous manhood and its race-building mission. *The Big Five* emphasises that the truest patriots are those prepared to forsake city life to settle in the liminal north. Its message is that the major reason for northern emptiness is a failure of the colonising spirit. The Australian people are not living up to their racial mission and their failure to do so might jeopardise their survival.

Conducted along these lines, the 'Empty North' debate invited reproach and recrimination, just as it fostered invidious contrasts between 'energetic' Asia and 'complacent' Australia. This Asia was invoked as a reminder that the wider world was unlikely to view Australians as the youthful and enterprising people they often considered themselves to be. Australians were unmasked by the Asian comparison. They stood revealed as a complacent, self-satisfied and comfortable people, peculiarly immune to warnings about the Asian cloud looming on their horizon. The *Sydney Morning Herald* wondered, portentously, whether Australia's 'sunshine prosperity' had given its people 'rose-coloured mediums of perception which have no power to focus cloud'.[32]

Many of the key pre-occupations of 'Empty North' propagandists were repeated in one of the best known of the Japanese invasion stories, *The Commonwealth Crisis*, first serialised in the *Lone Hand* in 1908.[33] Kirmess was determined to reveal the dangers of skilful Japanese diplomacy which he perceived as more of a danger than Japan's large population. Clever Japan might gain control over the Territory by persuading the world that it could convert those empty spaces into a region of astonishing productivity, thereby emphasising the point that the defence of Australia was increasingly an intellectual task. Kirmess's story, *The Commonwealth Crisis*, begins at a time in the future when the Japanese have already established a foothold in the north. The task of removing them falls to the 'White Guard', a band of race patriots, forced from official indifference to their cause, to act in isolation. Their ranks are recruited almost exclusively from the rural population of Queensland. City men are of little use; they display 'all the symptoms of indolent culture, love of play, indulgence in luxuries'. Here, once again, was the characteristic disapproval of commerce and consumption, the product of a feminised, decadent city culture. As for the White Guard:

> A finer body of men never took the field to do battle for Aryan ideals. It was composed of the sturdy sons of the Australian bush, set off by just a dash of a cosmopolitan element.[34]

In *The Commonwealth Crisis*, the race-conscious Americans came to the aid of endangered white Australia, just as they did in Lane's 'White or Yellow?' Kirmess believed that the Americans were more aware than the British that Australia was a rich prize in need of protection. American expression of this sentiment was particularly strong in 1908, the year of the visit of the 'Great White Fleet'. Winning American approval is a vital element in the White Guard's international strategy.

Hopkins, Pratt and Kirmess were all convinced that the Japanese were determined to colonise the Northern Territory. They may not have known that the Japanese had once been invited to help colonise the 'Empty North' and had firmly refused that offer. Wilton Hack, missionary and theosophist, had presented an ambitious colonising plan to the Japanese Government in the late 1870s. Hack, impressed by the industry and frugality of the Japanese, believed that a community of up to 400 Japanese farmers, miners and skilled craftsmen might well form the basis for a number of prosperous settlements in the Northern Territory. The South Australian government had given Hack modest financial backing and had supported his representations to the Japanese. The Japanese Government, however, distracted by clan rivalries and political instability, feared any exodus of skilled workers. In 1877, they officially rejected Hack's proposal.[35] For those wanting to use the Japanese threat as one of the grounds for the transfer of the Northern Territory to the Commonwealth, it was hardly helpful to be reminded that the Japanese once were indifferent to its charms.

The Northern Territory Acceptance Bill was passed in December 1910. By the time Federal parliamentarians came to debate the Bill, the 'Empty North' had attracted an avalanche of comment both at home and abroad. Australia was famous for being empty. The incoming Labor Prime Minister, Andrew Fisher, believed that the transfer of the Northern Territory to the Commonwealth would serve as a decisive defeat for those who still held out for the use of coloured labour in northern Australia. This act signalled to the world that Australia was determined to develop the entire continent along racially exclusive lines. This would complete white Australia. Those supporting the transfer, including

Alfred Deakin, who played a prominent role throughout the debate, insisted that while the Northern Territory remained empty and undefended it posed a clear threat to the integrity of the rest of Australia. The *Sydney Morning Herald* summed up some of the dangers in terms reminiscent of the plots of the *The Big Five* and *The Commonwealth Crisis*: 'It is undeniable that an enemy could establish himself anywhere along our northern seaboard, and be in possession for weeks before we had heard of him'.[36]

The Northern Territory Acceptance Bill was represented as a critical development in the creation of a 'national' approach to defence. Deakin, supporting the second reading of the Bill, maintained that 'the question has been, not so much commercial as national, first, second, third, and last. Either we must accomplish the peopling of the Northern Territory or submit to its transfer to some other nation'.[37] Loss of the Northern Territory might mean loss of Australia itself in circumstances that would prove grossly humiliating to national pride. All commercial considerations including the vexatious question of compensation, were trivial when measured against the twin threats that an empty north was thought to pose to security and to Australia's international reputation. These were the big issues. Supporters of the Bill took care that they should remain central.

One of the attractions in evoking the Asian threat was that it needed little detailed argument to support it. Deakin's reference to transferring the Territory to 'some other nation' was characteristically vague. He appeared to feel no obligation to specify how such a transfer might be accomplished. His supporters were frequently just as vague. Lieutenant-Colonel Sir Albert Gould, a Free Trade advocate from New South Wales, President of the Senate and a long-standing member of the West Maitland Volunteers referred sweepingly to the fine rivers on the northern coast allowing any 'foreign Power to obtain ingress and secure a foothold'.[38] Similarly, Edward Findley, a Labor Senator from Victoria, when using Theodore Roosevelt's warning that 'an unmanned country invites disaster' again chose not to specify exactly how the disaster might unfold.[39] An interjection from Labor Senator Edward Needham, John Curtin's brother-in-law from Western Australia, provided something more concrete: 'The cable news of the annexation of Korea by Japan appearing this morning should hasten the passage of this Bill'.[40] If Korea could be annexed, why not the Northern Territory?

The debate on the Northern Territory Bill continually brought up the vexed question of European entitlement to the Australian continent. Acceptance of the challenge of northern settlement was seen as an essential step in the ongoing attempt to consolidate and justify white possession. Egerton Batchelor, a Labor parliamentarian from South Australia claimed that 'the only genuine right to a country is that which effective occupation, and settlement give'.[41] At the back of these claims was the nagging suspicion that the Northern Territory, in Labor

Senator Patrick Lynch's words, 'presents physical features and climatic conditions which are specially attractive to the Oriental races'.[42] But this again raised the old moral dilemma: how could a people unsuited to tropical settlement continue to justify the exclusion of industrious peoples who were acknowledged to be better adapted to northern Australia's climatic conditions? Senator De Largie, Labor, Western Australia believed:

> The more we apply ourselves to developing [the Northern Territory] ... the greater will be the credit to the white race in Australia, who will thereby establish a better claim to hold this great island continent than had the black race whom we have superseded.[43]

This was one of the very few references to Aboriginal Australia through the long course of the debate, despite the fact that the Aboriginal population of the Northern Territory at that time was estimated at close to 20,000 people.[44] Yet it is notable that De Largie did not assert that European claims to Australia were beyond refutation. His comments left open the possibility that Australians might not be able to establish a claim appreciably stronger than that of the people they had dispossesed. It was evident that in 1910 an unchallengeable case for sole 'white' possession of the continent remained to be made.

Changes then occurring in Asia were regularly mentioned during these debates. A number of parliamentarians took the view that the threatening rise of Asia was largely the fault of the West. Mr Patrick Glynn, barrister and Free Trade representative from South Australia, warned: 'Hong Kong is nearer to Port Darwin than is Adelaide or Sydney, and the East is awakening to military activity'. He reminded Parliament how the nations of Western Europe had civilized Asia into 'moral restlessness and military activity' leaving Australia alone to face an unprecedented circumstance.[45] Alfred Ozanne, Labor, Victoria, also described an awakening East casting 'a hungry eye' on the Territory which 'offers so much attraction to them by reason of its climatic conditions'. He was backed in these opinions by his Victorian Labor colleague, James Mathews.[46] Meanwhile, veteran New South Wales Free Trader, Sir Joseph Cook, cautioned that the 'Asiatic shadow is becoming bigger every day'.[47] Clearly a new and pressing entity ('Asia' or 'the East' or 'the coloured nations to our north') was making its presence felt in national deliberations. Australians were now confronted by a new geo-political reality. Henceforth it would be impossible to ignore the presence of Asian nations in their region. More to the point, it appeared that Australia's colonising performance was being monitored and evaluated as never before.

While the proponents of the threat from the north dealt with vague, but frightening images of invasion, transfer and dispossession, opponents of the Bill had to be more specific. Their task was to demonstrate that the threat from the north was wildly exaggerated. They also maintained that the construction of a transcontinental railway line, sought by South Australia in recompense for loss of the Territory, would prove to be extremely expensive and of little economic worth.   Debating the Bill in the House of Representatives, Mr William McWilliams, a Free Trade member for Franklin, Tasmania, who later became the first leader of the Country Party, was scandalised by the 'bald and vague' statements used by supporters of the Bill.   'There would be no chance of this Bill passing', he insisted, 'if it were not for the bogy of invasion' (Plate 16).[48]

McWilliams pointed out Malay fishermen had visited the coast of northern Australia for centuries, yet had never settled. There was no evidence that they were inevitably drawn to tropical Australia as if it were their natural habitat. McWilliams was just as sceptical of the alleged Japanese and Chinese interest in the Northern Territory. Why would any invader concentrate his attack upon Port Darwin, when there were so many other options available? Senator Sayers had previously made a similar point: 'Only a fool would think of landing an army at Port Darwin and marching it across the desert'.[49]

Another sceptic was the Labor Representative for Capricornia, Queensland, William Higgs. Higgs argued that the completion of the proposed railway through the Northern Territory would increase Australia's vulnerability rather than diminish it.[50] This was a much discussed issue. What was to prevent the enemy from using the rail link to travel to larger centres of population? The railway might only encourage invaders. William Findlayson, a Labor colleague from Queensland, endorsed this view. He could 'conceive no more satisfactory arrangement for an invader than for us to provide him with a railway line through the centre of the continent'.[51] Mr Palmer, a Victorian Liberal-Nationalist agreed, citing the use the Japanese had made of Russia's Trans-Siberian railway. Palmer explained that while Port Arthur had been in Russian hands this railway was a considerable asset, but when the Port fell to the Japanese, it accelerated the transportation of Japanese troops and hastened Russia's defeat.

It is apparent from the debate over the future of the Northern Territory that Australia was now thought to be a watched continent. Federal parliamentarians suspected that Australian actions were likely to be met by perhaps unwelcome Asian reactions.   Nevertheless, there remained profound disagreement and some well-informed scepticism about the likelihood of Asian invasion. What the debate did register was a persistent unease that the Australian colonising performance might be judged poor enough to warrant the 'transfer', to use Deakin's term, of the Northern Territory to another, more deserving nation. Invasion was certainly the more terrifying prospect, but dispossession on the grounds of moral negligence and incompetence could hardly be thought of as a much better outcome. The idea that the Northern Territory might be transferred to a more deserving nation persisted well into the 1930s.

Following the formation of the League of Nations there was growing speculation that territorial disputes and grievances would be settled by international arbitration. The 1920 Medical Congress Report on tropical settlement, discussed more fully in Chapter 11, recommended a negotiated agreement with Asian neighbours over the settlement of the tropical north by Europeans. Australia's failure to achieve the population expected was commonly cited as a potential source of world conflict which others might step in to resolve if Australians proved incapable of doing so. A steady stream of visitors and publicists told Australians that their selfish refusal to recognise the legitimate territorial aspirations of other countries in the region was dangerously provocative. On his world tour of 1921, Lord Northcliffe scolded Australians for ignoring population pressures in Asia, maintaining 'you go about your work and play as if the lust for territory had not all down the centuries been a cause of war ... the story of the overthrow of the weak by the strong'.[52] The *Montreal Star* responded to Lord Northcliffe's remarks by emphasising that Canadians should be as concerned as Australians at the 'highly explosive question' of northern settlement. It saw Australia as 'an outpost of the white race', an inevitable focus of attack in a fight Western nations could not afford to lose. The paper maintained: 'The Australians must fill Australia with the sort of people they want for neighbours; or the overspill of Asia will fill it for them whether they like it or not'.[53] Similarly, in 1925, the distinguished author Sir Leo Chiozza Money identified Australia, with its handful of large cities and its empty interior, as a grave peril to world peace.[54]

In 1926, Edwin Lewin, writing for the *Atlantic Monthly*, endeavored to show that despite its apparent geographical obscurity, the Northern Territory was 'in reality a world problem of the first importance'. He attributed the failure of white colonisation to the political and economic policies of the Commonwealth Government. Its White Australia policy ensured that tropical industries would fail to develop on an economic basis. The situation then raised the moral question of how long 'the white races are entitled to hold vast tracts of country which they are unable to utilize or develop ... when nearby are millions of fellow creatures who are clamoring for land and the "right to live"'.[55] In the same year, the British author, Fleetwood Chidell, announced that under Japanese supervision, northern Australia would support two hundred million people. He unveiled a new scheme for Japanese settlement, predicting that if Asian nations were denied access to Australia's north, 'a great world struggle will break out in the Pacific'.[56] The American author, Warren S Thompson, developed similar themes in *Danger Spots in World Population*, where he predicted that a 'low-pressure' country like Australia 'is certain to prove attractive to peoples in high-pressure areas'.[57] Their claims for fair access to the world's resources would be hard to resist. In all of these commentaries there was a view that Australians had forfeited the world's sympathy by merely playing at the stern game of settlement.

In July 1933, Australian newspapers carried reports of a speech made in England by the Dean of Canterbury, the Rev Hewlett Johnson on the management of the Northern Territory. The Dean had argued that in order to reduce international tension, nations should take a 'statesmanlike' approach to help ease Japan's population pressures and give part of the Northern Territory to Japan. His remarks had received generous and enthusiastic applause from his English audience.[58] A H Charteris, Professor of International Law at Sydney University, dismissed the Dean's comments as insubstantial, but was disturbed by the applause they had received. It confirmed a suspicion he had held for a long time that the White Australia Policy and management of the Northern Territory were interpreted in England as evidence of national selfishness. Australians were thought of as a people incapable of acting in a statesmanlike way on the international stage, requiring others to act internationally on their behalf.[59]

The *Sydney Morning Herald* reported a 'storm of indignation' following the Dean's comments and carried a range of hostile responses from leading public figures, including Prime Minister Joseph Lyons. The *Daily Telegraph* was equally scathing.[60] The Australian High Commissioner in London, former Prime Minister, Stanley Melbourne Bruce, noted that the Dean's comments were totally opposed to Australian policy and that 'Australia was perfectly capable of colonising the whole continent'.[61] The episode was yet another reminder that highly placed critics of the 'Empty North' might contemplate its transfer to more deserving nations. In the process, the Northern Territory was marked by patriotic Australians as an unambiguously and distinctively Australian region. To give it away as the Dean of Canterbury proposed was tantamount to giving away Australia itself.

Chapter Ten

Lilies and Dragons

In December 1900, the *Town and Country Journal* ran a fascinating article on 'The Contempt of Asiatics for Europeans' in which gendered meanings of the East-West encounter were primary considerations. The writer confidently assumed that while there were obvious differences between Asian societies, there was nevertheless an 'Asiatic' mind. The 'Asiatic' was presented as a person of bright intelligence who was quick-witted, inventive, adept at 'abstract reasoning' and in anticipating the thoughts of those he dealt with. The meeting between the 'Asiatic' and the European was seen as an encounter similar to that between a 'clever woman' and an 'average and slightly stupid man'.[1] It was inferred that the clever woman would inevitably outwit and dominate the man. Was the Western male, the former lord and master, threatened by an increasingly claustrophobic future in which 'Asian' and female 'otherness' formed a collusive partnership?

Before considering the threat, we might first consider some ideals of femininity entrenched in Western culture. In the late nineteenth and early twentieth century, it was commonly thought that a properly brought-up young woman was a 'creature whose only reason for being resided in her beauty and her reproductive function'.[2] The ideal, represented by George du Maurier's Trilby or Tennyson's 'The Lady of Shallot', was a passive woman, self-sacrificing and submissive to the higher authority of the male. Her proper place was the 'private sphere'; only the male could inhabit the public realm.[3] William Acton, a leading British physician, maintained that the modest woman 'seldom desires any sexual gratification'. Although she might dutifully submit to her husband's embraces, were it not for the 'desire for maternity' she would far rather forego his attentions.[4]

The double standard of Victorian morality was soon contested by pioneers in the new science of sexology, including Havelock Ellis in Britain, Iwan Bloch in Germany and August Forel in France. These men believed that sex was a natural function. They promoted the ideal of a companionate marriage, where heterosexual couples found mutual sexual satisfaction within a monogamous relationship. Their views rapidly gained in popularity during the early decades of the twentieth century.[5] Marie Stopes' sex manual, *Married Love*, became a best seller in Britain while Margaret Sanger and Mary Ware Dennett expounded similar themes in the United States.[6] In Australia, the 'new sexology' was promoted by the mother-daughter team of Agnes and Rosamond Bentham from South Australia, by Lillie Goodisson, founder of the Racial Hygiene Association of New South Wales and by Marion Piddington, author of *Tell Them! or, The Second Stage of Mothercraft*.[7]

The 'new sexology' had its determined opponents. Throughout the English-speaking world, the influential Social Purity Movement, often with feminist support, resisted moves for sexual reform, fearing that the introduction of birth control would only lead to the sexual exploitation of women.[8] The Social Purity Movement called for a society free from 'vice'. Puritanical in outlook, these reformers condemned the evils of prostitution, pornography, venereal diseases, alcoholism and crime and argued that men must adopt the strict moral codes by which women had to live. Sex, they maintained, was for procreation.[9] In *Bulletin* circles, their views attracted much anxious mockery from those fearing red-blooded Australian manhood was about to be tamed and feminised. But the *Bulletin* was also no happier with the 'new woman' emerging after the easing of social and political restraints on women and the opening up of employment opportunities outside the home. In her varied manifestations as bachelor girl, career girl or flapper with her 'red lips, nails and hair', she seemed a threat to young manhood.[10] The prospect of this 'pleasure-seeker' becoming a good wife and mother seemed remote. Even August Forel, an exponent of the 'new sexology' thought things could go too far. In 1906 he warned that dislike of maternity was a social evil which rapidly diminished the 'power of expansion of a race'. If unchecked, the consequences were dire; the affected race would be 'supplanted'.[11]

In this era of rapid social change, it seemed to men that women were capable of any perversity and might even be attracted to Asian men. In 1895, W T Stead claimed that 'for reasons chiefly physical', some white women preferred Chinese men. He believed this was encouraged by the Chinese, who had 'no scruples' about mixed marriages.[12] A deeper fear was that Asian men might use their relations with white women to retaliate against past humiliations and abuses of white imperial power. As European dominance of the East began to wane, guilt and fear of retribution appeared to rise. Speaking in London before the first world war, George Morrison reminded his audience that the distinguished British diplomat, Sir Robert Hart, had prophesied that 'the day would come when the Chinese would repay with interest all the injuries and insults which they suffered at the hands of European Powers'. Kipling made the same point to Australian reporters on his visit in 1891.[13] There were fears that perhaps that day was drawing closer.

Fear of racial betrayal by frivolous white women is a prominent theme in *The Coloured Conquest*, by T R Roydhouse, published in 1903.[14] At the start of this novel, the world looks very rosy. The narrator, Frank Danton, a fine Australian, is newly engaged to Mabel Graham. They make a splendid couple; handsome, healthy, optimistic about their future. It is no coincidence that we first meet them as they visit the Japanese Training Squadron docked in Sydney harbour. Danton is alarmed by the effusive welcome given the Japanese as 'the youth and beauty' of Sydney flock to see the warships. He is particularly troubled by the 'attentions of foolish girls' whose admiration for the Asian visitors is, he feels, quite unbecoming. Mabel is no better than the rest. She too admires the handsome bearing and fine uniforms of the Japanese naval officers.

At one of Sydney's best suburban addresses, Danton meets the Japanese officer, Taksuma Moto, who speaks quite unguardedly about Japanese plans to conquer the white races. His complacent North Shore audience laughs in a good-humoured way at such boastful talk, unable to see the danger lying ahead. The fashionable society of urbanised Australia is pictured as a corrupt world of excess which has lost control of the lives of the rising generation of young women. In her flirtatious dealings with the Japanese, Mabel and the other 'foolish girls' are being permitted to enter the dangerous territory of inter-racial sexuality risking, Roydhouse warns, the dangers of violation and enslavement.

How close to reality was the mood of fraternity when the training squadrons dropped anchor? It is difficult now to interpret the sexual dynamics in meetings between young Australian women and Japanese officers, but it certainly struck the writer of the 'Women's Page' in the *Sydney Morning Herald* that the behaviour of the girls was uninhibited. 'Australian girls', she wrote, 'show a want of reserve with the Japanese that they would never dream of exhibiting with English-speaking officers'.[15] For their part, she felt that a number of the Japanese exhibited more of an eye for female beauty than she had expected to find at such gatherings. There was something intoxicating in the mix of the accomplished, magnificently uniformed Japanese and the exuberant young women of the sunny south (Plate 17).

The theme of inter-racial sex recurs throughout *The Coloured Conquest*. Few whites realise the potent threat until a civic reception is held for the Japanese in the polished surroundings of Sydney's Australia Hotel. Sydney's best people attend. There is pleasant chatter, with expensive drinks and much good humour. Then a Japanese naval officer presents Mabel Graham with a red rose. Guests pause. In a scene so tense that several Australian men allow their cigars to go out, the officer predicts that she will soon be his. This is not a marriage proposal. Danton knocks the foul rogue to the floor. He swears he will shoot Mabel rather than allow a Japanese to lay a finger upon her. Roydhouse implies that a Japanese conquest will lead directly to the violation of white women. Yet in characterising Mabel Graham he also suggests there may be some Australian women who would prefer Japanese men. Could there be a fifth column of Madame Izàns?

In Roydhouse's novel, the clever Japanese outwit their opponents, dispose of the British Fleet and invade Sydney. They now want fifty million settlers to occupy Australia and New Zealand within fifty years. They set to work immediately on a population program. 'Fair Lily Colonies' are established where the loveliest women are forced to breed with the most handsome men. The children of these unions are moved to the state crêche, the boys will work on farms and the best-looking girls will be assigned to serve Japanese men. Only Danton remains free, literally 'the last of a dishonoured race'. By this outcome, Roydhouse emphasised that the fate of the weak white population after a Japanese invasion would parallel the fate of Australian Aborigines at the hands of the British. By their weakness white Australians had forfeited their right to hold the continent.

The misogynist idea that women would readily betray the Australian national interest informed the *Bulletin*'s attempt to explain the reception accorded to the Japanese Training Squadron in 1906. When the *Bulletin* eventually acknowledged this welcome, it was forced to concede that it was both enthusiastic and sustained.[16] Disliking this evidence of approval, the *Bulletin* drew upon mass psychology for an explanation. Crowd behaviour had attracted a good deal of attention in the late nineteenth century, notably from the novelist Emile Zola and the sociologist Gustave Le Bon. Le Bon in *The Crowd*, drew direct parallels between the behaviour of the modern urban crowd and the behaviour of women. Both went to 'extremes'.[17] Another contemporary theorist insisted that 'the crowd is woman, even when it is composed, as almost always happens, of masculine elements'. The American, Homer Lea, author of *The Valor of Ignorance* and *The Day of the Saxon*, expounded similar views, describing the national 'mob-mind' as 'feminine, hence without reason'.[18] On similar grounds, the *Bulletin* had no difficulty in characterising the crowds welcoming the Japanese as both urban and essentially feminine in nature.

For the *Bulletin*, the conduct of the urban crowd triggered deeply held fears. The journal identified a condition it called 'love of freakishness' which it knew to be 'a trait of city character'. What might appear to be affection and genuine interest in the Japanese was nothing of the kind; it was a manifestation of a perverted city taste for the freakish and the abnormal. These were a people seeking the kinds of distraction provided by the circus. Their impulses were intensified by what the *Bulletin* called 'feminine gush'. The *Bulletin* maintained that city character was primarily a female phenomenon. As it explained to its readers: 'woman, in the mass, is still very little guided by reason, and prone to pursue what is new'.[19] What was 'new' was dubious and certainly included the West's love affair with enchanting Japan. The fascination with Japan which had been so prominent in Anglo-Australian circles by the 1890s, was now diagnosed by the *Bulletin* to be both feminine and feminising. The *Bulletin* felt that the welcome accorded to the Japanese squadrons was as unguarded as it was unthinking. It was another worrying sign of how decadent urban Australia had become (Plate 18).

In the face of this 'feminine and semi-feminine fuss over Japanese visitors', the *Bulletin* saw it as a clear male prerogative to resist the Japanese and oppose the forces of mass psychology, firmly identified with women and the city. It believed that manly resistance, at once taciturn and undemonstrative, was a prerequisite for the survival of a white Australia. In the race conflict the *Bulletin* believed was sure to come, women would recognise that silent white men with backbone would be their saviours and masters. In these characterisations, rural manhood had firmly drawn attributes and fixed boundaries, whereas the 'feminine' was mixed, formless and unstable and certainly not to be relied upon in the crucial business of separating Australia from Asia.

As Juliet Peers has noted, the *Bulletin* was intellectually up to date with late nineteenth century forms of misogyny.[20] Many of its ideas on the differences between men and women are also found in the writings of European theorists on sex and race at that time such as Otto Weininger, Viennese author of the influential, *Sex and Character*. In *Sex and Character*, Weininger argued that man was evolving from an early brutish, bisexual state to a higher plane. At this more evolved level there was a sharp dichotomy between the 'truly male' man who was both highly intelligent and deeply spiritual and the 'completely feminine' woman who was very beautiful but 'materialistic and brainless'.[21] Any assertiveness from the 'new woman' and the emerging feminist movement was taken as a sign of evolutionary reversion; these were masculinised women 'sinking back to the hermaphroditism' of the 'indeterminate primal state'.[22] Similar reversion and degeneracy occurred when a man began 'to show himself effeminate'.[23] These ideas became profoundly entangled with racial identities since Weininger further insisted that 'Jews, blacks and orientals had, through inbreeding or the inability to respond to evolutionary impulses, become effeminate and consequently degenerated'.[24] Such degenerationist theories were widely disseminated. Homer Lea warned that Western lifestyles had produced a 'national effeminacy' bringing with it 'tribes of theorists' and 'feminists' and all the 'necrophagon of opulent decadence'.[25] Feminism was read as a sure sign of a culture so decadent and commercial that it almost invited a cleansing invasion.

To the proponents of these degenerationist ideas, it seemed apparent that the more Australia allowed itself to become urbanised and feminised, the more vulnerable it would become to processes of merging, blending and mixing, to asianisation. Women, were viewed with great suspicion. They were given many of the elusive properties of water. They were gushing, tidal, uncontrolled, all-engulfing. They were reputed to be prey to moral instability and at the mercy of powerful and dangerous biological drives. They bled. They were painted in attitudes of lassitude, floating through the air, collapsing 'hopelessly ecstatic' in the waves or among the leaves of the forest floor.[26] Sydney Long, in 'Spirit of the Plains' painted in 1897, presented them as 'bush spirits', emanating from the uncivilized world.[27]

Accounts of the awakening East drew heavily on similar metaphors of fluidity and tidal change. Asia was also seen as both oceanic and threatening. Flowing crowds swirled out of its cities and poured over the countryside. Waves of sibilant whisperings sped through its bazaars. The noisy, abundant market-places of Asia were overflowing with uncontrolled humanity. The tide was on the turn, the East was finding its voice. This voice moreover, was suave, clever and articulate, drawing on rich intellectual traditions. It was quite at home in the sinuous turns and back alleys of complex eastern philosophies. In this subtle, infinitely flexible and feminised world, a white man might easily become bewildered. The gathering forces of Asia represented the ultimate crowd, the greatest engulfing deluge to threaten the West. When West engaged East in the context of the invasion novels, this meeting often had attributes of a male-female encounter. For decades the manly West was seen as more than a match for the feminised, corrupt and ineffectual East. But as imperial powers declined and women at home became more assertive, something more began to emerge. There was a sense that the old order was changing and that roles could change between men and women and between the white and the coloured world. As calls for a more 'manly' nationalism to counteract these trends grew stronger, there was also a growing fascination with earlier times, when men were very clearly men and 'women were property'.[28] Women had to be kept within boundaries.

The newly emerged feminist movement claimed that there was much that needed to be done in Australia to improve the status of women. The *Bulletin* writer A G Hales, however, believed that the West was already dangerously progressive in its attitudes. He felt that to go further down that path ran the distinct risk of creating a community so sensitised to women's interests that it might ripen into full decadence.[29] Hales, a prolific and popular author, was described by Randolph Bedford as one of the 'big men' of the Australian outback, 'a picturesque figure and good Australian'.[30] He was a vociferous protectionist who had supported the Labor platform in the 1890s and early 1900s and was heavily involved in the development of the mining industry as investor and journalist. Hales was a man's man who was not alone in his beliefs about women. Many men at the time believed that in the West, women were already sufficiently revered. Madison Grant, Chairman of the New York Zoological Society, Councillor of the American Geographical Society and author of *The Passing of the Great Race or The Racial Basis of European History*, published in 1916, thought that one of the distinguishing features of European civilization was chivalry towards women. He found the lofty codes of knighthood 'peculiarly Nordic'. Moreover, he believed that chivalry was unknown outside Europe and would never develop there. Nordic decline, he argued, would drastically weaken chivalry, leaving white women vulnerable to the 'lower' races.[31] E L Piesse made similar comments in an article on 'White Australia' published in 1921. He maintained that 'practically alone the Aryan races give the woman the right to determine her existence in her own way'. Piesse believed that whereas women were the 'flowers of Aryan culture', the 'savage races' treated women as mere 'instruments of men's pleasure' and would sometimes kill their female children. He was convinced that the treatment of women was one of the 'distinctive marks of a civilised race'.[32]

Hales's views on the privileged position of European women are evident in his invasion novel, *The Little Blue Pigeon*, published in 1904. This story warned of a powerful coalition of Asian interests, centred on Japan and China, and known as 'The Yellow Bond'. Japan, it was suggested, would achieve world domination by defeating Russia, establishing naval dominance in the Pacific and forcing Australia to open its doors to a tidal flow of Asian immigration. As a war correspondent, Hales had supported the Russians during the Russo-Japanese war, in part because he believed that the Russians might help check Japanese territorial ambitions. The 'Little Blue Pigeon' of the book's title was a tiny, doll-like figure, born into a samurai family. The spirit of martial honour, so dear to Western renditions of samurai traditions, coursed through her veins. Yet the novel also insisted upon the subjection of women as one of the unalterable traditions of the East:

> Womanhood in the land of the chrysanthemum does not rank on a level with the womanhood of European lands. Woman is still a chattel and a thing of small account ... and will remain so until the yellow blood has ceased to run.[33]

When the 'Little Blue Pigeon' enters the service of her Oriental lord and master, she prostrates herself before him, 'as the women do in the East'.[34] To underscore these points, Hales has his 'Pigeon' fall in love with a fine Englishman. She then learns for the first time that she is more than a mere piece of 'household furniture'. This novel experience was quickly generalised to all Western males, for whom a woman was 'something higher and nobler' than she was for males in the East.[35] Hales suggests that Australian women had better appreciate their men, for if Japan invaded Australia, the degradation of Australian women would surely follow. At this time, common representations of Eastern women as 'chattels' were regularly reinforced by commentaries reminding readers of Eastern practices like suttee and foot binding.[36]

Mrs Rosa Campbell Praed, in *Madame Izàn*, had suggested that Japanese men were capable of the highest expression of chivalry.[37] The Australian journalist, Helen Jerome, chose to differ. The status of women in Japan was her central concern in *Japan of To-day*, published by the New South Wales Bookstall Company in 1904. Jerome thought Japan had been presented to the Western world in remarkably idealised terms. She had criticised Australian enthusiasm for the Japanese during the Training Squadron visit of 1903.[38] On her visit to Japan, Jerome had found Japanese men extremely rude, without 'the remotest conception of the treatment due to a woman'. She argued that the Japanese man had 'much to learn before he can with safety clasp hands with his Western brother'.[39] Jerome had observed women in Japan treated with 'huge contempt'.[40] Since she believed the emancipation of women was a crucial measure of civilisation, Jerome judged Japan not to be a civilised society.

The treatment of women by Asians reappears as a theme in Ambrose Pratt's *The Big Five*, a novel of Asian invasion set in the 'Empty North'.[41] When the remnants of an exploratory party are captured by the leaders of an Asian settlement in northern Australia, the treatment of Lady Trevor, the only woman in the team, becomes an important issue. The party's leader, Jim McLean, is made aware of 'Eastern' attitudes in a discussion with his captor, a Malay prince. The Prince, demanding absolute silence from women, had removed the tongues from all his female servants. McLean's 'civilised susceptibilities' are badly shocked. In their captors' presence Molly Trevor and McLean 'orientalise' their relationship to attract less attention and to avoid damaging McLean's prestige. Molly Trevor stands before her captors 'pale, but still' and bows 'submissively'. She refers to McLean as 'my Lord Prince' and 'Highness'.[42] Impressed by her docile manner, Prince Kassim invites her to join his harem. Ever the philosopher, he advises McLean that regular beatings make women wise. The English, he thinks, are foolish for not beating their wives. Allusions to harems, ritual beating and female mutilation reinforced Orientalist accounts of the degraded condition of Eastern women. Such set pieces emphasised the submissiveness the East demanded from its women and the uncompromising codes that would be enforced in Australia if 'Asian' gender relations were allowed to become the norm. Such scenes also encouraged masculine fantasies of submissive, silently obedient females.

The threatened enslavement of the Molly Trevors, Cissie Saxbys and Mabel Grahams of the invasion novels drew upon a tradition of nineteenth century art and literature of 'eroticised female carnage'.[43] Esteemed academicians created mighty canvasses depicting rape and pillage in which helpless women, generally naked and often bound, found themselves at the mercy of heftily primitive men, rudely claiming what was theirs by right of conquest. In a related genre, the harem and the slave market provided endless opportunities to depict female enslavement as the mark of the East. One compelling example is Edwin Long's 'The Babylonian Marriage Market', completed in 1882 and when sold, the most expensive work of art in nineteenth century London.[44] The Trustees of the Art Gallery of New South Wales were keenly disappointed when they failed to obtain this treasure for their collection.[45] Paintings which depicted the way the Orient regarded women permitted disapproval of the cruelty of the East, while encouraging the male gaze to travel appraisingly over the naked bodies of women about to be sold into slavery. For the Western male, one of the clearest examples of maintaining boundaries around womanhood was the harem.[46]

In Pratt's *The Big Five*, Molly Trevor was given a choice between a life of beating and enforced silence in the harem, or of marriage and maternity in progressive Australia. Ambrose Pratt's attempts to interpret the 'mind' of the East were taken one step further when he adopted the persona of Chinese student and traveller, K'ung Yuan Ku'suh, purported author of *The Judgement of the Orient*, an account of the first world war written from a 'Chinese' perspective.[47] Pratt attributes K'ung with some very definite views about men and women. K'ung judges a nation's honesty according to whether its conduct is honorably male or manipulatively female. According to K'ung, where the female principal is dominant, dishonesty, envy and a 'grasping spirit' shaped national policy. A female nation was invariably unscrupulous: 'It will get always that which it wants if it can, and by any means it can'.[48] K'ung interprets the Great War as a battle between 'female' Germany dominated by envy and greed and 'masculine' England, a nation still governed by a sense of justice. The Great War is analogous to the unceasing, age-old 'war between the sexes'. In this war, Nature ensures that women are enslaved by their procreative imperatives. By answering her biological drives, Woman becomes ruthless and pitiless. She becomes crafty, manipulative and untiring. Woman is the crueler sex.

These ideas, presented by Pratt as the wisdom of the Orient, acquire an intriguing status. Pratt's Chinese persona permits him to articulate and connive at views on women which he first attributes to the East and then reclaims as ancient wisdom. The orientalised Pratt, garbed no doubt in the flowing robes of a wispily bearded Chinese sage, was permitted a greater freedom to develop a hostile critique of the role and influence of women than was the case for hum-drum Ambrose Pratt, Australian novelist. In adopting his Chinese persona, we can assume that Pratt appreciated philosopher K'ung's greater freedom both to treat women (and to discourse upon their place in the great scheme of things) in an 'Eastern' manner. Randolph Bedford found similar value in this approach. In a short story published in 1923 he allows his character, the Chinese sage Quong Sue Duk, to express a few truths about women who were 'creatures moulded out of faults'. They may bring life, but 'they bring death also'.[49]

By the end of the nineteenth century, women were beginning to resist their marginalisation in European society. Dijkstra has argued that as men perceived the disparity between their sexless feminine ideal and the corporeal reality of women now beginning to assert a 'sexual presence', they were overcome by a misogynist horror. This could transmute an assertive woman into an 'embodiment of evil'. Dijkstra has also pointed out the link between late nineteenth century '*erotic* fantasies about the deadly nature of female sexuality' and the development and dissemination of racist thinking.[50] The disdain, distrust and horror men could feel for women seems to have been greatly compounded if the woman was Asian.

One enormously popular writer who perpetuated many of the ideas common about Asian women at this time was 'Pierre Loti', pseudonym of Louis Marie Julien Viaud, the French sailor, adventurer, and member of the *Academie Francaise*. Loti's stories tended to follow a set formula where a handsome sailor travels to a distant land and becomes enthralled by an Oriental woman. The woman is invariably portrayed as a mere object for male 'delectation', existing only to please the men she attracts. Her image is usually one of 'indolence, sexual expertise and voluptuous degradation'.[51] While he pictured Japan as 'a fairy-like and enchanted country', Loti was particularly disparaging about Japanese women. In *Madame Chrysanthème*, Loti's narrator briefly marries little Chrysanthème, a young girl whom he has chosen as a 'plaything to laugh at'. Asleep, he finds her 'extremely decorative', but awake, her face is 'quite ugly'.[52] But Loti dismissed even the most noble Japanese women he met as 'great rare insects', claiming that without their elegant robes and sashes, a Japanese woman was nothing but 'a diminutive yellow being, with crooked legs and flat, unshapely bust'.[53] Irene Szyliowicz contends that Loti debased Asian women in this way to 'enhance a weak sense of male identity'. In Japan, he played the superior white male.[54]

Later, in the popular literature and art of the early twentieth century, the Asian woman becomes not merely indolent, available and voluptuous as in Loti's novels, but a more sinister figure, a 'woman of death' who can tempt and 'stifle' a white male until he dies of her love.[55] In *Tales of Chinatown*, published in 1916, Sax Rohmer created Lalá Huang, a dark and arresting woman with mixed European, Chinese and Kanaka blood. With her lustrous dark eyes and inviting smile, she is a vampire who lures men to strange deaths.[56] In *The Yellow Claw* Rohmer created 'The Lady of the Poppies', a 'demoniacal' Eurasian beauty with the 'grace of a gazelle', the 'witch-eyes' of a sorceress and a soul 'old in strange sins'. She was an 'exquisite, fragrantly youthful casket of ancient, unnameable evils' who lured men to an opium-induced stupor. An even better known version of this type was Fah Lo Suee, daughter of another Rohmer character, the dreaded Fu Manchu. Fah Lo Suee combines three essential traits: 'exotic sensuality, sexual availability to the white man, and a treacherous nature'.[57] She reappeared in American pulp fiction as Sanguh Liang-ghu, assistant to the Master of the New York Underworld and as the Dragon Lady in Milton Caniff's adventure comic strip, *Terry and the Pirates*.[58] In film, she was the vampire Sally Lung, the half Chinese, half French temptress in Cecil B De Mille's *The Ten Commandments*.[59] In opera, she was Princess Turandot whose pastime was the decapitation of male suitors.[60] Aubrey Beardsley created Japanese-influenced illustrations for Oscar Wilde's play, showing Salome as a similar, essentially evil *femme-fatale*. Rupert Bunny, the Australian artist, also portrayed an eastern Salome in 1919 while sinister women of varied Oriental or Asian aspect make appearances in the illustrations for children's literature of this period, including works by Edmund Duclac, Arthur Rackham and Heath Robinson.[61]

One of the period's most enduring and culturally powerful images of female evil, however, was that of the Chinese Empress Dowager, Tzu Hsi. She was the most demonic figure of them all. As cruelty incarnate, she fitted Ambrose Pratt's reading of woman's capabilities to perfection. A monstrous figure, her terrible excesses, cruelties and gross appetites affirmed what men suspected 'Woman' might become if granted the unrestrained exercise of power. In *Dragon Lady: The Life and Legend of the Last Empress of China*, the historian, Sterling Seagrave, has uncovered much of the reality behind this potent myth.[62]

Seagrave outlines what little is known of the historical Tzu Hsi. She was a nonentity until, as an imperial concubine, she bore the Emperor, Hsien Feng, a son, Tung Chih. Minutes before his untimely death, Hsien Feng, indicated that succession to the throne should pass to Tung Chih. In addition, he ordered that his wife Tzu An would rule jointly with Tzu Hsi as Dowager Empresses during his son's minority. The two women, however, were figureheads; power continued to reside with their Manchu advisors. When Empress Tzu An died in 1881, Tzu Hsi remained as titular head of state until March 1898 when she retired to make way for a new young Emperor. Then she was quickly restored as Regent after the ill-fated Hundred Days Reform Movement. Her regency encountered further troubles with the rise of the Boxers and the siege of the Legations in Peking. After the siege was lifted, the Empress Dowager fled Peking, but she returned after the signing of the Peace agreement, to live quietly in the Forbidden City until her death in November 1908.

Little is known about her real nature. For most of her life she appears to have been a 'dutiful widow' who would have been 'executed in a flash if she had been promiscuous'.[63] The evidence suggests that this woman was never a reptilian, sexually insatiable schemer who had poisoned her way to a position of absolute power in the Forbidden City. Yet she was portrayed overwhelmingly in these terms. The impression of Tzu Hsi given in the Western press of the time, in travelogues, diplomatic reports and in fictional accounts of the Manchu court was invariably menacing. Seagrave has shown how, in the terror following the Reform Crisis, anti-Manchu Chinese reformers, seeking someone to blame, focused 'an extraordinary outpouring of slander' on the Empress Dowager.[64]

Most Westerners in China at that time knew relatively little about the inner workings of the Manchu court, but were quick to circulate on allegations of Manchu depravity and decadence. Seagrave has traced an elaborate relay of reports, originating among anti-Manchu forces, from whence they travelled to the *Times* in London and the *New York Times*. From these distinguished newspapers, tales of the 'Dragon Lady' and her evil ways spread quickly throughout the English-speaking world (Plate 19).[65] No rumour of atrocity was too bizarre or outlandish to gain credence. Letters from Europeans living in China related even more wickedness:

> I suppose you have heard of the kidnapping scare ... Five thousand boys and five thousand girls are needed for immolation of the new railway! ... The Empress Dowager has given her assent ... The Chinese believe that no great work can be successfully executed without a human sacrifice in some form.[66]

In Singapore, the slanders about Tzu Hsi were repackaged for a British audience by the Chinese propagandist, Lim Boon-Keng, author of *The Chinese Crisis from Within*, published in 1901.[67] He considered the Empress Dowager responsible for all of China's ills. As Lim Boon-Keng had attended medical school in Edinburgh with George Morrison, the *Times* correspondent in Peking, Lim was able to use this association to pass on his 'dowager abuse'.[68] Morrison also heard numerous tales of Manchu decadence from his 'unofficial editor and advisor' Edmund Backhouse, a gifted linguist who saw in the Empress Dowager an opportunity to weave labyrinthine tales of intrigue and sexual licence. With Backhouse's help, Morrison, himself a considerable gossip with a substantial appetite for tales of sexual excess, developed his own portrait of Tzu Hsi as a wicked Manchu ruler. He blamed her for all the events of the Boxer Rebellion and the siege at Peking, reporting in the *Times* in 1900: 'One of the sages of China foretold that "China will be destroyed by a woman"'.[69]

Later, Backhouse, with the aid of John Ottway Percy Bland, Shanghai correspondent for the *Times*, wrote a highly influential biography of Tzu Hsi, *China under the Empress Dowager*, published in 1910.[70] The book proved 'a great success' as it seemed to provide 'the first documented and readable public account' of Tzu Hsi's reign.[71] Tales of the decadent Manchu Court 'appealed naturally to the intellectual decadence of the European *fin de siécle*'.[72] In *China under the Empress Dowager*, close descriptions of Tzu Hsi's character came from the diary of the court official Ching-Shan 'who had continual opportunities for studying her a close quarters'.[73] In a good mood he had found her 'the most amiable and tractable of women' but when angry her rage was 'awful to witness'. He warns foreigners that one word from Tzu Hsi could destroy them so completely that 'neither dog nor fowl be left alive, and no trace be left of their foreign buildings'.[74] Bland and Backhouse similarly described her 'vindictive ferocity' claiming she never learnt to control her terrible moods and passions or to forego the 'hideous barbarities' of the Forbidden City. She was said to be 'extremely superstitious', to be 'addicted to pleasure' and it was even charged that she had borne a son by a 'eunuch'. Nevertheless, they maintained she had courage, shrewdness and a 'certain simplicity and directness' of manner. The success of her career was attributed to her possession of 'that mysterious and indefinable quality which is called charm'.[75] Further tales of the

Empress Dowager and her wickedness appeared when *Annals and Memoirs of the Court at Peking*, also by Backhouse and Bland, appeared in 1914. Again it portrayed Tzu Hsi as an iron-willed tyrant whose crimes included 'the whole range of nymphomania, debauchery and homicide'.[76]

For many years, *China under the Empress Dowager*, was 'regarded as a classic' and was regularly cited by Western writers.[77] But in 1976, the historian, Hugh Trevor-Roper, revealed both it and its sequel to be entirely fraudulent biographies. Backhouse had systematically created a vast body of forged documents designed for sale and to back up his lurid inventions. These clever fabrications deceived experts through their 'minute and scrupulous detail'.[78] Ching-shan's diary, a 'masterpiece of the forger's art' formed the centrepiece of one of the great hoaxes of the time.[79]

Given the powerful mix of myth and misrepresentation developing around the figure of the Empress Dowager, it was not surprising that fabulous accounts of Tzu Hsi appeared in the Australian press. In February 1900 the *Sydney Morning Herald* reported a Chinese *coup d'état* with wild rumours that the Emperor had died, or had been stabbed or bow-stringed or poisoned or perhaps had committed suicide.[80] A few weeks later the paper circulated a letter from Canton explaining how China had sunk into corruption, blaming this ruin on sinister powers exerted by 'the ignorant and arrogant Empress Dowager'.[81] In May it was reported that the Empress Dowager was seeking to destroy the Emperor's tutor and other reformers, while editorials claimed that she had ordered the 'extermination of all foreigners'.[82] The *Review of Reviews* presented an outline of 'The Chinese Tragedy' in July 1900. The Empress Dowager was described as 'the only man in China who is a woman'. She was the Chinese version of Catherine of Russia and exhibited 'all the vices of Messalina'. In a later issue, the journal presented a lurid account of her life story.[83]

The *Argus* talked to local Chinese and found that although branches of the Reform Party had spread to Melbourne, there was 'a great disinclination amongst leading Chinese residents ... to discuss the question'. But the 'reign of terror' of the Dowager Empress was hardly forgotten. Stories were told of 'Chinese reformers from San Francisco being beheaded upon return to China'.[84] A headline in July announced: 'The Emperor and Dowager: Reported to be Poisoned'. Two days later, their fate seemed clear: 'The Emperor died, and the Empress is reported to have become insane', but not long after the *Age* noted that the Dowager Empress, though allegedly insane and poisoned, had 'resumed the Imperial authority'.[85] Understandably, the *Argus* found the situation in Peking nothing but a 'dark enigma'. But whether the 'vixenish Dowager' was 'mad or sane, in captivity or upon the throne,' she remained an enemy beyond the pale. The paper cited a letter to the *Times* from Professor Robert K Douglas, a well-known scholar, who had advised the Foreign Powers to capture and imprison the Empress Dowager, 'the root of all evil' in China.[86]

Continued stories of the Empress Dowager's iniquities emerged in her obituaries. The *Sydney Morning Herald,* summarising her career, noted that when she became a concubine, she had used 'all the arts and artifices in which her sex in the East excels' to gain power and influence.[87] The *Daily Telegraph* described her as 'scheming and ambitious', reporting that since the Reform Crisis of 1898 she had held 'undisputed sway in China'. But it also noted the 'general and genuine sorrow expressed' in the Chinese community in Sydney after the news of her death. All Chinese shops were closed and their flags flew at half mast.[88]

The 'Dragon Lady' in Australia, as elsewhere in the Western world, became a figure in whom Western males could read some of their own darkest fears and fantasies about the 'mysterious' East and the nature of Woman. The Empress, so elaborately forged and fabricated by the West, inhabited a world unrestrained by any known moral code. A China capable of creating a woman so evil was also a civilisation that would stop at nothing to achieve its ends. The Empress was an all-powerful figure whose domination of China could be seen as a step in the larger plan of world domination. That she was also, as in the title of one more fictitious account of her life, *The Woman Who Commanded 500,000,000 Men,* played upon male castration fears of all-consuming women.[89] Male power was of no account in the face of the despotic Empress, a warning of the terrible havoc that women created when the evil powers that resided in them were given free rein.

Chapter Eleven

Taking the Heat

In 1939 the American Geographical Society published a comprehensive review of the literature on European settlement in the tropics by the Australian geographer, A Grenfell Price.[1] Grenfell Price outlined some key questions which lay people had recently asked scientists: 'Why in general have the whites failed? Are they beginning to make progress? Can they hope for ultimate success?' Price could discover no agreement among scientists on these questions. Instead he uncovered a persistent unease about whether there was any future for permanent white settlement in tropical zones.

A recurrent idea evident in commentaries on tropicality from the 1890s was that white Australians, particularly white women, might fall prey to degeneration, nervous instability and intellectual decay if they attempted to settle in the more tropical parts of the continent. As 'high' civilizations were then thought to flourish only in hospitable temperate zones, it seemed logical that European civilisation could not hope to reach its highest possibilities in hot Australia. A withered, exhausted version of European civilisation might struggle into existence, sharpened here and there by infusions of fresh blood from the old country or braced into higher standards by the chillier winters of Tasmania but, longer term, the outlook appeared discouraging. White Australia seemed a problematic experiment.

Much of the anxiety about the degenerative effects of heat had developed from the British experience in India. B J Moore-Gilbert has noted how India soon came to be 'regarded as the "white man's grave"'. The Calcutta-born British novelist, Thackeray, had seven uncles and aunts who died young in India; little wonder that he was sent back to England at the age of six. At that time cholera and typhoid were dread diseases which took a high toll.[2] In an age before Pasteur, when the source of these deadly diseases remained unknown, contagion was often thought to arise directly from the heat itself.

James Johnson expressed this view in *The Influence of Tropical Climates on European Constitutions*, published in 1836. He noted how Europeans in India readily fell victims to the climate and urged such precautionary measures as the wearing of turbans to protect against 'solar heat', the re-wearing of carefully dried but unwashed linen to moderate the flow of 'cuticular discharge' and the avoidance of mangoes, cold fluids, alcohol and exercise.[3] Johnson warned that if a European was fortunate enough to survive his early years in India, his 'successors would *gradually degenerate*'.[4] Sir Ranald Martin, perhaps the leading mid-nineteenth century authority on tropical medicine, was also convinced of the dangers of heat. In the *Influence of Tropical Climates in Producing the Acute Endemic Diseases of Europeans*, published in 1861, he revealed that heat 'was the great moving power of all other subordinate sources of disease'.[5]

Many at this time believed in a 'racial environmentalism' which suggested that each race, being the accumulated, historically-formed expression of a distinctive set of energies and capacities, functioned best within its own climatic zone and would degenerate outside this region.[6] In the 1890s, Charles H Pearson lent support to degenerationist fears in *National Life and Character: A Forecast*. Pearson speculated that even the extermination of whole populations of native peoples in India would not ensure the success of European settlement because 'the climate would be fatal in a generation'. This discussion gave rise to Pearson's astonishing index entry: 'India, its people too numerous to be exterminated'.[7] In Australia, where many tropical areas awaited settlement, ways were sought to escape the predicted decline of the white race in the tropics. Some thought Australians could learn to adapt to their tropical climate. Others maintained that Australia's north was a healthy place, quite unlike the deadly tropical regions of Asia and Africa. Others again, Pearson among them, believed that it was too early to determine the future of northern Australia.

Walter Coote, author of *Wanderings South and East*, published in 1882, believed that Australia's climate was very healthy. He was particularly impressed by Toowoomba in Queensland. The heat could be intense, but this was not at all injurious since the air was 'fine and bracing'. Altogether he found Toowoomba, 'as healthful and even invigorating as that of any place in the world'.[8] Similarly Miss Shaw, writing in the 1890s for the London *Times*, found that a temperature of 100°F had a very different meaning in Australia than in England. In Australia she felt 'permeated with sunshine' in a way that was 'supremely wholesome'.[9] In making these observations both authors were aware that vigour and wholesomeness were not conventionally associated with hot climates and that their favourable comments about the climate might well have been met with scepticism. Then again, travellers were very different from settlers.

Most experts on the relationship between climate, civilisation and the formation of character remained unconvinced that extreme heat could be beneficial over the longer term. Nineteenth century race theorists invariably drew sharp, unforgiving distinctions between races from cold as against tropical regions. They argued that in the tropics abundance discouraged effort. Where nature was so generous, the individual did not have to plan for the future. On these grounds, Sir Charles Dilke denounced the labour-saving banana as the 'curse of the tropics'.[10] Cold climates were said to hone and sharpen talents by creating conditions of privation that demanded planning for scarcity. In a Lamarkian extension of these ideas some theorists contended that the energies and abilities generated in cold climates became part of the racial inheritance. By contrast, 'tropical races' were thought to suffer from an ingrained languor and a child-like inability to plan for the future. They also might be given some delightful characteristics — cheerfulness, spontaneity, sociability — but they rarely received credit for intellect or energy, attributes routinely conferred upon Anglo-Saxons.

White settlement of Australia coincided almost exactly with the coinage of the term 'Caucasian' in 1795 by the German natural historian, J F Blumenbach. Blumenbach assigned a formative role to the Caucasus mountains, not only in shaping a set of supposedly distinctive Caucasian racial aptitudes, but also in minimising that awkward debt to Asian origins central to accounts of the Aryan race. The 'Caucasian' was presented as a distinctively European racial type, moulded, energised and hardened in mountainous terrain, purified by the cold and spiritually elevated by mountain vistas. Nearness to 'God above' and the blinding whiteness of snow was supposed to intensify the identification of this race with purity, strength and nobility of purpose.[11] To the Romantics, the favoured settings for the flowering of Caucasian energies were 'small, virtuous and "pure" communities in remote and cold places: Switzerland, North Germany and Scotland'.[12] Australia could claim remoteness, but its climate, geography and convict origins seemed quite inimical to the perpetuation of Caucasian energies and virtues. In 1899, the Rev R Wardell warned that sunny Australia would produce only 'voluptuous and pleasure loving and easy-going' characters. He thought a better case could be made for New Zealand.[13]

Writing on *The Control of the Tropics* in 1898, the celebrated social scientist, Benjamin Kidd, reiterated the view, then common in European intellectual circles, that throughout history the 'development of the race has taken place outwards from the tropics'. He compared supposedly stagnant, morally undeveloped tropical races with dynamic European ones, thrusting their way northwards into ever more demanding climes. Kidd concluded it would be a real 'blunder' to settle whites in the tropics.[14] The arctic explorer and popular author, Vilhjalmur Stefansson, supported the idea that civilisation was travelling north. In *The Northward Course of Empire*, he published a map plotting 'the path of supremacy' taken by highly civilised societies as they moved from Upper Egypt in 3,000 BC to Paris and London in 1900 AD. The change in location equated to a decline in mean temperature from 25°C to 10°C. The *Sydney Morning Herald* was one of many papers which approved these views.[15] In similar vein, Madison Grant maintained that hard winters had helped the Nordic race eliminate its 'defectives' although overcast skies and long winters had also rendered 'the delicate nervous organization of the Nordics' sensitive to sunlight.[16]

When William Z Ripley surveyed the literature on tropical settlement in the late 1890s he found an 'almost universal opinion' that 'true colonization in the tropics by the white races is impossible'. Nevertheless, if whites had access to 'a permanent, servile, native population' some permanent forms of settlement might be achieved.[17] Almost thirty years later Ripley's views were still considered sufficiently authoritative for the Australian economist, G L Wood, to go the trouble of answering his objections to white settlement in the tropics point by point.[18] Suggestions of reliance upon 'servile natives' particularly affronted Australian democratic sensibilities, for wherever there was a servile native, there was also likely to be a despotic European, corrupted by excessive power and indolence. Alfred Deakin and Louis Esson were both shocked by the excesses of the British ruling class in India. Esson deplored the ultra-conservative Anglo-Indian who 'kicks his "bearer", pushes any natives he sees off the earth, and sows trouble with both hands'.[19] Randolph Bedford had been similarly shocked by the British imperial lifestyle in Ceylon and was wholly opposed to any attempt to settle the Australian tropics along similar lines. He was convinced that the Australian tropics must be developed by white labour even if the weight of expert opinion, as summarised by Ripley, was against this idea.[20]

Ripley had also supported the contention that tropical heat promoted undisciplined sexuality. He believed that 'surexcitation of the sexual organs' was an inevitable physiological by-product of life in a sultry climate.[21] This idea had a considerable history. In 1836, James Johnson had expressed concern at widespread belief that a tropical climate 'excites certain passions in a higher degree than in temperate regions', believing this a poor excuse for a relaxation of religious standards and moral disciplines. His major fear was that white men would engage in 'vicious and immoral connexions with native females' and that this in turn would lead to racial degeneration.[22] In common parlance, such men had gone 'troppo' or 'native' and were characteristically portrayed as unshaven wasters.

In tropical climates, women and children were thought to be at particular risk. The mortality rate among the children of soldiers in eastern India in the 1860s was estimated by Trevelyan to be as high as 88 per thousand per year.[23] It therefore became the standard practice among British settlers in India not to leave women and children to endure the fierce summer heat, but to send them 'home' (as with Thackeray and Kipling) or to the cooler climate of the Hill Stations.[24] *Health in India for British Women*, a popular medical text, warned that white children raised in India would show 'early signs of degeneration'.[25] Similarly, a Parliamentary Select Committee on Colonisation and Settlement in India was told by a respected medical witness in the late 1850s that British children reared in India's heat would be 'enfeebled' and would lose much of their 'Saxon energy'. As for their progeny they 'would be found deteriorated in all English or European attributes'.[26]

English children in India could not be expected to thrive. An Australian visitor, Sir James Penn Boucault, Judge and ex-premier, quickly became concerned by the English children he had seen in India. They were:

Plate 3: Front cover of the Melbourne edition of James Hingston, *The Australian Abroad on Branches From Main Routes Round the World*, 1885. Mitchell Library, State Library of New South Wales.

Plate 4: Kishengarh horsemen standing on their saddles to salute the Viceroy, Lord Curzon, at the Delhi Durbar in 1903. *Sydney Mail*, 13 December 1911. State Reference Library, State Library of New South Wales.

Plate 5: Ceremonial India made regular appearances in the Australian press. Here the King is replying to an address at Bombay. *Town and Country Journal*, 31 January 1912. State Reference Library, State Library of New South Wales.

Plate 6: Chinese landing at Cooktown, Queensland, in 1875. Mitchell Library, State Library of New South Wales.

Plate 7: Chinese gamblers playing at Fan-Tan. Gambling among the Chinese attracted considerable comment in the late nineteenth century press. *Town and Country Journal*, 30 April 1881. State Reference Library, State Library of New South Wales.

Plate 8: Thomas McIlwraith, Queensland politician, disporting himself with local women on his visit to Japan. The women, whose national characteristics are rather uncertainly established, are displaying the feminine wiles commonly attributed to the women of the 'Orient'. Cover, *Boomerang*, 29 December 1888. State Reference Library, State Library of New South Wales.

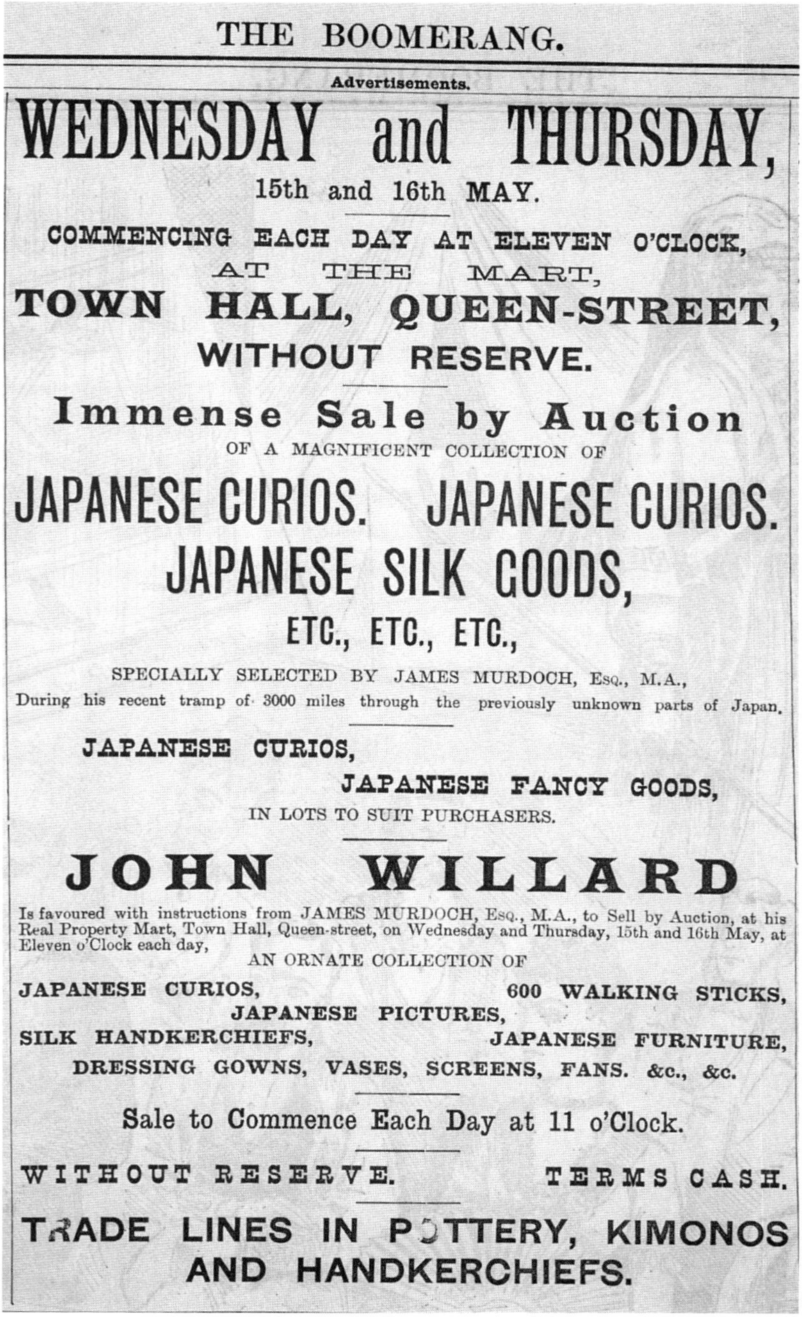

THE BOOMERANG.

Advertisements.

WEDNESDAY and THURSDAY,

15th and 16th MAY.

COMMENCING EACH DAY AT ELEVEN O'CLOCK,
AT THE MART,

TOWN HALL, QUEEN-STREET,

WITHOUT RESERVE.

Immense Sale by Auction

OF A MAGNIFICENT COLLECTION OF

JAPANESE CURIOS. JAPANESE CURIOS.

JAPANESE SILK GOODS,

ETC., ETC., ETC.,

SPECIALLY SELECTED BY JAMES MURDOCH, Esq., M.A.,
During his recent tramp of 3000 miles through the previously unknown parts of Japan.

JAPANESE CURIOS,
JAPANESE FANCY GOODS,
IN LOTS TO SUIT PURCHASERS.

JOHN WILLARD

Is favoured with instructions from JAMES MURDOCH, Esq., M.A., to Sell by Auction, at his Real Property Mart, Town Hall, Queen-street, on Wednesday and Thursday, 15th and 16th May, at Eleven o'Clock each day,

AN ORNATE COLLECTION OF

JAPANESE CURIOS, 600 WALKING STICKS,
JAPANESE PICTURES,
SILK HANDKERCHIEFS, JAPANESE FURNITURE,
DRESSING GOWNS, VASES, SCREENS, FANS. &c., &c.

Sale to Commence Each Day at 11 o'Clock.

WITHOUT RESERVE. TERMS CASH.

TRADE LINES IN POTTERY, KIMONOS AND HANDKERCHIEFS.

Plate 9: Advertisement for the Brisbane auction of James Murdoch's collection of Japanese curios. The auction suggests that there was a substantial demand for Japanese arts and crafts, although the 600 walking sticks must have gone a long way to satisfy the local market. *Boomerang*, 11 May 1889. State Reference Library, State Library of New South Wales.

Plate 10: Seventeen year old Sophie Blundell, daughter of Martin Petrie Blundell, Manager of the Bank of Australasia, dressed as a Japanese. The photograph was taken by an older sister of Sophie's in the family home, 'Chastleton', Chastleton Avenue, Toorak, Melbourne, in 1898. The Japanese screen and surrounding decor suggest the appeal of things Japanese among wealthy Anglo-Australian families of the 1890s. Photograph courtesy of Rodney Cummins.

Plate 11: Frederic Villiers, well-known British War Correspondent on his tour of the Australian colonies. Villiers later reported the Russo–Japanese war. *Sydney Mail*, 18 May 1895. State Reference Library, State Library of New South Wales.

Plate 12: His Excellency Admiral Shimamura, Commander of the Japanese Training Squadron, 1903. It is hard to reconcile the *Bulletin*'s dismissive comments about the Japanese with photographs of the Japanese officers published in the Australian press. It was for this reason, perhaps, that the *Bulletin* published no photographs of the Japanese during the Squadron visits of 1903 and 1906. *Australasian*, 19 May 1906. National Library of Australia.

Plate 13: American sailors from the Great White Fleet wrestling a bear for the camera, a rather more playful image than those generally shown of the Japanese. The poor bear died not long after in a shipboard accident. *Town and Country Journal*, 19 August 1908. State Reference Library, State Library of New South Wales.

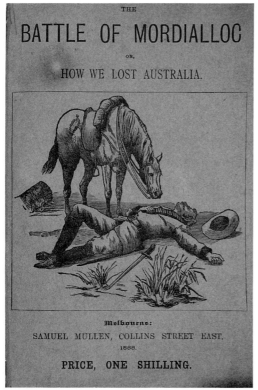

Plate 14: Front cover of *The Battle of Mordiallioc*, locating a story of Asian invasion in a stereotypically Australian setting. Mitchell Library, State Library of New South Wales.

THE

COLOURED CONQUEST

by

"RATA"

ONE SHILLING.

Plate 15: Front cover of *The Coloured Conquest*, by 'Rata' [T R Roydhouse], an invasion novel published by the New South Wales Bookstall Company. Roydhouse was editor of the *Sunday Times*, a Sydney paper, from 1893 to 1913 and was later Sydney correspondent for the Melbourne *Argus*. Mitchell Library, State Library of New South Wales.

Plate 16: Alf Vincent's ' "The Thin White Line" or our Northern Coast Defence' is a characteristic *Bulletin* comment on vulnerability and the proximity of Asia. *Bulletin*, 18 July 1907. National Library of Australia.

Plate 17: The artist Fred Leist's impression of a glittering Government House reception for the Japanese Training Squadron. *Sydney Mail*, 17 June 1903. National Library of Australia.

Plate 18: A photograph of Japanese officers with Sydney women during World War I, the kind of scene that generated inflamed comment in the *Bulletin* and *Truth*. Mitchell Library, State Library of New South Wales.

Plate 19: One of many drawings of a suitably sinister-looking Empress Dowager of China. *Review of Reviews*, 15 August 1900. Mitchell Library, State Library of New South Wales.

poor, persecuted, coloured humanity.

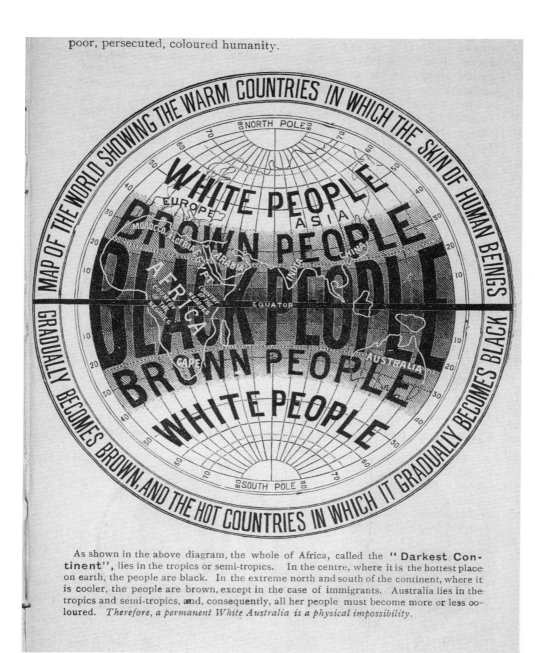

As shown in the above diagram, the whole of Africa, called the " Darkest Continent", lies in the tropics or semi-tropics. In the centre, where it is the hottest place on earth, the people are black. In the extreme north and south of the continent, where it is cooler, the people are brown, except in the case of immigrants. Australia lies in the tropics and semi-tropics, and, consequently, all her people must become more or less coloured. *Therefore, a permanent White Australia is a physical impossibility.*

Plate 20: E W Cole's map of the world showing his understanding of the relationship between skin colour and climate. E W Cole, *A White Australia Impossible*, 3rd edn, Melbourne, no date. Mitchell Library, State Library of New South Wales.

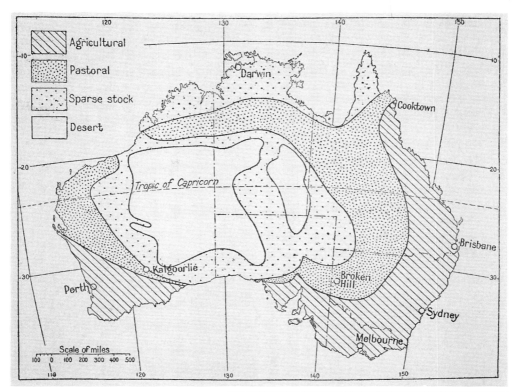

Plate 21: One of Griffith Taylor's many maps of Australia showing large areas of the continent as either arid or unsuitable for farming. Taylor's maps in major newspapers showing large expanses of 'arid' and 'useless' country generated sharp controversy in the 1920s. *Foreign Affairs*, July 1927. State Reference Library, State Library of New South Wales.

Plate 22: Map of Australia with European countries superimposed. This was a common motif in the early twentieth century and was used to emphasise Australia's emptiness and potential for settlement. Cover, *Millions Magazine*, 1 July 1921. Mitchell Library, State Library of New South Wales.

Plate 23: The English actor Bransby Williams impersonates Dr Fu Manchu at the Sydney Tivoli. The evil Chinese doctor would appear to have been sufficiently well-known to Australian audiences by the mid-1920s to be included in Williams' repertoire of stock characters. *Pacific*, 7 August 1924. Mitchell Library, State Library of New South Wales.

Plate 24: 'Will somebody tell him?', a cartoon satirising Professor Griffith Taylor's suggestion that Australians might benefit from inter-marriage with the Chinese. *Daily Telegraph*, 25 June 1923. State Reference Library, State Library of New South Wales.

Plate 25: Advertisement for Wombat Boot Polishes in the Netherlands East Indies. *Inter-Ocean*, January 1924. Mitchell Library, State Library of New South Wales.

Plate 26: Drawing of an impressive Chinese Department Store in Shanghai, suggesting the commercial potential of trade with China. *Millions Magazine*, 1 November 1919. Mitchell Library, State Library of New South Wales.

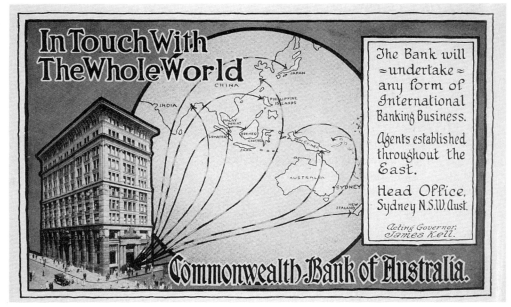

Plate 27: Advertisement for the Commonwealth Bank in Asia. *Inter-Ocean*, January 1924. Mitchell Library, State Library of New South Wales.

Plate 28: The growing number of publications on the Pacific in the inter-war years included some expensively produced journals. Cover, *Java Gazette*, July 1932. Mitchell Library, State Library of New South Wales.

thin pale and cadaverous, with the dull gleam of death in their suffering little eyes ... I wished, oh how I wished that I could take them to Mount Lofty [his home in South Australia].[27]

Frances Hodgson Burnett also pictured the unhealthy effects of India on a British child in her children's classic, *The Secret Garden*, first published in 1911. Mary Lenox was born and raised in India, where both parents die of cholera. With her 'little thin body' and 'yellow face', she is a rude and disagreeable girl. Several months exposure to England's climate and some energetic gardening at Misselthwaite Manor restore her health and manners. She has been saved from Indian heat.[28]

In India, Ceylon and Malaya, the Hill Station served as an important sanctuary and sanitarium, as well as a home-away-from home for British officials pining for thatched cottages and rose gardens. In Australia, Tasmania served as a similar summer retreat for wealthy Anglo-Australian families, a theme developed in Martin Boyd's novel, *Lucinda Brayford*.[29] One enduring argument in favour of such settings was the presumed benefits of a cooler climate. In 1863, a Parliamentary Commission was so persuaded of this fact that it recommended that one third of all British troops in India should have access to a Hill Station on a rotating basis.[30] The cooler climate of a Hill Station, while not actually curing disease, were seen to have restorative effects. Sufferers from debility, enervation and nervous disorders were considered particularly responsive. The Hill Station also allowed officials to maintain, in a colonial setting, the conspicuous displays of energy and command that accompanied belief in racial supremacy. It was the place for top dogs to maintain the vigour of their bark.

'Rajah' Inglis, tea-merchant, politician and colourful raconteur was among those who succumbed to India's terrible heat. He became an object-lesson on the perils facing the white man in the tropics. In 1875 Inglis was working in Oudh, in the far north of India, setting up indigo vats, clearing the land and behaving, in his own estimation, as a sturdy pioneer until he was struck down with recurrent fever, rheumatic pain and weakness. He took a course of salt-water baths without improvement. An elaborate regime of treatments ensued. 'Salicene, salycilic acid, hot baths, liniments, all kinds of medicaments were tried, but all were unavailing'.[31] Inglis, expecting an early death, left for Australia. Within months, sunny Australia's 'wonder-working air' had restored him. Inglis, convinced of the health benefits of this climate, then settled down in Sydney which, although often hot, avoided the extreme temperatures of the North-West Frontier.

In Australia the debate on climate was soon sharply divided between those who agreed that whites could never settle successfully in the tropics and those who argued that the Australian tropics would prove an exception to the rule. Dr Richard Arthur maintained that colonisation of the tropics by Caucasians was an impossibility.[32] He supported his case by reference to the medical writings of Major Charles E Woodruff, a surgeon in the United States Army. Woodruff, who had seen considerable army service in the Philippines, was the author of *The Effects of Tropical Light on White Men*, published in 1905.[33]

Woodruff contended that skin pigmentation was the key to long-term survival in the tropics. Unprotected white skin exposed to the 'actinic rays' of tropical light soon resulted in damaged nerve tissue and tropical neurasthenia leading to 'lost nerve stability'.[34] These arguments were freely linked to the influence of climate on the rise and fall of civilisations, a topic that invited — and in Woodruff's case received — some heroic generalisations. Woodruff held that 'climate kills off a race which has migrated too rapidly into a region too light for it'.[35] He saw the decline of the Australian birth-rate, the subject of a Royal Commission in New South Wales shortly before the publication of his book, as evidence that the white population was dying out. This was to be expected 'when white men are so far out of their zones'.[36] Under the influence of Woodruff's theories, Richard Arthur argued that suitably pigmented Southern Europeans, not Nordic or Caucasian types, should be encouraged to settle the Northern Territory.[37]

Jack London, for many years one of America's most popular novelists, was another convert to Woodruff's views, which suggests that they may well have reached a wide audience. When Jack London arrived in Australia in December 1908, he was by no means a robust exemplar of strenuous manhood. A sick man, he limped into Sydney after a period in the Pacific islands with skin peeling from his badly swollen hands. He was plagued by attacks of nervous apprehension and was quickly admitted to a hospital, coincidentally in Dr Richard Arthur's North Sydney electorate. London wanted to return to the 'nervous equilibrium' he enjoyed in California's climate, but he first sought to recover his vital energies in Tasmania.[38] After reading Woodruff, London became convinced that throughout his trip to the Pacific Islands he had been 'torn to pieces by ultra-violet rays'.[39] In *The Mutiny of the Elsinore*, published in 1913, London's narrator notes with approval Woodruff's contention that the 'blond races' would be supplanted in America by swarthier southern Europeans.[40] London may well have argued the same thing about northern Australia, where the heat was at least as severe.

Few white communities at the turn of the century remained immune to fears of decay, particularly since social darwinist explanations of fitness and survival had by that stage become pervasive. Against all the public talk of Australia's splendid future and the wonderful opportunities that awaited northern settlement, doubts about the climate persisted; this new community might yet suffer a decline of standards. Some expressed a concern that even if whites formed thriving communities in Australia's north, over time tropical conditions would turn these people black. This fear was expressed by Dr Nesbit, who argued that in the tropics a white man 'must become a blackfellow, or at least, a brunette'.[41]

E W Cole used similar logic to argue that a White Australia Policy could not be successful because white people in the tropics became 'coloured' (Plate 20).[42] No less worrying was the persistent concern that highly vulnerable white women would be unable to settle in the tropics. For, as Sir Herbert Gepp noted, 'no population can thrive unless the men have their women with them'.[43] Even Lord Lamington who had many positive things to say about Queensland's climate had to agree that in tropical settings white women could not have children without injuring their health.[44] Such a conclusion then brought the fear that if white settlement failed, other races, better equipped to handle tropical conditions might take over.

In 1911, the Ninth Australasian Medical Congress gathered in Sydney and authorised a full inquiry into the 'permanent settlement of a working white race in Tropical Australia'.[45] The war delayed completion of the Report until 1920.[46] By then the Congress was prepared to give a cautious endorsement of tropical settlement. The investigating Committee had been unable to find any 'insuperable obstacles' for such development and even noted that the 'absence of semi-civilised coloured peoples in Northern Australia' made the task of northern settlement more straightforward.[47] Otherwise the considerable Aboriginal presence in the Territory was ignored and no reference was made to Aboriginal health. Yet in response to the spirit of international arbitration surrounding the creation of the League of Nations, the report urged that efforts should be made to 'promote an understanding with neighbouring civilised races, other than white, whereby the mutual advantage of the avoidance of hybridism and the perpetuation of pure races be made the basis of international agreement and mutual co-operation'.[48]

Dr J H L Cumpston, Director of the Commonwealth Department of Health, commended the Report, affirming there was no evidence that residence in tropical Australia caused physiological harm. But he warned that maintenance of a white Australia required 'immaculate cleanliness' at both the personal and the communal level, another warning against 'hybridism' and the mixing of races, practices deemed 'unclean'. Higher standards of personal hygiene and public health should be bolstered by strict quarantine measures to control tropical diseases.[49] The message from the Congress was clear: tropical settlement by whites was quite possible but it was an experiment that would need to be very carefully monitored.

Despite these cautious scientific views, Dr Richard Arthur's articles to the press and his submission to the Congress revealed that degenerationist anxieties were still being widely circulated well into the 1920s. Such concerns were evident in the submission made by Dr Nisbet who addressed the Congress on behalf of his father, a medical practitioner with thirty years experience in the 'Tropical North'. Nisbet senior maintained that many of his patients, particularly women, complained of tiredness, irritability and an inability to concentrate upon intellectual tasks. Where men were engaged in healthy outdoor work, women were confined indoors in dreadfully hot conditions. Nisbet warned that when they dropped their standards, dressed in kimonos or neglected their hair, invariably horrific results would follow. Nisbet considered it imperative that women be allowed to recover their energies in the cooler south.[50] Otherwise, Australians might breed 'degenerate generations willing to live on rice and bananas', people no longer British 'but North Australians resembling the Levantine type'.[51] Levantines were then characterised as treacherous, volatile, politically unstable types, betraying marked Mediterranean and Asian influences.[52] They were certainly classified as an inferior, hybrid race. The evils of the banana have already been noted; the kimono, in this context, was yet another sign of the loose living that would follow asianisation. Here was the degenerationist fear in a nutshell. In the words of another contributor, a 'tragedy ... hangs over a woman's life in the tropics'.[53]

Yet by the 1920s, the degenerative effects of tropical heat were no longer acknowledged by the medical establishment. Bacteria and parasites were now known as the source of many greatly feared tropical diseases. Vectors like the mosquito rather than a sultry climate were emerging as the cause of concern. Medicine was also revealing that exposure to sunlight had definite benefits; sunlight killed anthrax and tubercular bacilli, and could be used to treat rickets and tuberculosis.[54] In 1922 Britain's Medical Research Council appointed a 'Committee on Sunlight' to report on these effects.[55] Doctors recommended treatments of 'helio-hygiene' for their tubercular patients and began exposing them to sunlight in the cool mountain air or at the beach.[56] They called for urgent action on the problem of 'urban light starvation' to abolish the 'diseases of darkness', particularly tuberculosis and rickets, in the polluted industrial cities of Europe.[57] As the benefits of sunlight became better known in Europe, warm climates could seem much healthier, not least to soldiers returning from the first world war with dreadful memories of the horrors of frostbite and frozen trenches.[58]

Changing attitudes to the benefits of sunlight had a particularly strong influence on women. In the late nineteenth century, when a cult of invalidism was prevalent, many middle-class women would not step outside for fear that sunlight might taint a pallid complexion.[59] But in the early twentieth century outdoor activities like bicycling and bathing became popular. By 1914 Coco Chanel, an arbiter of taste in the world of fashion, had devised bathing costumes for French society ladies wanting to bathe at Deauville. A decade later, British *Vogue* showed the first sunlamp and encouraged life on the beach. By the late 1920s the socialite Méraud Guiness was able to note, 'We practically live in bathing suits and coconut oil'. A vibrant tan had now became, not only a sign of health, but highly fashionable. These developments were not slow to take on in Australia, a continent of beautiful beaches. In Arthur Adams' novel, *The Australians*, published in 1920, Madge, a young Australian devotee of sunbathing and surf had a tan 'of the richest and clearest brown' whereas Edna, her English friend had 'livid' white skin. Edna's ghastly pallor made Madge think of 'those dead-white insects' found under stones.[60]

Through the 1920s, there was a growing expectation that the quality of Australian sunlight might change the Australian character. Nina Murdoch hoped for the day when the Australian sun thawed 'the ice of our Northern ancestry' and Australians became more 'Latin in appearance and temperament'. Murdoch hoped her countrymen would reject 'Anglo-Saxon self-consciousness and dread of emotion', which she clearly linked to the English climate, embracing instead 'colour and joy and graciousness'.[61] What were once vital Caucasian virtues were now seen as cultural limitations, signs of coldness, formality and a sickness of mind and body. Pallor became a sign of illness. A Mediterranean style was represented as altogether livelier, richer and more warmly human. Exposure to the sun conferred health, vitality and lust for life.

But there always remained some experts who cautioned against hot climates. In 1917, Dr William Nicoll announced that tropical Australia 'will never *under present circumstances* support a permanent population of *exclusively* European character'. For whites resident in the tropics he recommended 'a liberal vacation' to be taken 'at least every second year during the hot season'.[62] In the 1920s, Ellsworth Huntington, the Yale University geographer, also urged caution on the question of tropical settlement. He based his case on data ranking different climates against their potential to generate and maintain civilisation. Australia's tropical north faired poorly. It was too close to Java at the bottom of the scale. Even Tasmania, deemed the most favourable Australian climate for intellectual performance, fell well below the perfect score accorded to England. Huntington concluded the level of civilisation in Australia was higher than could be expected on the basis of climate. This result was not reassuring: Australian civilisation was largely maintained by the recent arrival of migrants from cold climates and degenerative effects were already insidiously at work.[63]

Where Ellsworth Huntington was urbane and conciliatory, Griffith Taylor, who was appointed to the Foundation Chair of Geography at Sydney University in 1920, confronted error wherever it was to be found. Taylor poured scorn on proponents of tropical settlement although he was routinely attacked in the press and occasionally in Parliament for his views.[64] Taylor argued that a tropical climate reduced the efficiency of white workers. This was one good reason for doubting the potential of tropical settlement. But another even more important barrier, Taylor maintained, was Australians' desire for comfort. He believed that it was very unlikely that white women, in particular, would want to move to the tropics while it remained possible to settle in more comfortable temperate regions of Australia.

Taylor backed these views with a theory of homoclimes, in which he compared regions of similar climate and rainfall throughout the world to assess potentialities for development. The unpopularity of Taylor's views may have owed something to the fact that his homoclimes emphasised Asian affinities in a society that liked to think of itself as British. Taylor likened Townsville to Calcutta, Brisbane to Fuchow [Fuzhou] or Hong Kong and Sydney to Shanghai. Somewhere between Sydney and Melbourne Australia underwent a transition from Asiatic to Mediterranean homoclimes since Melbourne was linked with Oporto in Portugal. Only Hobart had a climate that could be thought of as English.[65] Geographically considered, most of Taylor's Australia was Asian.

In the winter of 1924, Freda Sternberg joined Vilhjalmur Stefansson's expedition to Central Australia and the Northern Territory to see for herself whether white women 'can make homes and rear families' in the tropics. Her answer was emphatic. 'They can, and they have.' She was impressed by the 'healthy, contented appearance' of the women she met in stations along the way.[66] Another view to please supporters of tropical development could be found in Raphael Cilento's *The White Man in The Tropics*, published in 1925 when Cilento was Director of the Institute of Tropical Medicine in Townsville. Cilento argued that white settlement in the tropics was a matter of controlling disease rather than adapting to climate. Accordingly, he wanted Australians to dismiss the lurid associations which had gathered around the word 'tropical'. The word evoked too many images of sweltering mangrove flats, miasmic swamps, hostile 'savages' and regions too dangerous to inhabit. Cilento maintained that such reports were far removed from contemporary reality. He attempted to present the development of tropical Australia as a modern, twentieth century exercise in colonisation, in which the guiding hand of science would play a prominent role. Nonetheless, it was a momentous story. 'These settlers,' Cilento wrote, 'some of them the second and third generation, make up altogether the largest mass of a population purely white settled in any part of the tropical world, and represent a huge, unconscious experiment in acclimatization ...'.[67]

Others also showed appreciation of this new experiment. Professor Priestley of Sydney University declared in 1929 that North Queensland 'offers an experiment on a grand scale to test whether climate alone is responsible for loss of health'.[68] Similarly, in his novel, *The Australians*, Arthur Adams, former editor of the *Lone Hand*, had one character (squarely based on Randolph Bedford) declare:

> The sun gets into your blood and this is the first white race that has had that experience since the world began. Australia is the largest-sized and the most tremendous experiment ever tried in race-building, and Australia knows it.[69]

Although this swaggering Bedfordism hardly stands close scrutiny, it captures the post-war desire to see the colonization of Australia in thoroughly complimentary, race-building terms. There was bravura tone to much of the developmental rhetoric of the 1920s. Former Queensland premier E G Theodore struck this very note in praising his State: 'The land, the climate, and the conditions are in every sense suitable to the permanent settlement and propagation of a healthy, virile, white race'.[70] Defiant talk of Australia becoming the proud home of a 'healthy, virile, white race' became a mantra of the 1920s. After the Great War, alleged links between Caucasian virtues and cold climates were regarded more sceptically. The Europe that had fought itself to a bloody standstill no longer seemed the best example of civilisation. In these circumstances, Australian sunlight, far from seeming to be a problem, could now be celebrated and enjoyed. If nothing else, a warm climate could come as a relief from the miasma of gloom and pestilence hanging over a European landscape gutted by war. Trench warfare had given hard winters a dreadful reputation.

Randolph Bedford continually argued that Australian heat was energising and enlarging, while cold shrivelled the spirit. 'It is the people with the greatest capacity for enjoyment who love the sun', Bedford thundered. 'The man who hates heat is half-dead already'.[71] In his *Explorations in Civilisation*, Bedford condemned the depressing effects of the English climate. He had a point. As he wandered the streets of London on bitter winter mornings he surely saw more huddled battlers trying to get warm, than 'globe-trotting' geography professors energising themselves by exposure to cold. Bedford's defence of Australian heat, moreover, embraced the entire continent. He would not accept the description of any part of Australia as tropical if that brought associations with Asia. He dismissed the idea that the heat of northern Australia was degenerative: 'There's no enervation — as in Java or Singapore. It's Australian not tropical heat'.[72] Bedford was determined to believe that Australian heat conferred health, vitality and strength and had nothing at all in common with tropical Asia. He pushed his case further by maintaining that it was time to get on with the business of removing dark, tropical rainforests to allow the therapeutic Australian sunlight to fully extend its healthful influence on the people and the land.

A similar position was taken by the energetically pro-Australian *Smith's Weekly*. It attacked Taylor and the recent American fad of climatology which unjustly condemned hot climates as unsuitable for white settlement. *Smith's Weekly* roundly dismissed such thinking as 'an amusing piece of special pleading for their own pneumonia and blizzards'.[73] Taylor was dismissed as a person of gloomy views, a dangerous and unsuitable prophet. It was implied that he could hardly be anything other than a poor judge of the Australian climate because he had spent his first eleven years in England. Like Richard Arthur, he had obviously missed out on the enlarging Australian experience of having the sun enter his blood as a child. The *Bulletin* also endorsed the health-giving properties of Australian sunlight. In 1922 it argued: 'Our Great North is a dry, clean, healthy sort in which the white man flourishes much better than in the big southern cities'. The *Bulletin* believed that Australia should turn aside from urban civilisation and 'live up to our glorious destiny as the model white tropical State of the globe and of history'.[74] In pressing this claim, the *Bulletin* remained optimistic about the potential of Australia's primary industries and in Australia's capacity to absorb massive population increases. Mastery of the tropics was now the great Australian challenge.

A rather different perspective on the effects of the Australian climate was developed by the artist Hardy Wilson. In a semi-autobiographical novel, *The Dawn of a New Civilisation*, published in 1929, Wilson followed the fortunes of architect Richard Le Measurer. Le Measurer, searching for artistic inspiration, is first convinced that the semi-tropical climate of Sydney is damaging. It has destroyed the capacity for originality in the local population so that 'the planting of a British stock in Sydney would be accounted a failure'.[75] But he later perceives that Australia is geographically positioned at the end of Asia and that 'the soil of Australia is Oriental'. (Arthur Adams might have agreed, since he believed there was 'something almost Japanese in the eucalypt').[76] If Australia was under an Oriental influence then this might present unique opportunities for a new creativity. Le Measurer travels to China and returns convinced that the future lies in a blending of the cultures of East and West. A new cultural movement would develop in which Australia and America, as white Pacific nations, would play leading roles.[77] This was to be a cultural, not a physical blending. Wilson's views were supported by Henry Boote, editor of the Sydney *Worker* and at that time an effective and widely read essayist and poet. 'As a race of Western origin, evolving its culture in an Eastern environment', Boote wrote, 'the Australian nation must consciously orientalise its thought and its art'.[78] Where others had used climate to argue for a white Australia, Wilson and Boote made climate one of the reasons for Australia to become orientalised.

The great climate debate persisted well into the 1930s. In October 1937, a Report was presented to the Commonwealth Parliament on 'Land and Land Industries of the Northern Territory of Australia'.[79] Although the Report considered the White Australia policy fundamental and 'beyond compromise', it repeated serious concerns about the climate of tropical Australia. Darwin was described as 'enervating', 'very trying' and 'debilitating'. Active, physically fit males could be expected to withstand these conditions, but not so white women. The Commonwealth Health Laboratory in Darwin had revealed 'an amazingly high percentage of anaemia amongst females', accompanied by 'general malaise, lassitude and discontent'.[80]

This was the old problem. Permanent white settlement could not be established in the Northern Territory while women's health was jeopardised. In 1937, women still made up less than 30 percent of the Territorean population. What could be done? Diets could be improved by increasing the supply of fresh green vegetables to provide more of the vitamins necessary for red blood cell production. Here was an irony. As the report readily admitted, until 1911, when the Territory had passed into Federal hands and Chinese had been rigorously excluded, the Chinese had been particularly successful in supplying the Territory with vegetables. Now that Europeans seemed unable or unwilling to meet local requirements for fresh produce, it was proposed to allow the Chinese back in to re-establish their market gardens. The report also recommended the introduction of 'eastern natives' as domestic servants, a move designed to guard 'the health of white females'.[81] Such recommendations, despite assurances about the importance of the White Australia Policy, can only have added to the concern that Europeans and particularly European women were unsuited to life in the tropical north.

In 1900 it appeared that if Australia was not to become a fully realised Caucasian society, it ran the risk of degenerating into a tropical culture displaying a number of what were freely referred to as 'Asian' characteristics, not least a certain weary enervation and lack of ambition. The prestige of Caucasian civilization and the cold climates which had supposedly nurtured it, stood very high, just as tropical climates and societies were given a correspondingly low rating. But by the 1920s, terms like 'Caucasian' and 'Anglo-Saxon' were being linked much more freely to coldness and conformity. Warmth had become more desirable both as a personality trait and as a preferred climate. Australia could now be thought of as a country that might avoid the frosty formality of the Caucasian, without succumbing to tropical enervation. There was a Mediterranean middle course in which warmth and vitality were pictured as life-enhancing strengths. From the 1920s, the Australian tropics were also increasingly thought of as environments in which Europeans could be expected to develop permanent settlements. Even so, by the late 1930s the stigma of tropicality had not been removed altogether as both the Payne Report into Northern Settlement and Grenfell Price's magisterial survey of the tropical world demonstrate.

Today, theories about the effects of climate on racial character and civilisation are no longer analysed with the passion evident in the debates of the nineteenth and early twentieth century. Life in tropical areas has been transformed by the medical control of diseases, better housing, refrigeration and air conditioning. Temperature and comfort are no longer conditions over which settlers have relatively little control. Yet attempts in the inter-war years to characterise Australian climates and to infer how climate would shape white settlement, highlight both the ambiguous nature of northern Australia well into the twentieth century and the perceived close connection between climate, civilisation and racial character. Geographically, it was possible to see Australia as a continent which was as much 'Asian' as 'European' which encouraged the belief that Australia might yet evolve into a society with an Orientalised future. If Australians could not hope to become exemplary Caucasians and did not want to be characterised as a people subject to 'Asian' climatic influences, the Mediterranean option, if washed down with a glass of wine, could be represented as an acceptable alternative.

Chapter Twelve

Space Becomes Place

In 1910 it was still widely believed that Australia needed to attract millions of white settlers. Australia's 'emptiness' seemed a constant reproach which could only be removed by a population influx of 'Asian' proportions. But by the 1930s, estimates of Australia's optimal population had declined sharply and this was accompanied by a significant change in the understanding of Australia's emptiness. Australia now became a continent of vast open spaces and eerie silences, a harder, drier, browner land, requiring settlers able to withstand its climatic extremes, immense distances and great loneliness. It was now clear that in the spatial distribution of its population, Australia was unique, differing dramatically from most of Asia. The reduction of Australia's potential population also changed the debate over Asian populations. If climate, soil quality and lack of water would restrict Australia's population in the twentieth century to 20 million rather than the previously predicted 200 million, Australia could no longer be pictured as an empty continent, able to absorb Asia's excess millions. The more Australia was perceived as a continent with its own unique flora, fauna and landscapes, the harder it was to imagine it as a continent inevitably destined for Asian settlement.

By the 1920s, it was clear that the nature of the Australian continent could be very deceptive. Land that superficially appeared promising, all too often proved quite unsuited for settlement. Arguments about settlement began to change. Rather than suggesting that Australians lacked the will and imagination to settle their empty continent, it now seemed smarter to focus on the many difficulties that new settlers could be expected to face. An unforgiving climate and poor soil would naturally ensure a low population density. It could be argued that in prohibiting non-Europeans entry to the Northern Territory and Central Australia, Australians were not denying others access to desirable lands. Australians could no longer be so readily accused of selfish indifference to the world's problems. Reviewing Griffith Taylor's *Environment and Race* in 1927, Frederic Eggleston asked: 'Is it not obvious that if our country has fabulous riches in the interior, our ethical claim to exclusive possession is so much the weaker?'[1] In 1933 Professor K H Bailey of Melbourne University noted an increasing satisfaction as 'geographers exploded the opinion' of Australia's 'limitless economic resources'.[2] It was a relief to learn that Australia had little for other nations to covet. Ideas of lush, limitless Australia began to give way to accounts of a harsher continent requiring unique survival skills.

Bailey drew attention to the findings of an American authority on population and food supply, Professor Edward East, author of *Mankind at the Crossroads*, published in 1923. East scoffed at the idea of Australia as 'a perpetual fountain of plenty' able to absorb one hundred million people as predicted by figures like W M Hughes, the former Prime Minister. East dismissed such talk as baseless speculation and 'stupid politics' in view of the turbulence of the Far East.[3] In a picturesque turn of phrase, East described Australians as a people 'living on the rim of a soup-plate'. While the rim had its fertile spots, the bowl was only a barren desert denied regular water. By this criterion, the area suited to settlement could be reduced to the size of Spain or even Italy.[4]

Sydney University geographer, Griffith Taylor, was prominent among academic specialists seeking to persuade Australians that much of their country was barren, a view that initially met considerable resistance. Taylor criticised settlement schemes that ignored Australian geography and the political realities of Australia's relationship with its region.[5] Taylor's controversial views drew a great deal of criticism in the 1920s. In May 1922, the *Bulletin* denounced what it considered his bleak theories and unsound advice in an editorial on 'The Jeremiad of the Prophet Taylor'. The *Bulletin* was particularly appalled by Taylor's insistence that the immediate development of the north was a foolish mission. How, the *Bulletin* asked, would we go about explaining such a policy to the 'crowded and hungry' nations of Asia. Would we say:

> Let the nations take notice that, as far as the northern part of our estate is concerned, we are retiring from the Empire-building business indefinitely: and let them also be warned that they will have to keep off the grass.

The *Bulletin* believed that Asia was unlikely to accept such 'impudent and humiliating doctrines'.[6] It still believed that the only argument about Australia's development that might prove acceptable to Asia was that comprehensive settlement of the entire continent was Australia's first priority.

This was the old chestnut. How could a case be made for a sparsely settled white Australia in a world growing more crowded and more pressed for resources? How could Australians accept that 'our' numbers would remain comfortably small, while 'theirs' soared? The *Sydney Morning Herald* tackled this question directly in an editorial in 1925. The *Herald* had proved more receptive than the *Bulletin* to the arguments of geographers such as Griffith Taylor. It was prepared to acknowledge Taylor's contribution to the debate over the settlement potential of the Australian continent since he had 'the inexorable laws of science on his side'. But drawing on J W Gregory's recently published book, *The Menace of Colour*, the *Herald* was convinced, nonetheless, that the world faced an impending battle for resources which would be conducted along racial lines.[7] If it came to a fight, it seemed probable that the non-European races would win. The *Herald* supported Gregory's call for an arbitrated settlement of resource distribution, allocating Europe, North America and

Australia to the white races. The rest would have to be persuaded to take Asia, Africa and South America. Gregory advised that the best answer for people looking towards Australia's 'Empty North' was to direct their attention to other sparsely populated regions of the world, many of which were in Asia.

Sharply divided opinions over the nature of the Australian landmass and its development potential suggest that, well into the 1920s, Australia remained an ambiguous inheritance. Much remained to be learned of Australia's diverse environments and the kinds of skills and adaptive capacities required to settle them. Even the terms best describing Australia aroused bitter controversy, as seen in the protracted debate over whether central Australia should be described as desert. This started with new understandings of Australia coming from geographical surveys. In November 1921 the *Sydney Morning Herald* published Griffith Taylor's 'White Australia: Rainfall and Settlement'.[8] This included five maps describing central Australia as 'arid' and indicating that only a relatively narrow coastal strip of Australia had reliable rainfall. Taylor defined a desert as any region receiving less than 10 inches of rainfall a year (Plate 21). By this criterion, more than forty percent of Australia was desert.

These opinions fired up that Australian patriot, Randolph Bedford. He raged about professors who 'keep alive the lie of the Great Australian Desert'.[9] Bedford wanted the term 'desert' barred from the Australian lexicon. He was sure most of Australia was entirely suited for development. A little irrigation was all that was required. Bedford invited those who doubted its benefits to admire the splendid grass cover on the Kalgoolie racecourse. If this could be achieved with irrigation, the potential of areas like Lake Eyre was staggering. It could readily become world's greatest rice field.[10] Arthur Adams took a similar view, maintaining that the desert regions of Australia would disappear as soon as settlers moved in to cultivate the land.[11] In this view, to label Australia's sparsely settled regions as desert country was no more than a libellous admission of ignorance about its potential.

These were instructive denials. We have seen that Randolph Bedford was adamant Australia should not be regarded as a country with regions that were typically tropical. To Bedford, allusions to 'the tropics' called to mind places like Java and Singapore, with all their attendant problems: enervation, 'surexcited sexual organs', the 'decay of the white man'. Allusions to central Australia as 'desert' raised another series of disturbing images: burning sands, desolation, endless arid dunes, camels, oases, a monotony so terrible that it required a Rudolph Valentino to dispel its awfulness. American cultural historian, Ella Shohat has argued that the desert was commonly 'presented as the essential unchanging decor of the history of the Orient'.[12] The distinguished geographer, Edgeworth David, certainly believed that some of the considerable resistance to the use of the term 'desert' in Australia came from those who associated deserts with howling wildernesses of sand inhabited by Arabs.[13] From the 1830s

European artists had used the Moslem cultures of North Africa and the Middle East as the backdrop against which they developed an Orientalism centred on desert landscapes, religious fanaticism and a sexualized East epitomised by representations of the harem and veiled Eastern women.[14] Bedford was no more prepared to accept depictions of central Australia as 'desert', with these Oriental associations, than he was prepared to concede that parts of Australia might be described as tropical. Neither desert nor tropical orientalism had any place in Bedford's vision of the Australian future. To have Australia's future represented in such terms was a powerful denial of his preferred vision of a productive, populous and enterprising Australian nation.

Shohat also maintained that 'the Westerner, as the antithesis of the Oriental desert, is associated with productive, creative pioneering, a masculine redeemer of the wilderness'.[15] Bedford, whose chest measurements were almost as impressive as big Jim McLean's in *The Big Five*, was assuredly a masculine redeemer of wilderness for whom no land was too poor for development. He had seen the Kalgoolie racetrack. He knew the potential of Lake Eyre. He imagined levels of productivity in Australia on a scale the world had never seen before. Bedford foresaw a succession of triumphant victories over regions that ignorant professors had dismissed as useless desert.

The passions aroused by use of the term 'desert' are apparent in the extended correspondence on 'Arid Australia' which appeared in the columns of the *Sydney Morning Herald* in 1924.[16] The controversy was helped along by an editorial which noted how 'popular attention' was beginning to focus on this issue.[16] The editorial discerned two schools of thought on the nature of central Australia: the view espoused in the most recent *Times Atlas* which declared one third of Australia to be 'barren desert' of no commercial value and that of confident souls such as the Member for the Northern Territory, Mr Nelson, who thought central Australia contained some of 'the best pastoral country in the world'. To Nelson, it was a country of astonishing potential, ripe for development. The *Sydney Morning Herald* concluded that while the potential was still to be determined, the pessimistic assessments of the 'barren desert faction' were definitely mistaken.[17]

This judgement catapulted Taylor to his desk. The *Sydney Morning Herald* published his letter the following day.[18] He rejected the editorial and declared that the views of politicians and propagandists were less important than considered scientific opinion which used empirical factors like rainfall, temperature and geology to objectively classify land as desert. Using the classifications of a leading American climatologist, Taylor listed the world's major deserts in order of size. The four largest were the Sahara, central Australia, the Gobi desert in Turkestan and the desert area of Arabia. This placed Australia in company that made some observers distinctly uncomfortable. Taylor's letter re-affirmed that Australia had a classic Oriental desert at its very heart, a conclusion that could only cast grave doubt on past predictions of population-carrying capacity and economic potential. Indeed, Taylor warned yet again that to spend money seeking to develop these regions would prove to be a waste of resources.

Taylor reiterated his major points in a widely reported public lecture. He divided participants in the debate on Australia's 'great arid area' into two camps: 'the haphazard observer, well-meaning, optimistic and sure of a popular hearing ... and the scientific researcher'.[19] Taylor was concerned that the glowing descriptions of the former camp would only damage Australia's reputation over the longer term. If central Australia was so alluring, what would others think when it remained so sparsely populated? The 'others' Taylor had in mind were clearly the Asian nations to Australia's north. Their shadow fell heavily over the debate.

The *Sydney Morning Herald* debate continued fiercely at several levels. Firstly, there was a solid core of public opposition to Taylor as an academic theoretician, a mere scientist, pronouncing on subjects better left to 'practical men' who really knew the facts. These claimed the truth could only come from those with 'actual experience of travelling over the land' and never from 'the easy armchair of a professor of geography'.[20] But Taylor had certainly travelled extensively throughout Australia, taking accurate measurements as he went and his opinions were his own, not those of his armchair. Second, there was a vigorous body of correspondents who, like Randolph Bedford and Arthur Adams, considered use of the word 'desert' in an Australian context to be both inaccurate and unpatriotic.

Major-General William L'Estrange Eames entered early into the debate on the side of the practical men. Eames was the promoter of the Northern Australian White Settlement Association which planned to settle one hundred thousand Britishers in northern Australia.[21] This was precisely the kind of scheme that Taylor believed would produce yet another costly northern failure. Eames maintained that everyone knew that development had its problems. A professor was not needed to point them out. Australia needed spirited, practically-minded people who were prepared to roll up their sleeves and get down to work. Eames was tired of the theorists and wanted some action. 'Are we going to run true to British bulldog strain and emulate the grand work of our parentage', he thundered, 'or are we going to sink into insignificance as the vassals of some of our more enterprising coloured neighbours?'[22] Eames belonged to the Britons-never-never-will-be-slaves school of development.

A G Stephens, the well-known literary critic, also entered the debate on behalf of the patriots. He argued that Taylor, by dwelling so much on deserts, had 'written Australia down'. Stephens maintained that while 'actual population lags so far behind visible resources', it was essential that 'Australia should be written up'.[23] Some correspondents had no trouble with this. Expert opinion notwithstanding, they could still dream big dreams. One suggested dates were the ideal crop for the region to the north-east of Lake Eyre:

> Imagine, if you please, long avenues of date palms, each 60 to 80 feet high, and the growers' homesteads, stores, recreation sheds, cheaply covered with palm leaves, and the homes filled with wealthy and contented families.[24]

The area he had in mind for this venture was not so very far from where Randolph Bedford had located the world's greatest rice producing region.

While the *Sydney Morning Herald* often disagreed with Taylor, it nevertheless made room for him and other critics of 'Australia Unlimited' to put their case. The same could not be said for other sections of the press, including the *Bulletin* and *Smith's Weekly*. The *Daily Telegraph* was convinced that vast populations would live abundantly in Australia's now sparsely populated regions so unfairly dismissed by gloomy professors and their dismal followers. In an editorial on 'Central Australia' in 1924 it suggested that the Darling basin would eventually carry a population of 100 million people. Australia, it claimed, had more good soil than America.[25] The *Sun* also believed that it was quite wrong to label Australia as desert. Despite the views of science, this constituted 'anti-Australian propaganda'.[26] The *Sun* was particularly incensed by the idea that inland Australia should be compared with the Sahara.

In 1924, Dr Stefansson, famous arctic explorer and author of *The Northward Course of Empire*, presented a surprisingly cursory report to the Commonwealth government on central Australia which played into the hands of the desert-denying school of commentators. Stefansson claimed to have seen no country in Australia that could be called desert. Passing over local experts, including Taylor, he suggested that the Commonwealth might like to invite him back in the following year for another look, accompanied by an American who shared his views.[27] The Member for the Northern Territory, Mr Nelson, who constantly criticised Griffith Taylor for his 'perpetual slander of Central Australia' was overjoyed by Stefansson's findings and promptly called upon the Prime Minister to supply Taylor with a copy of Stefansson's report.[28] Nelson remained convinced that central Australia contained some of the richest country in the world and that Taylor's scientifically-based judgments were entirely wrong.

Buoyed by Stefanssson's findings, Nelson set out on a trip from Alice Springs to Darwin on a motor bike, to see this rich country for himself. When he failed to appear in Darwin an Aboriginal tracker was sent out to find him. Nelson had not fared at all well. His tell-tale tracks 'zig-zagged about the bush in a hopeless fashion'. The country had been appallingly dry and hot. Was it a desert perhaps? Nelson had run out of water and was forced to drink lubricating oil from his motor bike. He had even scratched out a farewell note to his wife believing he was about to be called to serve another constituency.[29]

Criticism of Taylor with his pessimistic talk about 'arid Australia' also extended to the Western Australian government. It withdrew his school text book because it referred to parts of Western Australia as desert. Government officials claimed this to be an inaccurate, harmful description of land ripe for development and closer settlement.[30] But again, in ignoring Taylor's warnings the Western Australian government came to pay a heavy price. Their great Empire settlement schemes failed spectacularly in the 1920s. This became a national scandal and provided yet more tinder-dry fuel for the critics of 'Australia Unlimited'.[31]

Senator James Guthrie may be taken as representative of public figures who saw it a duty to maintain an air of pugnacious optimism about Australia's potential. Born into a pioneering pastoral family, Guthrie considered himself an authority on immigration, land settlement and Australia's primary products. He had been selected to accompany a British Empire Parliamentary Delegation to South Africa as a Senate representative for the Nationalist Party. This experience had confirmed his view that Australia should definitely remain white. He returned from South Africa a confident expert in all matters relating to race and settlement. In 1925, Guthrie argued the case for white Australia in *Stead's Review*.[32] He maintained that Nature had kept Australia at a distance from 'the breeding ground of teeming hordes of the various coloured races' and drew the conclusion that empty, yet bountiful Australia must have been designed by Providence as 'a white man's country'. While Guthrie did admit an Aboriginal presence, he believed that if the Creator had intended Australia to remain Aboriginal, the country would have been more densely populated along Indian lines.

Guthrie was no less convinced that Australia's three million square miles constituted 'the richest portion of the globe'. Australia was fertile, rich and big: 27 times larger than Great Britain, almost as large as Europe or the United States and 28 times the size of Japan (Plate 22). Moreover, the Australian climate was 'infinitely better' than that of other countries. Accordingly, Guthrie was unconvinced by those who argued that much of Australia was desert. He admitted to some 'comparatively dry' regions, but argued that no part of the continent was unsuited for development and settlement. But unless Australians got to work and brought in vastly more people (and here he was talking only of white people), 'somebody else' might feel entitled to step in and take over. 'World opinion', Guthrie declared portentously, picking up the familiar theme of international intervention in Australian affairs, 'will not tolerate a dog-in-the-manger policy regarding the world's empty spaces'.

Through the 1930s the costs imposed by the various Empire settlement schemes, most of them based on logic not unlike Senator Guthrie's, were subjected to close scrutiny by economists. A consensus emerged that during the 1920s, borrowings to fund settlement schemes had substantially increased

Australia's indebtedness. As the Depression took hold, it became clear that the gap between the rhetoric of Empire settlement and its reality was unconscionably wide. The nation had been left to service an enormous debt.[33] In Victoria, disgruntled settlers took the Government to court on the grounds that the promotional literature which had induced them to immigrate had proved grossly misleading.[34] Settlers drifted from the land and emigration took over from immigration. Whereas in the 1920s Griffith Taylor's utterances had often been dismissed as bleak pessimism, by the 1930s they were just as often hailed as skilled prophecy. In 1937, W G K Duncan noted that the press was inclined to welcome cautious predictions about Australia's potential as a 'useful public service' when a little over a decade earlier they had been 'denounced as something akin to treason'.[35]

Through the 1930s there was also a growing insistence that Australia should acknowledge more realistically the qualities of its colonising performance. Australians had in fact often triumphed over their country's difficult conditions. As estimates of the optimal population Australia could support declined sharply between 1910 and 1930, Australia's colonising performance began to look more commendable. The new, more congratulatory tone is apparent in a contribution made by A G B Fisher, Professor of Economics at the University of Western Australia, to a symposium on immigration held in Canberra in 1937:

> Instead of talking about boundless natural resources, and at the same time insinuating that they had constantly refused to make the best use of them Australians would do better to realize the natural limitations of their country, at the same time as they congratulate themselves upon the excellent job they have done with rather indifferent material.[36]

Fisher joined the growing chorus of experts who condemned 'ecstatic' accounts of Australia's potential by the superior patriots. Expert opinion now declared the ecstatic patriot a pest. Professor Wadham, an authority on agriculture and rural development hoped, though rather unrealistically, that he would no longer be forced to listen to 'outbursts of oratory on the illimitable potentialities and unbounded resources of the Commonwealth'.[37]

Although the Great Depression proved a turning point in the development of a stronger critique of ideas that Australia had unlimited capacities, this trend in the views of expert opinion was apparent before the Depression took effect. J B Brigden, Professor of Economics at the University of Tasmania, was prominent among the pessimistic professors. In an article in *Stead's Review* in December 1925, he noted that the discipline of political economy called for cold-blooded examination of questions that were often 'subjects of popular emotion, of class feeling, and of common controversy'.[38] Academic authorities should realise that their concern for economic and 'social costs' could make them appear 'disagreeable' people, lacking vision on the topical questions of immigration and population growth. Brigden's concern was to establish a proper balance between the supply of new immigrants and the investment of capital required to ensure their productive absorption into the Australian economy, then experiencing high levels of unemployment. He calculated that it would require a total of ten million pounds to sustain an inflow of 35,000 immigrants to Australia.

Cautious estimates of immigration intake and Australia's optimum population were also a prominent feature of a volume of essays entitled *The Peopling of Australia*, edited by P D Phillips and G L Wood, and published with the assistance of the Institute of Pacific Relations in 1928. Phillips and Wood noted that some clear points of disagreement were evident between expert opinion and the 'general Australian viewpoint'. While extravagant population projections were still commonplace in the wider community, the editors pointed out that the contributors to their volume were much more restrained. Their estimate of an optimum population for Australia fell between 20 million and 40 million people, to be attained over a period of 100 years. This was far short of the 100 million or more still commonly cited by public figures unburdened by expertise.[39]

In his introduction to a second volume of essays on *The Peopling of Australia,* published in 1933, P D Phillips was more outspoken.[40] He curtly dismissed those who had formed their opinions of Australia's population carrying capacity by simply glancing at a map and drawing airy conclusions about Australia's vast population potential. Phillips wanted his readers to acknowledge that Australia had already achieved a commendable population increase. Its population was increasing faster than in any other countries with the exception of Canada, the Netherlands, and Japan. Nevertheless, critics were still apt to condemn Australia for not receiving more immigrants. Senator Guthrie, for example, considered Australia worryingly under-populated, arguing that immigration was a mere trickle when it should have been a mighty stream.[41] But Phillips insisted that many of the extravagant immigration schemes of the recent past had failed because they had emphasised great potentialities but had not calculated the actual costs in bringing out settlers. For example, the Millions Club had urged the creation of a 'million farms for a million farmers' throughout the 1920s yet in all their literature they had made no mention of what it cost to establish settlers on the land.[42]

Turning to the question of northern development, Phillips asked why Asian nations to the north had not seized their opportunity to develop this region. This was a question some parliamentarians had also asked during the debates over the Northern Territory Acceptance Bill in 1910. Phillips concluded that geographical and climatic limitations made the area 'economically sterile'. It was not simply a problem of attitude.[43] In addition, Phillips regarded it as highly unlikely that Japan would want to develop the Territory or have the skills to do so, a very different view from that of Richard Arthur who believed the Japanese would take to Australia like ducks to water. In fact, Phillips maintained that

Australians had already developed a pastoral industry particularly well suited to these areas of low economic potential. The privations and isolated working conditions of the industry had created a uniquely adaptable community, unlikely to find an equal among immigrants from 'Eastern races'.[44] Here was a new regard for the bush skills and flinty determination which had helped sustain the pastoral industry in difficult and unpredictable outback country. Phillips challenged the old refrain that enterprising Asia had the skills, capacities and disciplines to outperform hedonistic Australians.

A similar approach was also taken by Sydney Upton in an article written in 1934 for *United Empire*. Upton maintained that the 'early pioneers were no fools, nor were they shirkers'. The slow development of the Northern Territory was not the result of economic conditions or some failure of will to settle, but could be squarely attributed to the shortage of water. The rainfall, Upton believed, was always 'too low, too seasonal or too erratic' and, moreover, the soil was largely infertile. It was a largely 'sterile' area and this would remain the case whether settlement was attempted by coloured or white people.[45]

The growing recognition that Australia confronted settlers with some particular and demanding environments created room for a more sympathetic interest in the way Aboriginal populations had adapted to difficult country. The writings of Eleanor Dark and Xavier Herbert assumed that Aborigines had acquired a knowledge of the land based on generations of close observation and profound respect for the spirit of place, philosophies quite at odds with the view that Australia was an empty space which needed to be filled as quickly as possible with as many settlers as could be jammed within its capacious borders.[46] In acknowledging that Australia was a dry continent with large expanses of desert, it also became at once a more distinctive country and one more profoundly marked by its Aboriginal inhabitants. Knowing Australia became more fully implicated in knowing Aboriginal responses to the land.

The two volumes of *The Peopling of Australia* represented expert opinion drawn from specialised, technically demanding areas of research. Unsupported population projections were now subject to increasing scrutiny. Even so, extravagant rhetoric persisted. In 1935, Dr L Dudley Stamp writing for the prestigious British journal of science, *Nature*, reported there was still 'a wide divergence of opinion' on reasons for the slow settlement of tropical Australia.[47] By 1937 W Wynne Williams, Fellow of the Royal Geographical Society, had become exasperated at the persistent belief in the potential of the Northern Territory. Williams had seen 'the bogey of the empty spaces' reappear so often that he was almost resigned to 'its enduring resurrections'. It seemed immune to scientific evidence. Williams noted how the popular press, particularly the *Sun*, still seized every opportunity to praise this 'miserable tropic realm'. But Williams could conclude on one genuinely positive note: 'Australia is fortunate in possessing such a worthless tropical territory fronting the populated East'.

Why? Because 'the dreadful combination of swamp and waterless interior' that separated the centres of population from Australia's north was about the most effective barrier imaginable against populous Asia.[48]

Williams would certainly have been provoked by a series of five articles appearing in the *Sydney Morning Herald* between December 1935 and June 1936 which represented the 'Empty North' as 'Our Paramount Problem'.[49] One solution was that Australia might give the unoccupied Territory to the British Government for their unemployed. This view was supported by reference to the familiar fear that an 'Empty North' would provoke Asian nations to invade. These five articles drew a devastating response from Edward Masey, a regular contributor to the Australia First publication, the *Publicist*.[50] Masey reviewed Australia's limited capacity for settlement and concluded, after a thorough review of the scientific evidence, that a population of 30 million a century hence would be a sensible population outcome. Masey also expressed a new concern for the impact of settlement on the environment. He argued that Australia could not be filled with countless millions without doing enormous damage to fragile, arid country. Francis Ratcliffe addressed similar concerns in his beautifully written and influential book, *Flying Fox and Drifting Sand*, published in 1938.[51] Concerns that overpopulation would cause severe environmental degradation were substantiated by reports coming from the recently appointed Soil Erosion Commission.[52] The findings of this reputable body suggested that arid Australia, far from disappearing with the advent of settlers, threatened to expand dramatically. Grazing and pastoral development had not made arid Australia disappear as the optimists had maintained. On the contrary, existing deserts were growing into ever larger areas of windswept desolation.

Masey also believed that Australia need not fear any population influx from the crowded countries of Asia. Asia, he maintained, could solve its own population problems by expanding into the many sparsely populated areas present within its own region. Masey identified Japan as the only expansionist nation in Asia, but he considered that its main interest was in markets not territories; Manchukuo would satisfy these more immediate needs. Masey dismissed the 'distorted patriotism' of enthusiasts for massive population growth who seemed obsessed by imagined threats from Asia.[53]

Ion Idriess, the popular novelist, outback enthusiast and all-round Australian fitted Masey's picture of the 'distorted' patriot rather well.[54] Through the 1930s, with the considerable help of the *Sun* newspaper, Idriess became an important figure in articulating an anti-urban, rural settlement message. Idriess concocted a vast engineering scheme to reverse the rivers of Australia, making them flow into the interior of the continent to exploit the mighty catchment area provided by Lake Eyre. From late 1936 the *Sun* gave considerable publicity to the scheme and endeavored to find high-level government support for it.[55] Idriess believed that his 'Plan' could enable Australia to support 'millions more people'. It hardly needed to be said that these would be eager, white settlers. 'The crowding of the Australian population into a few great coastal cities', Idriess warned 'is a danger to our prosperity and to our economic and national life ... As our population is spaced now our national existence is in deadly peril'.[56]

Idriess's scheme promised a massive growth of prosperous rural communities and the validation of masculine energies through rural labour. As was so often the case with those who sought to populate central Australia and bring it to productive life, a warning was also sounded about what might become of the continent if these visionary schemes failed to be implemented. If Australians chose not to put this plan into action, Idriess warned that 'some other more enterprising nation' would certainly do so.[57] The Japanese were not mentioned directly, but in a book published in 1941 outlining Australia's need for a vastly increased population it was hardly necessary to do so. Once again, Australians were warned that failure to effectively settle their country might mean that it would be taken from them, either directly by more enterprising Asian nations or through international intervention.

While Idriess discounted Australian cities, others had begun to see their importance. In the 1928 volume of *The Peopling of Australia*, the Commonwealth Statistician, C H Wickens, noted that the period between 1880 and 1921, which had seen rapid urbanisation, had also brought a remarkable increase in the life expectancy of the Australian population. He remarked that while many lamented the 'drift to the cities', there was no evidence that the trend had damaged the 'progressive longevity of the population'.[58] E T McPhee, another contributor to the 1928 volume and a colleague of Wickens in the Commonwealth Bureau of Census and Statistics, also defended the urbanisation of the Australian population on economic, social and cultural grounds.[59]

But through the inter-war years the city remained the subject of much hostile commentary. Many imagined the corrosive effects of city life upon the more strenuous patriotic virtues, creating populations at once decadent and feminised. Overseas critics, like Lord Northcliffe, Chiozza Money and Fleetwood Chidell, all pushed variations upon this theme.[60] In the demonology of the invasion narrative, the city was invariably represented as a weak link in the chain of Australian defence. While the idea that cities had commendable strengths appealed to social scientists, popular commentary still characterised the city as the refuge of failed patriots and rootless consumers, the site of effeminate manhood and aggressive feminism. Rhetoric about the need to populate the empty spaces of Australia was invariably linked to unease about the city as a degenerate social environment, a place to be avoided. McPhee warned that the Australian problem was not that cities would grow bigger, although he was certain this would be the case, but that Australians would continue to believe they would be better off without them and would therefore fail to make adequate plans for their unavoidably urban future. The process of redefining and explaining the city was part of the larger task of redefining Australia itself and of defending Australia's record of settlement.[61]

The debates of the 1930s led to a greater appreciation of the forces behind urban growth. One of the most incisive contributions was W D Forsyth's *The Myth of Open Spaces*.[62] Forsyth predicted that twentieth century patterns of immigration would prove very different from those of the nineteenth century, when immigrants were attracted into territories of low population density as metropolitan powers developed their colonial possessions. These populations had shifted from densely populated to sparsely populated regions. Forsyth argued that this trend would now be reversed. Twentieth century populations would be drawn back to centres of economic opportunity, to cities rather than to hinterlands, to centres of metropolitan power rather than to remote colonies. Fuelling this shift would be a movement of capital from primary through secondary to tertiary industries. Economic progress would not flow from further geographical expansion but from social change which included the development of new skills and capacities in urban centres. In this view, urbanisation was not a peculiarly Australian disorder nor was it a sign of decadence and a deadly peril. Rather, it was a universal process of demographic change grounded in economic logic.

Forsyth dated the realisation that a dramatic change in the pattern of settlement was underway to the period of the Great Depression. While Forsyth readily conceded that there were still empty lands, he maintained that they were empty for good reasons: substantial problems of climate, water supply, soil quality or remoteness. The constraints were not merely a failure of will or a selfish impulse to deny opportunities to others. Australians were not guilty of neglecting vast potentialities. Nor did Forsyth accept that Australia's settlement record was so poor that it called the Australian entitlement to the continent into question. There were no grounds upon which guilty Australia deserved the censure of the international community. There had been mistakes, gross mistakes, but they were largely the result of trying too hard to settle large populations in inhospitable areas of the continent, not of trying to achieve too little.

The shrinking and drying of the Australian land mass caused dramatic decreases in population projections. This in turn cast a new light on Australia's obligations to the crowded nations to her north. After examining several predictive models, Forsyth concluded that Australia's population would peak at just under nine million in 1981 and then begin to decline. Australia had undergone a change from an immeasurably rich continent of unlimited potential to a uniquely fragile one facing severe constraints upon further development. In these circumstances, Forsyth felt that Asian immigration was unlikely to be an acceptable option in the foreseeable future. In particular, the constraints limiting Australia's growth meant that it could never provide a solution to the problem of over-crowding in Asia. Australia's potential contribution would only ever amount to a drop in the ocean. The problem of global over-population, Forsyth argued, had to be addressed at its source within those countries in which over-crowding was a major problem.

These reformulations of Australia's potential might appear to have had the effect of further distancing crowded Asia. Not so. Australia was now obliged to contribute to the solution of Asia's problems in other ways. Forsyth believed that Asia's greatest need was an inflow of capital, skills and new techniques to aid industrial development which would in the longer term reduce the rate of population growth while increasing the standard of living. He maintained that these strategies, coupled with an increased flow of trade, would do more to improve conditions in Asia than any plan for emigration. He urged Australia to accept that it had an important role to play in promoting these outcomes.

If Asian problems had to be solved in Asia, with whatever assistance the international community could provide, it followed that Australia would have to develop appropriate expertise if it was to perform the kind of supporting role that would be needed in the post-war world. Within Australia, Forsyth maintained, Asia-awareness had to shift from anxious speculation about invasion by hordes from the north, to a more focused examination of the specific needs and circumstances of particular Asian societies.

Chapter Thirteen

The Evil Doctor

The terrible destructiveness and huge population losses of the first world war revived and, in the American case, intensified, concerns about the vulnerability of white societies. As President Woodrow Wilson considered America's entry into the war, one of the factors weighing heavily on his mind was the damage that the loss of American lives would inflict upon 'white civilisation'. In February 1917 he advised his Cabinet that he wanted America kept out of the conflict 'to keep the white race strong in order to meet the yellow race'. Although the need to defeat Germany eventually became the over-riding priority, Wilson carried his anxieties about the 'yellow race' through the final years of the war and into the Versailles Peace Conference of 1919.[1]

One powerful and influential expression of this widely held concern over the vulnerability of white civilisation was *The Rising Tide of Color*, written by the Harvard historian and race theorist, Lothrop Stoddard, and published in the immediate aftermath of Versailles.[2] Stoddard's arresting title appropriated and further popularised the tidal metaphors common to the race debate over the preceding half century. Stoddard argued that the Great War had profoundly weakened the white race, severely reducing both its numbers and morale. In contrast, the 'yellow races', largely untouched by the conflict, had been emboldened by the damage they had seen the West inflict upon itself. Stoddard's book attracted considerable notice in Australia well into the 1930s. It added weight to the popular view that Australia needed to press ahead with substantial immigration programs as a protection against an invasion flooding in from the Asian nations to Australia's north.

Stoddard's ideas were hardly new. He readily acknowledged his indebtedness to Charles Pearson's *National Life and Character*, re-issued for the American market in 1913, when fear of Japan was running high.[3] Stoddard described *National Life and Character*, in one of several approving references, as an 'epoch-making book'.[4] Many of Stoddard's arguments recapitulated ideas that had been circulating at earlier stages of the race debate, not least his view that there were two sharply contrasting worlds, 'coloured' and 'white'.[5] This division had been a commonplace in the Australian press from the 1890s. Its characteristic expression is found in an editorial in the *Daily Telegraph* on 'The Yellow Peril' in 1904 where the paper stated that for practical purposes the world could be divided into 'white' and 'coloured' races. Until recently, the white race had been clearly dominant, but there were signs of sudden change. The transformation from extreme lethargy to intense activity evident throughout

Asia was attributed 'to the stimulus of racial passion, worked up by some psychic influence like that now operating on the Japanese'. It was assumed that the changes found in the Japanese when they overcame the Russians at Port Arthur in 1904 would now spread rapidly throughout the East. The white world, the *Daily Telegraph* claimed, would have to adjust to a period of seismic change.[6]

Australia's isolation and tiny population provided fertile soil for such racial anxieties. These fears appear to have struck Australian commentators earlier, and more forcefully, than their American counterparts, for whom ideas of invasion and coloured hordes retained a more abstract, theoretical dimension. American invasion anxieties, as distinct from the fears of invasion which had developed in California and which were West Coast rather than national in focus, were commonly linked to domestic concern over the impacts of immigration upon Anglo-Saxon America. One of the earliest American exponents of invasion fears was Homer Lea. Lea's *The Valor of Ignorance* warned Americans, albeit in complicated prose, of the dangers of Japanese invasion. Lea also had lessons for Australia. His book portrayed a rapidly shrinking world, reduced by science and technological change into a 'little ball' in which increasingly 'mankind is being crowded and jostled together'. Australia was thus inexorably moving 'closer and closer to the shores of Asia' and it would be impossible for it to remain uninvolved in its regional conflicts.[7] Just as urgent for Lea was the battle of modern life which he feared displayed all the elements of advanced decadence: urbanisation, calls for equality of the sexes, dependence on modern technologies, contempt for the soldier, declining birth-rates.[8] It was a long list. Lea maintained that while the Saxon had once stoutly resisted these corrosive tendencies, the rot was now well advanced in Saxon communities.

Stoddard expressed and exploited similar racial anxieties. F Scott Fitzgerald, in the opening pages of *The Great Gatsby*, satirises the uncritical acceptance by wealthy elites of 'The Rise of the Colored Empires' by 'this man Goddard'. Fitzgerald suggests Stoddard and his readers were not interested in the complex ambiguities of more rational discussion of race issues. They were already convinced: 'It's all scientific stuff; it's been proved'.[9] Stoddard knew the white race was in trouble and he knew why. It had all started with the Japanese victory at Port Arthur. This event had 'dramatized and clarified ideas which had been germinating half-unconsciously in millions of colored minds, and both Asia and Africa thrilled with joy and hope'.[10]

Although the coloured world was reluctant to act upon its new knowledge given the white world's formidable power, Stoddard knew 'the legend of white invincibility' had finally been destroyed.[11] Once again this was hardly very original. Richard Arthur, himself an accomplished mimic of current pessimisms, had expressed such sentiments in very similar language in Australia almost a decade earlier. Arthur had criticised the Anglo-Japanese Alliance because it had allowed the Japanese to defeat Russia. After this crucial event 'every bazaar in remotest Asia talked of the overthrow of the great white Czar by the brown people of the Pacific Isles. The prestige of the white man was shaken'.[12]

Stoddard maintained that while the Russo-Japanese war had had a dazzling impact on 'the coloured mind', this was as nothing compared to the impact of the Great War. The white world, which had once put up such an imposing show of unity, was now locked into 'an internecine death grapple'. Stoddard believed that as the first world war dragged on, 'fear of white power and respect for white civilization' had collapsed.[13] The white world, Stoddard argued, was now in decline, both in relative numbers and in influence. And as Europe fragmented, the coloured world grew more unified:

> welded by the most fundamental of instincts, the instinct of self-preservation, into a common solidarity of feeling against the dominant white man, and in the fire of a common purpose internecine differences tend, for the time at least, to be burned away.[14]

These themes of welding together, of solidarity and the burning away of differences recur throughout *The Rising Tide of Color*, as well they might, since the belief in a unified, increasingly cohesive 'coloured world' was central to Stoddard's purpose. The Asia Stoddard described was a world transformed, energised, unified. It was a world of excited gatherings, whispered conversations and knowing glances. The news was sweeping through the bazaars of Asia that the East could now triumph over the West. Stoddard's story was one of terrific drama, a globally significant tale whose impact, he was certain, would be felt dramatically and decisively in all countries bordering the Pacific. Stoddard assigned White Australia a critical role in the coming struggle as a racial blood donor. Australia's task would be to help maintain an unpolluted stream of 'clean, virile, genius-bearing blood'.[15] In this discourse, there was both a fear of growing Asian numbers as well as a sharp anxiety that the 'mind' of Asia seemed more confident, more aware of its possibilities and common purposes. Stoddard told of an articulate, scheming and increasingly clever Asia, plotting the downfall of a divided and demoralised white race.

Publication of *The Rising Tide of Color* drew rapid responses in Australia, although Australia was by no means Stoddard's central concern. He nevertheless pointed unmistakably to its endangered future as a white nation. It was nice to be noticed, even by an American author predicting that Australia was a lost continent, about to be submerged by a tidal flow from Asia. Among prominent Australians who approved Stoddard's book was Sir Joseph Carruthers, a conservative politician and a leading figure in the 'One Million Farms for One Million Farmers' campaign. Carruthers reviewed and recommended *The Rising Tide of Color* for the *West Australian* in September 1921 and a month later for the *Sydney Morning Herald*.[16] Other opinion quickly agreed with Carruthers' firm recommendations. An unlikely ally, the *Worker*, suggested that Stoddard's book 'should be in every library and School of Arts'.[17] This may indeed almost have come to pass. By the early 1930s, K H Bailey, Professor of Public Law at Melbourne University confirmed that *The Rising Tide of Color* had been in 'great demand' throughout Australia.[18] At the end of the 1920s, the *Bulletin* ran a cartoon, authorised by the Queensland Sugar Industry Defence Committee, which showed an Asiatic figure looking upon an empty Australia placed near the centre of an ocean labelled 'the rising tide of colour'. Stoddard's central idea had become instantly recognisable.[19]

Stoddard's account of world events also had its impact in Australian naval circles. In October 1921, Captain W H Thring circulated a report entitled 'Notes on the Racial Aspect of the Pacific Problem'. Thring was a prominent figure among those who developed Australian naval policies for the Pacific after the war and his views carried some weight.[20] Thring emphasised the great turning points in the decline of the white race: the Russo-Japanese war, the rising influence of the Moslem world (one of Stoddard's key themes) and the Great War. These developments had given 'Asiatics ... confidence in the power of the coloured races to throw off the White man's yoke'.[21] They had always had the numbers, now they had a growing confidence that they could win the coming power struggle where minds would matter as much as numbers.

Thring directed his confidential report to E L Piesse in the Commonwealth Intelligence Department, believing this body would need to follow up on his report. His concluding statement urged the Intelligence Department to take 'careful note of the effects on history of the great invasions such as those of Attila, Tamerlane, Jenghis Khan etc. to say nothing of the minor inroads of the Assyrians, Medes and Persians, Saracens and Turks'.[22] This is reminiscent of earlier commentaries by Francis Adams and William Lane where similar episodes in world history were also thought to have immediate modern applications. Although Piesse was well-read and had an interest in history, it may be doubted whether Thring's report sent him flying to consult the Assyrian section of his nearest library.

Stoddard's views did not go entirely unchallenged in Australia. In 1927, a contributor to the *Morpeth Review* noted that a widespread anxiety had developed in the Australian community about the extent to which 'coloured' populations were overtaking the 'white' populations of the world. He believed that these concerns were based on erroneous figures purporting to show that Asian populations were doubling at a much faster rate than Europeans, encouraging fears that Europeans would be 'swamped' and European blood diluted. The writer thought *The Rising Tide of Color* and another of Stoddard's books, *The Revolt against Civilisation*, were 'more responsible than any other publications for this distorted representation of population problems'.[23] There followed a detailed critique of Stoddard's population figures and the false conclusions he had drawn from them. Unfortunately the problem of combating Stoddard's influence required more than a rejection of his figures. There remained the powerful tidal metaphors, the passionate attacks on mixed blood and the sheer drama of his story.

Stoddard's work was followed by a British exposition on the race question *The Clash of Colour: A Study in the Problem of Race*, written by Basil Mathews and first published in 1924.[24] The title owed something to Stoddard and if it was an attempt to capitalise on the extraordinary popularity of Stoddard's book, it was a roaring success. Conflict between the white and coloured races, also the theme of J W Gregory's *The Menace of Colour*, could be guaranteed a substantial readership. *The Clash of Colour* had rushed to its fifteenth impression by the end of 1925. While Mathews acknowledged the 'brilliancy' of Stoddard's book, he challenged its central premise that race was the key to human history. Mathews was much more hopeful about political settlements and solutions and the exercise of goodwill.

Even so, Mathews' views on the declining prestige of the white man had much in common with Stoddard. Again, the Japanese victory over Russia was identified as a turning point in race relations, marking the time when Asia had exposed Europe's vulnerability, amid considerable rejoicing. The Great War, Mathews argued, took the process several steps further. Like Stoddard, Mathews described the first world war as a 'white civil war', and he noted how it had called 'the white man's hypnotic authority' into question.[25] Mathews argued that white authority had received its final blow in 1923, when the Turks had dictated the terms of the Treaty of Lausanne. According to Mathews, the electric circuitry of Asia lit up with the news: 'The Treaty of Lausanne was discussed in every bazaar in India, by the night fires of Arab sheiks, and in student debates from Cairo to Delhi, Peking and Tokyo'.[26] News of the collapsing prestige of the white man raced through the bazaars of Asia. For Homer Lea, these whispered communications were the signs of a shrinking world. 'So jammed together are the races of the world that one hears the whisper of the other'.[27] This was a congested, relentlessly crowded world, scrambling for space and dominance.

While the West appeared in decline and with its best stock dwindling, the East appeared to be growing ever larger, more powerful and more articulate. Of particular concern were the Chinese. They were often presented as an indestructible race, immune to decline and far too numerous ever to be displaced. These fears were amplified by the widespread notion that Asians were much cleverer than Europeans. They seemed to have access to special powers. While Alfred Deakin was critical of the 'credulous Oriental mind' he nevertheless perceived the power of its 'prophecies and omens' and 'mysterious warnings'.[28] This was the psychic East, linked by its own mysterious circuitry and fuelled by mystic religions and powerful occult teachings. The East was credited with powers of intuition and modes of knowing and communicating quite beyond the West and, for all his abilities, utterly beyond the Caucasian male. The mind of the East had been awakened to its powers. There was no corner of the earth that escaped the notice of alert Asian eyes. Espionage had become, so Stoddard believed, the very breath of their being.

One of the most persistent of the stereotypes, and one frequently deployed by Stoddard, was the famous inscrutability of the East. The Shakespearean adage that one could read the mind's construction in the face was all very well when dealing with people and with faces known to the observer but was much more difficult where cultural contact was minimal. As C Spurgeon Medhurst claimed in 1925: 'No white man has ever successfully explained the contents of the brain behind the wax-like face of the yellow man'.[29] Inscrutability, impassivity, smoothness all recur as adjectives used to describe the difficulties of grasping what the East was thinking and feeling. The East was commonly represented as an unfathomable culture of subterfuges, masks and intricate disguises.

Cultures which had perfected the arts of concealment could be expected to produce the most accomplished spies. Spying was believed to be an Eastern forte and Australia was commonly represented as a country in which Eastern spies were particularly active. As we have seen, William Lane was convinced that the four Chinese Commissioners who toured the Australian colonies in 1887 were spies, sent to assess Australia's potential as a Chinese colony. The rise of Japan then shifted the focus of concern. It became a general assumption that one of the principal occupations of the Japanese in Australia was espionage. Richard Arthur and the *Bulletin* both maintained that the Japanese Training Squadron of 1906 was crawling with spies.[30] In 1908, in an article in the *Lone Hand*, Walter Kirton described a Japanese school for spies he had visited in Shanghai. He noted that: 'It is from this college that the Japanese Government recruits its Intelligence Department in its campaign of political and commercial conquest of the Chinese Empire'. Presumably, if they could so easily infiltrate China, 'notebook in sleeve and eyes open for anything useful', they could similarly infiltrate Australia.[31]

In 1909 the press seized upon a story that four Japanese disguised as showmen were working as spies in vulnerable North Queensland. Further investigation revealed that they were actually the showmen they purported to be.[32] The *Sun* generated a much more colourful story in 1911 when it reported that New Caledonia was swarming with armed Japanese spies wearing military overcoats. Although the wearing of military overcoats suggests neither expert concealment nor Oriental cunning, the *Sun* noted that the Japanese was 'a sphinx' and that 'the Japanese brain is a curious product of latter-day education and profit by example'.[33] By this period the spy novel had achieved considerable popularity in Britain, a fertile source of many of Australia's ideas and anxieties.

The Millions Club, where the 'rising tide of colour' was a popular concern, took up this theme in 1921 when it claimed that Japanese spies, disguised as fishermen, were at work in nearby New Caledonia. The evidence was compelling: there were cameras, there were people who spoke more than one language, there were others who were too intelligent to be fishermen. Among them were men with 'well cared for hands, finely manicured nails and the well-dressed appearance of gentlemen'.[34]

A powerful acknowledgment of Australian concerns about Japanese spying came from the former Head of the Pacific Branch in the Prime Minister's Office, E L Piesse, who delivered a paper to a conference of intelligence officers on Japanese espionage in Australia in 1924. As with most things Piesse wrote this was a carefully measured, historically-informed presentation. He noted that Japanese espionage had become a 'very familiar' topic to intelligence officers. There were regular reports about spying in the newspapers. There were also not infrequent official inquiries, often enough coming up with innocent explanations for apparently suspicious behaviour. These reports covered the suspect activities of Japanese pearl divers and fishermen along with other incidents suggesting that well-educated Japanese had carefully placed themselves in strategic locations along the coast north of Sydney. Piesse believed that a case could be made that Japanese were collecting information that might be useful in the event of an attack upon Sydney. But he found no evidence that the Japanese government had authorised any of these activities. If sensitive information was being gathered, Piesse felt it was more likely to be the action of entrepreneurial individuals than the action of Japanese government spies. Had the Japanese Government been involved in spying, he believed they would have employed willing Europeans rather than their own conspicuous nationals.[35]

While Piesse cautiously conceded that there were some grounds for concern, he acknowledged that the Australian public seemed ready to believe that each new allegation of Japanese espionage proved that their country was under close scrutiny. He maintained that the formation of the Australian Intelligence Corps, 'the first systematic military intelligence body in Australia', was significantly influenced by fear of Japanese actions in Australia; reporting incidents that had come to public notice was 'certainly the main stimulus to its work'. Piesse argued that Australian fears were based upon a widespread misconception, fuelled by a lack of historical knowledge, that the Japanese were a peculiarly aggressive people with designs upon Australia. By the mid 1930s, when the international situation had changed dramatically, Piesse warned that a newly militarised Japan had indeed become a direct threat to Australian security. But from the different vantage point of 1924, Piesse rejected the idea that Japan was determined to invade. He favoured a more subtly modulated account of Japanese history, economic policies and emigration patterns, strongly influenced by James Murdoch's views, which suggested that while Japan was a determined power, it was not bent on indiscriminate conquest.

Piesse's carefully elaborated refusal to accuse the Japanese of systematic espionage in Australia merely demonstrates that the public often saw things differently. Ellsworth Huntington, the American geographer who visited Australia in 1923 was in no doubt that fear of Japanese spies was widespread. 'I was astonished to find', he wrote in *West of the Pacific*, 'how many intelligent Australians were really concerned over this matter'.[36] While Piesse was obviously concerned at the public willingness to see the Japanese as spies, he could also see that powerful stereotypes were at work, which quickly turned apparently innocent behaviour into something evil and full of menace. In an attempt to lighten the occasion and dispel dark suspicions, Piesse told his audience of intelligence officers:

> The fact that a Japanese has a camera & a note book & is using them is no evidence that he has improper objects. The Japanese are an alert, curious, inquisitive people, & everywhere they go they ask questions, & take photographs & make notes, to satisfy their own curiosity'.[37]

But where Piesse saw intellectual curiosity, others found disturbing evidence of Oriental cunning and insidious plans to conquer the white world.

The Australian publicist, E George Marks, fed the note of fear and suspicion in *Watch the Pacific! Defenceless Australia*, published in 1924. He warned that Asia's 'envious eyes' were studying the Pacific in general and Australia's empty spaces in particular.[38] Following up these concerns in *Pacific Peril*, he quoted Lothrop Stoddard's warning that 'Australia is the focal point where the extending forces of East and West confront each other most sharply and irreconcilably'. For Marks, the menace of the Orient could hardly be overstated.[39]

The demonic powers of the East soon became embodied in the evil villains of popular fiction, villains who had a hunger for world domination and who lusted after white women. An early example of the sinister Oriental in the popular novel was Yen How, the leader of invading Chinese hordes in M P Shiel's *The Yellow Danger*, published in 1898.[40] Yen How, the son of a Japanese father by a Chinese woman, is a 'man of remarkable visage'. Nearly bald, but with a majestic brow, he has brooding, meditative eyes and skin that is a 'specially dirty shade' of yellow. With a degree in Medicine from the University of Heidelberg, his 'big brain' knows about all subjects Eastern or Western. Yen How embodies the East and cherishes 'a secret and bitter aversion to the white race'. He aims not only to invade and dominate Europe but to possess one white woman by any means, fair or foul.[41]

Other popular writers soon mined this profitable vein producing a host of Oriental villains. One of the best known was Wu Fang, who appeared in books by Roland Daniel in the 1920s and 1930s.[42] Another was Chu-Sheng, an evil Chinese dwarf and deaf-mute.[43] Oriental criminals featured prominently in British boys' magazines such as the *Thriller* and were also essential ingredients in American pulp fiction.[44] Here were gathered criminals such as Dr Yen Sin, known as 'the Yellow Doctor' or 'the Crime Emperor' who called down on his enemies the curse of the Dragon's shadow, which caused physical degeneration, madness and death. Or Mr Lu, the 'Blue Scorpion' who called himself 'the Man with the Jade Brain'.[45] Among the race heroes seeking to defeat the criminals of the Orient was 'The Shadow' who crossed swords with Shiwan Khan. The satanic Khan, 'a new menace of the Orient', styled himself 'The Golden Master', ruled the secret Kingdom of Xanadu and was a direct descendent of the fearful Genghis Khan. He had a 'snakelike body' and used hypnotic powers to control the minds of his enemies.[46]

While evil Oriental villains remained enormously popular, there were also more benign Chinese figures. In 1925, the American novelist and playwright, Earl Derr Biggers introduced Charlie Chan to the reading public in *The House Without a Key*. Five more Charlie Chan books quickly followed. These were used as the basis for numerous radio programs and comic strips as well as for a series of 29 Hollywood films, mainly from Fox Studios, which appeared between 1926 and 1942, starring Warner Oland or Sydney Toler. Charlie Chan was never portrayed by a Chinese actor.[47] Biggers had attempted to create an 'amicable' Chinese who supported law and order. Charlie Chan is a 'wise, smiling, pudgy' man of Hawaiian American-Chinese ancestry, who walks with a woman's 'light and dainty steps'. He wears Western clothes and is invariably courteous and charming. But his bright eyes betray a 'razor-sharp' intelligence.[48] Chan speaks a stilted, broken English and is renowned for his 'quasi-Confucian' sayings, many of which confirm the submissive role expected of women. Chan's drift can be gathered from his saying: 'Good wife best household furniture'.[49]

While Charlie Chan was the benign, though slightly effeminate, Americanised Orient, co-opted to serve law, order and patriarchy, Dr Fu Manchu was an altogether more sinister proposition. While Charlie Chan largely supported white supremacy, Fu Manchu embodied 'yellow power'. Fu Manchu, the Chinese doctor who sought to overthrow the white world, was the creation of Sax Rohmer, pseudonym of popular British novelist Arthur Sarsfield Ward. Fu Manchu made his first appearance in popular fiction in 1913, when Rohmer published *The Mystery of Dr Fu Manchu*. This book, printed for an enthusiastic American audience as *The Insidious Dr Fu Manchu*, appeared in over forty editions both in hardcover and paperback. Another 14 novels followed, making the evil doctor a household name, 'the living embodiment of the yellow peril'.[50] By 1934 Rohmer could plausibly claim that millions of people knew the wicked Chinese character who had turned him from a struggling journalist into one of the wealthiest writers of the inter-war years.[51]

Dr Fu Manchu's career was popularised through film, a medium partial to the depiction of sinister Orientals. In 1915, a Pathe serial, *The Romance of Elaine*, featured the fiendish Wu Fang, while in 1916, the equally vicious Ali Singh appeared in William Randolph Hurst's *The Yellow Menace*.[52] Dr Fu Manchu made his screen debut only a few years later in 1923, in a series of short British films starring Harry Agar Lyons. Their success was shortly followed by three Paramount productions: *The Mysteries of Dr Fu Manchu* (1923), *The Return of Dr Fu Manchu* (1930) and *Daughter of the Dragon* (1931), all starring Warner Oland. In 1932, MGM brought out *The Mask of Fu Manchu* with Boris Karloff, while in 1940 there appeared a fifteen part series, *Drums of Fu Manchu*.[53] Photographs from these productions reveal that no stone was left unturned in creating a figure of sinister portent.[54] Australians also had a chance to see this evil genius played by Bransby Williams at the Tivoli theatre in Sydney.[55] While it is difficult to know how readers or audiences might have responded, the consistent representation over many years of a figure combining fearsome intelligence with occult powers suggests a complicity in the portrayal of the Chinese as remarkably dangerous adversaries. Dr Fu Manchu presented a figure in whom European audiences could read some of their own anxieties about the 'awakening East' and 'the rising tide of colour' generically coded as the 'Yellow Peril' (Plate 23).[56]

By any measure, Dr Fu Manchu was a remarkable figure. No reader was in any doubt that he was a man of phenomenal intellect: his 'massive' head and the 'amazing frontal development of his skull' were unmistakable clues.[57] These observations situate the Dr Fu Manchu narrative within discourses on craniometry, the so-called 'science' of racial measurement. At about the time that Dr Fu Manchu made his first appearance the 'scientific phrenologist', Dr Bernard Hollander, informed a distinguished audience at the Authors' Club, London, that the massive brains of cultivated Chinese indicated that they were a people of great intellectual ability who would come to have a considerable impact upon the world.[58]

Dr Fu Manchu was described 'as the most evil and most wonderful man' the world had ever known.[59] His evil was apparent in his persistent attempts to overthrow western civilisation and become Emperor of the World. He was also a super-scientist, the most skilled medical figure in world history, a brilliant madman and a genius capable of anything. 'Genius' in this context provides another racially-coded reference, since it was a common argument among race theorists like Stoddard and Huntington that the West, in destroying its Nordic stock, had all but destroyed the primary source of Western genius. Their teacher in these doctrines was Sir Francis Galton, author of *Hereditary Genius*, and inventor of the term 'eugenics'.[60]

Dr Fu Manchu's mind was said to be a 'wonderful' instrument. Popular literature of the time exhibited a marked fascination with brains. Writers were constantly creating hierarchies of world intellect and comparing Eastern and Western minds. There was a constant struggle to win the services of top brains and little uncertainty about who owned them. Estimates of brain capacity were also much in evidence in Australian attempts to assess the progress of the Japanese. In 1906 the *Bulletin* still clung to the hope that the Japanese were unoriginal copyists whose achievement would soon come to an abrupt end. Their limited brains, according to the *Bulletin*, had taken them as far as they could go.[61] The anthropologist J MacMillan Brown held the opposite view. He argued that the Japanese had been shaped by 'the long winters of the north temperate zone', a similar environment to that which had made north-west Europe 'the brain and master of the world'. Brown believed that in modern Japan a new Asian brain had emerged, one that the European world should fear. This was 'a brain that may be its final master'.[62] The step from academic anthropology to popular fiction was not necessarily a large one.

Dr Fu Manchu's plans to control the world and eliminate the white race were invariably foiled at the eleventh hour by the solid work of Sir Denis Nayland Smith, Ex-Commissioner of Scotland Yard. The battle between Nayland Smith and Fu Manchu was a constant test of wits, though each observed strict rules of gentlemanly conduct. Summing up his old opponent, Fu Manchu believed that although Nayland Smith's reasoning powers were limited, he had remarkable intuitive gifts and could be ranked 'in the seven first-class brains' of his race.[63] Nor did Nayland Smith underestimate Dr Fu Manchu's brain. He describes attributes that would certainly have made the evil doctor stand out in a crowd: 'A brow like Shakespeare and a face like Satan. Eyes of the true cat green ... He speaks every civilized language with near perfection, as well as countless dialects. He has the brains of any three men of genius embodied in one man'.[64]

In *The Bride of Fu Manchu*, published in 1933, the evil doctor tries to manufacture a virus that would wipe out Europe. He is aided in his plan by a piece of brazen medical wizardry which allows him to bring a selection of the world's top men back from the dead. Representing 'the finest brains in science, military strategy and politics' the world had ever known, these men will be set to work on Fu Manchu's devilish schemes, drugged and manipulated into his service and little better than slaves.[65] This motif draws upon a venerable tradition in orientalist writings in which powerful Asian figures routinely enslaved those who fell victim to their terrible powers. If there was a modern warning running through Sax Rohmer's novels, it was directed to the dire possibilities that would flow when the evil disposition of the old Orient was harnessed to the destructive capabilities of modern science and a medically engineered future. Whereas the West used science to improve the human condition, Fu Manchu, it was argued, sought to harness the power of science to control the world. No horror was beyond him.

Fu Manchu further strengthened his already mighty powers by using some esoteric ancient practices known only to the East. We learn that although the great doctor rarely slept, he would sometimes be found in a trance-like state, his room permeated by the smell of incense. This was not 'a streak of effeminacy in an otherwise great man'. Not at all. This was the cunning use of potent perfumes for inspiration and renewal: 'The Delphic Oracle was so inspired; incense cunningly prepared, such as the *khyfi* of the ancient Egyptians, can exalt the subconscious mind'.[66] Fu Manchu was also the most accomplished hypnotist in the world and often consulted occult law for inspiration to maintain his world-destroying powers. The knowledge that Fu Manchu never slept was also a reminder that the East was ever watchful, ever alert, supplied with endless reserves of energy and patience. Poor Nayland Smith was run ragged, knowing that his great adversary was always on the job; the ceaseless machinations of the East required constant watchfulness.

Fu Manchu was also a master of disguise. He managed to be everywhere and to see everything. As Nayland Smith explained to his assistant: 'He is behind us, under us, and over us'.[67] He was also able to conceal his thoughts and emotions behind a mask of impassivity. His was a world of secret societies, nocturnal activities, clever feints, artful disguises, wily deception, hidden passages, espionage. In his capacity to defy normal rules of time and space, Dr Fu Manchu presented a neat analogue for the apparent ubiquity of the rapidly multiplying and seemingly inexhaustible Asian races. They were thought to be everywhere, looking into everything, appearing where they were least expected and least wanted, over-running the earth.

What Fu Manchu planned to do with the world once he had it under his control is never very clear, although the relegation of women to submissive roles evidently demanded in the Orient was vital to his program. He maintained that one of the West's major defects was the way it encouraged women to participate in public life, fostering inappropriate notions of equality. The doctor regarded this with outright contempt: 'The myth you call Chivalry has tied your hands and stricken you mute'.[68] He had a different way of doing things, more consistent, he thought, with old Chinese customs. There were older methods including the use of whips, where necessary, to bring women into line.

In attributing to Dr Fu Manchu intellectual powers beyond even the cleverest Europeans, Rohmer developed one of the more persistent tropes in the Orientalist repertoire. The notion that the Asian 'other' possessed powers beyond the European added to the unease already freely associated with superior numbers and their supposed race-mind and psychic gifts. The power of the Chinese to combine ('one hundred work as one') was a variation upon this same fear. These remarkable attributes contributed to anxieties about Asian ubiquity. They could appear anywhere and in apparent defiance of normal laws. The combined impact of huge populations, formidable brains and occult powers was rendered yet more dreadful when linked to other aspects of modern change: the sense of a contracting world, more crowded, more urbanised, with less distance between 'white' and 'coloured' races. The declining prestige of the white man contributed to this sense of spatial congestion. Somewhere in the outer darkness, unseen and largely undetected, 'they' were plotting. Clever 'Orientals', blessed with infinite patience, were undoubtedly planning their final, devastating assault on a weakened white race.

Chapter Fourteen

The Blood Tells

From the beginning of the twentieth century, as the world's population increased and as movement between societies and races quickened and intensified, the opportunities for race mixing, for merging and mingling, grew more common and more readily imagined. From the 1920s there was concern that 'the prestige of the white man' was in decline and with it the power to control populations and maintain racial and sexual boundaries on strictly Western terms. At the same time, racist theories and opinions were attracting stronger criticism. The argument began to be heard that societies which insisted upon racial purity would be overtaken by more culturally dynamic, racially diverse communities.

Lothrop Stoddard coined the term 'mental Eurasianism' to describe the culture of mixed-race people. To him they were outsiders, cultural nomads, having 'no civilisation, no country, and no history', a condition destructive to themselves and harmful to the progress of civilisation. Indeed, Stoddard feared they spelled the end of civilisation itself.[1] In his account of mixed-race union, the separate inheritances from West and East were thought to be in a state of constant conflict within the individual, just as in society, East and West fought a battle for supremacy. There could be no room for accommodation or compromise. Collapse, decline, decay, degeneration, deterioration, mongrelization, mongrel chaos: Stoddard deployed an imposing array of ugly terms to describe the dreadful consequences of mixed-race union. He described half-castes as 'unhappy beings' whose every cell was 'a battle ground of warring heredities'.[2]

Latin America provided Stoddard with some of his most drastic examples of these evils. In mixed-race Latinity, Stoddard found a 'verbal abundance', as well as 'grace, verbal elegance, quibbles even and artistic form'.[3] To some, these might appear attractive qualities, but to Stoddard they were marks of degeneracy — effeminate characteristics that had no place in a 'masculine' world. Stoddard believed that actions spoke much louder than words. He was deeply suspicious of too much talk and unstable cleverness, too much show and artifice, too much performance and gesticulation. He found in Latin America an admixture of blood so extreme, bringing such a confusion of cultures that he could not believe the formation of a unifying national consciousness was in any way possible. Disordered blood surely led to disordered politics. To Stoddard, Latin America represented a 'mongrel chaos' which he found worthy of Rome in the period of its sharpest decline.

Stoddard found the opposite qualities in the Nordic race, the embodiment of purity and race distinction. He was influenced in this belief by Madison Grant, author of *The Passing of the Great Race*, who idealised the Nordic sailor, soldier, adventurer and pioneer, but who feared the race was now in sharp decline, destroyed by factories, tenements and crowding.[4] To Grant, a modern city like New York was no more than a '*cloaca gentium*', presenting a freak show of 'racial hybrids'.[5] He feared that big, blond, adventuring Nordics were bound for extinction in America unless the country rapidly changed its immigration policies. Meanwhile, Australia and New Zealand remained important 'communities of pure Nordic blood', which could be called upon to help regenerate the once great Nordic race.[6]

George Meudell, an Australian who had made seven trips to America, would have agreed with Madison Grant's assessment of American hybridity. Writing in the late 1930s he maintained that in North America Anglo-Celtic peoples had been diluted by Teutons, Latins and Slavs.[7] The Americans were emerging as 'a synthetic race' with declining physical and mental aptitudes. They were slipping to a lower plane of development.[8] By contrast, Meudell remained proud of the 'pure-bred' Australian, although he feared that negligent Britain might allow Australia to be swamped by 'millions of [American] hybrids'.[9]

Stoddard blamed industrialisation for much of the Nordic decline. He argued that although the Nordic race had continually suffered losses through war and migration, it had nevertheless managed to retain its influence until the end of the eighteenth century. The industrial revolution brought a sharp decline as industry began to overtake agricultural production. Cities developed. Living conditions became more congested: 'The cramped factory and the crowded city weeded out the big, blond Nordic with portentous rapidity'.[10] As Nordic Europe declined, the Alpines and Mediterraneans took over most of Europe and North America. Stoddard believed that by the end of the nineteenth century, Europe had entirely succumbed to a decadent modernism resulting in a dramatic weakening of the white world.[11] A spirit of pervasive unrest, exacerbated by the seriously depleted state of the Nordic race was apparent on all sides. Finally, the Great War damaged the 'Great Race' almost beyond recovery.

Stoddard, like Grant and Meudell, attributed racial decline to industrialisation and the rise of noisily cosmopolitan cities. Stoddard believed that the modern city favoured the 'lower' races; urban complexity, crowds, noise and chaos mirrored the conflicted genetic condition of the 'half-caste'. The city was 'the half-caste' child of a civilisation grown corrupt and unclean. City-dwellers were routinely denigrated as voluble, devious, unreliable, degenerate. Cities were thought to encourage far too much mixing and mingling; too much talk, invention and experiment. Their parliaments were dismissed as places where verbosity overtook action and gestures replaced deeds. The city was seen as the site of racial betrayal. In contrast, rural folk were solid, dependably stable, patriotic. Only they were true nation-building material.[12] In 1934, Robert E Park, a well-known American urban sociologist, seeking to formulate general hypotheses about race-mixing, maintained that 'generally speaking, half-caste peoples are city folk'. He believed that great cities had always been the home of 'marginal man' who in an urban environment could play out the role of intermediary and interpreter between two cultures.[13]

But Australia, despite its high levels of urbanisation, wanted no mixed race cultures. From the 1880s, regular warnings were issued about the tragic consequences that would befall Australia if it ever became a hybrid, 'piebald' society. The nearby Netherlands East Indies already provided a cautionary example. In 1910, Mervyn Skipper, who had worked for the Eastern Extension Cable Company, felt able to write at first hand of the 'racial tragedy' of the Dutch in Java. His article in the *Lone Hand* is prefaced in bold type with a warning that the Netherlands East Indies 'swarms with half-castes' and that as the 'white blood runs thin — and thinner', the country would come to be ruled not by the Dutch, but by Eurasians. Skipper's article goes on to describe the thwarted lives, blighted hopes and social dislocation resulting from mixed-race unions. It was a 'tragedy' unfolding on Australia's very doorstep.[14]

Skipper maintained that whereas the Dutch had allowed themselves to become 'half-oriental', the British policed the colour line in the tropics unrelentingly. It had to be so. As far as Skipper was concerned, 'the man of mixed blood does not tend towards the higher, but to the lower type'. Indeed, Ripley, that great authority on race, had stated that 'a cross between races is all too often apt to be a weakling, sharing in the pathological disposition of each of its parent stocks'.[15] For those who agreed with this analysis, it followed that racial purity was vital to national strength.

The *Bulletin* agreed with Skipper's views. The journal took a hostile view of inter-racial marriages and was always on the lookout for evidence that the 'melancholy hybrid' was a 'tragedy' to himself and to his society. Neither melancholy nor tragedy had any part in what the *Bulletin* believed to be Australia's sunny future. In January 1919, the *Bulletin* warned that in a world where racial boundaries were less firmly maintained, Australia must be resolute to ensure racial purity. This meant Australians should support their Prime Minister, Billy Hughes, in denying the Japanese entry to Australia. This, the paper maintained, was 'the biggest and best school of thought' not only in Australia but probably also in Japan, a country well known for its racial exclusivity. The problem, as the *Bulletin* saw it, was not that the Japanese were inferior. On the contrary, their capacities were so great that many of the standard objections to inter-racial marriage were hard to sustain. 'The very distinction of the Japanese', the *Bulletin* argued, 'their force and intellectual gifts, make them a more serious menace in the eyes of those Australians who aspire to keep the race pure'.[16]

Returning to this question in May 1919, the *Bulletin* claimed that the British experience in India proved beyond doubt that when white and coloured co-existed, admixture of blood could not be prevented. This was evident despite the fact that the British were a particularly arrogant conquering race whose prohibitions against inter-racial unions were severe. A similar story could be told about the United States. The *Bulletin* noted that although the Negro was a lower type than the Japanese there were still 'women of the proudest white caste on earth' prepared to cohabit with black men. Here again the journal considered women the weak link. Given the demonstrated frailties of ordinary mortals, the only safe policy was to exclude non-Europeans from Australia altogether.[17]

In the early twentieth century, Eurasians were widely held to be inferior citizens, lacking both the intellectual force and the competitive energies commonly attributed to Europeans and the 'primitive' strengths associated with their non-European inheritance. The American author Edward Byron Reuter summarised their position. They stood between two civilisations, but belonged to neither: 'They are miserable, helpless, despised and neglected'.[18] They were also assumed to be excitable and terribly thin-skinned. These qualities of mixed-race people proved a fertile topic for women writing home from the East. A preoccupation with this theme developed where the burden of maintaining racial purity rested largely with women. Yet, as we have seen from the writings of William Lane, white males also suspected that women were susceptible to the blandishments of the East; they could be accused of blurring the boundaries between the races. No self-respecting white woman in the 1920s, knowing the social stigma attached to mixed blood and the distrust of their sex, could afford to be judged complacent about race-mixing. Edmund Piesse, in an adroitly argued defence of the White Australia Policy prepared for *Round Table* in 1921, emphasised the importance of women in defining and maintaining the boundaries of white society. Piesse believed white women in particular, had a 'self-protective instinct' which resisted mixed-race marriage. This he maintained was not intolerance but a 'protest against the debasement of that conception of marriage which white women feel to be vital to their dignity and happiness'. Piesse accepted that there were instances where this instinct was weak which allowed two races to combine to form a nation exhibiting the strongest qualities of each group. But, more often, the instinct was strong, making mixed marriage 'treacherous'.[19]

Gertrude Moberley's letters, published in Sydney in 1933, reveal a persistent concern about race and racial purity. She was a woman with eminently respectable connections, the daughter of the Reverend E G Moberley and the grand-niece of the Bishop of Salisbury. She knew the codes. During the first world war she worked in various Indian hospitals and on troopships carrying wounded Australian soldiers from East Africa and the Persian Gulf back to Bombay. In Durban she had been 'horrified' to see an Australian officer going about the city with a 'darkie lady'.[20] She later described one of her nurses as 'che che', the common term for Eurasians, and she described another as conspicuous for her 'golden hair and brown hands!' She referred to Eurasians as 'so many annas in the rupee', in direct reference to their degree of mixed blood.[21] But amid all the jokes and dismissive comments, Gertrude Moberley liked to add a worldly disclaimer that racial background was, of course, of no concern to her. But she noted how important it was not to 'let a Eurasian know that you know what they know you know'. To Gertrude Moberley, like so many white women of her time, people of mixed race were one of India's 'awful tragedies'.[22]

Gertrude Moberley perceived this 'tragedy' at first hand when one of her 'che che' nurses announced her engagement. Should her fiancee, a British Army Captain, be told the truth? He seemed ignorant of the fact that she was not an Irish girl, though Gertrude Moberley had soon tumbled to her background. The girl's lovely eyes spoke less of Ireland than of the alluring East. But someone soon told, and the Captain quickly broke off the engagement. Miss Moberley then felt 'so sorry' for the nurse, who then became another of India's tragedies.[23]

The sorrow expressed at this recurrent tragedy, however, did not often extend to practical help. At British schools established in the hills of India, parents often objected to the presence of mixed-race, Anglo-Indian students. The British writer, M M Kaye, in her memoirs of youth at Simla, *The Sun in the Morning*, describes how her parents removed both her sister and herself from their school when they began to exhibit accents similar to their Anglo-Indian class-mates. Indian schools tried to improve their reputation and social standing by imposing barriers to the admission of mixed-race students.[24]

The complexities of race are also to be found in the unpublished letters Dorothy Fry wrote to her family between 1919 and 1923.[25] Dorothy Fry, then in her twenties, was one of several young Australian typists working in Dutch, British or American firms in Batavia. She was a spirited, independent and modern young woman with definite opinions. Concerned to maintain her position, she kept a close eye on her bank account, while learning the ways of the world in a new, demanding location. She kept up with developments in Australia and was a keen reader of the *Bulletin* and *Smith's Weekly* and, at some cost, maintained her subscription to *Art in Australia*. She knew and enjoyed Australian poetry and wrote entertaining and observant letters. A secular tone and sceptical intelligence inform her commentaries. Dorothy Fry wrote with fond pride of Australians as a humorous, egalitarian and spirited people, whereas she found the English stiflingly class-conscious, insular and altogether too formal. Yet Dorothy Fry also inhabited an entirely racialised world, a world in which every human action had a racial meaning and in which each individual was ascribed a fixed racial identity. As a white woman, Dorothy Fry accepted the responsibility of maintaining racial boundaries.

Dorothy Fry's first contact with foreign soil was in Macassar. Going on shore, her party ventured into a narrow street where they found the 'niggers staring and laughing as much as we did'.[26] Fry was inclined to use the N-word in letters home to her father, although in her other correspondence the word 'native' was substituted. As soon as she arrived in Batavia she found much need for these terms as 'the colour question hits you at every turn you can't get away from it'.[27] Nevertheless, she found her 'first taste of the East' to be 'wonderfully interesting and strange' and she was soon recording the presence of people of every size, shape, race and colour.[28] She began to notice the 'tremendous number of halfcastes', though appearances could be deceptive. She found that some were almost impossible to detect.[29] But Dorothy Fry soon learned the ropes from a girl friend, who 'prides herself in her extreme sensitiveness to anything in the colour line'.[30] Soon Dorothy Fry found that she also had a trained eye that could unravel signs and clues to any mystery of racial identity.

Fry began to refer to a widely held opinion among the British residents, that 'pure Dutch' were extremely rare in the Netherlands East Indies. It was widely rumoured that the Dutch had become so racially mixed that not three white families were left in Holland. She considered it a disgrace that 'the breed' had been so diluted 'with the native strain':

> It is not fair to call the mongrel mixture of black and white and the appalling mixture of brown coffee & yellow results of coarse masses of flesh in the Dutch people — tho' it is said the whole race is now riddled with the black element.[31]

Dorothy Fry was particularly concerned that Dutchmen of mixed heritage who appeared and behaved as white, might marry Australian girls. These naive women might later make the humiliating discovery when their children were born that their husband had Malay blood. Java was quickly teaching Dorothy Fry that it was 'unthinkable to have an inferior black race mixing up with good British blood. The race would go down at once'. She had come to realize that no 'black person is to be trusted, the blood tells sooner or later'.[32]

Dorothy Fry became adept at discerning what the blood could tell. The discrimination started at her workplace. One girl, a capable typist, was considered beyond the pale when she was found to have a Scottish father and a 'native' mother. Dorothy admitted: 'Everyone feels sorry for her'. But little could be done: 'alas the colour is obvious, & she is never one of ourselves'.[33] She soon came across another equally difficult case: 'One very pretty girl with lovely grey eyes and black hair, sits near us', but she too had to be excluded from the social group: 'her lips are a little too full and her skin just too dark'.[34] The lovely eyes of this poor girl told the same terrible story as Gertrude Moberley's 'che che' nurse; both had to be treated, albeit with murmurings of regret, as social outcasts.

As her experience of Java grew, Dorothy Fry's sensitivity to 'colour' became even more acute. Uncovering racial identities from the subtlest of clues, hints, signs and silences required triumphs of detection that ranked alongside the best efforts of a Sherlock Holmes. Drawing the colour line called for endless practice and the constant refinement of skills. It was a collusive world which gave a particular shape and meaning to being 'one of ourselves'. Dorothy Fry drew the line not just at the Javanese and at anyone of mixed-race, but also at the Japanese. In a letter to her father in 1921, she notes that she has been reading Lafcadio Hearn's *Out of the East*. Although she had admired his sympathetic and informed account of the Japanese character, she had also found that these opinions had not softened her own anti-Japanese prejudices:

> somehow I never see the car-loads of dapper, wealthy, clever looking, & inscrutable & sly & lacking in all frankness, looking little Japs going to & from their offices without a feeling of disgust.[35]

She was aware that her prejudice was unacceptably intense, but how was she to explain that the mere sight of Japanese men in Batavia sickened her? She thought that it was 'because they are such a menace to Australia & one has in mind that they could overun Australia. I should think Australia has every & very good cause to fear the Japs'.[36] Yet Dorothy Fry was committed to openness and receptivity to new experience in what she considered a very Australian way. Racial exclusivity did not sit comfortably with this particular stance. She was forced to make efforts to defend her contradictory position:

> the more I see of orientals and coloured people generally, the less I like them. I am sure I didn't set out with prejudices & am surprised to find them growing steadily. I didn't think one's mind could close instead of expand with knowing fresh scenes & people.[37]

During her stay in Java she had come to believe, rather to her surprise, that the British had a lot in their favour. She felt this view however was 'frightfully narrow-minded' and that it would be better to be more cosmopolitan in her opinions. Yet she identified Norwegians, 'big and fair-haired, fresh-skinned and blue-eyed' as a people closest to her ideal type. Her racial preferences were becoming unmistakably Nordic. She also began to develop some definite views on the White Australia Policy, believing that purity of blood was the only basis upon which Australia could create an enduring nation. She feared once white blood had been spoilt or tainted, racial decline, lowering of standards and social chaos would inevitably follow. White prestige would be fatally compromised. Whites would be found doing jobs normally reserved for 'natives', while Eurasians and perhaps even 'natives', would do jobs that should be reserved for Europeans. Yet even as Dorothy Fry condemned the evils of race mixing, she frankly admitted that she was attracted by the variety and energy that appeared to spring from heterogeneity and difference. For all her Nordic certitudes, she experienced considerable confusion and unease at her growing intolerance. While it was easy enough to discard the shysters, ruffians and dodgy schemers encountered in mixed-race Batavia, some of the sweet and able typists who worked in her office could not be so readily dismissed as 'mongrels'.

Mary Gaunt, Australian traveller and author of *A Woman in China* and *A Broken Journey* was no less insistent on racial purity.[38] She was unhesitating in pointing out transgressions of the code. In the early 1920s, while stopping in Shih Chia Chuang in Shansi province, she encountered a striking young English woman, Mrs Chang, married to a British-educated Chinese man. Mrs Chang was a lady in distress, without sufficient money to complete her travel to Peking. Although Mary Gaunt's hosts, men from the British American Tobacco Company, did not hesitate to offer their assistance, Mary Gaunt did not feel charitable. She saw a woman who had 'committed the unpardonable sin of the East, the sin against her race, the sin for which there is no atoning'.[39] There is a whiff of the set speech about this comment and in the pronouncement that the woman had become an outcast forever:

> in marrying a Chinese, even one who had been brought up in England, she had exiled herself ... Her little child may not go to the same school as the foreign children, even as it may not go to the same school as the Chinese. She has committed the one error that outclasses her, and she is going to pay for it in bitterness all the days of her life.[40]

Other respectable women travellers held similar views. In January 1925, Janet Mitchell, Education Secretary for the YWCA in Melbourne, joined the Australian delegation to the First Conference of the Institute of Pacific Relations in Honolulu. Mitchell was very interested in immigration especially where it touched on the 'colour problem'. Although she had corresponded with YWCA workers in China and Japan and believed that young women 'are fundamentally the same everywhere, irrespective of colour, creed, and class', when she came to Honolulu, that racial melting-pot, she found she could not support the racial intermarriage she found there. She thought it brought out 'the worst features of both races' and found no comparison between the magnificent full-blooded Hawaiians that she saw out surfing or fishing, and the 'wretched half-castes' working on the sugar and pineapple plantations.[41] Mitchell also noted how the Japanese discriminated against mixed marriages and seemed comforted that the 'feeling of racial superiority was not confined to the white races'.[42]

In 1915, Australians of the better sort had a chance to comment on a high-profile mixed-race marriage between Martanda Bhairava Tondaiman, the Rajah of Pudukkotai, a dashing and wealthy, English-educated Hindu prince and Molly Fink, the vivacious, fair-haired daughter of Sir Theodore Fink, deceased owner of the *Herald and Weekly Times*. In Martanda, Molly had found a man of 'warmth, generosity and maturity, but also of polish and refinement found in few Australian men of the time'.[43] Molly's mother approved the match and the couple were wed at the Melbourne Registry Office in Melbourne in August.

The best people were not impressed. The Governor-General, Ronald Munro Ferguson, declined an invitation to the wedding breakfast at the Menzies Hotel. The Press sneered:

> Mrs Newly Wed brought her coffee-coloured husband to proudly present him to her envious acquaintances. What was her surprise to find them not envious! All agree that he is a charming and cultured man to meet — but not to marry ... Several calls which the newly-married pair have paid have not been a huge success.[44]

When the couple returned to India in 1916, the question of precedence proved a difficulty for the British Government. The Government of India was told that the lady would not be officially received. When the Rajah was later also told that the succession of his Eurasian son to the Princedom was unacceptable, he abdicated and went to live with his wife in Cannes until his death in 1928.[45] Even for wealthy and powerful couples, miscegenation remained inadmissable.

Given the strength of feeling on mixed-race marriage, it is not surprising that it formed a common theme in the popular fiction of the 1920s. The numerous detective novels by Australian author, Arthur Upfield, published through the inter-war years, featured the mixed-race detective Napoleon Bonaparte who could track as expertly as an Aboriginal, but who had the reasoning ability of a white man. Blacks tracked, whites reasoned. But Bonaparte was judged unusual. In Upfield's books, other people of mixed-race are routinely described as both touchy and inferior.[46] Their difficulties were presented more sympathetically in the work of Louise Jordan Miln. Miln, who published novels with evocatively Eastern titles — *By Soochow Waters*, *Flutes of Shanghai*, *The Soul of China* — was perhaps the most widely read writer of popular fiction set in China before the advent of Pearl Buck. In *The Vintage of Yon-Yee*, published in 1931, the reader encounters Lois Allingham, the beautiful daughter of a proud English father and an exquisite Chinese mother.[47] Though charming and sociable and at ease in both cultures, Lois finds as she grows older that her mixed blood becomes an increasing problem. There is no suggestion that her 'Chinese blood' is inferior. On the contrary, Miln provides numerous assurances that the Chinese are a powerful, enduring and civilised race. 'Chinese blood is very strong', one of her English characters asserts: 'It is the strongest and most characteristic of all bloods'. He added: 'mix it with any other blood, and it hits back even in the fourth or fifth generation or after'.[48] The difficulty for Lois Allingham lies in the incompatible mixture of her two strong strains of blood, which 'clashed and quarrelled' more and more as she grew older. Her 'half-caste' condition becomes a torment. Lois exhibited a condition which the British sociologist, Herbert Spencer, considered an inevitable product of inter-breeding: 'a chaotic constitution'.[49] At the end of the novel the tragic heroine rejects both her Chinese and her European suitor. She will remain single as she cannot bear to perpetuate mixed blood.

In A L Pullar's *Celestalia*, published in Melbourne in 1933, the Chinese-Italian heroine Talia, shows a similar reluctance to perpetuate her inheritance of mixed blood; it would always be an 'insuperable bar' to marriage.[50] Other aspects of the mixed race 'tragedy' are also to be found in American popular fiction of the time. In this literature, as William F Wu has noted, miscegenation invariably led to violence, terrible misfortune or death. In a typical story published in 1921, a young woman kills herself and her baby when she finds out that she is half-Chinese and that she has passed on some Oriental features to her child.[51]

The archetypal story of this inter-racial tragedy is *Madame Butterfly*, a short story by American author, John Luther Long, published in the 1890s, which formed the basis for a play by David Belasco and then for Puccini's famous opera. The play was first performed in Sydney at Her Majesty's Theatre in 1903, not long before the visit of the Japanese Training Squadron, while the Australian premiere of the opera, *Madame Butterfly*, was staged seven years later at the Theatre Royal, Sydney and at Her Majesty's Theatre, Melbourne. Audiences were enthusiastic. The *Sydney Morning Herald* acclaimed a performance which drew out 'the cumulative tragedy of the fateful situation'. The *Bulletin* was less impressed, scoffing at the difficulties that arose when a 'stout Frenchwoman' tried to portray 'a stoical little slave-woman of Japan'.[52]

In the not very numerous films of the early twentieth century which deal with Asians, the predominant theme is the tragedy of inter-racial love affairs. Here again there were no happy endings. In Thomas Ince's *Typhoon* (1914), a love affair between a Japanese diplomat and a young French woman ends with her murder and his suicide. In *The Red Lantern* (1911) the half-Chinese heroine also kills herself.[53] Even the more sympathetic film by D W Griffith, *Broken Blossoms* (1919) starring Lilian Gish, ends in tragedy. Although the 'Yellow Man' in the story is a figure of 'peace and honour', it is clear that in falling in love with a young Western girl, he has broken a major taboo. Although their love is never physically consumated, both die at the end of the movie.[54] *The Bitter Tea of General Yen* (1932) portrayed a platonic love affair between a Western woman and the Chinese warlord, General Yen. The woman finds the General both 'alluring and disgusting'. But her love match also ends in disaster when the General commits suicide. Hollywood clearly 'brooked no miscegenation'.[55] But screen-writers also began to learn that there was popular appeal in the titillation of interracial sex. They found that they could present this possibility, but avoid the taboo, by ensuring the plot had a twist — the heroine at the last moment is discovered to be white! This device was adopted in both *Broken Fetters* (1916) and in *East is West* (1918).[56]

In 1922, *Stead's Review*, an Australian journal with a healthy circulation of around 7,000 copies a month, expressed discontent with the prevailing ideas of mixed-race tragedy. In 1921, the journal had presented a sympathetic account of the marriage between Lafcadio Hearn and his Japanese wife, Setsuko.[57] It now criticised the 'time-worn cant' that half-breeds inherited the vices of both races and the virtues of neither. *Stead's Review* believed that the time had come for a more dispassionate examination of the scientific evidence on 'The Mingling of Races'.[58] On reviewing the findings of leading authorities, including Viscount James Bryce, Sir Harry Johnson, Professor Sir Ray Lankester, A J Macdonald and Sir Sydney Olivier, the journal concluded there was very little solid evidence for the racial decline so often blamed upon 'blood mingling'. Degeneracy in mixed race children was attributed to neglect and ill-treatment by prejudiced Europeans rather than to any 'divine dispensation' favouring racial purity. One authority, Sir Sydney Olivier, author of *White Capital and Coloured Labour* went so far as to claim that interbreeding often produced a 'more competent vehicle of humanity', because the combination of racial aptitudes and capacities from different stock was likely to produce a more richly blended and attractively complex human being.[59]

The idea was that pure blood might be thought of as narrow and impoverished struck at the heart of the White Australia doctrine, which had always identified purity of race with moral, intellectual and physical superiority. While the discussion in *Stead's Review* may not have had a noticeable impact upon public opinion, the fact that it appeared at all indicates the presence of a disclaiming voice, another sign that once secure racial boundaries were under threat.

Yet the idea that race mixing provided a strength which distinguished enterprising nations from somnolent ones had always attracted some support in Australia. J Currie Elles is a case in point. In 1906, Elles presented a lecture in Sydney to the British Empire League. He contrasted the invigorating receptivity of the British Empire to a broad range of cultural influences with Australia's narrow, suspicious response to anything foreign. Elles then argued the case for hybridity and cultural mixing as the great energising forces behind successful nations. He pointed to the contemporary Englishman who came from a 'salad of mixed French, Saxon, German, Dane, Spanish, Italian and other nations'.[60] Elles could quote many other examples where an admixture of races had proved just as beneficial. Elles made a strong case for open mindedness and cultural receptivity. 'It is the intercourse with virile races and their gradual amalgamation', he maintained, 'which cements and builds up the real nation'.[61] Elles was convinced that in the future, vigorous cultural exchange was likely to become increasingly important. In a world becoming smaller each year:

> any attempt to thwart the natural aspirations of all countries in these advanced times, must result in a stoppage of progress, if not in the absolute collapse of the country adopting such short-sighted tactics.[62]

Elles was cautious about recommending Asian immigration, but he certainly welcomed the implementation of a broad immigration policy which, in guaranteeing the rights and freedoms of immigrants independent of nationality would secure their commitment to the development of Australia and their loyalty to the flag. Elles wanted to see Australia develop into a great trading nation. But he warned that it could not do so with insular, fearful and defensive policies and with leaders ignorant of the great Asian civilisations.[63] In 1913, J MacMillan Brown made a similar case for race mixing and a relaxation of Australia's immigration policies, arguing that without this change Australia risked insularity and stagnation.[64]

Percy Grainger, composer, pianist and man of startling originality and linguistic prowess was among those for whom race and racial characteristics were matters of fundamental importance. Though recently described as 'a racial bigot of no small order', Grainger remains hard to classify.[65] He was certainly a Nordic enthusiast (he described Nordics in his 'blue-eyed English' as the 'blue-gold-rosy-race'), basing his views on the writings of Madison Grant and Lothrop Stoddard.[66] Indeed, he carried around an article of Stoddard's on the major racial groupings of Europe, which he whipped out and consulted whenever a matter of racial identity needed clarification.[67] He was convinced that Nordics were in danger of becoming extinct and lamented their passing not, he claimed, on grounds of their superiority, but because the world would be a poorer, less diverse place without them, sentiments he was happy to extend to any rare species including the 'duck-billed platypus'. Comparing the fate of the 'Great Race' with that of the platypus was not a view to be found in the solemn warnings of either Madison Grant or Lothrop Stoddard. While Grainger thought his own Nordic purity had been corrupted by the blood of his 'dark-eyed' father, he also defended 'ALL KINDS of race-blends' and 'ALL racial experiments'.[68]

The Nordic character of the Australian population was analysed in a study by J Lyng, published in the 1920s. Lyng was convinced that Nordics were superior to all other races. He believed they combined creative energy with migratory zeal and made wonderful 'warriors, sailors, pioneers and explorers'. Lyng calculated that Australia was almost 80 percent Nordic. The rest were mainly 'stolid' Alpines and quick, but superficial Mediterraneans, who were 'less amenable to discipline'. While he was convinced of Nordic superiority, Lyng nevertheless denounced racial uniformity as 'soul-destroying'. He advocated 'the blending of individuals — Mediterraneans, Alpines, Nordics, and even coloured peoples' into a 'composite body' which, in its diversity would work for the common good, making 'life rich and full and worthwhile living'. As with Grainger, this was an unusual juxtaposition of Nordic enthusiasms and advocacy of race blending.[69]

The possible benefits of racial mixing also intrigued the intrepid Griffith Taylor. As might be expected, Taylor dismissed prevailing ideas about racial purity, especially the 'Nordic fetish' of Madison Grant and Lothrop Stoddard, as patently absurd. He thought Australia should not remain a home largely for Western Europeans. Instead, he believed that racial mixture was not only inevitable but also beneficial. He proposed that Australians might inter-marry with the Chinese and thought this likely within fifty years. But in making this suggestion he tended to overlook its contentious nature, while never doubting that the Chinese would be willing to inter-marry to obtain their 'place in the sun'. He believed the Chinese had formidable skills and capabilities, greatly improved educational prospects, immense resources and were now exerting a growing influence in the region to Australia's north.[70]

In June 1923, Taylor took a march into the enemy camp and accepted an invitation to speak at Sydney's Millions Club, a group whose extravagant views on immigration and population growth he had systematically criticised. The theme of his illustrated lecture was typically modest: the evolution and migration of the human race. He criticised racial purists, pointing out that all major races were very mixed. He also confronted the problems of racial stereotyping through his favorite party trick. He presented a slide showing Robert Louis Stevenson with his Samoan cook and noted that from an ethnological point of view the cook was a more intellectual type than the famous author of *Treasure Island*. But in relation to the Australian Aborigines, Taylor held to the dominant beliefs of his time, maintaining that the Aborigines were a lowly racial group whose 'full-blooded' people would soon die out.[71]

Taylor drew attention to Australia's geo-political vulnerability and the urgent need to reach a peaceful accommodation with countries in their region. He claimed that it would be far better for Australia to admit a modest number of 'cultured Mongolians' rather than to become an enemy of China, a country that would inevitably become a Great Power. Taylor maintained that there should be no concern about inter-marriage between whites and 'Mongolians'; the 'Mongolian race' was of a high racial character, closely related to the 'Alpine group' to which whites supposedly belonged. In the past, this admixture had produced 'a strong, virile race' that was at least the equal of its parts. This would again occur when Australians married Chinese. Such inter-marriage provided a viable alternative to the White Australia Policy. Taylor asked his audience to realise that it also 'might not be a calamity'.

Taylor's views drew sharp criticism from the *Daily Telegraph*, the *Sun*, *Smith's Weekly*, and *Hermes*, the Sydney University student newspaper. The *Daily Telegraph* published a cartoon showing Professor Taylor blessing a marriage between an obese Chinese man and a handsome white woman, its caption stressing the appalling nature of this event, while awakening deeply embedded anxieties about the violation of white women by lustful orientals (Plate 24).[72] The *Sun* presented a line drawing showing Taylor cradling an ugly, half-caste infant, with caricatured Chinese features. The paper called Taylor's proposal 'repugnant'.[73] *Smith's Weekly* depicted 'Australia's Taylor-made Future' as a nightmare of miscegenation, endorsing the 'chaotic constitution' view of racial mixing when it maintained that 'the yellow half-caste ... partakes of all the vices and none of the virtues of the two racial strains, perpetually at war in his mental make-up'.[74]

Hermes followed conventional opinion by declaring that the 'tragedy of the East' was its mixed-race population'.[75]

Attacks of this kind contributed to Taylor's decision to accept a Chair of Geography at the University of Chicago in 1928, though he continued the debate in his books, insisting that there had always been more race mixing than the race purists supposed. He took as examples Britain and Japan where, in each case, a 'foundation stock' had been invaded and displaced by a different racial groupings. These were not examples of racially pure societies, as was commonly supposed, but brilliant advertisements for racial mixture, since these were 'two of the most enterprising nations of our times'.[76] Taylor believed that one of the fatal weaknesses of Aboriginal Australia, particularly the Tasmanian Aborigines, was their long isolation from this stimulus of racial admixture.

Taylor also argued that many cultural differences were frequently and mistakenly described as racial in origin. He viewed race as a biological category and believed that significant biological differences between races were hard to demonstrate scientifically. Racial differences between Europeans and 'Japanese, Chinese, Indians and Amerinds' had been shown to be biologically insignificant, which Taylor found very encouraging; it indicated that 'race prejudice' was based not on biology but on cultural differences that might be readily abolished. He anticipated and welcomed a rapid narrowing of the divide which separated white Australia from Asia and, in particular, from China.[77]

What of economic objections to an 'invasion by hordes of lower-paid, more industrious Asiatics'?[78] Taylor admitted that while it might be natural to want a policy of exclusion, he doubted it was sensible. Taylor argued in favour of a modest intake of Chinese on a quota system, believing that their presence would stimulate industrial competition and demonstrate Australia's commitment to racial equality. Such a 'far-seeing' immigration policy might also help reduce the 'race prejudice and national jealousy' which Taylor saw as the chief obstacles to world peace.[79] In the longer term, Taylor believed that the 'whole trend of racial history' was developing towards 'an amalgamation of peoples in the next few centuries on a scale never before accomplished'.[80] Taylor hoped that Australians, situated as they were in the Asia-Pacific region, would be in the vanguard of change.

Taylor asked Australians to consider two fundamental questions about their future: the costs of remaining an isolated society wedded to illusory notions of racial purity and the possible benefits that might flow from a measured relaxation of racially discriminatory immigration policies. Taylor saw the White Australia Policy as essentially misguided. This was a recipe for cultural stagnation, the Rip Van Winkle option. Instead, Australia needed closer contact with Asia, including some Asian immigration, in order for it to become a more fully energised and enterprising society. Closer engagement with Asia could create a keener, more competitive Australia, an Australia willing to engage the world.

Chapter Fifteen

Money for Jam

Early in 1919 the *Bulletin* quoted T W Heney, editor of the *Brisbane Telegraph*: 'Every Australian business-man should carry a map of China in his head'.[1] Heney wanted Australian business men to learn more about China and the possibilities it offered for trade. The *Bulletin* disagreed, arguing that European ideals differed from those of Asia and that Europeans were designed for a 'grander progress'. The *Bulletin* believed European differences from Asia related 'to the home and the outlook upon life'. The *Bulletin* saw these values as critical: 'to save that is to save the world'. Tempting though Chinese markets might seem, the White Australia ideal had a value far in excess of 'all the dollars to be gathered in a thousand years from Tong-king to Manchuria'.[2]

Soon after the *Bulletin's* dismissive response to trade with China, *Commerce*, the Official Organ of the Sydney Chamber of Commerce, concluded that the trade potential of the East was 'enormous'.[3] Even so, *Commerce* warned that before the Great War, both British and continental manufacturers had put a great deal of effort into these markets; during the war America and Japan had also entered the field as major players. Where did that now place Australia?

Commerce was not optimistic about Australia's prospects. It quoted a trade representative who declared that Hong Kong traders agreed that Australia had lost the trading 'opportunity of a lifetime'. An importer, commenting upon Australia's 'amazing indifference to market requirements', identified four prominent Australian failings: terrible packaging; indifference to complaints about poor quality products; dreadful labelling and lack of knowledge about 'exporting methods, billing, invoicing, shipping, insurance and so forth'. Similar complaints had come from India, China, the Philippines and the Netherlands East Indies.[4]

Though many agreed that Australian trade in the East needed better management, moves to develop Australian commercial representation in Asia were faltering. Some of the earliest initiatives came from private firms. In 1920, Holden and Frost Limited in Adelaide, forerunners of General Motors Holden in Australia, dispatched two representatives to Asia looking for export opportunities for leathergoods, boots and machinery. Later, with the support of the South Australian Premier, they sent Arthur Markham on a six month trip to search out buyers for South Australian flour, particularly in Singapore and the Netherlands East Indies. Persistent efforts by this company led to the establishment in 1921 of an Australian shipping service suitable for carrying flour to Java and Singapore. Unfortunately, by 1924 this service was no longer considered profitable.[5]

There were also moves from Western Australia, which was only 'two or three days' by steamship from the 'Indian Near East' although the two populations were largely ignorant of each other.[6] In 1921 a delegation of Western Australian businessmen visited the Straits Settlements and Java in order to establish the trade potential. Dorothy Fry was pleased to see them as she believed there was a promising market for Australian exports.[7] The delegation came away convinced by the impressive trading opportunities but urged that a co-ordinated national response was required to properly develop trade with the East. The *West Australian* supported the need for such an approach, noting that it was imperative for Australia to 'rehabilitate' its reputation in the East where Australian commodities already had 'a bad name'.[8]

For some time the Prime Minister, W M Hughes, had maintained that the way to develop Asian trade was through the appointment of federal trade representatives. In 1921, without prior British approval, Hughes appointed Edward S Little as Commonwealth Trade Commissioner in the Far East, to be based in Shanghai. As Sandra Tweedie has noted, it was an appointment that reflected expanding federal powers.[9] Little was an Englishman and an ex-missionary who had corresponded with Hughes on the prospects for eastern trade. This initiative was strongly attacked by the protectionist *Age*, somewhat disapproved of by the *Sydney Morning Herald* but applauded by the *Daily Telegraph* which supported free trade principles.[10] Overall, the appointment proved controversial. Complaints came from Australian residents in Shanghai that Little was not an Australian yet had near diplomatic status, that he was pretentious and had become too involved in Chinese politics.[11] Nevertheless, Little impressed the *Sydney Morning Herald* as a 'man of dynamic energy' whose knowledge of Chinese enabled him to travel without an interpreter.[12]

Speaking to the Sydney Chamber of Commerce in 1921, Little emphasised how political changes in the East were opening up new possibilities for Australian trade. 'The great centre of the world's activities', he argued, 'had shifted to the Pacific'. He reported that the Chinese were making great progress in industry, education and the development of modern transport; the Chinese now 'wanted what we wanted'. Little believed that they were ready to start spending their money on some of the comforts of life.[13] But Australia must take advantage of the 'immense trade possibilities'. This could not be done without considerable effort and in the face of stiff competition from other countries: 'If we want a share we must go and fight for it'.[14] Little may have received some support from the Sydney Chamber of Commerce, but not from the New South Wales Trades and Labor Council which passed a motion dissociating itself from his mission. TLC spokesman, Mr Carden, felt that trade with China and the encouragement of Chinese capitalism would not improve working conditions in China or Australia.[15]

At a Melbourne Conference of Commonwealth and State Ministers held in October and November, 1921, the State Premiers finally agreed that it was time 'to organise a serious national effort to open up the East'.[16] In particular, agreement was reached to allow the Commonwealth to control the inspection and grading of goods to reduce the export of inferior products.[17] The conference also agreed to Hughes's proposal to appoint commercial representatives in Asia. The Commonwealth Government had first mooted this idea in 1917 but it had not been acted on. When the conference reconvened in January 1922, Hughes presented his choice for the new position. He wanted E T Sheaf appointed as Trade Commissioner to South-East Asia, based in Singapore.[18]

Sheaf was duly appointed and given a huge area of responsibility: Manchuria, North and South China, the Philippines, Indo-China [Vietnam], Siam [Thailand], Malaya, Burma, India, Ceylon [Sri Lanka] and Mesopotamia. Although Sheaf had thirty years experience in Asia, he had to concede that this was an enormous task. He wanted to divide this territory into zones, each with its own trading centre. Sheaf was known to W M Hughes, but not particularly well qualified for his new role. Born in England, he had lived in Victoria for fourteen years while managing a citrus farm. He lacked Asian language skills but had been the representative for the American film company, Kodak Ltd., an enterprise which had taken him to Java, Malaya, Siam, North China and particularly to India. Nevertheless, his knowledge of Australian export products and their possible markets was questionable. He tended to reply to questions with generalities.[19] But by his own account, he was a much travelled man. He spoke to the *Sydney Morning Herald* of Australia's great opportunities, noting that from Singapore 'Australia is by far the nearest white exporting country to these great markets by many thousands of miles'. Why then was Australia's performance in the region so disappointing? At the time of his appointment, Sheaf had two crucial messages for Australian exporters: first, they should clearly understand that Australian goods in Asia were sold in direct competition with the best products from the rest of the world and second, that successful marketing demanded knowledge of the needs and expectations of both Asian and expatriate European buyers.[20]

Another indication that trade with the East was on the federal agenda was the official visit to China by the Tasmanian Senator, Thomas Bakhap. His trip was designed to report on trade prospects between Australia and China and to investigate Little's activities in Shanghai.[21] Bakhap's report on 'Trade between the Commonwealth and China' was tabled in the Senate in September 1922.[22] Bakhap's career contains a number of surprises which throw a fascinating light on Chinese-Australian relations. He was born in the Benevolent Asylum, Ballarat, in October 1866, the son of Margaret Hogan, an 18 year old Irish girl. His father was unknown. Within two years of Thomas's birth, Margaret Hogan married the Canton-born, George Bak Hap. The family moved to Tasmania where Bak Hap became a grocer and herbalist. Thomas was taught Cantonese by his step-father and was said to speak it fluently. He had also acquired basic Mandarin. Bakhap encouraged the view that he was half-Chinese, which is consistent with his life-time interest in matters Chinese, but not with the historical record, which Hilary Rubinstein has researched with care. The appealing notion that Bakhap was half-Chinese and deserves to be thought of as the first non-European to serve in an Australian Parliament, perpetuated recently by Eric Rolls, is unsupported.[23]

Throughout his life, Bakhap maintained a steady affection for the Chinese people and their culture. Though he was suspicious of Japanese intentions in the Pacific, Bakhap was convinced that Australians needed to learn Chinese and Japanese in order to develop effective trading ties in the region. At the same time he was an enthusiastic imperialist, a prominent conscriptionist during the first world war and a supporter of closer ties with the United States of America. In 1923 the newly elected Prime Minister, Stanley Melbourne Bruce, described Bakhap as one of Australia's foremost authorities on China. Bakhap was a lively spirit whose elegantly written report reveals a person at once patriotically Australian, yet quite at ease with Chinese merchants and Chinese customs. It might strain credulity to describe a trade report as a charming essay, but this is nevertheless the case.[24]

While Bakhap was confident that Australia could find new export markets in China, his report made it clear that the Commonwealth faced some solid competition. Other nations were already exploiting the possibilities of closer integration with 'the tremendous commercial fabric' of China. Bakhap found that Britain, America, Canada, Japan, France and Sweden had all established substantial representation. The Americans, as might be expected, maintained Consuls or Consuls-General at twenty major centres throughout China, all of which appeared to be well staffed. Bakhap was particularly struck by the fact that the Canadians had established a Commissioner eight years previously and now showed every sign of becoming an important participant in the China trade.[25] By contrast, Australia had belatedly appointed Little as its Trade Commissioner in Shanghai but did almost nothing to support his activities. In particular, Australia would not direct any aid to establish a direct shipping link between Shanghai and Australia, which might have greatly advanced the China trade.[26] For his part, Sheaf had such a vast portfolio that he had little time to extend to China. He was soon forced to concede that 'India, Burmah, Ceylon, the Philippines and China are beyond the personel touch of my commission'.[27] Bakhap warned that despite the considerable scale of the British presence in China, Australia should not rely on this representation as there were bound to be some conflicts of interest.[28]

Bakhap respected the skill and ingenuity of the Chinese and believed that many imports into China would soon be replaced by cheaper domestic manufactures. This meant that only the most innovative and intelligent trading nations would succeed in the China trade. For Bakhap, China was a formidable test of the adaptive capacities, cultural knowledge and intelligence of the trading community. But he also thought Australia had some advantages. There were important contacts among Chinese business-men in Hong Kong, Shanghai, Canton [Guangzhou] and Tientsin with some previous Australian experience. Bakhap maintained that Australia had 'no better supporters in any country' than the Chinese who had spent time in the Commonwealth. Their large department stores with their 'lifts, roof gardens, picture shows, restaurants, menageries' and their elaborate illuminations, had been based on their experience of Australian department stores, but now they often exceeded the best that Australia had to offer.[29] Bakhap wanted a Trade Commissioner in Hong Kong to help cultivate these links.

Bakhap also pressed other initiatives: a branch of the Commonwealth Bank in Shanghai and a direct shipping link to Shanghai on the grounds that the practice of sending goods to Hong Kong and then trans-shipping them to Shanghai was slow, clumsy and expensive. He was discomfited by the comparison between the 'floating palaces' that plied the trade between China and North America and the humble vessels on the China to Australia run. He made further specific comments on the opportunities for expanded wool, wheat and timber exports. Bakhap also believed there were lessons to be learnt from a close study of Chinese culinary practices. He saw possibilities in the export of fish, shrimps and wine.[30] In 1924, Sheaf also saw great possibilities in a fish trade with the East. He predicted that an Australian fishing industry developed to supply the Asian market would one day employ hundreds of workers.[31]

On one thing Bakhap was insistent: Australian manufacturers had to improve the presentation and marketing of their products. 'It cannot be too constantly repeated', he observed, 'that China is not a market into which the refuse and rejects of manufacturing processes can be profitably dumped'. This was already an old story, all too familiar to trade veterans like J B Suttor.[32] Bakhap also made it very clear Australia needed strong policies and unwavering commitment if it was to successfully compete in the struggle for the China trade. He thought the Commonwealth should use the determined spirit shown by Australian troops landing at the Dardanelles to win its share of the China market.[33] Unhappily for Australia-China relations, Bakhap became ill while he was still in China and died shortly after his return to Australia in August 1923.[34] He had very little opportunity to follow up the recommendations in his report. Moreover, despite Bakhap's knowledgeable and insightful proposals there is little evidence that they were ever acted upon or taken seriously at government level.

Yet Sheaf's appointment and Bakhap's mission indicated that there was some awareness within the newly elected Bruce-Page government that trade with the East needed to be co-ordinated. In 1922, members of Sydney's mercantile community heard the Federal Minister for Trade and Customs, Mr

Rodgers, affirm the 'positive necessity' to open new markets for Australian products. Rodgers promised a new determination to provide better credit facilities and to overcome problems of marketing. 'It would be the aim and ambition of the National Government', he insisted 'to put into the markets of the East good goods, behind which would stand the honour of the nation'. His sentiments were warmly applauded.[35] But although Rodgers looked East for greater trading opportunities, the British Empire still constituted his preferred community of trading nations. He looked for the day when the nations of the Empire would come together to determine 'an Empire food and raw material policy'. His statement mirrored Prime Minister Bruce's firm commitment to British imperial connections.[36]

Rodgers' references to 'good goods' had drawn appropriate applause. There would not have been one person present who had not heard stories that reflected badly on Australian products and practices. The pages of *Commerce* give intriguing glimpses of a nation struggling to match its trade performance to its rhetoric. Trade with the East always seemed smaller and more difficult to sustain than geographical circumstances might suggest. As in Bakhap's report, the Australian position was often contrasted with that of Canada. Although Canada seemed less well placed to develop trading links with Asia, it always appeared to be doing more and doing it better.

E S Little, the Australian Trade Commissioner in Shanghai was particularly critical of Australia's wavering commitment to developing Eastern trade. His core complaint remained the absence of a direct shipping line between Australia and China: 'It is surely unnecessary to enlarge upon the impossibility of building up any permanent trade or intercourse with a complete lack of facilities for either'.[37] Little was in no doubt that Australia had to overcome a solidly ingrained prejudice against its own goods which had built up during and immediately after the war years. In a briefing document prepared for Senator Bakhap, Little remarked: 'Every importing Hong has complaints of the way in which Australian goods come to hand'. All complained that they had lost money dealing with Australian manufacturers whose goods often arrived late or damaged or both.[38]

One specific example of the problems Little faced is given in an arresting discussion on the subject of jam. Jam was in demand by expatriate Europeans and had growing acceptance among affluent Chinese. It provided a test case for new Western products in the China market. Little maintained: 'As the wealth of the country increases and the standard of living continues to rise, the demand for these products is bound to grow'.[39] Nevertheless, Little could point to some Australians who had already decided that the market for jam in China was not worth pursuing. He also knew that Britain, America, Canada, France and Germany saw a market worth cultivating. Why were Australians, who had some of the finest fruit in the world, unable to see this too? Little knew there were many good Australian jams, but none of them were ever on sale in China.

The European manager of a foreign provisions store in Tientsin had told him that Australian jams looked so alarming he would not stock them. They arrived in hefty tins often leaking a sticky ooze that damaged and discoloured the labels, causing ink and images to form ugly splodges. The spread of rust helped complete this disturbing picture. Canadian jam was another story. It almost made Little swoon: 'The bottle was of a fine shape, the glass clear, the fruit showing through bright and without a flaw, the metal cover clean and without a stain or trace of rust and the label artistic and striking'.[40]

In another report to the Federal Government early in 1923, Little invoked the example of the entrepreneurial Canadians who had just established an elaborate salesroom in Shanghai. It was such a well-managed, modern and appropriately funded venture that an Australian business-man had left the display 'with a sense of complete despondency' at the contrast with the disorganised and uncompetitive Australian approach to marketing.[41] Henry H Cohen, a Melbourne business man who had established himself in Shanghai as the representative of several large Melbourne trading companies, was also very critical of Australia's poor performance in China. He too pointed to Canadian successes in markets that he believed should have been dominated by Australian interests. Cohen accused Australia of 'peacefully slumbering while this wonderful trade was being snapped up by other countries'.[42]

One of the issues that attracted persistent comment from Trade Commissioners was the need for trade marks that were likely to strike a responsive chord in foreign cultures (Plate 25). Many firms hoped to achieve a marketing edge by using Australian fauna as trade marks. This was misguided. Asian consumers often assumed that they were being offered tinned koala or platypus, delicacies for which they were unprepared. Sheaf catalogued some of the dangers in choosing a 'cho' or trademark for use in Eastern markets. In China, the horse was a 'token of evil', the colour yellow had a 'sinister meaning' but red was the 'sign of good luck'. Also if one was trading with Moslems, 'the mark of a pig was impossible'.[43] Sheaf was impressed by the need to find striking images for Australian goods, something sufficiently eye-catching to improve market share. For India, he suggested, the use of 'various loud types of female beauty, European or Indian'.[44] Mrs T R Bowman, President of the National Council of Women, deplored the idea, astonished that a representative of the Commonwealth should 'conceive much less suggest anything in trade relations with coloured races that might appear to lower the status of womanhood in Christian countries'. The Board of Trade agreed with these criticisms and advised Sheaf to reconsider his proposals.[45]

The notion that Australia was developing a concerted drive into Asia, spearheaded by its Trade Commissioners, Little and Sheaf, proved to be remarkably short-lived. Little resigned just over a year after his appointment, amid wildly contradictory reports about his integrity and effectiveness. The

Australian Trade Commissioner Service in China produced a document detailing press reactions in China to Little's dismissal. It noted that 'Australia's reputation has been most badly damaged and drastic action in the direction of justice is demanded if Australia is to be regarded, for years to come, as even approximating ideas of western fair play and honest democratic government'. There followed substantial extracts, all of them condemning the decision to remove Little, from the *North-China Daily News* and the *China Press* in Shanghai, the *Central China Post* in Hankow, the *Daily News* in Chefoo, the *Tsingtao Leader* in Tsingtao, the *Peking and Tientsin Times* in Tientsin and the *Telegraph* and the *Daily Press* in Hong Kong. All seemed persuaded that Little was a person of great integrity and ability who had suffered a terrible injustice.[46]

At home, Parliamentary debates told a different story. Here it was alleged that Little had accepted the position of Trade Commissioner while he still acted in a business capacity for Little Brothers Ltd. of Shanghai. This firm, although listed in his son-in-law's name, was run by Little himself. Little was accused of feathering his own nest. One speaker referred to Australian trade representation in Shanghai as a 'pantomime', another noted that leading business interests in Melbourne were so disillusioned with Little's performance that they had sent their own representative to the East.[47] During Little's brief period of office, trade with China had actually declined.[48] During the parliamentary debate on Little's dismissal, Sheaf had also came in for some adverse criticism. The veteran Trade Commissioner, J B Suttor, however, escaped the general odium and was cited as a reliable source of commercial information. By that time he had been twenty years in Japan, returning to Australia in June 1922.[49]

Some of the difficulties of Sheaf's position were set out in a detailed response to a commercial enquiry from the Universal Products company of Melbourne in September 1924. This was more than a year after the removal of Little and at the time Sheaf must have suspected that his own days as Trade Commissioner were numbered. In twelve carefully typed pages, Sheaf advised Universal Products to be very cautious about committing themselves to Eastern markets. In recent years, he believed, some quite false expectations about trade with the East had developed, attributable to people making superficial judgments about complex trading cultures that it would take a lifetime's study to understand. Armed with little knowledge, these freshly-minted authorities all too often spoke freely to the Australian press about the 'vast possibilities' and 'unlimited markets' that awaited Australian enterprise in the East. Sheaf warned that, in matters of trade with the East, it was better to be safe than sorry. He then provided detailed comments on prospects for particular Company products, giving additional background information to help them decide what to do. It was a measured, detailed, helpful letter, but it was not an unrestrained endorsement of Australia's trading future in the East.[50]

Sheaf came to be very critical of 'loose statements' that the East, particularly China, could provide 'unlimited markets'. Such statements would never bear 'the acid test of facts and figures'.[51] Here he may have been referring to some of the bulletins sent out by his colleague Little, who remained committed to 'the myth of the immensity of the Chinese market'.[52] Pointing out the great poverty of many people in the East and their frequent isolation from reliable forms of transport, he argued that for trade purposes relatively small numbers were left. The idea of millions of people just waiting for Australian trade was 'nothing but a fallacy' (Plates 26, 27).[53]

Sheaf's fears for his position proved justified. In January 1925, *Commerce* abruptly announced that his appointment had been terminated.[54] When the Bruce-Page Government had consulted the States as to whether there was support for the position, they had largely been opposed. Only Western Australia acknowledged that Sheaf's efforts had been of value.[55] *Commerce* noted that the Prime Minister, S M Bruce, had declared that the decision did not in anyway adversely reflect on Mr Sheaf. Improvements in trade were simply not sufficient to justify his continued appointment. Instead of relying on a trade office, exporting houses would be now be encouraged to send their own commercial travellers into the region. *Commerce* noted that Sheaf had produced a number of valuable reports on trading opportunities and had done what he could using photographs and drawings to indicate where the presentation of Australian goods fell below the standards of Australia's competitors.[56] While *Commerce* implied that it was surprised by the decision, it had earlier reported that the Minister for Trade and Customs favoured accredited and Government subsidised commercial travellers who would represent groups of firms in the East. Sheaf warned the Director of the Commercial and Industrial Bureau of the Board of Trade that without an official Trade Commissioner, Australia ran the risk of having its reputation besmirched: 'In many of these Eastern ports there are gangs of shady adventurers, living no honest man can understand how, and, unfortunately for the Commonwealth, prominent among them is a large proportion of Australians'. Sheaf believed that his Singapore office had done a lot to discourage such types.[57]

Soon after Sheaf's dismissal, Stirling Taylor, Director of the Commonwealth Board of Trade, prepared a chart detailing Australia's best export trade for the year of 1924. Despite a trade deficit, Britain gained the the 'best customer' title. Australian imports from Britain stood at £63 million against £45 million in exports to Britain. The value of American exports to Australia at £34 million was five times higher than US imports from Australia. Japan was rated 'a very good customer' taking £11.5 million of goods from Australia, where Australia took goods to the value of only £3.5 million from Japan. The Chinese market was thought to have been practically untouched, while trade with the Straits Settlements and the Netherlands East Indies was considered unimpressive.

Reporting the findings, *Commerce* concluded: 'Perhaps the outstanding disclosure is that Australia does less business with the markets nearest its shores — India, Straits Settlements, Dutch East Indies, China, and Japan — than she does with the British market, 10,000 miles away'.[58] On these figures, Sheaf may have been judged a failure, but they might just as easily have been used to make the case that nearby markets needed more attention. Yet as the Great Depression struck the Australian economy, the benefits of the Japanese market became very apparent. Wool exports to Japan helped cushion the economic ravages of the Depression and served as another reminder that trade with the East could hardly be overlooked. In October 1930, *Commerce* reported a wide-ranging meeting between the Minister for Markets, Mr Parker Maloney, and delegates with an interest in Eastern trade.[59]

The urgent need to re-assess this trade is evident in two comprehensive reports published in 1932. One was written by Herbert Gepp, an influential Consultant on Development to the Commonwealth Government, the other by Professor A C V Melbourne of Queensland University.[60] These Reports mark a new thoroughness in the examination of Asia's trade potential together with a new determination to create those structures needed to place trade with Asia on a secure footing. Moreover, they now related success in trade to a need for a detailed knowledge of Asian societies and cultures and also sought to repair Australia's previously tarnished trading reputation in Asia. By the 1930s the link between trade performance and cultural knowledge of Asian societies, while hardly a commonplace of the time, was becoming more widely accepted.

Gepp and Melbourne were in agreement on the importance of Eastern markets and the urgent necessity to improve the level and quality of Australian representation in Asia. Gepp reported that he continually met people perplexed that the Commonwealth had no official representatives in Asia to supply information about Australian exports, markets and business practices. There were no organisations equipped to 'tell the story of Australia or of its products'.[61] Gepp called for the prompt establishment of a standing committee or committees to review and promote trade in Asia. He also recommended 'high-class' diplomatic appointments to China and Japan, backed by suitable commercial envoys. He suggested that an Australian Trade Delegation should soon visit the East, believing that Australia was beginning to realise that its political and economic future would be 'influenced materially by Pacific Affairs'.[62]

A C V Melbourne was similarly convinced of the need for Australia to develop its own policies in relation to the East. He argued that Australia's reliance on Britain was no longer appropriate and moreover was ineffective in developing Australia's reputation as a trading nation. Australia was still conducting itself in Japan and China as if it were 'a mere dependency of the British Crown'. This was not in Australia's long term interest. Even worse, Australia had failed to develop consistent trade policies. Throughout the 1920's Australian approaches to Asian trade had been characterised by erratic switches of direction. Melbourne maintained:

> Japan and China are natural markets in which Australia may reasonably expect to sell her products; geographically they are Australia's nearest neighbours; and Australia would profit considerably from an increased personal contact between Australians and the people of the East.[63]

But for the reference to 'the East', these now appear modern sentiments, more attuned to the 1980s than the 1930s.

Between December 1931 and April 1932, Melbourne visited China, Japan and Korea on a fact-finding mission for the Queensland Government. He stayed at the Cathay Hotel in Shanghai but found the situation in the city so 'very miserable' that he doubted he would ever want to return: 'The place is the last word in disease and filth, aggravated I suppose at the present by the fact that over a million refugees are in the International Settlement'.[64] Melbourne had wanted to secure financial committments for a new Sino-Australian Trading and Manufacturing Corporation to be funded jointly from Chinese and Australian backers. But the disturbed state of affairs in Shanghai precluded this outcome.

Once back in Australia Melbourne wrote a 'personal and confidential' letter to Prime Minister Lyons setting out the eight preliminary steps necessary to expand Australian trade with the East.[65] These included the establishment of the Sino-Australian Trading and Manufacturing Corporation in China and a similar Japan-Australia Trading Company in Japan; a commercial agreement between Australia and Japan; tariff and most favoured nation negotiations; the appointment of trade commissioners in Tokyo and Shanghai, improved banking facilities and the immediate appointment of an Australian Economic Mission to Japan and China. Melbourne stressed that it was vitally important that Australians dealt directly with Chinese and Japanese financiers, rather than working through intermediaries. Though Melbourne was disappointed that more did not come of his recommendations, his expertise on trade with the East was recognised in his appointment as Chairman in 1933-34 of the Federal Advisory Committee on Eastern Trade.

Some of the recommendations forwarded to government by Gepp and Melbourne were adopted, if in modified forms: there was a mission to the East in 1934 led by Sir John Latham, though it was called a Goodwill Mission, not an Economic Mission as Melbourne had suggested.[66] In addition, trade commissioners were appointed to Tokyo, Shanghai and Batavia in 1935.[67] Melbourne, however, became increasingly concerned and sometimes irritated at Government unwillingness to develop an independent Australian presence in China and Japan. The initial response of the Lyons government to the trade commissioner proposal was to attach promising but relatively junior Australians to the staff of British consulates. Melbourne was very critical of a proposal that he felt could only intensify a position of dependence. He thought it was time for Australia to develop its own foreign policy and its own standing in the region.[68]

Nevertheless, there was solid opposition within the Australian commercial community to the appointment of trade commissioners. In October 1932, the Council of the Sydney Chamber of Commerce rejected the idea, arguing that trade commissioners had proved unsuccessful despite the fact that their official publication, *Commerce*, had previously supported the efforts of Sheaf and Little. The Chamber now believed that exporting firms themselves, rather than Government-appointed trade commissioners, were better placed to develop trading relations. Indeed, the Chamber also expressed its concern that government officials might well hamper trade by 'inspiring government regulations to the detriment of established commercial channels and usages'.[69]

Having lost the battle, *Commerce* eventually claimed that it had persuaded the government to use the trade commissioners more as 'diplomatic representatives' than as commercial agents.[70] Advertisements for positions for three trade commissioners to the East attracted a wide field of applicants. The papers of A C V Melbourne contain brief summaries from 213 of these people. This was not the complete list as other names were also under consideration. Though the biographical records are not at all detailed, some broad outlines emerge: 54 of the 213 applicants (25%) spoke an Asian language; Malay or some form of Chinese predominated, while Hindi ran a strong third. Twenty-four (11%) of the applicants spoke a European language. Nearly half (44%) of all applicants had business, administrative or journalistic experience in the East, including 28 who had had experience in China, 17 in Malaya, 13 in India, ten in the Dutch East Indies, six each in Japan and Burma.[71]

For all its sketchiness, the list is also full of interest. D G Donald of Amalgamated Wireless had continuously resided in the East between 1916 and 1926. He had had studied Chinese business methods and had travelled extensively through China, Manchuria, Japan, Hong Kong, Java, Siam, Singapore and Malaya. W M Gray, 38, had worked in Japan, Korea, China and Russia. Gray, who spoke Japanese fluently, was also proficient in Russian and French and could make himself understood in Mandarin, Korean and Persian. E F Mackie, also 38, who worked in China from 1918 to 1930 for the British American Tobacco Company, had a close knowledge of Chinese markets as salesman, organiser, inspector and advertiser. He had travelled extensively through China and Inner Mongolia, spoke Mandarin and could recognise over 3,000 Chinese characters. A H Donecker had toured China and Japan 'reorganising Dalgety's interests in the East'. By age 29, R C Slessor had lived in China for more than three years where he had studied Mandarin and Chinese culture at the Chinese University of Nanking [Nanjing] and also gained business experience. Slessor knew Shanghai and Hong Kong 'intimately'. On return, he had commenced work for the Sydney *Sun*. At 52, R Zions had been Manager of the London Java Trading Company for nine years. He spoke Dutch and Malay and had knowledge of shipping, trading, banking and Dutch law. A R Duncan was secretary of the Japanese Chamber of Commerce in Melbourne. These abruptly summarised lives suggest that Australia had a number of figures with experience in the East, a subject that invites further historical research.

One name missing from the list was A C V Melbourne. Melbourne certainly sought a position as trade commissioner, particularly to Japan. Much to his astonishment, Melbourne learnt that the government considered him too anti-Japanese to be suitable for appointment. The Japanese Consul-General in Sydney, Mr Murai, assured Melbourne that the anti-Japanese allegation was 'utterly absurd'.[72] In the event, the position was given in June 1935 to Major E Longfield Lloyd. Lloyd had an army background, an excellent wardrobe, discretion, service in the Commonwealth Investigation Branch and some Japanese to his credit. He could rely on Latham's support and had also benefited from the success of the Goodwill Mission of which he was a member. Although Lloyd had none of Melbourne's drive or creative energy, he was a gentleman and had never been outspoken about the need for an independently Australian approach to relations with Japan. He would clearly do the job that he was asked to do.[73] In the same month Vivian G Bowden was appointed as trade commissioner to China while Mr Charles E Critchley was appointed as trade commissioner to the Netherlands East Indies.[74] Bowden was an 'old China hand' who had been Managing Director of A Cameron and Co. (China) in Shanghai, but had little experience of Australian exports. Critchley, however, had previously held the position of assistant trade commissioner in Canada.[75]

Ian Clunies Ross was another convert to the view that Australia's future lay in the Asia-Pacific region. Clunies Ross later became the Director of the F D McMaster Animal Health Laboratory at the University of Sydney and had research interests in parasitology. He had become enthusiastic about Japan, having spent the year of 1929-1930 in a Research position at the Institute of Infectious Diseases, Tokyo.[76] In 1935-36, Clunies Ross toured Korea, Japan, China and Manchukuo, Japan's puppet state in Manchuria, to carry out a survey of the wool industry on behalf of the Federal Council of the Graziers' Association. In Shanghai, he met Eleanor Hinder who had been working in Shanghai from 1926 and at the time of her meeting with Clunies Ross was chief of the Industrial Division of the Shanghai Municipal Council, where her responsibilities included the monitoring of labour conditions and the promotion of regulatory practices. Hinder was characteristically forthright in her opinions of the Graziers' Association: 'I poured my scorn on the parochial viewpoint of the said organisation, which greedily wants more wool sales and will do nothing towards promotional activities'. She noted that Clunies Ross was 'astounded' by the rapid growth of wool exports over the past three years (Figure 15.1). Both discussed further ways to encourage the trade. Clunies Ross favoured the distribution of hand operated spinning wheels but Hinder dismissed this as impractical, suggesting the distribution of knitting needles with a hank of wool. She remarked that Clunies Ross appeared taken aback by her suggestion and added: 'Men do lack imagination of a practical kind'.[77]

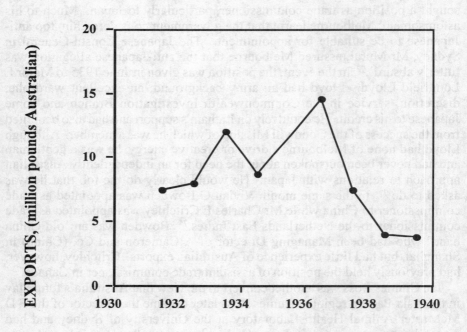

Figure 15.1: Australian wool exports to Japan from the financial year 1931-32 until 1939-40. Data from: Sandra Tweedie, *Trading Partners, Australia & Asia 1790-1993*, Sydney, 1994, p 241.

Given the growing Japanese demand for Australian wool, *Commerce* maintained a steady commentary about the need to cultivate Japan as a major trading partner. 'Continued large sales of Australian wool to Japan throughout the depression and since', *Commerce* reported, 'have effectively aided the financial recovery of the Commonwealth'.[78] In the financial year 1935 to 1936, Australia exported wool worth $14,598,000 to Japan.[79] At the same time there was a dramatic intensification of Japanese efforts to secure a trade agreement with

Australia. In September 1935 His Excellency Mr Katsuji Debuchi, a distinguished Japanese diplomat, visited Australia, accompanied by Peter Russo, an Australian living in Japan, who travelled as his adviser. Debuchi reminded Australians that for some time Japan had been the second largest buyer of Australian wool and predicted that it would soon become Australia's principal wool buyer.[80]

Through the latter half of 1935 and in direct response to the Debuchi visit, plans were made for an Australian business delegation to visit Japan early in the following year, when it was hoped international tensions might have subsided.[81] For those with their gaze fixed on commerce, the trading relationship between Australia and Japan seemed extremely auspicious. There seemed to be more visits, more expressions of goodwill, dinners and toasts to the future than ever before. The year 1935 ended with a display of Australian products in the Takashimaya Department Stores in Osaka. On the surface, the reception of the display seemed entirely favourable, but some discontent was expressed over Australian prejudices. One major wool purchaser was aggrieved that Japanese buyers received no better treatment than minor customers when they traded for Australian wool, while the manager of the Osaka branch of the Yokohama Specie Bank recalled the 'bitter experiences' of Japanese bankers in the early 1920s in their financial dealings with the Commonwealth.[82]

The May 1936 issue of *Commerce* admitted that while recent difficulties had arisen in the trading relationship with Japan, negotiations for a Trade Treaty had now 'greatly improved'. *Commerce* maintained, as it had done for a number of years, that 'any disturbance of the friendly relations between Australia and Japan would be injurious to each'.[83] It announced the publication of a goodwill report, the result of a Pacific Economic Inspection Party visit from Japan in April 1935.[84]

This was a handsome 240 page volume bearing profuse messages of goodwill from leading figures in Australia, Japan and New Zealand. Sir John Latham had contributed the leading article.[85] This publication was exquisitely timed, for its arrival in Australia coincided almost exactly with the sudden announcement on 22 May 1936 of a Trade Diversion policy, which now gave preference to British over Japanese textiles in Australian markets. The Japanese responded with a sharp reduction in their imports of Australian wool (Table 5). The matter dragged on until December 1936 when a new trade agreement was signed, though with quotas applying both to the volume of wool imported by the Japanese and to Australian imports of Japanese textiles. The Trade Diversion policy highlighted the competing pressures that were acting upon the Lyons government.[86] Was Japan the way forward to a new trading future or were Australia's interests better served by protecting the trading relationship with Britain?

Chapter Sixteen

Pacific Citizens

As the twentieth century burst upon a waiting world, the well-known American author, Hubert Howe Bancroft, predicted a mighty future for the Pacific.[1] He foretold that the region would soon be converted to a new centre of world power by Anglo-Saxon enterprise. Bancroft observed that as early as 1852, when Japan remained 'wrapped in barbaric conceit' and Australia was the 'land of the black bushman', William H Seward, later American Secretary of State under President Abraham Lincoln, had seen the Pacific Ocean as 'the chief theater of events in the world's great hereafter'.[2] Commodore Perry's mission to Japan in 1853 was taken as an early sign of this recognition of an emerging Pacific future. Another was the opening of the Panama canal in 1914, a project energetically promoted by President Theodore Roosevelt.[3] In 1902 Archibald R Colquhoun, one of the leading British writers on the Far East, declared that the 'great struggle of the twentieth century' would occur in the Pacific.[4] Frank Fox, former editor of the *Lone Hand*, made a similar point in *The Struggle for the Pacific*.[5]

Heightened awareness of the potential of the Pacific fostered a trans-Pacific community of writers and intellectuals who charted the commonalities of the region and its many lines of division and potential conflict. In 1913, one of these figures, J Macmillan Brown, writing in the *Sydney Morning Herald*, described American plans to develop a new American Asiatic Institute. This 'powerful body' would analyse 'the Pacific and Eastern Asia'. Brown, who feared the Japanese might assimilate the 'white races' to the Orient, 'as the lamb is assimilated to the wolf', urged the Americans to include all the white nations of the Pacific in the proposed Institute, where they could give each other mutual support.[6] At the same time, Brown argued that the Institute should become a racially diverse organisation, prepared to push 'white nations' into adopting 'conciliatory methods and tones' in dealing with racial issues. The advent of the Great War prevented further development of the American Asiatic Institute, but it did not stop further calls for education and conciliation in Pacific affairs.

The war caused a sharp decline in German commerce in the Pacific. This presented openings for new competitors to enter the field, opportunities that were largely exploited by the United States and Japan. Their products became increasingly prominent in Australian stores. Towards the end of 1916 one commentator observed that warehouses all over Australia were filling up with Japanese manufactured goods, a development that caused him some unease. In 1928, the American author, Nicholas Roosevelt, depicted the changing balance of power in the Pacific (Figures 16.1 and 16.2). Before 1914, the power of Japan and the United States was relatively low. From 1915 onwards their influence increased dramatically. In contrast, the power of the United Kingdom, which had been dominant before 1914, now markedly decreased. Russia had a period of rising influence between 1890 and, despite the set-back of the Russo-Japanese war, maintained this position until 1915, when its power in the Pacific also fell sharply.[7]

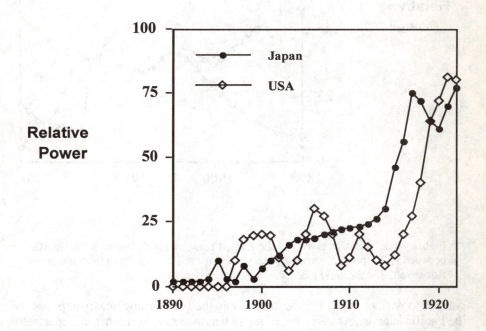

Figure 16.1: Relative power of Japan and the United States of America in the Pacific between 1890 and 1922 on an arbitrary scale of 1 to 100. Redrawn from Nicholas Roosevelt, *The Restless Pacific*.

Another sign of a growing Pacific awareness in Australia was the appointment in 1917 of James Murdoch to a Lectureship in Oriental Studies at Sydney University. To those who saw no necessity for such a position, Murdoch pointed out that Australia could hardly ignore a discipline expanding rapidly in Germany, Britain and America. He explained that his teaching and research work would focus on Australia's near Pacific neighbours: Japan, China, India, the Dutch East Indies and the Philippines, countries 'whose needs may be

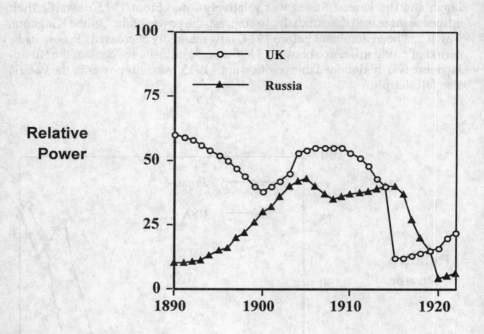

Relative
Power

Figure 16.2: Relative power of the United Kingdom and Russia in the Pacific between 1890 and 1922 on an arbitrary scale of 1 to 100. Redrawn from Nicholas Roosevelt, *The Restless Pacific*.

catered to with profit'.[8] He did not include the 'wide-flung yeasty expanse' of the Pacific Islands. As suspicion of Japan was then running high, the Department of Defence asked Sydney University to announce the new appointment. They did not want it widely known that Murdoch had been brought from Japan to teach Japanese at the Royal Military College, Duntroon, though he was aware that both the Department of Defence and commercial interests wanting to develop Eastern trade had backed his appointment.[9]

Murdoch worked closely with Edmund Piesse, Director of the Pacific Branch of the Prime Minister's Department. Writing to Piesse in 1919, Murdoch pointed out the need for a clear policy towards Japan as a necessary basis for an independent Australian foreign policy attuned to the role that Pacific trade would come to play in Australian affairs.[10] Murdoch also believed that the modern citizen should know something of the great civilisations of Japan, China and India. He supported the teaching of Asian languages in Australian High Schools and helped introduce Japanese at Fort Street High School, Sydney. It pleased him when, in 1919, the first of these students took their intermediate examination in Japanese under the guidance of their teacher, Mr Miniechi Miyata.[11]

Murdoch wanted Sydney University to become a leading school of oriental studies but his death in 1921 set back this cause. It also denied students the final volume of his history of Japan covering the momentous Meiji period. Professor Mungo MacCallum, Shakespeare scholar and close friend, noted in his obituary that Murdoch had clearly understood what many denied: 'that Australia is primarily a Pacific, and therefore an Eastern power'. MacCallum, like Murdoch, believed Australians needed 'a thorough knowledge' of their Pacific neighbours.[12]

In 1919, a new journal, the *Pacific*, was published in Sydney to encourage interest in the nations bordering the Pacific. Although the *Pacific* gave editorial support to the White Australia Policy, it also argued that Australia's proximity to Asia made it one of 'the most fortunate of nations'. But the advantages of this location could only be realised if Asian cultures were well understood. The *Pacific* urged the inclusion of Asian history in the school syllabus, with Asian 'languages and writings' as electives. In 1923, it maintained: 'we have more to gain by a proper understanding of Asia and the people thereof than can ever come to us through the most intimate knowledge of Europe and America'.[13] Arthur Sadler, Murdoch's successor, supported these views, contending that 'the real civilisation of art, literature and thought' was Oriental.[14]

The *Pacific* sought to correct a cultural bias against Asia in the values and practices of the wider Australian community. The journal's attempts to present 'Asia' in a positive light was sometimes coupled with dismissive comments about 'average' Australians. 'Asianists' writing for the *Pacific* ran the risk of substituting the established caricatures of the backward East and the progressive West with new caricatures contrasting clever Asia with backward Australia. There were better, more convincing ways to encourage a greater interest in Asia-Pacific affairs. The *Pacific* could expect more success when it argued for an Australian role in promoting peace at a time when tensions between America and Japan were increasing.[15]

An even more ambitious trans-Pacific publication, the beautifully illustrated Sluyter's *Monthly East Indian Magazine*, made its first appearance in May 1920. Sluyter's was later retitled *Inter-Ocean* and then became the *Java Gazette* (Plate 28). Published in Batavia, the journal was intended for those 'businessmen in America, British India, Australia, Japan and China' who recognised the Pacific as an 'extraordinarily important Commercial Sphere'.[16] Through the 1920s, it published commentaries on Pacific cultures. Articles on Australia included regular contributions from the economic journalist, H D Newby and the Commonwealth Trade Commissioner, E T Sheaf.[17]

Other journals promoting the idea of a new Pacific era included *Mid-Pacific Magazine*, which ran from 1911 to 1936, when it was retitled *Pan-Pacific*. It carried regular commentary on Australia. *Pan Pacific Progress: A Magazine of International Commerce and Service*, run by American business interests Los Angeles, maintained that 'the greatest movement in civilisation ... will take place on the Pacific Coasts'.[18] One of its patrons was David Starr Jordan, warrior against race suicide and friend of David Stead, the opinionated father of the Australian novelist Christina Stead.[19] *Stead's Review*, no relation, also published commentaries on Asia through the 1920s, including bylines from its Asia correspondent, John Brailsford. *Stead's Review* was the first Australian journal to regularly publish articles by Asian intellectuals including the text of a powerful speech by Yasuke Tsurumi given to the Pan-Pacific Club, Tokyo, analysing Japanese responses to the anti-Japanese American General Immigration Act of 1924.[20] As another indication of the growing interest in the Pacific as a region for study and comment, the number of books dealing with the Pacific region catalogued by the Library of Congress rose dramatically after 1900 (Figure 16.3).

Journals dealing with the Pacific region invariably promoted the cause of 'understanding' among Pacific nations. Griffith Taylor also saw this as one of his aims as Professor of Geography at Sydney University, an appointment which initially complemented Murdoch's focus on the Orient. In November 1923, Taylor maintained that Australian students needed to study the resources and capabilities of their own country in a Pacific context. How many Australians, he asked:

know anything of Java, of the Malay States, of the Philippines, Papua and the Melanesian Islands; to say nothing of those huge populations of China and Japan some two or three weeks away from our northern frontier.[21]

From October 1920, the *Sun* published a series of articles on Taylor's field research in the Netherlands East Indies which described the resources, racial character and strategic significance of the region. Taylor urged Australian scientists to compare Timor with the fertile islands of Java, Sumatra and Borneo in order to gain a better appreciation of the difficulties of white settlement in northern Australia. Travel in the name of science became a dominant motive of his life, providing the title for his autobiography, *Journeyman Taylor*.[22]

Taylor belonged to a growing community of international scientists with Asia-Pacific interests. The Pan-Pacific Union, which originated in Honolulu in 1917, organised a major forum, the Pan-Pacific Science Congress, for the exchange of views between these experts. The first Pan-Pacific Science Congress was held in Honolulu in 1920.[23] In 1923, Taylor joined the Second Congress, held in Melbourne and Sydney. This included a delegation of Japanese scientists, whose presence coincided with the great Kanto earthquake, an event that received extensive media coverage in Australia.[24] Prominent among the Americans at the gathering was Ellsworth Huntington whose book, *West of the Pacific*, published

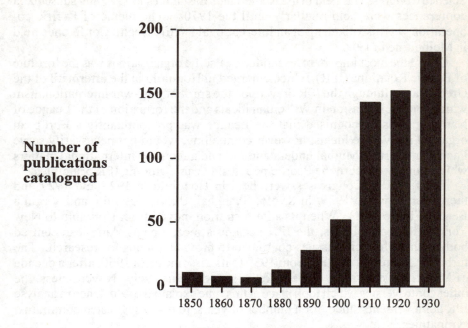

Number of publications catalogued

Decade beginning in the year

Figure 16.3: Number of publications catalogued as dealing with the Pacific region by the Library of Congress, Washington DC, in the years 1850 to 1939. Publications which dealt with only one Pacific nation or with only a limited area of the Pacific coast have not been included.

in 1925, treated issues of climate, settlement and race as common Pacific themes.[25] Huntington believed that the development of the Australian continent was best understood in relation to settlement issues around the Pacific littoral, particularly in China and Japan.[26]

In 1926, Taylor joined 14 Australasian delegates to the third Pan-Pacific Science Congress in Tokyo, where a new Pacific Science Association was created. Taylor's account of the meeting and of his extensive travels through the East later appeared in the *Sydney Morning Herald*.[27] He was particularly impressed by an evening he and other Australian colleagues had spent as guests of a Japanese scientist; this had been a rare opportunity to see the interior of a

Japanese home and to meet Japanese people socially.[28] The fourth Pan-Pacific
Science Congress was held in the Netherlands East Indies in 1929 and subsequent
conferences were held regularly until the 1970s. The theme of Pacific co-
operation was also taken up at an International Pacific Health Conference held
in Melbourne in 1926.[29]

One of the most important and enduring Pacific organisations was the Institute
of Pacific Relations (IPR), which emerged in Honolulu in the aftermath of the
Great War. Although the IPR drew upon the spirit of post-war internationalism
which found expression in Wilsonian ideals and the formation of the League of
Nations, it also recognised that the League was predominantly a European
organisation whose ideals, however compelling, would not necessarily serve
Pacific interests. 'Mutual understanding' and a focus on international matters
which 'vitally concern the Pacific peoples' became guiding IPR principles.[30]

The first IPR Congresses were held in Honolulu in 1925 and 1927 and
thereafter, down to 1939, in Kyoto, Shanghai, Banff, Yosemite and Virginia
Beach (Figure 16.1). When its administration moved from Honolulu to New
York in the early 1930s, the IPR became a more openly American-centred
body, although Pacific issues continued to provide a focus for research. The
turbulent history of the IPR from 1939 to its dissolution in 1960, after a decade
of McCarthyist assaults lie beyond the scope of this study. Nevertheless, the
bitter controversies which took place at this time explain the reluctance to analyse
IPR achievements since, for a number of years, to do so suggested communist
sympathies.[31]

In 1921, the agreements reached at the Washington Conference between
Britain, France, the United States and Japan, created new mechanisms for the
regulation of regional disputes in the Pacific. At the same time, the Treaty for
the Limitation of Naval Armaments which was signed by Britain, the United
States and Japan, effectively replaced the Anglo-Japanese Alliance, and again
promised to maintain peace. These new developments encouraged the hope
that a Pacific community of nations was an achievable goal.[32] By 1928, C
Hartley Grattan could declare that high-sounding predictions about the Pacific
becoming the 'principle arena of international politics' had been heard so often
they had become platitudes.[33]

Herbert Croly, editor of *New Republic*, claimed the Washington Conference
had provided the first ever 'sketch of a Pacific regional community'. Fearing
this 'sketch' might all too soon be erased, Croly lent his considerable authority
to the ideals embodied in the IPR: the development of a 'society of nations' in
the Pacific 'bound together by an internationalized body of water'. To achieve
its ends, Croly urged the Institute not to exert a direct influence on the politics
of Pacific nations but to use indirect methods of 'inquiry, study, and consultation'.
For those who heard the call, modern internationalism was a captivating ideal.
No one has captured the spirit of this 1920s era more compellingly than Frank

Moorhouse in *Grand Days*. The life of his main protagonist, Edith Campbell Berry, resonates strongly with the outlook and experience of certain IPR figures, not least Persia Crawford Campbell.[34]

The Institute's delicate mission was brilliantly laid out in a series of letters from J Merle Davis, General Secretary of the IPR to the Chairman of its Pacific Council.[35] Davis, a tall, spare and persuasive man, had been born and raised in Kyoto. Between April and September 1926 he toured Pacific countries to publicise the work of the IPR. In Japan, Davis argued that the IPR might prove a useful forum for the discussion of Pacific issues but warned that the Japanese should not be preached at.[36] He noted that in the past four years, two disasters had struck Japan: the Kanto earthquake and the discriminatory US Immigration Act of 1924. Whereas the earthquake had spurred the rebuilding of a devastated Tokyo, the US Immigration Act had wounded Japanese pride in a manner that was harder to repair.[37] Japan had long respected the United States; its first diplomatic mission of the modern era had been sent to Washington DC in 1860 and since that time many Japanese had studied in America.[38] The Japanese now found the American legislation insulting and perplexing. At the Pan-Pacific Club, founded in Tokyo in 1924, Davis heard Yasuke Tsurumi's sombre appraisal of Japanese responses to the US legislation. Davis could well understand that Japan now felt particularly vulnerable to American power.

In China, Davis was saddened by the poverty of the people, by European arrogance and the lack of effective government. Shanghai was reduced to an armed camp where Chinese were treated as second class citizens. Regardless of social class, they were ignored in banks and commercial houses and shut out of clubs and restaurants. Yet Davis considered the Chinese a 'marvelous people' with much to teach the West. Davis feared the IPR would be a much depleted body without Chinese participation.[39]

In Sydney, Davis met some of the key Australian students of Pacific affairs, including the Head of the NSW Branch of the IPR, Sir Mungo MacCallum and its Chairman, Professor Griffith Taylor. Taylor later recalled how Davis, the 'enlightened Internationalist', had spoken of 'the Circle of Fear' in the Pacific and 'the harm it was doing to world relationships'.[40] Davis was impressed by the calibre of those he met, including Archibald Charteris, an authority on international law and immigration, the economists, R C Mills and G L Wood, and A L Sadler, a cultural historian of Japan. Davis already knew of the group's Honorary Secretary, Persia Campbell, through her work on Chinese immigration.[41] Davis also met Brunsdon Fletcher, author of *Problems of the Pacific* and editor of the *Sydney Morning Herald* and R W Cambage, President of the Australian National Research Council. He knew both as influential supporters of the IPR.[42]

Janet Mitchell, Honorary Secretary of the Victorian branch of the IPR, organised a busy schedule for Davis in Melbourne, including meetings with the

Victorian Attorney General, Frederic Eggleston and Sir William Harrison Moore, President of the League of Nations Union. Davis spoke with key figures in academe, including P D Phillips, a respected writer on Pacific affairs and to prominent people in the business community, the labour movement and the press.[43] The newspapers carried positive accounts of the IPR's work.[44] Davis also briefed Prime Minister S M Bruce's Private Secretary on the aims and objectives of the IPR and noted that J G Latham, the Commonwealth Attorney General, whom he had been unable to meet, nevertheless 'heartily endorsed the Institute'. Latham, Eggleston and Piesse were experienced internationalists and were Australian members of the British Empire Secretariat in Paris at the end of the war. Davis also addressed an audience of 1,800 people at Wesley Church and reached a further 50,000 by radio broadcast.[45]

Although satisfied with his Australian tour, Davis had found it was 'no special asset to be an American'. Australia faced an influx of 'vulgarities of all sorts' from America and there was ill-feeling that Americans had grown rich while allowing others to bear the brunt of the fighting during the Great War. It was suggested in some quarters that the IPR was merely a front for American interests. Yet Davis thought that IPR aims were largely understood and appreciated, although he doubted the 'average' Australian had much interest in the Pacific. Some of the 'wisest men' in the Commonweath had expressed their concern over this insularity, welcoming a body that might make Australians more aware of their 'responsibilities and opportunities' in this region.[46]

Australia intrigued Davis. He could understand its emphasis upon the White Australia policy but thought international respect for this aim would have been greater had Australians settled their large continent more quickly and effectively. Like so many others, Davis was worried by the contrast between 'empty' Australia and 'teeming' Asia. But he appreciated the difficulties of tropical settlement, doubting white women could maintain reproductive health in tropical heat. He also noticed a 'self-conscious and nervous attitude' towards Japan, adding: 'the mere mention of the name makes people start and look unhappy'.[47] He was told that suspicion of Japan had been manufactured by certain politicians and sections of the press.

Janet Mitchell, Education Officer in the Melbourne YWCA and cousin of George Morrison, was the only Australian woman to attend the founding IPR Congress in 1925 (Figure 16.1).[48] In Honolulu, she joined representatives from the United States, China, Japan, Canada, New Zealand, Hawaii, the Philippines and Korea. It was an inspiring international event which set Mitchell on a new path as a journalist. In the next decade she was to file news reports from eastern Russia, Mongolia, Japan, the Philippines and China.[49]

In 1927, the Australian delegation to the second IPR Conference was headed by Frederic Eggleston, who later became Australia's first ambassador to Nationalist China. In his address to the conference, Eggleston acknowledged the 'immense complexity' of the Pacific, but warned delegates not to 'argue from European analogies or be dominated by a European psychology'.[50] Their task was rather to create new Pacific responses and approaches to regional issues. While promoting regional stability and peace, Eggleston also emphasised that Australians sought to develop their unique continent in their own way. The proceedings from the second IPR conference were quickly published as *Problems of the Pacific*, edited by the New Zealand economist, J B Condliffe, then Research Secretary of the IPR.[51] Edmund Piesse considered this to be the most informative examination of the region ever published, a judgment which carried some weight.[52]

Frederic Eggleston again led the Australian delegation to third IPR Conference held in Kyoto in 1929.[53] Ian Clunies Ross, an urbane young scientist then completing his year's research at the Institute for Infectious Diseases in Tokyo, was among those attending. In a chatty letter to his mother, he described the other Australian delegates, adding that Kyoto was a dream of 'old world civilised loveliness'.[54] Again Eggleston congratulated the IPR on its work, which was helping Australians to become 'better citizens of the Pacific world'. Eggleston also admitted, tellingly, that Australians would need to improve the living conditions of Aborigines, an admission that Australia's record on race relations was likely to come under close scrutiny in future Asia-Pacific forums. But Australian problems were largely swept away by the unremitting tensions between the Chinese and Japanese delegations, an unmistakable discord which precipitated one of the most powerful debates Eggleston had ever heard.[55] The episode highlighted the IPR's difficulties in endeavouring to define and understand the nature of Pacific citizenship, while mitigating the numerous threats to this ideal.

As with Clunies Ross, Kyoto created a profound impression on Eggleston. He spent as much time as possible visiting its temples and shrines, where the gardens were in brilliant autumn colour, gratifying 'instincts long starved'.[56] He might also have enjoyed Kyoto's Gion district, with its narrow, stone streets, lanterns, tiny bars and teahouses where there was always a chance of sighting a fabled geisha gorgeously attired, passing by with tiny steps, her face painted a startling white. Along the famous Philosophers' Walk, with its gliding stream, flanked by cherry trees, Eggleston pondered the sharp differences between Australia's newly emerging society and the deeply ritualised human landscape of Japan.

The fourth IPR Conference was held in Hanchow [Hangzhou] and Shanghai, China in 1931. Now the tensions between Japan and China, inflamed by the Manchurian crisis, almost destroyed the gathering.[57] It was hastily moved to the International Quarter in Shanghai; the safety of the Japanese delegation could not be assured in Hangzhou. Janet Mitchell, attending her second conference, was struck by the fact that the IPR had become a much more imposing event than had seemed possible in 1925.[58] While impressed by the leader of the

Japanese delegation, Dr Inazo Nitobe, liberal internationalist and author, her 'outstanding personality' was Dr Hu Shih, the leading Chinese educationist and reformer.[59] Mitchell spent most of her time at the Conference with Miss Wu Yih-Fang, an educator from Nanking [Nanjing] and Sophia Chen-Zen from the National University, Peiping. Although she valued these contacts, Mitchell now doubted the IPR's influence as a force for peace. The divisions between the Chinese and Japanese had become so intense that continuing conflict appeared inevitable. Despondently she accompanied her old friends, Dr and Mrs Stuckey, on a trip north to Peiping [Beijing] before proceeding to Manchuria to investigate the effects of the Japanese occupation. Later, she published a novel based on her experiences in Harbin. The collapse of the Washington Treaties and Japan's withdrawal from the League of Nations in 1933 contributed to Mitchell's growing conviction that the Pacific was becoming a centre of world conflict.

Although the IPR began to lose its Pacific focus after the 1931 Conference, its meetings continued to be attended by Australian delegates. In retrospect, it is apparent that IPR activities, particularly in the years from 1925 to 1931, helped create a group of Australians who were attracted by the prospect of Australia developing closer links with the Asia-Pacific region.[60]

In 1934, the Australian Government sent a Goodwill Mission to the East, led by Sir John Latham, the Commonwealth Attorney General. When viewed against the background of IPR activities over the preceding decade, this was not quite the singular initiative that it might first appear to have been. The work of the IPR had done a great deal to create an atmosphere in which the Goodwill Mission could be presented as a timely gesture.[61] Its primary purpose was 'psychological'. It visited the Netherlands East Indies, Cochin-China [Vietnam], China and Japan and was, in Latham's words, 'the first mission of a diplomatic character which the Commonwealth of Australia has sent to foreign countries'. The stability of the Pacific and the peaceful resolution of conflict in the region were singled out as matters that concerned Australia very closely.

While Eric Rolls has characterised Latham as a haughty and ineffectual anglophile, there is no question that he was a very senior and distinguished political figure, hardly noted for his warmth, but with a background in foreign affairs dating from the Paris Peace Conference.[62] He was accompanied on the Goodwill Mission by E Longfield Lloyd, then an officer in the Commonwealth Attorney General's Department and by A C Moore from the Department of Trade and Customs. Two journalists, Frank Murray of the Sydney *Sun* and F M Cutlack from the *Sydney Morning Herald* and Latham's wife and daughter also accompanied the Mission.[63]

The Goodwill Mission generated considerable publicity. The *Osaka Mainichi*, a leading Japanese newspaper, printed a substantial supplement on Australia.[64] Melbourne University graduate and linguist, Peter Russo, working close to 'the pulse of Japanese student life' at Tokyo University of Commerce, noted how for weeks after the visit University clubs 'discussed Pacific relations, the importance of a thorough understanding with Australia, and the necessity of having closer cultural ties between the two countries'.[65] Many years later, Russo described Latham as a 'British Empire forever man' who saw Australia's role in the East as largely a matter of supporting British foreign policy. Moreover, Latham was sceptical about the technological capacities of the Japanese, raising a 'scornful eyebrow' when Russo begged to differ. Russo also complained that Longfield Lloyd went out of his way to be taken for an English gentleman at official gatherings in Tokyo.[66] Latham might well have considered Russo too overtly Australian in manner and style to hold any official posting, whereas Longfield Lloyd was obviously considered an utterly loyal and dependable fellow. As Ruth Megaw has noted, Latham was reluctant to concede that the British imperial order might prove impermanent.[67]

Russo's friend, A C V Melbourne, was prominent among the intellectuals of the 1930s who wanted Australia to develop a more informed relationship with Asia. Melbourne, however, operated largely outside the framework of the IPR. He promoted an Australian-based foreign policy, not because he was anti-British, but because he believed that Australia had to raise its profile in the region. In his voluminous letters to people of consequence he maintained that attempts to expand exports to Asia would fail if undertaken in a cultural vacuum. Melbourne sought government support for the creation of a School of International Relations in Canberra and for quality Australian journals covering Asia-Pacific issues.[68] Academic exchanges had been part of Melbourne's brief on his 1931 tour of China and Japan, but distracting trade discussions and turbulent conditions in China meant that little was achieved.[69] After a second visit in 1936, Melbourne reported in more detail on the encouraging prospects for academic exchanges with China and Japan.[70]

Ian Clunies Ross was among the first to appreciate the benefits of establishing close research links with Asian colleagues. He spent a formative year in Japan in 1929-30 acquiring a greater knowledge of Japan and the region, interests fostered by his friendship with Professors A L Sadler and Griffith Taylor.[71] By the early 1930s, Clunies Ross saw the need for a thorough examination of Australia's relationship with Asia. He used his considerable charm and powers of persuasion to assemble an impressive list of contributors for his book, *Australia and the Far East: Diplomatic and Trade Relations*, published in 1935 in conjunction with the Australian Institute of International Affairs (AIIA), the Australian Branch of the IPR. *Australia and the Far East* sold well, was soon reprinted and generated a steady flow of royalties for the AIIA. It became one of the landmark studies of Australia's interactions with Asia.[72]

Australia and the Far East located trade issues within the broader framework of cultural diplomacy.[73] Clunies Ross had been impressed by a recent British report which had praised American foresight in promoting US culture in China. The Americans had used their Boxer indemnity to finance a scholarship program

Table 1: Australian Delegations to IPR Conferences 1925-1939

Date	Place	Delegation (* Leader)	Affiliation
1925	Honolulu 30 June-14 July	Stephen Henry Roberts*	Melbourne University
		Fred E. Brown	Graduate Melbourne University
		H Duncan Hall	Sydney University
		J T Massey	Australian YMCA
		Janet Mitchell	YWCA, Melbourne
		Dr E J Stuckey	Medical Missionary, China
1927	Honolulu 15 July-19 July	F W Eggleston*	Former Attorney General, Vic
		Persia Campbell	Industrial Commission NSW
		C H Currey	Sydney Teachers' College
		H Duncan Hall	Syracuse University, NY
		G L Wood	Melbourne University
1929	Nara and Kyoto 23 October- 9 Nov	F W Eggleston*	Solicitor, Melbourne
		Tristan Buesst	Secretary, RIIA, Vic.
		Persia Campbell	Industrial Commission of NSW
		A H Charteris	Sydney University
		C H Currey	Sydney University
		Mrs Harry Emmerton	Melbourne
		Eleanor Hinder	National YMCA, China
		Ian Clunies Ross	Infectious Diseases, Tokyo
		A L Sadler	Sydney University
		Georgina Sweet	President, YWCA, Melbourne
		G F Taylor	*The Age*, Melbourne
1931	Hangchow [Hanzhou] and Shanghai 21 October -2 Nov	Sir William Harrison Moore*	Melbourne University
		Tristan Buesst	Secretary, RIIA, Vic.
		H W Gepp	Development and Migration Vic.
		Eleanor Hinder	National YMCA, China
		Janet Mitchell	YWCA, Sydney
		Mrs Ernest Scott	Melbourne
		Dr E J Stuckey	Medical missionary, China
		Mrs E J Stuckey	Missionary, China
		Muriel Swain	Labor Statistician, Sydney
1933	Banff 14 August- 26 August	Ernest Scott*	Melbourne University
		Mrs Ernest Scott	Melbourne
		Alfred T Stirling	Barrister, Melbourne
		Georgina Sweet	President, YWCA, Melbourne
1936	Yosemite 15 August-29 August	F W Eggleston*	Solicitor, Melbourne
		D. B. Copland	University of Melbourne
		Constance Duncan	Bureau of Social and International Affairs
		E C Dyason	Engineer, stockbroker, Melbourne
		W M Gray	AIIA, Melbourne
		J F Nimmo	University of Melbourne
		Miss B A Rouch	Bank of NSW, Sydney
		Jack Shepherd	Hon. Secretary, AIIA
		N B Tindale	University of Adelaide
1939	Virginia Beach 18 November- 2 Dec	Jack Shepherd*	Columbia University, NY
		John J Crawford	Sydney University
		H Duncan Hall	League of Nations, Geneva
		John Dyason	Businessman, Melbourne

which, over a twenty year period, had created an American-educated Chinese elite.[74] The British Report suggested this strategy had yielded impressive economic results and concluded that Britain had fallen far behind America in cultural diplomacy. While scholars would now dispute these trade claims, it could hardly have escaped Australians that they had barely embarked upon cultural diplomacy in Asia.[75] Clunies Ross outlined initiatives to broaden Australia's relations with Japan, including academic exchanges of the kind developed by the Americans.[76]

The IPR not only helped create a community of interest around Asia-Pacific concerns, it also made a dramatic impact on Australian research in the social sciences. Contributions from S H Roberts, A L Sadler and Ian Clunies Ross to *Australia and the Far East* drew upon work already prepared for IPR conferences. One of the first studies to document Australia's growing trade with the Pacific after the first world war, Nancy Windett's *Australia as Producer and Trader, 1920-1932*, was the product of a 'generous financial partnership' between the IPR and the London School of Economics.[77] The IPR quickly became a genuinely international forum. Of particular interest is the fact that through the inter-war years the fields of Australian Studies and Asian Studies, broadly defined, developed alongside each other. As an example, one can take IPR-funded research in the 1930s on 'food supply, demography and land utilization'.[78] From this program there emerged not only Lossing Buck's influential study, *Land Utilization in China*, but also S M Wadham and G L Wood's, *Land Utilization in Australia*, published in 1939. Wood had been involved in earlier IPR-funded projects: *The Peopling of Australia*, *The Pacific Basin*, and *The Peopling of Australia, Further Studies*, published between 1928 and 1933.[79] His 'comprehensive' geography of the Pacific was welcomed by Frederic Eggleston, who hoped Wood's ideas would help create 'a Pacific sense' among Australians. The two volumes of *The Peopling of Australia* brought together a number of Australia's leading social scientists.[80]

Research in the inter-war years on Australian population, settlement and resource management was often presented at IPR forums by speakers conscious of the need to convince Asian delegations that Australia was a geographically distinct continent, with limited population-carrying capacity. This need to explain Australia to an Asian audience often led, quite literally, to the creation of an Australia that was not meant to appeal to Asian nations seeking settlement opportunities abroad. The complex art of keeping Asians out was accompanied increasingly by the realisation that it was no longer appropriate to appear bigoted in wanting to do so. There needed to be convincing stories to tell about social cohesion, the delicacy of democratic institutions and the experimental nature of Australian egalitarianism. The pride IPR intellectuals took in creating a distinctive Australia, involved a growing recognition that 'Asia' could no longer be dismissed with an imperious wave of the hand. There needed to be a greater spirit of accommodation and a keener interest in Asian affairs, which for many intellectuals required a more educated public opinion in Australia.

IPR intellectuals often became missionaries for their cause, committed people seeking to change the way Australians thought about the region in which they were located. Consider Griffith Taylor, who maintained a high media profile on questions of climate, settlement, race and the future of the Pacific. In the 1930s, A C V Melbourne, Ian Clunies Ross, Janet Mitchell, William Macmahon Ball and S H Roberts all gave regular radio broadcasts on Pacific affairs.[81] But in attempting to broaden Australian sympathies, these intellectuals became more curious about Australian opinion itself and the nature of Australian values.

The IPR gave Australian intellectuals opportunities to build American networks at a time when American intellectuals were becoming increasingly concerned at the influence of the print media and the cinema on the future of democracy.[82] These issues soon began to interest the Australians. Cultural stereotyping and the nature of foreignness attracted considerable interest in IPR circles. In 1938, a paper prepared for the AIIA included among other influences, travel, radio and film on Australian constructions of the outside world. While the authors of the article were not clever enough to coin the term 'otherness', they nevertheless broadened the analysis of how awareness of foreign cultures developed in Australia. Even so, their model remained rather mechanical in proposing that ideas and impressions 'flowed' towards largely passive recipients.[83]

In 1938 A G Pearson from Melbourne University broke new ground in his examination of 'The Australian Press and Japan' at a symposium of the Victorian Branch of the IPR.[84] Pearson analysed media accounts of Japanese industrialisation as part of an inquiry into the 'psychological attitude towards the foreigner'. He found different class and sectorial interests were apparent within the media, with a clear division between the labour press and the major metropolitan dailies. His analysis may have been influenced by *Japan in American Public Opinion*, a comprehensive analysis of the American media published earlier that year.[85] *Press, Radio and World Affairs*, the volume in which Pearson's article appears, demonstrates how new approaches in the social sciences emerged when Australian researchers drew upon their knowledge of American scholarship to pose fresh questions about Australia's role as an Asia-Pacific nation.

One of the most convincing of these studies is Jack Shepherd's *Australia's Interests and Policies in the Far East*, published in 1939 by the IPR when the author was just twenty-six years old.[86] A former student of S H Roberts, Shepherd's promising career was cut short by his premature death in 1944. In *Australia and the Far East*, Roberts had provided an overview of the Australia's relationship with Asia. Shepherd now expanded this into the first comprehensive history of Australian relations with Asia. He argued that between 1932 and

1935, Australians had become more alert to prospects for closer economic, political and cultural ties with the 'Far East'. Shepherd examined the implications for Australia becoming, in the current phrase, 'part of Asia' and concluded that Australia might indeed derive substantial benefit. But after the Trade Diversion dispute of 1936 and the Sino-Japanese conflict in the following year, prospects for such regional collaboration virtually disappeared.

Nevertheless, Shepherd remained convinced that Australia had to make a long-term commitment to the Asia-Pacific region. Prejudiced responses to Asian nations and cultures had to be replaced by a 'real knowledge and appreciation' of Asian history, cultures and 'current problems and policies'.[87] Shepherd had been encouraged by an address given by Prime Minister Robert Menzies in May 1939 in which Menzies spoke of the need to build a spirit of Pacific community through the development of 'real machinery for the cultivation of friendship'. Menzies urged 'mutual understanding, through extensive personal contact' among countries of the region. Shepherd went further in calling for 'a vigorous effort' to study, not only the cultures of Japan and China, but also the history and 'present problems of all the Pacific countries' and especially 'Australia's relations with them'.[88]

The question of Australia's obligations to the Pacific region were taken up by Sir Robert Garran, the constitutional lawyer. As a member of the British Empire Secretariat at the Paris Peace Congress, Garran had worked closely with John Latham on the question of League of Nations Mandates. He was also a contributor to the AIIA volume, *Australia and The Far East*. Arguing the case for a national 'School of Oriental Studies', Garran praised the IPR for its work in elucidating Pacific affairs.[89] He wanted Australia to build on these developments, arguing that Australia was 'clearly destined' to have close relations with the 'countries of the Orient' not only diplomatically, but 'commercially, and humanly'. The term 'humanly' echoed Eggleston's ideal of Pacific citizenship, which Garran expanded upon in a decisive way: 'I believe that Australia's great role in international relations is that of interpreter of the East to the West, and of the West to the East. We have the opportunity, and the duty, of making a close study of the Orient'. But Garran also stressed there were 'many Orients' containing distinctive and separate cultures. Garran clearly expressed the hope that Australia might create a significant role for itself on the international stage through its interaction with the Asia-Pacific. This view resembled that of Bancroft, although with a crucial distinction: Australians had to develop a much more educated awareness of Asian cultures and their contribution to world civilisation than the patronising Bancroft would have considered necessary.

In 1937 the AIIA began publication of a new bi-monthly review, with a ying-yang logo, *The Austral-Asiatic Bulletin*. It aimed to make Australia 'more curious about the Orient, of which she is part'. Its editorial board, chaired by Frederic Eggleston, included the academics W Macmahon Ball, P D Phillips and

Ernest Scott and the Melbourne business figure, E C Dyason. The first issue included articles by three IPR veterans, E L Piesse, A L Sadler and Ian Clunies Ross.[90] Other contributors included Georgina Sweet, Douglas Copland, Herbert Gepp and the American, Edgar Snow. Yasuke Tsurumi, another contributor, was surprised to find, on visiting Australia, that so many people were learning Japanese.[91] Articles examined trade, Australian defence and foreign policy and Asia-Pacific cultural relations. Regional correspondents filed regular reports and there was a comprehensive book review section. In the 1930s, it had become a common complaint that Australian interest in international affairs was slight. That may be so, but there was nevertheless a well-travelled, well-informed group of internationalists who saw the Asia-Pacific as a region of vital importance to Australians and the world at large.

Chapter Seventeen

Conclusion

From the mid-nineteenth century traders, travellers, intellectuals, missionaries and artists generated an increasing volume of comment on the character and destiny of the East. Much of the commentary was derivative, drawing often upon highly coloured narratives, many biblical in origin, of India and the Middle East. This was the setting for Edward Said's *Orientalism* — the Holy Lands of the Middle East — in which the European Empires of the nineteenth century fought for control of minds, territories and resources. In Said's argument, 'Orientalism' was the reason or permission Europe gave itself for being in the Orient. Prominent among those reasons was the 'lassitude' and 'backwardness' attributed to the East. This was the East as a hot, primitive, largely inert world, available for European colonisation. This Orient was one acted upon, rather than acting.

While the Australian travel writer, James Hingston, subscribed to the 'orientalist' reading of the Middle East, there was also in Hingston the carefully fabricated persona of the modern traveller, sceptically aware of the rich history of inflated claims that hung over the East and, increasingly, of the diversity of cultures that constitued the Asian world. For Hingston, knowledge of the diversity of Asian civilisations, preferably backed by travel, was an essential qualification for those who considered themselves to be truly modern. Hingston travelled as an enthusiastic ironist who believed that one of the great teachings of the East was the impermanence of all things, a prominent theme in *The Australian Abroad* and one well-suited to Hingston's interest in the rise and fall of civilisations.

One of the recurrent images of nineteenth century orientalism was of majestic ruins, crumbling to nothing in searing deserts or overgrown by vines and creepers in forbidding jungles. The modern inhabitants of this Asia were commonly reduced to the status of primitive remnants of a now remote, but once great civilisation. Asia represented mankind's turbulent past, Europe its impressive future. Hingston, however, doubted this comforting dichotomy, realising that China and Japan could not be easily accommodated within such a neat schema.

When Hingston turned to China and Japan he saw not a defeated, disorderly Asia, but a powerful combination of immensity, racial uniformity and, in the case of Japan, exquisite taste. Both civilisations had shown themselves to be strong and remarkably enduring. While it seemed clear to Hingston that China was in decline, he believed that Japan was a model society, deserving high praise. He enthused over Japan's Elizabethan energies and creative force. Curiously, Elizabethanism had a considerable hold on late nineteenth century literary culture in Australia. The *Bulletin* liked to represent itself as a swashbuckling enterprise, full of bold literary sword play. Piracy seemed a dashingly red-blooded pastime and dressing as pirates was a favourite bohemian pursuit. And who had not marvelled at the story of good Sir Francis Drake, calmly finishing his game of bowls, before turning to fight the Spanish Armada? By the late nineteenth century, however, it was clear that Japan had also developed something of a reputation as an Elizabethan civilisation. Elizabethan Japan was a disconcerting discovery for Australian observers of the East.

One version of Elizabethan England showed a roystering world of laughing male drinkers with big appetites, wenches on hand as required. In this turbulent world, only the fittest and most urgently procreative could expect to survive. It could seem to those close to the *Bulletin* that Australia seemed to be in the process of proscribing powerful Elizabethan energies at precisely the time that Elizabethan Japan was building its military power and seeking a role for itself as *Dai Nippon* — Great Japan. Australia seemed an increasingly feminised and sedentary culture at a time when Japan was taking a sternly masculinising path. And, through it all, Britain, so it could seem, was carefully instructing Japan on how to become a modern Imperial Power. What was worse, Britain itself, appeared to be losing its Elizabethan inheritance. In 1912, H E Pratten, Australian businessman and politician was driven to comment:

> The decadence of England must be serious if the Englishmen of today — the descendants of Drake and Frobisher ... are transferring their heritage of the right to rule the waves to the Asiatics.[1]

If Britain was declining, what would stop Imperial Japan from colonising Australia?

From around the 1880s, there were increasing claims in the radical press that the British Empire had stirred modern Asia into restless energy. According to this view, an interfering, meddlesome Empire had awoken a sleeping Orient stirring, in the process, dangerous territorial longings and ambitions among grievously overpopulated and often desperate peoples. By its imperious conduct in the East, Britain, it was argued, had helped bring forward a new round in the oldest and bloodiest of all conflicts, the battle between East and West. The great exponents of Empire were seen to be serving no higher goal than commerce and personal gain. This was an Empire of greed that would put Asian profits ahead of Australian security. In this analysis, British actions might put Australia in danger of being consumed in the fires of a terrible war with an Eastern foe. Burning Australian cities feature prominently in the invasion narrative. This was Asia configured as the enemy Australia would one day have to fight. In the telling of this story, the task of awakening a sleeping nation to this new 'Asia' at their door commonly fell to a lonely visionary more alert to ominous world events than his slumbering fellow citizens. But in each of these stories there was also an attempt to discover what had gone so badly wrong for the nation that it had ended up being controlled by Asia. Asia had begun its career as a versatile nightmare that would help serve the purpose of pushing a sleeping people towards nationhood.

By the 1890s, the future of the East had become one of the great topics of the age. As difficult as it might be to know the East, it seemed impossible to ignore. In one form or another the 'Eastern question' or the 'awakening East' or the 'yellow peril' demanded attention. The more the topic was discussed, the more likely it appeared that Australia's future would be influenced, perhaps decisively, by developments in Asia. The likely impacts of Asia on Australia covered a range of possibilities from speculations about invasion to reflections upon what Asia's proximity to Australia might mean. There was a growing realisation that for good or ill, Australia, perhaps more than any other European nation, might be progressively subjected to a range of asianising contacts and influences. Asia had made Australia special, though in a rather invidious way. While destructive Asia, figured as an irresistable human tide, was a prominent motif in our culture from the late nineteenth century, there was an uneasy awareness of Asia's power to beguile and charm the West into a state of false security. Australia might have to be on its guard against Asia. The *Bulletin* was shocked by the enthusiastic welcome accorded to the visiting Japanese Training Squadron in 1906, because it seemed that urban middle class Australia, particularly Australian women, felt that it was appropriate to flatter and encourage the visitors and, in so doing, decorate and embroider their suburban lives a little. The *Bulletin* wanted its readers to see the Japanese, not as a cultivated and progressive people, a view that had won considerable support among the cultural elites of late nineteenth century Europe, but as a formidable, 'lower race' who were best kept at a distance. The *Bulletin* made the case against Japan all the more forcefully, in the belief that *Japonisme* pervaded the Anglo-Australian elite and its imperialist supporters.

Repeated messages about Australia's proximity to populous Asia made Australia vulnerable to 'racial panics' over the imagined impacts that the Asian world and its mysterious European supporters and go-betweens might have on its future. But the idea that Australia was vulnerable to invasion, infiltration or the transfer of territory to one or other Asian power was also a commonly used strategy designed to catch public attention. Australians were advised that, with Asia watching, particularly educated Asia, they might need to lift their performance as a people. They were enjoined to raise their sights from the small, essentially domestic world of the suburb to the large arena of global change and possible race conflict. There was an insistent call for the nation to attend to the big questions of continental settlement, where the sweeping landscapes of rural Australia and the vastness of the 'Empty North' were said to provide a grander and more appropriate scale for Australian thinking and problem-solving than could be found in suburban drawing rooms. From the beginnings of the Commonwealth in 1901, the question of Australia's performance as a nation was linked to the belief that Asia might emerge as a possible claimant to the vast and allegedly 'empty' continent positioned so invitingly on its doorstep. It seemed reasonable to hope that a strong, vigorous nationhood might help to keep Asia at bay whereas a weakly expressed nationality would surely encourage and embolden a watching enemy.

Even where Asia was represented as Australia's dominant threat, there was a suggestion that Australia's largely untried skills of diplomacy and persuasion would be tested and challenged by the coming encounter with Asia. This was sometimes represented as a necessary stimulus to nationhood. Proximity to Asia might sharpen Australian skills and help create a more populous, competitive and imaginative nation. Griffith Taylor was prominent among those who represented the rise of Asia generally, and China in particular, as a test of Australian adaptability. Notwithstanding the powerful hold of White Australia mentalities through the inter-war years, Taylor joined a small, though persistent minority who wondered if a rigid adherance to doctrines of racial purity was the best way to serve Australia's long-term interests. Through the inter-war years, Taylor depicted successful nations as outward-looking and capable of drawing strength from an admixture of peoples, whereas nations which allowed themselves to become culturally enclosed risked stagnation. Taylor wondered if doctrines of racial purity, which had been routinely represented as one of Australia's greatest strengths, might emerge in the near future as a damaging disadvantage to a Pacific nation.

It has generally been in the interest of those who believed that Australians needed to know more about Asia to emphasise that Australians were poorly equipped to understand their immediate region and that the little they knew was either dated or wrong. The irrelevance of past conceptualisations of Asia and the urgent need to modernise Australian opinion about Asia was the burden of almost every invasion narrative from William Lane onwards, just as it was central to those arguing for closer engagement with Asia from the 1930s to suggest that the attitudes of the past were no longer relevant to modern conditions. This idea persists. By definition, the reformist cause was prosecuted by those who wanted knowledge of Asia to increase at an accelerating pace. It was not thought important or useful to draw attention to the history of Australia's interaction with Asia unless it was to show how abjectly the nation had performed. William Macmahon Ball set high standards for dismissive generalisations about Australia's awareness of the world when he declared in 1936 that Australian ignorance of Pacific affairs was more appropriate to 'desert tribesmen' exhibiting a 'lowly state of mental growth' than to the citizens of a modern democracy.[2] Australians could be safely dismissed as a people in whom ignorance of Asia was embedded in the national character. Exceptions there may have been, but they could be easily set aside as aberrant.

Australians today, backed by a larger, more widely travelled and better-educated population, should hesitate before accusing the four million insecurely established and predominantly Anglo-Celtic settlers of 1900 of developing an irrational fear of Asia and especially so at a time when the basic structures of national life were still in their infancy. The idea that Australia was a continent under threat seemed all too rational for those who saw the world as a place in which the strong preyed upon and eliminated the weak. Australia's distance from Europe, tiny population, high levels of urbanisation and declining birth-rate seemed unmistakable signs of a community at risk either of takeover or of an accelerating exposure to Asian influences. Even so, the spectrum of 'Asianist' opinion is much broader and more imaginatively diverse than this nonetheless powerful motif might suggest. Australians encountered and documented multiple 'Asia's' in the period examined in this book. 'Asia' as the 'Antique Orient' provided one entry point to a contemplative world of the imagination in which the European, for the most part male, could indulge his intellectual and sensual impulses. In its studious forms this was the world of the philologist and student of religion. In its eroticised forms, the world of the harem, *Madame Chrysanthème* and salacious Japanese prints. There was the Asia opening to travel, the world of Cooks Tours, Burns Philp and the Orient Line. There was the Asia opening to trade with the West and developing a demand for products, particularly wool and horses, that Australia was positioned to supply. When rendered as the Eastern Question, Asia became one of the major topics for contemporary journalists. 'Chinese' Morrison moved seamlessly, with a stop or two in between, from Geelong to Peking to become a powerful figure in this world. The possibility arose, however indistinctly, that some Australians might make a name for themselves as interpreters, mediators or entrepreneurs in newly emerging Asia. Some, like Ambrose Pratt, turned from committed exponents of 'yellow peril' doctrines before the first world war to advocates of closer engagement with the Asia-Pacific region in the inter-war years.

Where Asia was commonly depicted in threatening attitudes, the forms in which these threats appeared, their logic, rationale and appeal are themselves complex and culturally revealing. Even to refer to an 'invasion threat' can be misleading when the spectrum of concern ran from direct military aggression to suspicions of a shadowy oriental presence. Nor should we assume that invaders were simply malign figures. They were often endowed with qualities that Australians were thought to lack. In the case of Japan, for all the concern aroused by its rise to military power there remained a considerable fascination with a culture that had apparently succeeded in reconciling its ancient traditions with the demands of a modern state. The writings of James Hingston, Mrs Campbell Praed and James Murdoch come to mind. All had been enchanted by Japan. The cult status that Japan had acquired among professional aesthetes like Douglas Sladen lived on, albeit in a rather more politicised and temperate forms, in public figures, including Frederic Eggleston, John Latham and Ian Clunies Ross. While stressing the strategic and economic significance that an industrialised Japan might have for Australia, their separate encounters with Japan moved them profoundly.

Japan had been a revelation of elegance and order, displaying many of the hallmarks of a unique and impressive civilisation. Behind public talk that the proximity of Asia was Australia's opportunity to become both an economic force in the region and a source of Asian expertise, there lurked a hope, not unlike Deakin's in relation to India, that Japan and Australia might form a special bond. It did not seem too much to hope that, scrubbed clean of Europe's ancient and disfiguring conflicts, Australians might one day turn themselves into the Europeans Asian leaders might learn to trust.

By the 1930s, there was an increasingly articulate group of internationalists, many of them associated with the Institute of Pacific Relations, who maintained that knowledge of Asian societies was vital to Australia's future as an independent nation. They began to tease out the need to give institutional expression to Australia's position as an Asia-Pacific nation. In these circles, the Pacific was routinely spoken of as a region of great strategic and commercial significance. And, increasingly, this was the world they travelled. Japan's emergence as a major market for Australian wool quickened the hope that the industrialisation of Asia would create millions of new consumers for Australian goods. Knowing Asia could be represented as both commercially astute and a searching test of Australia's adaptability. The Institute, after suffering a withering McCarthyist onslaught through the 1950s, was virtually excised from public memory, leaving behind, nonetheless, an impression of its supporters as a suspect fraternity of naive idealists and dangerous leftists. They, and their Asia-Pacific interests, had been tainted.

Though there were regular calls for Australians to be given more opportunities to study Asian languages, cultures and economic conditions before 1939, the institutional responses, with the exception of the IPR, remained sporadic. Even so, the appointment of James Murdoch to Sydney University — the world's foremost historian of Japan at the time of his appointment — or the teaching of Japanese at Fort Street High School, remain fascinating educational experiments. Then again, the publication in 1936 of A C V Melbourne's report on educational exchanges between Australian universities and universities in China and Japan, was an early formal statement of the need for systematic educational exchanges in the region. Melbourne's regular promotion of closer ties with Japan and China is a reminder that there were significant groupings of intellectuals with an interest in what was then generally termed Pacific Affairs within the universities and in the wider community. Through the 1930s, despite disputes over trade diversion and the growing threat of war, Australia's commercial, diplomatic and intellectual engagement with the Asia-Pacific region had grown stronger and more varied. A new architecture of engagement — a diplomatic mission, the appointment of trade commissioners, a brisker public debate, a growing commercial community with economic interests in Asia — had already been put to some of its most searching tests. But through it all, however, Sir Denis Nayland Smith continued to pursue the elusive Dr Fu Manchu.

Notes

Chapter One

1   Richard Austin Thompson, *The Yellow Peril 1890-1924*, New York, 1978, p 4.
2   'Sketcher' [William Lane], 'White or Yellow? A Story of the Race War of 1908', serialised in the *Boomerang*, 18 February 1888 to 5 May 1888; Kenneth Mackay, *The Yellow Wave: A Romance of the Asiatic Invasion of Australia*, London, 1895; Rata [T R Roydhouse], *The Coloured Conquest*, Sydney, 1903; Lothrop Stoddard, *The Rising Tide of Color Against White World Supremacy*, New York, 1921.
3   Reverend James Jefferis, 'Australia's Mission and Opportunity', *Centennial Magazine*, vol 1, August 1888-July 1889. See also Walter Phillips, *James Jefferis: A Prophet of Federation*, Melbourne, 1993.
4   See P D Phillips and G L Wood (eds), *The Peopling of Australia*, Melbourne, 1928, p 26.
5   *Australia To-Day*, 1 November 1912.
6   'Parabellum', [Ferdinand H Grautoff], *Banzai!*, New York, 1908.
7   'Viscount James Bryce', *Modern Democracies*, vol 2, London, 1921, p 290.
8   Alex M Nicol, 'How to People the Commonwealth: A Dream and a Reality', *Australia To-Day*, 1 December 1909.
9   Roderic Quinn, 'Australia: A Nation', ibid., 1 November 1910.
10 Roderic Quinn, Letter to editor, *Manly and North Sydney News*, 27 July 1907.
11 'People or Perish', cover illustration, *Millions Magazine*, vol 2, no 10, 15 October 1923. See also David Walker, 'Australia as Asia' in Wayne Hudson and Geoffrey Bolton (eds), *Creating Australia: Changing Australian History*, St Leonard's, NSW, 1997.
12 T P O'Connor, 'Is Australia Menaced?', *Sydney Morning Herald*, 6 July 1905.
13 John Foster Fraser, *Australia: The Making of a Nation*, London, 1910, p 24.
14 Reverend T E Ruth, 'Will Australia remain British?', *Millions Magazine*, 15 August 1924.
15 'Australasia' [Edward Gibbon Wakefield], *Sketch of a Proposal for Colonizing Australasia, &c, &c, &c*, London, 1829.
16 Fraser, op. cit., p 214.
17 Richard Arthur, 'The Question of Questions for Australia', *Australasian Review of Reviews*, no date, Richard Arthur Papers, MS 473, Mitchell Library, Sydney.
18 Hardy Wilson, *The Dawn of a New Civilisation*, London, 1929.
19 Quoted in Hardy Wilson, 'Cultural War', 11 May 1947, Q701/W, Mitchell Library, Sydney.
20 E J Dyer, 'Australia and the Asian-Pacific: An Address delivered in Melbourne Town Hall on October 21, 1895', Melbourne, 1895.
21 J Currie Elles, 'The Influence of Commerce on Civilisation', *Journal of the Institute of Bankers of NSW*, 30 April 1908.
22 A T Yarwood, *Asian Migration to Australia: The Background to Exclusion 1896-1923*, Melbourne, 1967; Charles A Price, *The Great White Walls are Built: Restrictive Immigration to North America and Australasia, 1836-1888*, Canberra, 1974; F Hawkins, *Critical Years in Immigration: Canada and Australia Compared*, Sydney, 1989.
23 Sean Brawley, *The White Peril: Foreign Relations and Asian Immigration to Australasia and North America 1919-78*, Sydney, 1995.
24 A C Palfreeman, *The Administration of the White Australia Policy*, Melbourne, 1967.
25 Ian Clunies Ross (ed.), *Australia and the Far East: Diplomatic and Trade Relations*, Sydney, 1935; Jack Shepherd, *Australia's Interests and Policies in the Far East*, [1939] New York, 1940.
26 Werner Levi, *Australia's Outlook on Asia*, Sydney, 1958.

27 D C S Sissons, 'Attitudes to Japan and Defence 1890-1923', 3 vols, MA thesis, University of
    Melbourne, 1956; 'Early Australian Contacts with Japan', *Hemisphere*, vol 16, no 4, April
    1972; 'Manchester v Japan: The Imperial Background of the Australian Trade Diversion
    Dispute with Japan, 1936', *Australian Outlook*, vol 30, no 3, 1976; 'Australian-Japanese
    Relations: The First Phase 1859-91', unpublished paper, School of Pacific Studies, Australian
    National University, 1980.
28 Eric Rolls, *Sojourners: the Epic Story of China's Centuries-Old Relationship with Australia:
    Flowers and the Wide Sea*, St Lucia, 1992; Eric Rolls, *Citizens: Continuing the Epic Story of
    China's Centuries-Old Relationship with Australia ... the sequel to the Sojourners*, St Lucia,
    1996.
29 Jill Roe, *Beyond Belief: Theosophy in Australia, 1879-1939*, Sydney, 1986.
30 Neville Meaney, *The Search For Security in the Pacific, 1901-1914*, Sydney, 1976; Neville
    Meaney, *Fears and Phobias: E L Piesse and the Problem of Japan: 1909-39*, Canberra, 1996.
31 Raynaldo C Ileto and Rodney Sullivan (eds), *Discovering Australasia: Essays on Philippine-
    Australian Interactions*, Townsville, 1993; Paul Battersby, 'No Peripheral Concern: The
    International Political Implications of Australian Tin Mining Investment in Thailand, 1903 to
    the 1950s', PhD thesis, James Cook University, 1996.
32 David Walker (ed.), 'Australian Perceptions of Asia', *Australian Cultural History*, vol 9, 1990;
    Alison Broinowski, *The Yellow Lady: Australian Impressions of Asia*, Melbourne, 1992; Robin
    Gerster (ed.), *Hotel Asia: An Anthology of Australian Literary Travelling to the 'East'*, Melbourne,
    1995; Maryanne Dever (ed.), *Australia and Asia: Cultural Transactions*, Honolulu, 1997.

Chapter Two

1   Margaret Steven, *Merchant Campbell 1769-1846: A Study of Colonial Trade*, Melbourne,
    1965, p 26.
2   ibid.
3   Robert Irving (ed.), *The History and Design of the Australian House*, Melbourne, 1985, p 46,
    cited in an unpublished paper by Peter Griffiths, 'The Influences of Cultural Diffusion upon
    the Australian House', Deakin University, 1996, p 9.
4   For entries on Chisholm, Coverdale and Fyans see Douglas Pike (general ed.), *Australian
    Dictionary of Biography, Volume 1: 1788-1850*, Melbourne, 1966. For Macquarie, ibid., vol 2,
    Melbourne, 1967; John Ritchie, *Lachlan Macquarie: A Biography*, Carlton, 1986, pp 29-49.
5   Marnie Bassett, *The Hentys: An Australian Colonial Tapestry* [London, 1954], Melbourne,
    1962, p 35.
6   ibid., p 138.
7   Philip Muskett, *The Illustrated Australian Medical Guide*, Sydney, no date, Introduction; Sir
    William Moore, *A Manual of Family Medicine and Hygiene for India*, 7th ed., London, 1903.
8   'The Famine in India', *Town and Country Journal*, 6 October 1877.
9   'Indian Famine Relief Fund', *Town and Country Journal*, 10 November 1877.
10 'Australian Horses for India', *Town and Country Journal*, 5 February 1870. See also discussion
    and correspondence, *Sydney Morning Herald*, January to March 1870.
11 A T Yarwood, *Walers: Australian Horses Abroad*, Melbourne, 1989, p 198. For early
    Australian trading links with Asia see 'The British Connection: Restricted Childhood' in
    Sandra Tweedie, *Trading Partners: Australia & Asia 1870-1993*, Sydney, 1994, pp 12-21.
12 R Martin and H Koda, *Orientalism: Visions of the East in Western Dress*, New York, 1994,
    p 11.
13 Beverley Kingston, 'The Taste of India', in David Walker (ed.), 'Australian Perceptions of
    Asia', *Australian Cultural History*, vol 9, 1990.

14 After spending ten years in India, Inglis came to Australia in 1877 where he prospered as a tea merchant. He was a prolific and popular author and prominent politician. For an account of his period in India see James Inglis, *Our Australian Cousins*, London, 1880, chp 1. For Inglis and the tea trade see James Inglis, *How a Great Firm Grew: The Story of the Tea Trade*, Sydney, 1901. Inglis's books on India, *Tent Life in Tigerland* and *Sport and Work on the Nepaul Frontier* were brought out in a single volume in Sydney, 1888. For a contemporary profile of Inglis see Mrs Charles Bright, 'Mr James Inglis', *The Cosmos Magazine*, vol 2, no 6, 29 February 1896. See also Inglis papers in the Mitchell Library, Sydney, MSS 6239, ML 1217/65. For erosion of the Chinese tea market in Australia in the 1880s see Tweedie, *Trading Partners*, op. cit., p 26.

15 Jenny Sharpe, *Allegories of Empire: The Figure of Woman in the Colonial Text*, Minneapolis, 1993, p 63.

16 Christopher Hibbert, *The Great Mutiny: India, 1857*, New York, 1978. See also Sashi Chaudhuri, *English Historical Writings on the Indian Mutiny, 1857-1859*, Calcutta, 1979; Patrick Brantlinger, 'The Well at Cawnpore: Literary Representations of the Indian Mutiny of 1857' in Patrick Brantlinger, *Rule of Darkness: British Literature and Imperialism, 1830-1914*, Ithaca, 1988. For more recent Indian approaches to the subject see Ranajit Guha and Gayatri Chakravorty Spivak (eds), *Selected Subaltern Studies*, New York, 1988. For Australian responses to the Mutiny see 'White Australia and the Indian Mutiny', in J V D'Cruz, *The Asian Image In Australia: Episodes in Australian History*, Melbourne, 1973, pp 11-31.

17 F K Crowley (ed.), *A Documentary History of Australia*, vol 2, Sydney, 1980, pp 357-8.

18 Stewart Firth and Jeanette Hoorn, 'From Empire Day to Cracker Night' in P Spearritt and D Walker (eds), *Australian Popular Culture*, Sydney, 1979.

19 James Hingston, *The Australian Abroad on Branches From Main Routes Round the World*, London, 1880, 2 vols, reissued in a single volume, Melbourne, 1885. For bibliographical information on Hingston and other Australian travellers abroad see Ros Pesman, David Walker and Richard White (eds), *Annotated Bibliography of Australian Overseas Travel Writing, 1830 to 1970*, Canberra, 1996.

20 Hingston, op. cit., p 291.

21 ibid.

22 ibid., p 265.

23 ibid., p 334.

24 ibid., p 282.

25 ibid.

26 ibid.

27 ibid., p 277.

28 ibid., p 335.

29 ibid., p 334.

30 ibid., p 265.

31 Thomas Playford, *Notes of Travel in India, China and Japan*, Adelaide, 1907, p 52.

32 'Women at the Well', *Town and Country Journal*, 2 January 1875.

33 T B Fischer, *A Month in India: The Collected Writings of T B Fischer*, Melbourne, 1914, p 118.

34 ibid., p 125.

35 Eleanor Rivett, *Memory Plays a Tune, Being Recollections of India 1907-1947*, Melbourne, no date, p 10.

36 Walter Murdoch, *Alfred Deakin: A Sketch*, London, 1923, p 170.

37 ibid.

38 ibid., and *Irrigated India : An Australian View of India and Ceylon, Their Irrigation and Agriculture*, London, 1893. Also J A La Nauze, *Alfred Deakin: A Biography*, Melbourne, 1965, pp 480-2, and Al Gabay, *The Mystic Life of Alfred Deakin*, Cambridge, 1992.

39 Deakin, *Temple and Tomb*, Melbourne, 1893, p 151.

40 ibid., p 2.
41 ibid., p 151.
42 Deakin, *Irrigated India: An Australian View of India and Ceylon, Their Irrigation and Agriculture*, London, 1893, p 11.
43 ibid., p 13.
44 Deakin, *Temple and Tomb*, op. cit., p 2.
45 ibid., p 51.
46 Max Müller, *India: What Can it Teach Us?* [Leipzig, 1884], Indian ed., Calcutta, 1934, p 7. See also Niraud C Chaudhuri, *Scholar Extraordinary: The Life of Professor the Rt Hon Freidrich Max Müller, PC*, London, 1974; Dietmar Rothermund, *The German Intellectual Quest for India*, New Delhi, 1986.
47 Beverley Kingston, 'The Taste of India', op. cit. See also Joscelyn Godwin, *The Theosophical Enlightenment*, Albany, 1994.
48 Deakin, *Temple and Tomb*, op. cit., p 2.
49 See entry on John Smith in Bede Nairn (general ed.), *Australian Dictionary of Biography, Volume 6: 1851-1890*, Melbourne, 1976.
50 Wilton Hack, 'Sketch of My Life: For the Instruction and Amusement of My Beloved Children', 30 July 1907, p 108, South Australian Archives, PRG 456/59. See also J Cross, 'Wilton Hack and Japanese Immigration into North Australia', *Proceedings Geographical Society of Australasia* (South Australia Branch), 1959-60.
51 Hack, 'Sketch of My Life', op. cit., p 83.
52 ibid., p 109.
53 Jill Roe, *Beyond Belief: Theosophy in Australia, 1879-1939*, Sydney, 1986, p 54.
54 Victor Kennedy and Nettie Palmer, *Bernard O'Dowd*, Carlton, 1954, pp 105-6.
55 Roe, *Beyond Belief*, op. cit., p 115.
56 Louis E Girard, 'The Genius of an Empire', *The Pacific*, 18 September 1924.

Chapter Three

1   Alfred Deakin, *Irrigated India, An Australian View of India and Ceylon, Their Irrigation and Agriculture*, London, 1893, pp 10, 12-13. See also Sir Charles Dilke, *Problems of Greater Britain*, London, 1890.
2   A W Jose, *The Growth of Empire: A Handbook to the History of Greater Britain*, Sydney, 1897, p 374.
3   ibid., pp 377-8.
4   ibid., p 369.
5   ibid., p 375.
6   Jenny Sharpe, *Allegories of Empire: The Figure of Woman in the Colonial Text*, Minneapolis, 1993, p 67.
7   W H Fitchett, *The Tale of the Great Mutiny*, New York, 1901.
8   W H Fitchett, *Deeds That Won the Empire*, Melbourne, 1897. For bibliographical information see Bede Nairn and Geoffrey Serle (eds), *Australian Dictionary of Biography, Volume 8: 1891-1939*, Carlton, 1981. *Deeds That Won the Empire* was enormously successful in its time: the British Admiralty made it compulsory in all warship libraries, it was in great demand as a school text, it was printed in Braille; Siegfried Sassoon records how his Nanny constantly read it to him during his childhood. See Robert H MacDonald, *The Language of Empire: Myths and Metaphors of Popular Imperialism, 1880-1918*, Manchester, 1994, pp. 62-64.
9   David Walker, *Dream and Disillusion: A Search for Australian Cultural Identity*, Canberra, 1976, pp 4, 79-81.

10 Fitchett, *Deeds That Won the Empire*, op. cit., p 140.

11 Fitchett, *Tale of the Great Mutiny*, op. cit., p 21.

12 ibid., p 97.

13 Tim Jeal, *The Boy-Man: The Life of Lord Baden-Powell*, London, 1989.

14 Deakin, *Temple and Tomb*, op. cit., p 145.

15 Gail Bederman, *Manliness & Civilization: A Cultural History of Gender and Race in the United States, 1880-1917*, Chicago, 1995, p 184.

16 John Ruskin, *Crown of Wild Olive*, London, 1866, pp 152-3.

17 G W Burston and H R Stokes, *Round About the World on Bicycles*, Melbourne, 1890, pp 86-90. R M Allen, a young Australian soldier had similar impressions; see R M Allen, *Mesopotamia and India: A Continuation of "Letters from a Young Queenslander"*, Brisbane, 1916, p 103.

18 Martyn Lyons and Lucy Taksa, *Australian Readers Remember: An Oral History of Reading*, Melbourne, 1992. For the general phenomenon of 'Kiplingitis' see R H Croll, 'Kipling in Australia', *Australian National Review*, 1 November 1937.

19 *Sydney Mail*, 21 November 1891, p 1132. For confirmation of Kipling's popularity in Australia see William H Wilde, Joy Hooton and Barry Andrews (eds), *The Oxford Companion to Australian Literature*, 2nd ed., Melbourne, 1994.

20 Helen Rutledge (ed.), *A Season in India: Letters of Ruby Madden: Experiences of an Australian Girl at a Great Coronation*, [Durbar, Delhi, 1903], Sydney, 1976.

21 In 1911, Sir Sidney Kidman also visited India for the Durbar as did a group of schoolboys from the elite King's School at Parramatta accompanied by their headmaster; see A T Yarwood, *Walers: Australian Horses Abroad*, Melbourne, 1989, pp 4-5.

22 Rutledge, *A Season in India*, op. cit. p 92.

23 Lindon Brown, *Letters from an Australian Abroad*, Parramatta, 1910, p 38.

24 Sir James Penn Boucault, *Letters to My Boys: An Australian Judge and Ex-Premier on His Travels in Europe*, London, 1906, p 17.

25 H Chalmers Miles, *Life in India and Scenes in the Mutiny being a Lecture delivered to the X C Officers and Men of the Royal Artillery and Royal Engineers in the Gymnasium Shed, Royal Artillery Park, Halifax, on Friday Afternoon, April 27th 1860*, Halifax, 1860, p 8.

26 Boucault, *Letters to My Boys*, op. cit., p 17.

27 Brown, *Letters from an Australian Abroad*, op. cit., p 29.

28 Burston and Stokes, *Round About the World on Bicycles*, op. cit., p 71.

29 Chalmers Miles, *Life in India*, op. cit., p 24.

30 Deakin, *Temple and Tomb*, op. cit., p 133.

31 Deakin, *Irrigated India*, op. cit., p 10.

32 Boucault, *Letters to My Boys*, op. cit., p 17.

33 This scenario is spelt out in Charles Stuart-Linton, 'The Navy and the Colonies', *Empire Review*, vol 12, November 1906. A copy of this paper, heavily marked by Arthur is held in the Richard Arthur Papers, Mitchell Library, Sydney, item 473.

34 Richard Arthur, 'A Stone in Empire Building', *Morning Post*, 6 October 1908.

35 Richard Arthur, 'Australia for the Anglo-Indian', Letter to the Editor, *Madras Times*, 13 May 1907, Richard Arthur Papers.

36 Richard Arthur, 'Back To The Land', 14 July 1907, Newspaper Cuttings, Richard Arthur Papers.

37 Richard Arthur, *Eastern Bengal and Assam Era*, 22 February 1908, Richard Arthur Papers.

38 Homer Lea, *The Day of the Saxon*, New York, 1912. Richard Arthur reviewed Lea's book in *Stock and Station Journal*, 29 November 1912, Newspaper Cuttings, Richard Arthur Papers.

39 Homer Lea, *The Valor of Ignorance*, New York, 1909. For a profile of Homer Lea see Dumas Malone (ed.), *Dictionary of American Biography*, vol 11, New York, 1933 and Clare Boothe, 'The Valor of Homer Lea', Introduction, Homer Lea, *The Day of the Saxon*, New York, 1942.
40 Clare Boothe, ibid., p 191.
41 ibid.
42 Lea, *The Day of the Saxon*, op. cit., p 69.
43 Cyril Pearl, *Morrison of Peking*, Melbourne, 1970, p 233.
44 See *Dictionary of American Biography*, op. cit.
45 Walker, *Dream and Disillusion*, op. cit. See also Peter Fitzpatrick, *Pioneer Players: The Lives of Louis and Hilda Esson*, Cambridge, 1995, pp 39-40.
46 Bradley FitzMaurice, 'Red Parasols Over an Antipodean Italy', MA thesis, University of NSW, 1986, p 21.
47 Louis Esson, 'From The Oldest World', *Lone Hand*, 1 May 1908; 'Colombo', ibid., 1 June 1908; 'Swadeshi and other Imperial Troubles', ibid., 1 July 1908; 'Japan's Jiu-Jitsu Diplomacy', ibid., 1 August 1908; 'The Golden Temple of the Sikhs', ibid., 1 September 1908; 'Benares', ibid., 1 October 1908.
48 Esson, 'From The Oldest World', op. cit.
49 ibid.
50 Louis Esson, 'The Decay of the Delhis', *Lone Hand*, 1 July 1908.
51 Esson, 'Swadeshi and other Imperial Troubles', op. cit.
52 ibid. A good account of this type of imperial behaviour can be found in George Orwell, *Burmese Days*, [1934], New York, 1962.
53 Louis Esson wrote a second series of articles for the *Lone Hand* under the title 'The Asiatic Menace'. They were: 'Japan, the Gamester', 1 September 1908; 'Japanese Imperialism', 1 October 1908; 'The Awakening of the Dragon', 2 November 1908; and 'Celestial Politics', 1 December 1908.
54 Esson, 'Swadeshi and other Imperial Troubles', op. cit.

Chapter Four

1 For an account of restrictive immigration legislation see Arthur R Butterworth, *The Immigration of Coloured Races into British Colonies*, London, 1898. See also Eric Rolls, *Citizens: continuing the epic story of China's centuries old relationship with Australia ... the sequel to the Sojourners*, St Lucia, 1996, p 2; 'The Exclusion of the Chinese', in T A Coghlan, *Labour and Industry in Australia: From the First Settlement in 1788 to the Establishment of the Commonwealth in 1901*, vol 3, London, 1918.
2 The figure of 7,000 is given by Marie M De Lepervanche, *Indians in a White Australia: An Account of Race, Class and Indian Immigration to Eastern Australia*, Sydney, 1984, whereas the figure of 800 is given in James Jupp (ed.), *The Australian People: An Encyclopedia of the Nation, its People and their Origins*, North Ryde, 1988.
3 *New York Times Book Review*, cited in Ian Buruma, *The Missionary and the Libertine: Love and War in East and West*, London, 1996, p 262.
4 William Z Ripley, *The Races of Europe*, London, 1899, p 561.
5 'Li Hung Chang. Character Sketch', *Review of Reviews*, 20 June 1895. See also Geoffrey Serle, *The Golden Age: A History of the Colony of Victoria, 1851-1861*, Melbourne, 1963, pp 323-324; Kathryn Cronin, 'On a Fast Boat to Queensland: The Chinese Influx onto Queensland's Goldfields' in Raymond Evans, Kay Saunders and Kathryn Cronin (eds), *Exclusion, Exploitation and Extermination: Race Relations in Colonial Queensland*, Sydney, 1975, pp 254-88; E M Andrews, *Australia and China: The Ambiguous Relationship*, Carlton, 1985, pp 18-21; 'Asian Immigrants to Western Australia 1829-1901' in Anne Atkinson

(compiler), *The Bicentennial Dictionary of Western Australians*, vol 5, Nedlands, 1988; Timothy Jones, *The Chinese in the Northern Territory* (revised ed.), Darwin, 1997, pp xi, 20-21. Male anxieties about floods and tides have been discussed by Klaus Theweleit in *Male Fantasies, Vol 1, Women, Floods, Bodies, History*, translated by Stephen Conway, Erica Carter and Chris Turner, Minneapolis, 1987.

6   See Patrick Brantlinger, 'Imperial Gothic: Atavism and the Occult in the British Adventure Novel, 1880-1914', *Rule of Darkness: British Literature and Imperialism, 1830-1914*, Ithaca, 1988, pp 227-54.

7   David Goodman, *Gold Seeking: Victoria and California in the 1850s*, St Leonards, 1994, pp 22-24; Elmer Clarence Sandmeyer, *The Anti-Chinese Movement in California*, Urbana, 1991, pp 16-17; Andrew Markus, *Fear and Hatred: Purifying Australia and California 1850-1901*, Sydney, 1979, pp 1-2.

8   Goodman, *Gold Seeking*, op. cit., pp 20-2.

9   E H Fraser (British Consul at Pagoda Anchorage) to G E Morrison, 14 February 1898, Lo Hui-Min (ed.), *The Correspondence of G E Morrison*, vol 1, 1895-1912, Cambridge, 1976.

10 Sterling Seagrave, *Dragon Lady*, New York, 1992, pp 46, 53.

11 Immanuel Chung-yueh Hseu, *The Rise of Modern China*, New York, 1990, p 219.

12 James Hingston, *The Australian Abroad*, Melbourne, 1885, p 57.

13 ibid, pp 94-5.

14 ibid., p 144.

15 ibid. See also Rev Dr E J Eitel, 'China and the Far Eastern Question', in *Papers Read Before the Royal Geographical Society of Australasia*, Fourteenth session, 1900-1, South Australian Branch. Eitel maintained that the Chinese were supported by a 'strong organising instinct of co-operation, by a national feeling of clannishness which gives the Chinese nation its cohesiveness, and enables the Chinese wherever they may be, to present a united front against opponents', p 95.

16 Eric Rolls, *Sojourners: The Epic Story of China's Centuries-old Relationship with Australia: Flowers and the Wide Sea*, St Lucia, 1992, p 462.

17 ibid.

18 Andrews, *Australia and China*, op. cit., p 20; Geoffrey Serle, *The Golden Age: A History of the Colony of Victoria, 1851-1861*, Melbourne, 1963, pp 323-8.

19 L E Neame, *The Asiatic Danger in the Colonies*, London, 1907, p 75.

20 Francis Adams, 'Daylight and Dark. White or Yellow: Which Is to Go? What the Chinese Can teach Us', *Boomerang*, 1 February 1888.

21 ibid.

22 ibid.

23 Ross Lloyd, *William Lane and the Australian Labor Movement*, Sydney, 1936.

24 John Miller [William Lane], *The Working Man's Paradise, an Australian Labour Novel*, [1892], Sydney, 1948.

25 Grahame Stewart [Graeme Douglas Williams], *Where Socialism Failed. An Actual Experiment ... With Illustrations and a Map*, London, 1912; Gavin Souter, *A Peculiar People: The Australians in Paraguay*, Sydney, 1968.

26 'Sketcher' [William Lane] 'The Case for the Anti-Chinese', *Boomerang*, 11 February 1888.

27 'Sketcher' [William Lane], 'Daylight and Dark. Opium Smoking in Brisbane', *Boomerang*, 21 January 1888. Other articles in Lane's series 'Daylight and Dark' include 'Sunday Night in a Chinese gambling Hell', *Boomerang*, 14 January 1888; 'The Fascinations of Fan-Tan', *Boomerang*, 28 January 1888; 'How the Chinese Live in Queensland', *Boomerang*, 4 February 1888.

28 'Sketcher', 'Opium Smoking in Brisbane', op. cit.

29 David Walker, 'Continence for a Nation: Seminal Loss and National Vigour', *Labour History*, no 48, May 1985.

30 'Sketcher', 'The Case for the Anti-Chinese', op. cit.
31 ibid.
32 Sing-wu Wang, 'The Organization of Chinese Emigration, 1848-1888 with Special Reference to Chinese Emigration to Australia', MA thesis, Australian National University, 1969. See also Sing-wu Wang , 'Diplomatic Relations between China and Australia prior to the establishment of the Chinese Consulate in Melbourne in 1909', reprinted from *Chinese Culture*, vol x , no 2, June 1969 and Rory Mungoven, 'The Imperial Chinese Commissioners', unpublished, September 1987.
33 *Sydney Morning Herald*, 11 May 1887.
34 *Sydney Morning Herald*, 16 May 1887.
35 'Sketcher', 'The Case for the Anti-Chinese', op. cit.
36 Rolls, *Sojorners*, op. cit., p 463.
37 Stuart Anderson, *Race and Rapprochement: Anglo-Saxonism and Anglo-American Relations, 1894-1904*, Rutherford, c1981, p 149.
38 ibid.
39 See Chapter 5.
40 Charles H Pearson, *National Life and Character: A Forecast*, London, 1893. See Douglas Pike (ed.), *Australian Dictionary of Biography*, vol 5, 1851-1890, Melbourne, 1974 ; John Tregenza, *Professor of Democracy. The Life of Charles Henry Pearson, 1830-1894. Oxford Don and Australian Radical*, London, 1968; William Stebbing, *Charles Henry Pearson, Fellow of Oriel and Education Minister of Victoria, Memorials by Himself, His Wife and His Friends*, London, 1900.
41 *Australian Dictionary of Biography*, vol 1, op. cit.
42 Pearson, *National Life and Character*, op. cit., p 37.
43 ibid., p 40.
44 ibid., p 41.
45 ibid., p 54.
46 ibid., p 90.
47 Theodore Roosevelt, 'National Life and Character', *Sewanee Review*, May 1894.
48 ibid., p 360.
49 ibid., p 364.
50 ibid., p 367.
51 George F Curzon, *Problems of the Far East*, (revised ed.), New York, 1896.
52 For details of Curzon see David Gilmour, *Curzon*, London, 1994.
53 Curzon, *Problems of the Far East*, pp 396, 399.
54 ibid., p 405.
55 ibid., p 410.
56 Brantlinger, *Rule of Darkness*, op. cit., pp 32-3.
57 Professor H A Strong, 'A Memoir and Portrait', *Charles H Pearson: Reviews and Critical Essays*, London, 1896. See also Bede Nairn (ed.), *Australian Dictionary of Biography, vol 6, 1851-1890*, Melbourne, 1976.
58 Strong, 'A Memoir and Portrait', op. cit., pp 36-7.
59 ibid., p 37.
60 George E Morrison, *An Australian in China*, London, 1895.
61 ibid., p 104.
62 ibid., p 224.

Chapter Five

1   William Elliot Griffis, 'Introduction', in Inazo Nitobe, *Bushido: The Soul of Japan*, Rutland, 1905, p xxii. For an excellent account of the first Japanese Embassy to the United States in 1860 see Masao Miyoshi, *As We Saw Them*, New York, 1994.
2   Hal Porter, *The Watcher on The Cast-Iron Balcony*, London, 1963, p 15.
3   ibid., pp 84, 87.
4   Charles MacFarlane, *Japan: An Account, Geographical and Historical, From the Earliest Period at Which the Islands Composing this Empire were Known to Europeans Down to the Present Time and the Expedition Fitted Out in The United States, etc.*, Hartford 1856, Book X.
5   ibid., p 279.
6   Toshio Yokoyama, *Japan in the Victorian Mind*, Houndmills, 1987.
7   Martin Bernal, *Black Athena: The Afroasiatic Roots of Classical Civilization. Vol 1. The Fabrication of Ancient Greece 1785-1985*, London, 1987, pp 239-40.
8   Sir Rutherford Alcock, *Art and Art Industries in Japan*, London, 1878.
9   ibid., p 2.
10   Terence Lane and Jessie Serle, *Australians at Home: A Documentary History of Australian Domestic Interiors from 1788 to 1914*, Melbourne, 1990, p 37.
11   ibid., p 5.
12   ibid., p 3.
13   Julia Meech and Gabriel P Weisberg, *Japonisme Comes to America: The Japanese Impact on the Graphic Arts 1876-1925*, New York, 1990, p 36.
14   Clay Lancaster, *The Japanese Influence in America*, New York, 1963, p 25.
15   Elizabeth Aslin, *The Aesthetic Movement: Prelude to Art Nouveau*, London, 1969, p 96.
16   For the *Australasian Sketcher* see Jessie Serle, 'Asian and Pacific Influences in Australian Domestic Interiors, 1788-1914', *Fabrications*, vol 4, June 1993.
17   Colta Fella Ives, *The Great Wave : The Influence of Japanese Woodcuts on French Prints*, New York, 1974, pp 11-12.
18   Charles R Spencer, *The Aesthetic Movement 1869-1890*, London, 1973, as cited in Gabriel P Weisberg 'Early Sources and The French Printmaker 1854-1882' p 1, and footnote 7, in Gabriel P Weisberg, Phillip Dennis Cate, Gerald Needham, Martin Edelberg and William R Johnson (eds), *Japonisme: Japanese Influence on French Art 1854-1910*, Cleveland, 1975.
19   Ives, *The Great Wave*, op. cit., p 12.
20   Weisberg, 'Early Sources and the French Printmaker', op. cit., pp 1, 3, 15.
21   Meech and Weisberg, *Japonisme Comes to America*, op. cit., pp 27-29. For the Arts and Crafts Society see Jackie Menzies, 'Never the twain shall meet ... Australian artists and the Orient', *Art in Australia*, vol 31, no 4, 1994. See also Gabriel P Weisberg, *Art Nouveau Bing: Paris Style 1900*, New York, 1986. For Conder see John Rothenstein, *The Life and Death of Conder*, London, 1938, p 133; Frank Gibson, *Charles Conder: His Life and Works*, New York, 1914, reviewed in *Nation*, 8 January 1914.
22   ibid., p 7.
23   Ives, *The Great Wave*, op. cit., p 20.
24   Lancaster, *The Japanese Influence in America*, op. cit., p 29.
25   ibid., p 29.
26   R Martin and H Koda, *Orientalism: Visions of the East in Western Dress*, New York, 1994, p 74.
27   Lane and Serle, *Australians at Home*, op. cit., p 217, plate 225. For a more restrained use of Japanese effects in Australian painting see Tom Roberts, 'Portrait of Mrs L A Abrahams', 1888, National Gallery of Victoria, Melbourne.
28   Meech and Weisberg, *Japonisme Comes to America*, op. cit., p 253.

29 Gerald Needham, 'Japanese Influence on French Painting 1854-1910', in Weisberg et al, *Japonisme: Japanese Influence on French Art*, op. cit., p 119.

30 ibid., pp 115-31.

31 Martin and Koda, *Orientalism*, op. cit., pp 73, 77.

32 Needham, 'Japanese Influence on French Painting', op. cit., p 120.

33 Martin Eidelberg and William R Johnson, 'Japonisme and French Decorative Arts', in Weisberg et al, *Japonisme: Japanese Influence on French Art*, op. cit., p 151.

34 ibid., p 149.

35 Victor de Luynes, *Rapport du Jury Internationale Classe 20: Rapport sur la céramique*, Paris, 1882, cited in Eidelberg and Johnson, 'Japonisme and French Decorative Arts', op. cit., p 147 and footnote 26.

36 Meech and Weisberg, *Japonisme Comes to America*, op. cit., p 34.

37 Menzies, 'Never the twain shall meet', op. cit.; Lady Barker, *Travelling About over New and Old Ground*, London, 1872, pp 344-5. For early Australian responses to the 'Orient' see Alison Broinowski, *The Yellow Lady*, Melbourne, 1992, pp 20-46.

38 'The Japanese Method of Silk Producing', *Town and Country Journal*, 11 March 1871, pp 300-301.

39 'The Press in Japan', *Town and Country Journal*, 15 August 1874, p 253.

40 Harold S Williams, *Tales of the Foreign Settlements in Japan*, Rutland, 1972, pp 158-9. See also John R Black, *Young Japan: Yokohama and Edo. A Narrative on the Settlement and the City From the Signing of the Treaties in 1858, to the Close of the Year 1879 with a Glance at the Progress of Japan During a Period of Twenty-One Years*, 2 vols, Yokohama, 1881.

41 J H Brooke, 'Impressions of Japan', *Argus*, 22 August to 28 October, 1867. See also Williams, *Tales of Foreign Settlements in Japan*, op. cit., pp 161-63.

42 *Japan Times Overland Mail*, 27 January 1869, cited in D C S Sissons, 'Early Australian Contacts with Japan', *Hemisphere*, vol 16, no 4, April 1972, p 14.

43 James Hingston, *The Australian Abroad*, 2 vols, London, 1880, p 1.

44 P K Morton, 'Trade with the East', *Argus*, 22 October 1895.

45 Hingston, *The Australian Abroad*, op. cit., p 87. For Japan as 'a wonderful country' and the Japanese as 'an ideal people' see Anon's articles reprinted from the *Advertiser*, as *Land of The Rising Sun*, Adelaide, 1893, pp 30-31.

46 Rev George O'Neill, *Life of the Reverend Julian Edmond Tenison Woods (1832-1889)*, Sydney, 1929, pp 355-360. See also Rev J E Tenison Woods, 'Notes of Travel', *Sydney Morning Herald*, 15 June 1887.

47 Hingston, *The Australian Abroad*, op. cit., p 96, See also Rudyard Kipling, *Letters from the East*, [1889], New York, c1890, p116.

48 Kipling, *Letters from the East*, op. cit., p 128.

49 Sydney International Exhibition, *Official Catalogue of Exhibits: Japanese Court*, Sydney, 1879. For responses to the exhibition see *Sydney Morning Herald*, 8 September 1879, first cited in Michael R Johnson, '"Complementarity and Conflict": Australian and Japanese Relations in the Nineteenth Century', BA (Hons), University of New South Wales, October 1981. An earlier exhibition was organised in Sydney by the architect John Smedley who visited Japan in 1869 and then exhibited Japanese paintings and craft items at the Sydney Metropolitan and Intercolonial Exhibition in 1877, see Darryl Collins, 'Asian Art in Australia. One Hundred and Fifty Years of Exhibitions. Connoisseurs and Collections', *Art in Australia*, vol 30, no 3, Autumn 1993.

50 *Official Catalogue of Exhibits: Japanese Court*, ibid., pp 1-91. See also *Official Awards Sydney International Exhibition*, 1879, Sydney, 1879; Collins, 'Asian Art in Australia', op. cit.

51 'Japanese objects acquired by the museum prior to 1900', unpublished catalogue, Powerhouse Museum, Sydney. For an account of these objects see Mary Mackay 'Objects, Stereotypes

and Cultural Exchange' in Maryanne Dever (ed.), *Australia and Asia: Cultural Transactions*, Honolulu, 1997.

52 J S [James Smith], 'The Japanese Exhibits and Japanese Art', *Argus*, 5 March 1881. For comments on nineteenth century ideas on the relationship between physiology and art see David Walker 'Modern Nerves/ Nervous Moderns', in S L Goldberg and F B Smith (eds), *Australian Cultural History*, Melbourne, 1988. For comment on Smith see Lurline Stuart, 'James Smith: his influence on the development of literary culture in colonial Melbourne', PhD thesis, Monash University, 1983.

53 The 'Mikado' was first performed in Australia at the Theatre Royal from 14 November 1885. Reviews can be found in the *Daily Telegraph* and the *Sydney Morning Herald* on 16 November 1885 and in the *Town and Country Journal*, *Sydney Mail* and *Bulletin* for 21 November 1885.

54 *Sydney Morning Herald*, 16 November 1885, p 7.

55 *Sydney Mail*, 14 November 1885, p 1054.

56 'Building à La Jap', *Boomerang*, 24 December 1887. 'Death of Judge Paul. Brief Sketch of his Life', *Brisbane Courier*, 10 December 1909.

57 Lane and Serle *Australians at Home*, op. cit., pp 218-19, 237-39, 331 and plates 228, 256, 378. Cullis Hill , Melbourne *Bulletin* 15 May 1885, as cited in 'Asian and Pacific Influences in Australian Domestic Interiors', op. cit.

58 Advertisement, *Boomerang*, 11 May 1889.

59 Conder, op. cit., p 27 and plate 1; Jane Clark, 'The 9 x 5 Impressionist Exhibition', *Golden Summers*, Melbourne, 1985, p 114. First cited in Ursula Prinster, 'From Empire's End: Australians as Orientalists, 1880-1920' in Roger Benjamin (curator and ed.), *Orientalism : Delacroix to Klee*, Sydney, 1997, p 45. *Australians at Home*, op. cit., p 238. See also 'Viva', *Sydney Mail*, 31 August 1889, cited in 'Asian and Pacific Influences in Australian Domestic Interiors', op. cit.

60 A E Aldis, 'A E Aldis's Room at "Killara", Glenferrie, Victoria, c1891, in *Australians at Home*, op. cit., p 257 and plate 281.

61 Douglas Sladen, *Twenty Years of My Life*, London, 1914, p 246.

62 ibid., pp 35-45.

63 ibid., pp 35, 36.

64 Douglas Sladen to Edmund Stedman, 12 April 1895, E C Stedman Collection, Special Collection, Butler Library, Columbia University Libraries, Columbia University, New York, NY, USA.

65 Sladen, *Twenty Years*, op. cit., p 36. Douglas Sladen, *The Japs at Home. Fifth Edition: To Which are Added for the First Time Some Bits of China*, London, 1895.

66 Douglas Sladen, *My Long Life*, London, 1939, p 347-56

67 Sladen, *Twenty Years*, op. cit., pp 43-4.

68 ibid., p 40.

69 George Meudall, *The Pleasant Career of a Spendthrift and His Later Reflections*, Melbourne, 1939, p 156.

70 'Cherry Blossom Season in Japan', *Town and Country Journal*, 28 February 1912. Accounts of holiday travel may be found in J H Want 'To Japan and Back'(6 parts), *Town and Country Journal*, 3 August 1889 to 27 September 1889; in the richly illustrated articles by 'Artistic Correspondent': 'From Sydney to China and Japan' (13 parts), *Town and Country Journal*, 7 June 1890 to 18 October 1890; and Mrs Ellen Beadnell, 'A Holiday in Japan', *Town and Country Journal*, 9 August 1911.

71 'Early Australian Contacts with Japan', p 17. Articles by James Murdoch were published in *Boomerang* on 9 March, 30 March, 20 April, 20 October, 30 November 1889; 17 May 1890; 3 January 1891, as cited in 'Attitudes to Japan and Defence 1890-1923', D C S Sissons, 3 vols, MA thesis, University of Melbourne, 1956. For biographical details of James Murdoch see

Bede Nairn and Geoffrey Serle (eds), *Australian Dictionary of Biography, vol 10: 1891-1939*, Melbourne, 1986.

72 A M [James Murdoch], *From Australia and Japan*, London, 1892.

73 A M [James Murdoch], *Ayame-san, A Japanese Romance of the 23rd Year of Meiji (1890)*, Yokohama, 1892. For a glowing review see 'Japanese Literature', *The Athenaeum*, 24 June 1893.

74 A M, 'Early Australian Contacts with Japan', op. cit., p 17.

75 James Murdoch, *A History of Japan*, 3 vol, New York, 1996.

76 W E Griffis, 'Reviews of Books', *American Historical Review*, vol 9, no 4, 1903.

77 James Murdoch, *A History of Japan*, vol 1, New York, 1964, p 2.

78 ibid., p 3.

79 ibid., p 12.

Chapter Six

1 Sandra Tweedie, *Trading Partners: Australia & Asia 1790-1993*, Sydney, 1994, pp 27-33. See also Ian H Nish, *The Anglo-Japanese Alliance: The Diplomacy of Two Island Empires: 1894-1907*, London [1966], 1985, p 10.

2 For Dyer's activities as a commercial agent see John Plummer, 'Australian Notes on Japanese Topics', *Japan Daily Mail*, 3 April 1895 and 'Japanese Topics in Australia', *Japan Daily Mail*, 26 April 1895.

3 'Trade with the East. The Proposed Japanese Treaty', *Argus*, 22 October 1895.

4 *Age*, 22 October 1895.

5 E J Dyer, 'Australia and the Asian-Pacific: An Address delivered in Melbourne Town Hall on October 21, 1895', Melbourne, 1895, p 3. Dyer's views on trade with the East were also discussed in 'Trade with the Philippines. Australian Products at the Manila Exhibition', *Sydney Morning Herald*, 4 May 1895 and in 'Japan: A New Commercial Competitor', *New Century Review*, vol 3, no 15, March 1898.

6 Dyer, 'Australia and the Asian-Pacific', op. cit., p 5.

7 W Madden, 'Trade With The East. The Proposed Japanese Treaty', *Argus*, 22 October 1895.

8 Cited in John Plummer, 'Australia and Japan', *Japan Daily Mail*, 16 May 1896.

9 Michael R Johnson, '"Complementarity and Conflict": Australian and Japanese Relations in the Nineteenth Century', BA(Hons) thesis, University of New South Wales, October 1981, pp 41-48. See also 'Japan. Market for Australian Products. Splendid Prospects. Mr Suttor's Views', *Sydney Morning Herald*, 4 April 1916.

10 Johnson, '"Complimentary and Conflict"', op. cit., p 42.

11 Details are given in John Plummer, 'Australian Notes on Japanese Topics', *Japan Daily Mail*, 18 April 1895.

12 For biographical details see Bede Nairn (ed.), *Australian Dictionary of Biography, vol 6: 1851-1890*, Melbourne, 1976.

13 Plummer, 'Australian Notes', op. cit.

14 Kurando Koga, 'Origin of Kanematsu Organization in Australia', *Kanematsu Geppo: Commemorative Number*, 15 August 1959, translated by Akira Ocdaira. See also Tadakatsu Inoue, 'Pioneering in Australian Direct Trade: The Life of Fusajiro Kanematsu, 1845-1913', *Kobe Economic and Business Review*, 22nd Annual Report, The Research Institute for Economics and Business Administration, Kobe University, 1976; Paul C Vincent, 'The Kanematsu Laboratories', *Medical Journal of Australia*, 29 April 1985; and John Plummer, 'Australian News', *Japan Daily Mail*, 23 September 1895.

15 Tweedie, *Trading Partners*, op. cit., pp 18-20; Plummer, 'Australian Notes', op. cit., 18 April 1895.

16 Inoue, 'Pioneering in Australian Direct Trade', op. cit., p 11; Tweedie, *Trading Partners*, ibid., p 34.
17 A T Yarwood, *Walers: Australian Horses Abroad*, Melbourne, 1989. See also 'Australian Horses in India', *Town and Country Journal*, 7 October 1882.
18 J B Suttor, 'Report on Java and the Dutch East Indies', *Bulletin no 26*, Intelligence Department, New South Wales, Sydney, 1908.
19 Plummer, 'Australia and Japan', *Japan Daily Mail*, 6 May 1896.
20 J B Suttor, 'Report on the Trade of Japan for the Year 1904', *Bulletin no 2*, Intelligence Department, New South Wales, Sydney, 1905.
21 Johnson, '"Complementarity and Conflict"', op. cit., Appendix II, p B 10; D C S Sissons, 'Australian-Japanese Relations: The First Phase 1859-91', unpublished, School of Pacific Studies, Australian National University, 1980.
22 Tweedie, *Trading Partners*, op. cit., pp 32,38,39.
23 John Plummer, regular column, *Japan Daily Mail*, 3 April 1895 to 22 February 1898. Australia and Japan Newspaper Cuttings 1895-1898, vol 56, Mitchell Library, Sydney. For biographical details see Geoffrey Serle (ed.), *Australian Dictionary of Biography, vol 11: 1891-1939*, Melbourne, 1988.
24 Elles first appears in Sand's *Sydney Directory* in 1888 as a merchant. In 1889 he is listed as a manufacturers' agent, then in 1890 as a stock and sharebroker, in 1891 as a share, bullion and finance broker and thereafter, until his retirement in 1925, as a stock and sharebroker. In 1890 he became founding chairman of the stock exchange of New South Wales. Later he was an honorary member of the NSW Institute of Bankers which published several substantial articles by Elles in its journal, *Journal of the Institute of Bankers of NSW*, between 1892 and 1910. For further details on Elles see Stephen Salsbury and Kay Sweeney, *Sydney Stockbrokers: Biographies of Members of the Sydney Stock Exchange 1871 to 1987*, Sydney, 1992. For further details on Colonel George Bell, see A B 'Colonel Geo W Bell (United States Consul)', *Cosmos Magazine*, 31 December 1895; *Who Was Who in America: A Companion Volume to Who's Who in America*, vol 1, 1897-1942, Chicago, 1942.
25 Plummer, 'Australia and Japan', *Japan Daily Mail*, 6 May 1896.
26 William Sowden, *Children of the Rising Sun: Commercial and Political Japan*, Adelaide, 1897, pp 9 and 19.
27 'Mr Frederick Villiers. A Famous War Correspondent', *Sydney Mail*, 18 May 1895.
28 Plummer, 'Australia and Japan', *Japan Daily Mail*, 27 June 1895.
29 Plummer, 'Japanese Topics in Australia', *Japan Daily Mail*, 9 August 1895.
30 ibid.
31 Plummer, 'Australia and Japan', *Japan Daily Mail*, 16 July 1896.
32 *Japan Daily Mail*, 16 May 1896.
33 *Japan Daily Mail*, 29 August 1895.
34 *Japan Daily Mail*, 17 January 1896.
35 *Japan Daily Mail*, 2 March 1896.
36 *Japan Daily Mail*, 10 February 1897.
37 *Japan Daily Mail*, 3 April 1895.
38 *Japan Daily Mail*, 6 May 1896.
39 ibid.
40 Plummer, 'Australian News', *Japan Daily Mail*, 23 September, 1895.
41 Plummer, 'Australia and Japan', *Japan Daily Mail*, 25 November 1896.
42 *Japan Daily Mail*, 6 May 1896.
43 *Japan Daily Mail*, 15 December 1896. Mary Hall in *A Woman in the Antipodes and in the Far East*, London, 1914, pp 176-177, praises the accommodation, service and meals provided on the Nippon Yusen Kaisha line.

44 I Takeda, 'Australia-Japan Relations in the Era of the Anglo-Japanese Alliance, 1896-1911,' PhD thesis, University of Sydney, 1984, p 36.

45 Plummer, op. cit., 15 December 1896.

46 Takeda, 'Australia-Japan Relations', op. cit., pp 36-7.

47 ibid., p 62.

48 ibid., p 68.

49 ibid., p 82.

50 'Report of The Annual General Meeting of the Sydney Chamber of Commerce', 27 July 1903.

51 Glen Walsh, 'John Bligh Suttor and the New South Wales Commercial Agency in the East', BA (Hons) thesis, University of Sydney, 1979, cited in Takeda, 'Australia-Japan Relations', op. cit., but original uncited. Sydney University has been unable to locate a copy of this thesis.

52 Takeda, 'Australia-Japan Relations', op. cit., pp 126-40.

53 ibid., p 98.

54 ibid.

55 J B Suttor, 'Report on the Trade of Japan, 1910', *Bulletin no 47*, Immigration and Tourist Bureau, New South Wales, Sydney, 1911, p 5.

56 J B Suttor, 'Report on the Trade of Japan, 1907', *Bulletin no 28*, Immigration and Tourist Bureau, New South Wales, Sydney, 1908, p 6.

57 J B Suttor, 'Report on the Trade of The Dutch East Indies, 1910', *Bulletin no 49*, Immigration and Tourist Bureau, New South Wales, Sydney, 1911, p 35.

58 ibid., p 14.

59 'Topical Talk', *Worker*, 18 January 1906.

60 Tweedie, *Trading Partners*, op. cit., pp 224-225.

61 'Sydney and the East. Unequalled Trade Openings', *Sydney Morning Herald*, 29 May 1908.

62 Colonel Geo W Bell, *The Little Giants of The East or Our New Allies*, Sydney, 1905; *The Empire of Business! Or How to People Australia*, Sydney, 1906.

63 Bell, *Report of The Proceedings at The Banquet to Colonel Geo W Bell (US Consul at Sydney)*, Sydney, 1896, p 10.

64 Bell, *The Empire of Business!*, op. cit., pp 39-40.

65 ibid., p 45.

66 Bell, *The Little Giants of The East*, op. cit., p 57.

67 '"Pisness is Pisness": Bumptious Blatherskite Bell. Bell Blusters, Bawls, Bellows. Baneful Bunkum about "Business", Maleficent Mouthings about Mongol Meekness. Colonel Bell's Intrusive, Insufferable, Ignorance. He Dennounces "High Wages" and Advocates Coloured Immigration', *Truth*, 27 May 1906. See also 'Jaw-Bell's Jap Jaw. A Yankee Colonel, Barracking for the Japs Proves Conclusively that in Australia Will Be Centered: The Empire of Business and Civilisation', *Truth*, 14 January 1906.

68 Moira MacKay, Assistant Archivist, University Archives, University of Glasgow, to David Walker, 8 July 1996.

69 J Currie Elles Esq., 'The Influence of Commerce on Civilisation', *Journal of the Institute of Bankers of NSW*, 30 April 1908.

70 ibid., p150.

71 *Sydney Morning Herald*, 10 July 1905. Also Rory Mungoven, 'James Murdoch: Professor of Japanese', unpublished notes, September 1987.

72 'Significant Speeches', *Sydney Morning Herald*, 19 July 1910.

73 For biographical details see Bede Nairn and Geoffrey Serle (eds), *Australian Dictionary of Biography, vol 7: 1891-1939*, Melbourne, 1979.

74 Randolph Bedford, 'White, Yellow and Brown', *Lone Hand*, 1 July 1911.

75 ibid.

Chapter Seven

1 *Advertiser* (Adelaide), 13 May 1903.
2 *Advertiser* (Adelaide), 8 May 1903.
3 *Advertiser* (Adelaide), 13 May 1903.
4 *Age*, 23 May 1903
5 *Argus*, 23 May 1903.
6 *Argus*, 24 May, 1903.
7 *Argus*, 18 May 1903.
8 ibid.
9 *Age*, 18 May 1903
10 *Sydney Mail*, 10 June 1903.
11 *Sydney Mail* , 17 June 1903.
12 'Our Japanese Guests' (editorial), *Sydney Morning Herald*, 6 June 1903.
13 *Sydney Mail*, 10 June 1903.
14 *Bulletin*, 13 June 1903.
15 *Argus*, 12 May 1906.
16 *Argus*, 14 May 1906.
17 *Age*, 15 May 1906.
18 *Argus*, 16 May 1906.
19 *Argus*, 18 May 1906.
20 *Argus*, 10 May 1906.
21 F A A Russell, 'Australian Problems: Australia and the East', *Sydney Morning Herald*, 25 July 1905.
22 Inazo Nitobe, *Bushido: The Soul of Japan*, Rutland, 1905; J D Storry, *Japan and the Decline of the West in Asia, 1894-1943*, New York, 1979, p 64.
23 E Ashmead Bartlett, 'Some Famous Men I Have Met', *Town and Country Journal*, 9 January 1918.
24 *Who Was Who 1929-1940: A Companion to Who's Who: Containing the Biographies of those who died during the period 1929-1940*, [1941] London, 1967, p 39.
25 Mark R Peattie, entry on General Maresuke Nogi, *Kodansha Encyclopedia of Japan*, vol 6, Tokyo, 1983.
26 'Japan's Warships. Arrive at Sydney. A Hearty Welcome', *Sydney Morning Herald*, 22 May 1906.
27 'Japanese Squadron: Entertaining the Officers: A Trip to Parramatta', *Sydney Morning Herald*, 24 May 1906.
28 *Sydney Morning Herald*, 26 May 1906.
29 'The Return of Our Allies', *Sydney Mail*, 23 May 1906.
30 *Sydney Mail*, 16 May 1906
31 'Rear Admiral Shimamura', *Australasian*, 19 May 1906.
32 'The Japanese Visit', editorial, *Sydney Mail*, 23 May 1906. See also 'Our Half-Century of Self-Government', editorial, *Sydney Mail*, 16 May 1906
33 'The Japanese Welcome', *Bulletin*, 24 May 1906.
34 Douglas Sladen, *Queer Things about Japan*, Fourth Edition, to which is added: 'Life of the late Emperor of Japan', London, 1913.
35 Victor Kennedy and Nettie Palmer, *Bernard O'Dowd*, Carlton, 1954, pp 105-106.
36 'A Japanese Invasion', *The Worker*, 3 May 1906.
37 *The Worker*, 17 May 1906.
38 *Truth*, 27 May 1906.
39 'The Japanese Welcome', op. cit.

40 Orlando H Baker to Robert Bacon, Dispatch # 147, vol 61, Dispatch Book 1/1900-6/1906, RG84 Records of Foreign Service Posts, Consular Posts, Sydney, Australia, 6 June 1906, National Archives and Record Administration, College Park, MD, USA.

41 ibid.

42 ibid.

43 One of the best analyses of the Great White Fleet visit to Australia remains Ruth Megaw, 'Australia and the Great White Fleet 1908', *Journal of the Royal Australian Historical Society*, vol 56, no 2, 1970. Other sources are Neville Meaney, *The Search For Security in the Pacific, 1901-1914*, Sydney, 1976; Richard Waterhouse, 'The Beginning of Hegemony or a Confluence of Interests: The Australian-American Relationship, 1788-1908', *The Australasian Journal of American Studies*, vol 9, no 2, 1990; James R Reckner, *Teddy Roosevelt's Great White Fleet*, Annapolis, 1988; and Robert A Hart, *The Great White Fleet: Its Voyage around the World, 1907-1909*, Boston, 1965. The best contemporary account is Franklin Matthews, *Back To Hampton Roads: Cruise of the U S Atlantic Fleet from San Francisco to Hampton Roads July 7, 1908-February 22, 1909*, New York, 1909.

44 For newspaper accounts of the invitation see 'The American Fleet. May Visit Australia. Invitation from Mr Deakin', *Age*, 24 February 1908 and 'United States Fleet. Invited to Visit Australia. Authorities Highly Gratified', *Argus*, 24 February 1908.

45 W H Fitchett, 'The Problem of Australian Sea -Defence', *Review of Reviews*, 20 December, 1901; Anon., 'The Problem of Australian Sea -Defence', *Review of Reviews*, 20 January 1902; Anon, 'The Admirals on Australian Sea-Defence', *Review of Reviews*, 20 February 1902.

46 James Edmond, 'The Australian Fleet', *Living Age*, 12 August 1911.

47 Alfred Deakin to Whitelaw Reid, Ambassador for the United States in Great Britain, 7 January 1908, File # 8258/45, State Department Records of the Cruise of the Atlantic Fleet to the Pacific, General Records of the State Department (RG 59), Numerical and Minor File, 1906-1910, microfilm # M862, National Archives and Record Administration, College Park, MD.

48 John P Bray, American Consul General, Melbourne, to the Assistant Secretary of State, Washington DC, 24 December 1907, File # 8258/123, ibid.

49 Alfred Deakin to John P Bray, 24 December 1907, File #8258/124, ibid.

50 Alfred Deakin to Whitelaw Reid, 7 January 1908, op. cit.

51 Elihu Root, Secretary of State, to President Theodore Roosevelt, 21 February 1908, File no #8258/143-145, op. cit.

52 Matthews, *Back To Hampton Roads*, op. cit., p 67.

53 ibid., p 70.

54 Roderic Quinn, "Hail! Men of America, Hail!", cited in Matthews, *Back To Hampton Roads*, op. cit., p 72.

55 'Dryblower' Murphy, 'The Lonely Kangaroo', cited in Matthews, *Back To Hampton Roads*, op. cit., pp 106-109.

56 Charles S Sperry to Edith Sperry, 28 August 1908, Charles S Sperry Papers, 1862-1912, Box 13 World Cruise Correspondence, Manuscript Division, Library of Congress.

57 Charles S Sperry to Edith Sperry, 9 September 1908, ibid.

58 'Our Fleet in Australian Waters', *Current Literature*, vol xlv, no 4, October 1908.

59 'Americans Guests of the Australians', *New York Times*, 21 August 1908.

60 Hugh H Lusk, 'A Visit of the Fleet to Australia', *Harper's Weekly*, 11 July 1908.

61 *New York Herald*, 22 August 1908.

62 'The White Australia Ideal', *The Times*, 9 August 1908.

63 V Chirol to G E Morrison, 21 January 1908 in Lo Hui-Min (ed.), *The Correspondence of G E Morrison vol I 1895-1912*, Cambridge, 1976.

64 G E Morrison to J M V J Ffrench, 22 September 1910, ibid.

65 'The Battleship Fleet and The Yellow Peril', *Japan Times*, 13 August 1908; 'The American Squadron and Radical Bias', *Japan Times*, 14 August 1908.
66 'Anti-Japanese Sentiment', *Japan Times*, 29 August 1908. See also 'In the Wake of the Battleship Fleet', *Japan Weekly Mail*, 5 September 1908. For a scathing critique of Australia's fears of Japan see 'Japan and Australia', *Nation (US)*, 3 September 1908.
67 Editorial, *Japan Times*, 29 August 1908.
68 'Japanese Press', ibid., 29 August 1908.

Chapter Eight

1 I F Clarke, *Voices Prophesying War: Future Wars 1763-3749*, (2nd edition) Oxford, 1992; Patrick Brantlinger, *Rule of Darkness: British Literature and Imperialism, 1830-1914*, Ithaca, 1988.
2 David Trotter, 'Introduction', Erskine Childers, *The Riddle of the Sands* [1903], Oxford, 1995, p ix.
3 Daniel Pick, *War Machine: The Rationalisation of Slaughter in the Modern Age*, New Haven, 1993, p 115.
4 Anon [Lieutenant Colonel Sir George Tomkyns Chesney] 'The Battle of Dorking', *Blackwood's Magazine*, May 1871, in Clarke, *Voices Prophesying War*, pp 26-35. 'The Battle of Dorking' was also published in Australia as *The Battle of Dorking: Reminiscences of a Volunteer*, Melbourne, 1871.
5 W H Walker [George Rankin], *The Invasion*, Sydney, 1877. Other early invasion novels at this time include: A Dekhnewallah, *The Great Russian Invasion of India: A Sequel to the Afghanistan Campaign of 1878-9*, London, 1879; P Colomb, J F Maurice, F N Maude, Archibald Forbes, Charles Lowe, D Christie Murray and F Scudamore, *The Great War of 189-*, London, 1893; Louis Tracy, *The Final War*, London, 1896; William Le Queux, *England's Peril*, London 1899; T W Offin, *How The Germans Took London*, London, 1900. For plot synopses see Everett F Bleiler, *Science Fiction: The Early Years*, Kent, 1990.
6 Chris Steinbrunner, Otto Penzler, Marvin Lachnan and Charles Shibuk (eds), *Encyclopedia of Mystery and Detection*, New York, 1976, p 243.
7 Trotter, 'Introduction', op. cit., p x.
8 Gail Ching-Liang Low, *White Skins/Black Masks: Representation and Colonialism*, London, 1996, pp 14-15.
9 Eric J Grove, 'Introduction', E Childers, *The Riddle of The Sands* [1903], Annapolis, 1991, p xxviii. For further analysis of the development of the British spy novel see David French, 'Spy Fever in Britain, 1900-1915', *The Historical Journal*, vol 21, no 2, 1978; David A T Stafford, 'Spies and Gentlemen: Birth of the British Spy Novel, 1893-1914', *Victorian Studies*, vol 24, no 4, 1981.
10 Clarke, *Voices Prophesying War*, op. cit., p 142. See also Trotter, 'Introduction', op. cit., p ix.
11 David Trotter, 'Introduction', op. cit., p xvii.
12 William Le Queux, *The Invasion of 1910*, London, 1905. See also Steinbrummer et al, *Encyclopedia of Mystery and Detection*, op. cit., p 244.
13 Nicholas Hiley, 'Introduction', William Le Queux, *Spies of the Kaiser: Plotting the Downfall of England* [1909], London, 1996, p viii.
14 A A Milne, 'The Secret of the Army Aeroplane', *Punch*, 26 May 1909.
15 Hiley, 'Introduction', op. cit., p xvi.
16 Daniel Pick, 'Tunnel Visions', *War Machine: The Rationalisation of Slaughter in the Modern Age*, New Haven, 1993, pp 115-35 with quotation p 121. Tunnel invasion stories included T A Guthrie, *The Seizure of the Channel Tunnel*, London, 1882 and C Forth, *The Surprise of

the Channel Tunnel, London, 1883. In a later American development of this theme G Edwards [G E Pendray] , *The Earth Tube*, New York 1909, described how the Eastern world attacked America through a vast subterranean tunnel, cited in I F Clark, *Tale of the Future: From the Beginning to the Present Day* (3rd ed), London, 1978.

17 Lang-Tung [F V White], *The Decline and Fall of the British Empire: Written for the Use of Junior Classes in Schools*, London ,1881, cited in Clark, *Tale of the Future*, ibid.; H G Wells, *War in the Air*, London, 1907.

18 R Valerie Lucas, 'Yellow Peril in the Promised Land: the Representation of the Oriental and the Question of American Identity', in Francis Barker, Peter Hulme, Margaret Iverson and Diana Loxley (eds), *Europe and its Others*, Colchester, 1985,p 44.

19 Lorelle, 'Battle of the Warbush', *Californian*, 2 October 1880.

20 Robert Wolter, *A Short and Truthful History of the Taking of California and Oregon by the Chinese in the Year AD 1899*, San Francisco, 1882.

21 Pierton W Dooner, *The Last Days of the Republic*, San Francisco, 1880; Otto Mundo, *The Recovered Continent. A Tale of Chinese Invasion*, Columbus 1898.

22 William F Wu, *The Yellow Peril: Chinese Americans in American Fiction 1850-1940*, Hamden, 1982, pp 12-29.

23 The key Australian literature on the Chinese as invaders includes Anon., *The Battle of Mordialloc, or How We Lost Australia*, Melbourne, 1888; 'Sketcher' [William Lane],' White or Yellow? A Story of the Race-War of 1908', *Boomerang*, 18 February 1888 to 5 May 1888; Kenneth Mackay, *The Yellow Wave: A Romance of the Asiatic Invasion of Australia*, London, 1895; Raymond Longford (director), J Barr, C A Jeffries (script writers), *Australia Calls*, Sydney, 1913. For an account of *Australia Calls* see *Bulletin*, 24 July 1913; Graham Shirley and Brian Adams, *Australian Cinema: The First Eighty Years*, revised edition, Sydney, 1982, p 32 ; Ina Bertrand (ed.), *Cinema in Australia: A Documentary History*, Kensington, 1989, p 100. Samuel Rosa in *The Invasion of Australia*, Sydney, 1920, provides one of the few systematic arguments against fears of invasion. For a survey of invasion literature see David Walker, 'Invasion Literature: The Yellow Wave: Moulding the Popular Imagination', *Asian Influences on Australian Literature: Proceedings of a Symposium*, Library Society, State Library of New South Wales, 1988. See also Robert Dixon, 'Imagined Invasions: The *Lone Hand* and narratives of Asiatic invasion', in Robert Dixon, *Writing the Colonial Adventure: Race, gender and nation in Anglo-Australian popular fiction, 1875-1914*, Cambridge, 1995; Neville Meaney, 'The "Yellow Peril": Invasion Scare Novels and Australian Political Culture' in Ken Stewart (ed.), *The 1890s: Australian Literature and Literary Culture*, St Lucia, 1996.

24 'Sketcher', 'White or Yellow?', *Boomerang*, 18 February 1888.

25 *Boomerang*, 25 February 1888.

26 *Boomerang*, 17 March 1888.

27 For a further discussion of the symbolism of dead virgins in late nineteenth century culture, see 'The Cult of Invalidism: Orphelia and Folly; Dead Ladies and the Fetish of Sleep', in Bram Dijkstra, *Idols of Perversity: Fantasies of Feminine Evil in Fin-de-Siècle Culture*, New York, 1986.

28 G E Morrison, *An Australian in China*, London, 1895, pp 100, 140.

29 'Sketcher', 'White or Yellow?', op. cit., 7 April 1888.

30 Anon., *The Battle of Mordialloc*, op. cit., p 67.

31 Obituary, 'Major-General Mackay: Death of Noted Cavalryman', *Sydney Morning Herald*, 18 November, 1935.

32 Mackay, *The Yellow Wave*, op. cit., p 352.

33 ibid., pp 382-3.

34 ibid., p 369.

35 'Sketcher', 'White or Yellow?', op. cit., 31 March 1888.
36 No stated author, *Mathew Phipps Shiel (1865-1947)*, Cleveland, 1979. For an account of Shiel's early life see 'M P Shiel 1865-1947' in E F Bleiler (ed.), *Science Fiction Writers. Critical Studies of the Major Authors from the Early Nineteenth Century to the Present Day*, New York, 1982. For his contribution to the literature of English decadence see Mathew Sturgis, *Passionate Attributes: The English Decadence of the 1890s*, London, 1995, pp 203-206.
37 M P Shiel, *Science, Life and Literature*, London, 1950, p 21.
38 M P Shiel, 'The Empress of the Earth. The Tale of the Yellow War', *Short Stories*, 5 February 1898 to 18 June 1898; M P Shiel, *The Yellow Danger*, London, 1898; M P Shiel, *The Yellow Danger*, New York, 1899. The story was later serialised as 'The Yellow Peril, a Tale of the Great Chinese War', *Illustrated Weekly News*, 30 June 1900 to 1 September 1900 and continued in *The Curiosity Shop*, 8 September 1900 to 13 October 1900 as cited in *Mathew Phipps Shiel (1865-1947)*, op. cit.
39 A Reynolds Morse, *The Works of M P Shiel: A Study in Bibliography*, Los Angeles, 1948.
40 M P Shiel, *The Yellow Danger*, New York, 1899, p 127.
41 ibid., p 301
42 ibid., pp 382, 386.
43 ibid., p 388.
44 J H Palmer, *The Invasion of New York or How Hawaii was Annexed*, New York, 1897, see Bleiler, *Science Fiction: The Early Years*, op. cit., p 584 ; L Netterfield [S J O'Grady], *Queen of the World; or Under Tyranny*, London, 1900, pp 538-9. For another British tale where China rules the world see James Barr, 'The Last Englishman', *Monthly Story Blue Book Magazine*, July 1906, ibid., p 39.
45 J. Morris, *What Will Japan Do?*, London, 1898, cited in Clark, *Tale of the Future*, op. cit.
46 For an Australian response to the Russo-Japanese War see E R Peacock, *Little Japan against Mighty Russia being a Popular Statement of the Far Eastern Question*, Melbourne, 1904. This book was dedicated to Peacock's 'esteemed friend and travelling companion' K Iwasaki, Consul-General for Japan, Sydney. For defence build-up and Asia-Pacific concerns see Neville Meaney, *The Search for Security in the Pacific, 1901-1914*, Sydney, 1976. For a general history of the period see Gavin Souter, *Lion and Kangaroo: The Initiation of Australia 1901-1919*, Sydney, 1976. For boyhood conscription see John Barrett, *Falling In: Australians and 'Boy Conscription' 1911-1915*, Sydney, 1979. For the establishment of the Military Academy at Duntroon see Colonel J E Lee, *Duntroon: The Royal Military College of Australia 1911-1946*, Canberra, 1952. For Federal control of the Northern Territory see Chapter 9. For a survey of Japanese immigration see [E L Piesse], 'Japanese Immigration into Australia: History of the Immigration Restrictions Act', *Stead's Review*, 1 August 1925.
47 For an early expression of concerns over Australia's rapid urbanisation see Adna Ferrin Weber, *The Growth of Cities in the Nineteenth Century: A Study in Statistics*, New York, 1899. For a discussion of concerns about effeminacy see 'Body/Border Lines', in Low, *White Skins/Black Masks*, op. cit., pp 13-35. For concerns over the emancipation of women and the decline of the birth-rate in Australia, see Judith A Allen, *Sex & Secrets: Crimes Involving Australian Women Since 1880*, Melbourne, 1990. For the Royal Commission on the Decline of the birth-rate in New South Wales, see Neville Hicks, *"This Sin and Scandal": Australia's Population Debate 1891-1911*, Canberra, 1978.
48 Mrs Rosa Campbell Praed, *Madame Izàn: A Tourist Story*, London, 1899.
49 ibid., p 10.
50 ibid., p 24.
51 Katie Spearritt, 'New Dawns: First Wave Feminism 1880-1914', in Kay Saunders and Raymond Evans (eds), *Gender Relations in Australia: Domination and Negotiation*, Sydney,

1992, p 325; Robert Dixon, 'The New Woman and the Coming Man: Gender and Genre in the 'Lost Race' Romance', in Susan Rowley, Susan Magarey and Susan Sheridan (eds), *Debutante Nation: Feminism Contests the 1890s*, St Leonards, 1993, pp 163-74. See also 'The Woman of the Future', *Review of Reviews*, 20 May 1895.

52 Praed, *Madame Izàn*, op. cit., p 140.

53 Ernest F Fenollosa, 'Man's Final Experiment', *Harper's Magazine*, cited in 'The Wedding of East and West', *Review of Reviews*, 15 January 1899.

54 ibid., p 198.

55 ibid., p 326.

56 Rata [T R Roydhouse], *The Coloured Conquest*, Sydney, 1903.

57 Carol Mills, 'The Bookstall Novel: An Australian Paperback Revolution', in David Walker and Martyn Lyons (eds), 'Books, Readers, Reading', *Australian Cultural History*, no 11, 1992.

58 A G Hales, *The Little Blue Pigeon*, London, 1904; Ambrose Pratt, 'The Big Five', *Lone Hand*, December 1907 to September 1908, then published as *The Big Five*, London, 1910; C H Kirmess, 'The Commonwealth Crisis', *Lone Hand*, 1 October 1908 to 1 April 1909, republished as *The Australian Crisis*, Melbourne, 1909; Randolph Bedford, 'White Australia, or The Empty North', Australian National Archives, Canberra; Frances Hopkins, *Reaping The Whirlwind: An Australian Patriotic Drama for Australian People*, Sydney, 1909; Jo Smith, 'The Girl of The Never Never; An Original Drama in Four Acts', unpublished script, c1912, Northern Territory Library. Short stories with a theme of Japanese Invasion include 'Veronica', 'Guarding Our Northern Gate', *Lone Hand*, 2 August 1909 and Evelyn Aldridge, 'The Deliverer', *Lone Hand*, 1 July 1910.

59 For Wodehouse see Brantlinger, *Rule of Darkness*, op. cit., p.235.

60 R W Cole, *The Death Trap*, London, 1907, in Bleiler, *Science Fiction: The Early Years*, op. cit. p 148; J Crabapple, *The War of 1908 for the Supremacy of the Pacific*, London 1908; A W Kipling, *The New Dominion*, London, 1908, cited in Clarke, *Tale of the Future*, op. cit. Marsden Manson, *The Yellow Peril in Action: A Possible Chapter in History*, San Francisco, 1907; Ernest Hugh Fitzpatrick, *The Coming Conflict of Nations, or, the Japanese-American War*, Springfield, 1909; M J Phillips, *In Our Country's Service*, Columbus, 1909; Johnston McCulley, 'When the World Stood Still', *All-Story*, August-December 1909. See also Rowan Stevens, 'The Battle for the Pacific'; Yates Stirling Jr., 'The Bombardment of the Golden Gate' and 'A Fight in the Fog'; W J Henderson, 'Joe Griffith's Great Jump' in Rowan Steven's, Yates Sterling Jr, et al., *The Battle for The Pacific*, New York, 1908. A Japanese invasion of America is also a theme of Melville Davisson Post, *The Gilded Chair*, New York, 1911.

61 'Parabellum' [Ferdinand H Grautoff], *Banzai!*, New York, 1908, p 193.

62 ibid., p 199.

63 ibid., p 286.

64 ibid., p 287.

65 ibid., p 293.

66 ibid., p 288.

67 Frank Fox, *Problems of the Pacific*, London, 1912, p 106, cited in Bradley Fitzmaurice, 'Red Parasols Over an Antipodean Italy: A Study of the *Lone Hand* and the People who Made It', MA (Hons) thesis, University of New South Wales, 1986, p 3.

68 Weber, *The Growth of Cities*, op. cit., p 138.

69 Professor J MacMillan Brown, 'East and West: Japan and the White Race', *Sydney Morning Herald*, 28 June 1913. See also J MacMillan Brown, 'The Pacific. American Asiatic Institute. Problems of the Future', *Sydney Morning Herald*, 31 May 1913 and editorial, 'Problems of the Pacific', *Sydney Morning Herald*, 31 May 1913. For Richard Arthur's

response to 'Problems of the Pacific' see Letters to the Editor, *Sydney Morning Herald*, 5 June 1913. For a profile of J MacMillan Brown see James Cowan, 'Famous New Zealanders. No 24', *New Zealand Railways Magazine*, March 1935. For a discussion of British concerns over the effects of the decadent environment of cities see Low, *White Skins/Black Masks*, op. cit., pp 15-21.

70   Arthur Adams, 'The Day the Big Shells Came', first published in the *Bulletin*, reissued in the *Call*, February 1909.

Chapter Nine

1   *Northern Territory Acceptance Act 1910, reprinted as at 31 December 1983*, Canberra, 1984.
2   Gail Bederman, *Manliness & Civilization: A Cultural History of Gender and Race in the United States, 1880-1917*, Chicago, 1995, p 194.
3   For biographical details on Octavius Beale see Bede Nairn and Geoffrey Serle (General eds), *Australian Dictionary of Biography, vol 7: 1891-1939*, Melbourne, 1979.
4   Theodore Roosevelt. General Records of the Department of State, Despatches From US Consuls in Melbourne, Australia, RG84, no 306, Microfilm T1&2, US National Archives, College Park, MD.
5   Alfred Deakin, cited in ibid.
6   Franklin Matthews, *Back To Hampton Roads: Cruise of the US Atlantic Fleet from San Francisco to Hampton Roads July 7, 1908-February 22*, 1909, New York, 1909, p 140.
7   Guy H Scholfield, 'The White Peril in Australasia', *Nineteenth Century and After*, vol 58, 1905.
8   'Australia's Problem. Peopling the North. "Times" on the Fisher Cabinet', *Sydney Morning Herald*, 11 July 1910.
9   William Sowden, *Children of the Rising Sun: Commercial and Political Japan*, Adelaide, 1897, p 8.
10   ibid.
11   J Langdon Parsons, 'The Northern Territory of South Australia: A Brief Historical Account: Pastoral and Mineral Resources', *Royal Geographical Society of Australasia*, Adelaide, 1901.
12   George Merrivale, *Report of the Annual General Meeting of the Sydney Chamber of Commerce*, 31 July 1907.
13   *Sydney Morning Herald*, 8 July 1906.
14   *Bulletin*, 10 November 1910.
15   Richard Arthur, (letter to ed), *North Sydney News*, 22 May 1906.
16   Richard Arthur, 'Immigration: The Salvation of Australia', *Commonwealth*, 30 June 1906.
17   ibid., and Richard Arthur, 'The Empty North', 10 January 1910, unidentified newspaper cutting, Richard Arthur Papers, MS 473, Box 3, Mitchell Library.
18   Arthur, 'The Empty North', op. cit. See also Richard Arthur, 'The Empire for Britons', *Sydney Morning Herald*, 15 January 1910. Herbert Easton to E C Buley, editor, *British Australasian*, 10 November 1907, explains grounds for the establishment of the British Immigration League. See also Herbert Easton to E C Buley, 14 January 1908; British Immigration League of Australia, MS 302, Mitchell Library, Sydney.
19   Herbert Easton, Letter to the editor, *British Australasian*, 9 February 1909.
20   Richard Arthur, Letter to Secretary, British Immigration League, London, 22 April 1907.
21   Richard Arthur to H B Stephens, editor of *Australian World*, London, 30 April 1907, Richard Arthur Papers, newspaper cuttings, op. cit.
22   Frances Hopkins, *Reaping the Whirlwind: An Australian Patriotic Drama for Australian People*, Sydney, 1909.

23 Ambrose Pratt, 'The Big Five', *The Lone Hand*, December 1907 to September 1908, republished as *The Big Five*, London, 1910.
24 Pratt, *The Big Five*, op. cit., p 86. H E Pratten likewise considered Port Darwin 'an Oriental port', see *Through Orient to Occident*, Sydney, c1912, p 5.
25 ibid., p 87-8.
26 ibid., p.88.
27 Cyril Pearl, *Morrison of Peking*,[1967], Ringwood, 1970, p 351.
28 Pratt, *The Big Five*, op. cit., p 111.
29 ibid., pp 180, 194.
30 ibid., p 200.
31 ibid., p 272.
32 'Australia's Need', *Sydney Morning Herald*, 27 December 1910.
33 C H Kirmess, 'The Commonwealth Crisis', *Lone Hand*, 1 October 1908 to 1 August 1909.
34 ibid., 1 March 1909.
35 'Project for Introducing Japanese Settlers into the Northern Territory, 1876-77', Letter-books 1876-77, File PRG 456/19, South Australian Archives. See also J Cross, 'Wilton Hack and Japanese Immigration into North Australia', *Proceedings, Royal Geographical Society of Australasia (South Australia Branch)*, 1959-60.
36 *Sydney Morning Herald*, 22 June 1910.
37 Alfred Deakin [House of Representatives], Northern Territory Acceptance Bill, Second Reading, *Hansard*, 12 October 1910, p 4425.
38 Lieutenant Colonel Sir Albert John Gould [Senate], ibid., 17 August 1910, p 1582. For biography see Joan Rydon, *A Bibliographical Register of the Commonwealth Parliament 1901-1972*, Canberra, 1975, p 90.
39 Edward Findley [Senate], ibid., 26 August 1910, p 2141. For biography see ibid. p 74.
40 Edward Needham [Senate], ibid., 26 August 1910, p 2142. For biography , ibid., p 165.
41 Egerton Lee Batchelor, [House of Representatives], ibid., 6 October 1910, p 4250. For biography, ibid., p 13.
42 Patrick Joseph Lynch [Senate], ibid., 21 September 1910, p 3470. For biography, ibid., p 138.
43 Hugh De Largie [Senate], ibid., 20 September 1910, p 3362. For biography, ibid., p 60.
44 Commonwealth Bureau of Census and Statistics, *Official Year Book of the Commonwealth of Australia*, Melbourne, 1911.
45 Patrick McMahon Glynn [House of Representatives], Northern Territory Acceptance Bill, op. cit., 12 October, 1910, p 4444. For biography see *A Bibliographical Register of the Commonwealth Parliament 1901-1972*, op. cit. p 89.
46 Alfred Ozanne and James Mathews [House of Representatives],ibid., 13 October 1910, pp 4551 and 4583 respectively. For biography, ibid., pp 172, 157.
47 Sir Joseph Cook [House of Representatives], ibid., 25 October 1910, p 5128. For biography, ibid., p 48.
48 William James McWilliams [House of Representatives], ibid., 13 October 1910, p 4573. For biography, ibid., p 152.
49 Robert John Sayers [Senate], ibid., 26 August 1910, p 2160. For biography, ibid.
50 William Higgs [House of Representatives], ibid., 13 October 1910, p 4589. For biography, ibid., p 106
51 William Findlayson [House of Representatives], ibid., 25 October 1910, p 5125. For biography, ibid., p 74.
52 Alfred Viscount Northcliffe, *My Journey Round the World (16 July 1921- 26 Feb. 1922)*, London, 1923, p 302. See also 'Lord Northcliffe on Australian Immigration', *Millions Magazine*, 1 October 1921.
53 *Daily Star*, cited in 'Peril of "Empty Australia" ' *The Literary Digest*, vol 71, 5 November, 1921.

54 Sir Leo Chiozza Money, *The Peril of the White*, London, 1925.
55 Evans Lewin, 'Northern Australia: A Local World-Problem', *Atlantic Monthly*, vol 137, April 1926.
56 Fleetwood Chidell, *Australia-White or Yellow?*, London, 1926, pp 156, 157.
57 Warren S Thompson, *Danger Spots in World Population*, New York, 1930, p 83. Reviewed in *Pacific Affairs*, September 1930.
58 'The Empty North: A Dean's Suggestions: "Give Part to Japan": Ridiculed in Australia', *Sydney Morning Herald*, 7 July 1933.
59 ibid.
60 ibid.; 'Dean Johnson, of Canterbury is So, SO Generous: Ready to Give Australia Away, Even unto the Japanese', *Daily Telegraph*, 7 July 1933.
61 'Our Land for Ourselves! Bruce Answers the Dean', *Truth*, 9 July 1933.

Chapter Ten

1 'The Contempt of Asiatics for Europeans', *Town and Country Journal*, 8 December 1900.
2 Bram Dijkstra, *Idols of Perversity: Fantasies of Feminine Evil in Fin-De-Siécle Culture*, New York, 1986, p 182. I would like to thank Juliet Peers for bringing this reference to my attention. Her current PhD thesis, 'The In/Credible Woman: Woman as Aberrant in Late 19th Century Australian Culture ', Deakin University, extends the range of cultural history writing in Australia and its many cross references to European art. For an excellent indication of her views see Juliet Peers, 'The Tribe of Mary Jane Hicks: Imaging Women through the Mount Rennie Rape Case 1886', in David Walker, Stephen Garton and Julia Horne (eds), *Crimes and Trials*, *Australian Cultural History*, no 12, 1993.
3 Dijkstra, *Idols of Perversity*, op. cit., pp 35-42; Jeffrey Weeks, *Sex, Politics and Society: The Regulation of Sexuality Since 1800*, 2nd edition, London, 1989, pp 81,87; Carl N Degler, 'Women's Sexuality in 19th-Century America' in *At Odds: Women and the Family in America from the Revolution to the Present*, Oxford, 1980, pp 249-78.
4 William Acton, 'The Functions and Disorders of the Reproductive Organs', London, 1875, as cited in Sheila Jeffreys (ed.), *The Sexuality Debates*, New York, 1987, p 62.
5 Sheila Jeffreys, 'Sex Reform and Anti-Feminism in the 1920s', in The London Feminist History Group, *The Sexual Dynamics of History: Men's Power, Women's Resistance*, London, 1983, pp 178-179; John Money, Herman Musaph, *Handbook of Sexology*, Amsterdam, 1977, pp 27-34, 38-41.
6 Marie Stopes, *Married Love*, London, 1918. See also June Rose, *Marie Stopes and the Sexual Revolution*, London, 1992, pp 93-4; Ellen Chesler, *Woman of Valor: Margaret Sanger and the Birth Control Movement in America*, New York, 1992, pp 66-67. On Sanger's links with British sexologists and her campaigns for sexual reform in the United States see Genevieve Burnett, 'Fertile Fields: A History of the International Birth Control Movement c1870-1970', PhD thesis, University of New South Wales, Sydney, 1999. For Mary Ware Dennett see Edward T James, *Notable American Women: A Bibliographical Dictionary*, vol 1, Cambridge (Mass), 1971, pp 463-465.
7 For the Benthams see Carol Bacchi, Alison Mackinnon, 'Sex, Resistance and Power: Sex Reform in South Australia c1905', *Australian Historical Studies*, vol 23, no 90, 1988. For Lillie Goodisson see Heather Radi (ed.), *200 Australian Women: A Redress Anthology*, Sydney, 1988, p 72; Stefania Siedlecky, Diana Wyndam, *Populate and Perish: Australian Women's Fight for Birth Control*, Sydney, 1990, p 116. For Marion Piddington see Geoffrey Serle (general ed.), *Australian Dictionary of Biography: vol 11: 1891-1939*, Melbourne, 1988; Marion Piddington, *Tell Them! or, The Second Stage of Mothercraft: A handbook for the Sex Training of the Child*, Sydney 1926.

8   For feminist hostility towards sexual reform see Linda Gordon, *Woman's Body, Woman's Right: A Social History of Birth Control in America*, New York, 1977, pp 95-115. For a comparative discussion of the attitudes of British, European and American liberal feminists towards the 'new sexology' see Genevieve Burnett, 'The Cuckoo Mothers: Feminism' in 'Fertile Fields', op. cit., Chapter 2. For Australian feminism and sexual reform see Bacchiand Mackinnon, 'Sex, Resistance and Power', op. cit., Judith Allen, '"Our Deeply Degraded Sex" and "The animal in man": Rose Scott, Feminism and Sexuality 1890-1925', *Australian Feminist Studies*, nos 7 & 8, 1988; Susan Sheridan, 'The *Woman's Voice* on Sexuality' in Susan Magarey, Sue Rowley and Susan Sheridan (eds), *Debutante Nation: Feminism Contests the 1890s*, Sydney, 1993, pp 114-24.

9   Weeks, *Sex, Politics and Society*, op. cit., p 84-93.

10 Beverley Kingston (ed.), *The World Moves Slowly: A Documentary History of Australian Woman*, Melbourne, 1977, p 41.

11 August Forel, *The Sexual Question; A Scientific, Psychological, Hygenic and Sociological Study* [1906], Revised edition, translated by C F Marshall, New York, 1925, cited in Dijkstra, *Idols of Perversity*, op. cit., p 216.

12 W T Stead, 'Topic of the Month. The Crime against China and Ourselves', *Review of Reviews*, 15 December 1895.

13 G E Morrison, 'The Awakening of China', Address to the Author's Club as reported in the *Morning Post*, cited in Cyril Pearl, *Morrison of Peking*, Ringwood, 1970, p 213; 'Mr Rudyard Kipling. An Interesting Interview', *Age*, 13 November 1891.

14 Rata [T R Roydhouse], *The Coloured Conquest*, [1903], Sydney, 1904, p 1.

15 'Japanese Episodes', *Sydney Morning Herald*, 30 May 1906.

16 'The Japanese Welcome', *Bulletin*, 24 May 1906.

17 For a discussion of crowds and crowd theory see Gustave Le Bon, *Psychologie des Foules* [Paris, 1895], published in England as *The Crowd* [1896], reprinted in Alice Widener, *Gustave Le Bon: The Man and His Works*, Indianapolis, 1979, pp 57-103; Daniel Pick, *Faces of Degeneration: A European Disorder, c1848 -c1918*, Cambridge, 1989, pp 4, 92-96 and 222-224. See also David Walker, 'Introduction : Australian Modern: Modernism and its Enemies', *Journal of Australian Studies,* no 32, 1993.

18 Gabriel Tarde cited in Pick, *Faces of Degeneration*, ibid., p 93; Homer Lea, *The Valor of Ignorance*, New York, 1909, p 138.

19 'The Japanese Welcome', op. cit.

20 Peers, 'The Tribe of Mary Jane Hicks', op. cit., p 141.

21 Otto Weininger, *Sex and Character*, London, c1906, pp 407 and 409, cited in Dijkstra, *Idols of Perversity*, op. cit., p 219. See also Max Nordau, *Degeneration*, 3rd edition, New York, 1895.

22 For accounts of the development of the Women's Movement in Australia, see Audrey Oldfield, *Woman Suffrage: A Gift or a Struggle*, Melbourne, 1992; Patricia Grimshaw, Marilyn Lake, Anne McGrath and Marian Quartly, *Creating a Nation*, Ringwood, 1994 .

23 Dijkstra, *Idols of Perversity*, op. cit., p 213.

24 Weininger, *Sex and Character*, op. cit., cited in Dijkstra, *Idols of Perversity*, p 220.

25 Lea, *The Valor of Ignorance*, op. cit., p 59.

26 Peers, 'The Tribe of Mary Jane Hicks', op. cit., p 141.

27 Dijkstra, *Idols of Perversity*, pp 70, 87 and 100. Male anxieties about floods and tides have been discussed by Klaus Theweleit in *Male Fantasies. Vol 1, Women, Floods, Bodies, History*, Stephen Conway, Eric Carter and Chris Turner (trans.), Mineapolis, 1987.

28 *Idols of Perversity*, op. cit., p 109.

29 The views are evident in A G Hales invasion novel, *The Little Blue Pigeon*, London, 1904.

30 Randolph Bedford, *Nought to Thirty Three*, Sydney, 1944. For biographical information on
    A G Hales see Bede Nairn, Geoffrey Serle (general eds), *Australian Dictionary of Biography:
    Volume 9: 1891-1939*, Carlton, 1983, pp 159-60.
31 Madison Grant, *The Passing of The Great Race or The Racial Basis of European History*,
    New York, 1916.
32 E L Piesse, 'White Australia', *Round Table*, vol 11, March 1921.
33 Hales, *The Little Blue Pigeon*, op. cit., pp 30-31.
34 ibid., p 152.
35 ibid., p 156.
36 For European reactions to the practise of suttee see Sir Edward Braddon, *Thirty Years of
    Shikar*, London, 1895, pp 144-145. For a harrowing accounts of the effects of foot-binding on
    young girls in China see 'Two Books of the Month. The Yellow Puzzle: What should be done
    with China?', *Review of Reviews*, 15 July 1899 and Mary Gaunt, *A Woman in China*, London,
    1914, pp 171-178. For further Australian comments on the degraded position of Japanese
    women see H E Pratten, *Asiatic Impressions*, Sydney, 1908, pp 29-30.
37 Mrs Rosa Campbell Praed, *Madame Izàn: A Tourist Story*, London, 1899. See chapter 8.
38 Helen Jerome, *Japan of Today*, Sydney, 1904, Preface.
39 ibid., p 91.
40 ibid., p 11.
41 Ambrose Pratt, 'The Big Five', *Lone Hand*, December 1907 to September 1908.
42 ibid., pp 275-6.
43 Dijkstra, *Idols of Perversity*, op. cit., p 111.
44 Sander L Gilman, 'Black Bodies, White Bodies: Towards an Iconography of Female Sexuality
    in Late Nineteenth-century Art, Medicine and Literature', in James Donald and Ali Rattansi
    (eds), *'Race', Culture and Difference*, London, 1992. See also Phillip Julian, *The Orientalists:
    European Painters of Eastern Scenes*, Oxford, 1977; Maryanne Stevens (ed.), *The Orientalists:
    Delacroix to Matisse*, London, 1984; Vern G Swanson, *Alma-Tadema: The Painter of the
    Victorian Vision of the Ancient World*, New York, 1977.
45 Ursula Prunster, 'From Empire's End : Australians as Orientalists, 1880-1920' in Roger
    Benjamin (curator and ed.), *Orientalism: Delacroix to Klee*, Sydney 1997.
46 Ella Shohat, 'Gender and Culture of Empire: Toward a Feminist Ethnography of the Cinema',
    Quarterly Review of Film & Video, vol 13, 1991.
47 K'ung Yuan Ku'suh [Ambrose Pratt], *The Judgement of the Orient. Some Reflections on
    the Great War made by the Chinese Student & Traveller K'ung Yuan Ku'suh*, New York,
    1916.
48 ibid., p 40.
49 Randolph Bedford, 'The Enameller's Shop: The Face of Quong Sue Duk', *The Pacific*, 17
    August 1923.
50 Dijkstra, *Idols of Perversity*, op. cit., p 401; Bram Dijkstra, *Evil Sisters: The Threat of
    Female Sexuality in Twentieth Century Culture*, New York, 1996, p 4.
51 Irene L Szyliowicz, *Pierre Loti and the Oriental Woman*, New York, 1988, pp 1, 15, 66, 117.
52 Pierre Loti, [Louis Marie Julien Viaud], *Madame Chrysanthème*, [1887], New York, 1910,
    pp 7, 10, 75, 158, 173, 198.
53 ibid., pp 142,169.
54 Szyliowicz, *Pierre Loti*, op. cit., p 57.
55 Dijkstra, *Evil Sisters*, op. cit., p 276, and Sax Rohmer, [Arthur Sarsfield Ward], *The Yellow
    Claw*, London, 1915, cited in *Evil Sisters*, p 277.
56 Sax Rohmer, 'The Daughter of Huang Chow', in *Tales of Chinatown* [London, 1916], London,
    1971, pp 16, 25, 33.
57 Sax Rohmer, *The Hand of Fu Manchu; The Return of Dr Fu Manchu; The Yellow Claw;
    Dope: 4 Complete Classics*, Secaucus, NJ, 1983, pp 234, 262,277; Sax Rohmer, *Daughter of*

Fu Manchu, New York, 1931 as cited in William F Wu, *The Yellow Peril: Chinese Americans in American Fiction 1850-1940*, Hamden, 1982, pp 191-2 .

58 Wu, *The Yellow Peril*, op. cit., pp 192-5. See also Gary Hoppenstand, 'Yellow Devil Doctors and Opium Dens: A Survey of the Yellow Peril Stereotypes in Mass Media Entertainment', in Christopher D Geist and Jack Nachbar (eds), *The Popular Culture Reader* (third ed.) Bowling Green, 1983, pp 171-85.

59 Dijkstra, *Evil Sisters*, op. cit., pp 331-3.

60 Dijkstra, *Idols of Perversity*, pp 202, 235 and 376. The first Australian performance of Turandot was in 1928 by the Nellie Melba and J C Williams Organisation. See Alison Gyger, *Opera for the Antipodes: Opera in Australia 1881-1939*, Sydney ,1990, p 259; John Cargher, *Bravo! Two Hundred Years of Opera in Australia*, South Melbourne, 1988, p 32.

61 See Brian Read, *Aubrey Beardsley*, New York, 1967, plate 290, 'John and Salome'; for other depictions of eastern women see plates 185 and 252. For the painting of Salome by Bunny see Benjamin, *Orientalism*, op. cit., pp 55 and 165. Patrick Bade, *Femme Fatale: Images of Evil and Fascinating Women*, New York, 1979, p 38.

62 Sterling Seagrave, *Dragon Lady: The Life and Legend of the Last Empress of China*, first published 1992, New York, 1993. The account given below of Tzu Hsi's life is based on Seagrave's biography.

63 ibid., p 103.

64 ibid., pp 194, 235, 251

65 ibid., p 266.

66 G Owen (London Missionary Society, Peking) to G E Morrison, 24 May 1897, in Lo Hui-Min (ed.), *The Correspondence of G E Morrison, vol 1 1895-1912*, Cambridge, 1976, pp 50-51.

67 Wen Ching [Lim Boon-Keng], *The Chinese Crisis from Within*, London, 1901, cited in Seagrave, *Dragon Lady*, op. cit., p269.

68 Seagrave, *Dragon Lady*, op. cit., pp 270, 272 and 281.

69 *The Times*, 13 October 1900.

70 J O P Bland and E Backhouse, *China under the Empress Dowager*, London, 1910, in Seagrave, *Dragon Lady*, op. cit.

71 Hugh Trevor-Roper, *The Hermit of Peking: The Hidden Life of Sir Edmund Backhouse*, London, 1976, pp 60-62, in Seagrave, *Dragon Lady*, op. cit., pp 13-14.

72 Seagrave, *Dragon Lady*, op. cit., p 285.

73 Bland and Backhouse, *China under the Empress Dowager*, op. cit., p 478.

74 ibid., p 259.

75 ibid., pp 90, 479, 481, 485, 490, 497.

76 Edmund Backhouse and J O P Bland, *Annals and Memoirs of the Court of Peking*, Boston, 1914; in Seagrave, *Dragon Lady*, op. cit., with comments on pp 11, 284-5.

77 Trevor-Roper, *The Hermit of Peking*, op. cit., p 2.

78 ibid., p 277.

79 ibid., p 285.

80 *Sydney Morning Herald*, 17 February 1900.

81 'The Far East: Peking', *Sydney Morning Herald*, 13 March, 1900.

82 'The Far East: The Dowager's Victims', *Sydney Morning Herald*, 3 May 1900, and editorials, 7 and 26 June 1900.

83 'Topic of the Month. The Chinese Tragedy', *Review of Reviews*, 15 July 1900; 'Character Sketches: I Tsze Hsi, Empress of China', *Review of Reviews*, 15 August 1900.

84 'Notes on the Situation', *Argus*, 7 July 1900.

85 *Age*, 7, 9 and 12 July 1900.

86 *Argus*, 12 and 21 July 1900.

87 'Empress Dowager of China: Death on Sunday: Foul Play Suspected', *Sydney Morning Herald*, 17 November 1908.

88 'Crisis in China; Death of the Emperor: Empress Dowager Mortally Ill', *Daily Telegraph*, 17 November 1908.
89 Charles Pettit, *The Woman Who Commanded 500,000,000 Men*, New York, 1929.

Chapter Eleven

1   A Grenfell Price, *White Settlers in the Tropics*, New York, 1939. For surveys of the debate on climate and settlement see David N. Livingstone, 'Human Acclimatization: Perspectives on a Contested Field of Inquiry in Science, Medicine and Geography', *History of Science*, vol 25, 1987; Helen R. Woolcock, '"Our salubrious climate": Attitudes to Health in Colonial Queensland', Chapter 9 in Roy Mcleod and Milton Lewis (eds), *Disease, Medicine and Empire*, London, 1988; Leonore Manderson, *Sickness and the State: Health and Illness in Colonial Malaya, 1870-1940*, Cambridge, 1996, pp 72-76; Michael Roe, *Nine Australian Progressives: Vitalism in Bourgeois Social Thought 1890-1960*, Brisbane, 1984; Jonathon Todd, 'Conceptualisation of the Body in Australia, c1880-c1925', BA Thesis, University of New South Wales, 1991; David Walker, 'Climate, Civilization and Character in Australia, 1880-1940', in David Walker and Michael Bennett (eds) 'Intellect and Emotion', *Australian Cultural History*, no 16, 1997/98. For a comment on climate in early America see Karen Ordahl Kupperman, 'Fear of Hot Climates in the Anglo-American Colonial Experience', *William and Mary Quarterly*, vol 41, April 1984. For the reaction of the British to the climate in India see 'Climate and the Colonial Condition', in Dane Kennedy, *The Magic Mountains: Hill Stations and the British Raj*, Berkley, 1996 pp 19-37. For excellent articles on tropical settlement in Australia and the Philippines respectively see Warwick Anderson, 'Geography, Race and Nation: Remapping "Tropical" Australia, 1890-1930', *Historical Records of Australian Science*, vol 11, no 4, 1997; 'The Trespass Speaks: White Masculinity and Colonial Breakdown', *American Historical Review*, vol 102, no 5, 1997.
2   B J Moore-Gilbert, *Kipling and Orientalism*, New York, 1986, p 35.
3   James Johnson, *The Influence of Tropical Climates on European Constitutions, including an Essay on Indigestion, or the Morbid Sensibility of the Stomach and Bowels*, London, 1836, pp 2, and 645-678.
4   ibid., p 2.
5   Sir James Ranald Martin, *Influence of Tropical Climates in Producing the Acute Endemic Diseases of Europeans*, [London, 1860], second ed., London, 1861, p 45, in Kennedy, *The Magic Mountains*, op. cit., p 20.
6   Gail Ching-Liang Low, *White Skins/Black Masks: Representation and Colonialism*, London, 1996.
7   C H Pearson, *National Life and Character: A Forecast*, London, 1893, pp 37, 376.
8   Walter Coote, *Wanderings South and East*, London, 1882, pp 9 and 11.
9   'Australasian Topics', *Review of Reviews*, March 1893.
10 'White Races in The Tropics', *Japan Times*, 9 August 1908.
11 Richard Dyer, *White*, London, 1997, p 21
12 Martin Bernal, *Black Athena: The Afroasiatic Roots of Classical Civilization. Vol 1. The Fabrication of Ancient Greece 1785-1985*, London, 1987, p., 209.
13 Reverend R Waddell, 'The Influence of Climate on Character. The Case for New Zealand', *Review of Reviews*, 15 August 1899.
14 Benjamin Kidd, *The Control of the Tropics*, New York, 1898, pp 51-52.
15 'New Worlds for Old. Stefansson's Creed. Views of Human Progress', *Sydney Morning Herald*, 7 June 1924. Vilhjalmur Stefansson, *The Northward Course of Empire*, New York, 1922, see map opposite title page; Vilhjalmur Stefansson, *Discovery, the Autobiography of Vilhjalmur Stefansson*, New York, 1964.

16 Madison Grant, *The Passing of the Great Race or The Racial Basis of European History,* New York, 1916, pp 34 and 153.
17 William Z Ripley, *The Races of Europe: A Sociological Study*, London, 1899, pp 584-585.
18 G L Wood, 'The Settlement of Northern Australia', *Economic Record*, vol 11, no 2, May 1926.
19 Louis Esson, 'From the Oldest Word. Swadeshi and other Imperial Troubles', *Lone Hand*, 1 July 1908.
20 Randolph Bedford, *Explorations in Civilisation*, Sydney, 1914, p 16.
21 Ripley, *The Races of Europe*, op. cit., p 562.
22 Johnson, *The Influence of Tropical Climates on European Constitutions*, op. cit., p 678.
23 Moore-Gilbert, *Kipling and Orientalism*, op. cit., p 36.
24 Kennedy, *The Magic Mountains*, op. cit.
25 Edward John Tilt, *Health in India for British Women*, 4th ed., London , 1881, cited in Kennedy, *The Magic Mountains*, op. cit., p 32
26 Captain John Ouchterlony, 'Third Report from the Select Committee (India) 1858', *Parliamentary Papers*, Session 1857-58, VII part 1, p 54, cited in *The Magic Mountains* , op. cit., p.33.
27 Sir James Penn Boucault, *Letters to My Boys: An Australian Judge and Ex-Premier on his Travels in Europe*, London, 1906, p 24.
28 Frances Hodgson Burnett, *The Secret Garden* [1911], New York, 1987, p 9.
29 Martin Boyd, *Lucinda Brayford*, first published 1946, Ringwood, 1985.
30 'Report of the Commissioners Appointed to Inquire into the Sanitary State of the Army in India', *Parliamentary Papers*, 19, 1863, pp 150-153, cited in Kennedy, *The Magic Mountains*, op. cit., p 26.
31 James Inglis, *Our Australian Cousins*, London, 1880, pp 1-3.
32 Richard Arthur, 'The Colonisation of Tropical Australia', *Transactions of the 8th Session, Australasian Medical Congress*, Melbourne, October 1908, vol 2.
33 Major Charles E. Woodruff, *The Effects of Tropical Light on White Men*, New York, 1905.
34 ibid., p 195.
35 ibid., p 244.
36 ibid., p 279.
37 'The Colonisation of Tropical Australia', op. cit., p 94.
38 Earle Labor, Robert C Leitz III and I Milo Shepherd (eds), *The Letters of Jack London, Volume 2 : 1906-1912*, Stanford, 1988, p 774.
39 David Mike Hamilton, *"The Tools of My Trade": The Annotated Books in Jack London's Library*, Seattle, 1986, p 297.
40 ibid.
41 'Globe Trotter', 'White Australia', *Daily Mail* (Brisbane), 4 September 1920.
42 E W Cole, *A White Australia Impossible*, Melbourne, no date.
43 Sir Herbert Gepp, 'Australia's Great Backyard', *Living Age*, vol 354, August 1938.
44 Lord Lamington, 'A Cheerful View of Queensland', *Review of Reviews*, 20 May 1902.
45 *Australasian Medical Congress: Transactions of the Ninth Session held in Sydney, New South Wales, September, 1911*, vol 1, Sydney, 1913. For a contemporary examination of scientific responses to the physiology of tropical settlement see Professor Osborne, 'Problem of Tropical Colonisation. From a Physiological Standpoint', *Argus*, 10 April 1909.
46 Australasian Medical Congress, *'Tropical Australia': Transactions of the Eleventh Session, Brisbane, 21-28 August 1920*, Brisbane 1921.
47 ibid.
48 ibid.
49 ibid.
50 'Globe Trotter', op. cit.

51 ibid.

52 Grant, *The Passing of The Great Race*, op. cit., p 140.

53 Australasian Medical Congress, *'Tropical Australia'*, op. cit., p 66.

54 C W Saleeby, *Sunlight and Health*, New York, 1924, pp 16-26; the impact of sunlight on anthrax was demonstrated in 1877 by Downes and Blunt, while Robert Koch in the United States showed its effect on tubercular bacilli. The effect of sunlight on rickets was first indicated by Dr Theobald Adrian Palm, 'The Geographical Distribution and Aetiology of Rickets', *Practitioner*, October and November, 1890, while in 1893 Dr Niels R Finsen in Denmark pioneered the use of sunlight in the treatment of cutaneous forms of tuberculosis.

55 Sir William M Bayliss, 'Introduction', Saleeby, *Sunlight and Health*, op. cit., p 10.

56 ibid., p 9. One of the early and very influential clinics for treatment with sunlight was established in 1903 at Leysen, Switzerland by Dr A Rollier, who published *La Cure de Soleil* in 1914, translated as *Heliotherapy*, London, 1923. See 'Cures by the Sun', *Sydney Morning Herald*, 28 February 1925.

57 Saleeby, *Sunlight and Health*, op. cit., pp 25-6. See also Leonard V Dodds, *Modern Sunlight*, London, 1930.

58 For a commentary on the new appreciation of sun and warmth after the first world war see Paul Fussell, *Abroad: British Literary Traveling Between the Wars*, New York, 1980.

59 Abba Goold Woolson, *Woman in American Society*, Boston, 1873, cited in Bram Dijkstra, *Idols of Perversity: Fantasies of Evil in Fin-De-Siècle Culture*, New York, p 27.

60 Edmonde Charles-Roux, *Chanel: Her Life, Her World-and the Woman Behind the Legend She Herself Created*, New York, 1975. Also G Howell, *In Vogue*, Harmondsworth, 1973, pp 13 and 86; cited in Jill Julius Mathews 'Building the Body Beautiful', *Australian Feminist Studies*, no 5, 1986, pp 17-34. Arthur Adams, *The Australians: A Novel*, London, 1920, p 103.

61 Nina Murdoch, *Seventh Heaven: A Joyous Discovery of Europe*, Sydney, 1930, cited in Ros Pesman, David Walker and Richard White (eds), *The Oxford Book of Australian Travel Writing*, Melbourne, 1996, p 134. For a fascinating exchange on the relative merits of Southern versus Northern European climates and Mediterranean versus Nordic qualities see the film *Queen Christina*, starring Greta Garbo, dir. Rouben Mamoulian, 1933.

62 William Nicoll, 'The Condition of Life in Tropical Australia', *Journal of Hygiene*, vol 16, December 1917.

63 Ellsworth Huntington, *Civilization and Climate*, New Haven, 1915.

64 Griffith Taylor, 'Our Tropical Spaces', *Forum*, 7 November, 1923; 'Tropical Problems. Climate, Health and Settlement', *Argus*, 14 October 1922; 'The Australian Tropics', *News Bulletin, Institute of Pacific Relations*, January, 1927; 'Geographical Factors Controlling the Settlement of Tropical Australia', *Queensland Geographical Journal*, vol 32-33, 1916-1918. For Taylor on Climate and Settlement see 'The Climate Factors Influencing Settlement in Australia' in Commonwealth Bureau of Census and Statistics, *Official Year Book of the Commonwealth of Australia, Containing Authoritative Statistics for the Period 1901-1917*, no 11, Melbourne, 1918; 'Geography and National Problems' in W R B Oliver (ed.), *Report of the Sixteenth Meeting of Australasian Association for the Advancement of Science, Wellington Meeting, January 1923*, Wellington, New Zealand, 1924, pp 433-87; 'Tropical Settlement by the White Race in Australia' in *Environment and Race: A Study of the Evolution, Migration, Settlement and Status of the Races of Man*, London, 1927; 'Conditions Affecting Tropical Settlement in Australia', in Griffith Taylor, *Australia: A Study of Warm Environments and their Effect on British Settlement*, London, 1940. For Taylor's reaction to his critics in parliament see Griffith Taylor, *Journeyman Taylor*, London, 1958, p 13.

65 Griffith Taylor, 'Australia's Future Population', *The Morpeth Review*, no 4, June 1928.

66 Freda Sternberg, 'White Women in the Australian Tropics', *Living Age*, vol 325, April 1925.

67 Raphael Cilento, *The White Man in the Tropics: With Especial Reference to Australia and its Dependencies*, Brisbane, 1925. See also R W Cilento, 'Australia's Problems in the Tropics', *Report of the Twenty First Meeting of the Australian and New Zealand Association for the Advancement of Science*, Sydney, 1932 ; R W Cilento, *Triumph in the Tropics: An Historical Sketch of Queensland*, Brisbane, 1959.
68 Professor H Priestley, 'Physiological Aspects of White Settlement in Tropical Australia', *The Australian Geographer*, vol 1, part 2, November 1929. See also Sir James Barrett, 'Can Tropical Australia be Peopled by a White Race?', *Margin*, vol 1, no 1, 1925.
69 Adams, *The Australians*, op. cit., p 30
70 E G Theodore, 'White Settlement in the Australian Tropics. Can White People Live There?', *Stead's Review*, 11 March 1925.
71 Bedford, *Explorations in Civilisation*, op. cit., p 173 .
72 ibid., p 9.
73 'The Man of the Week: Counsel for the Yellow Streak', *Smith's Weekly*, 14 July 1923.
74 See Ross Laurie , '"Not a Matter of Taste but a Healthy Racial Instinct". Race Relations in Australia in the 1920s: Racial Ideology and the Popular Press', MA thesis, Griffith University, 1989, p 51.
75 Hardy Wilson, *The Dawn of a New Civilisation*, London, 1929, p 71. See also Cyril Pearl, *Hardy Wilson and his Old Colonial Architecture*, Melbourne, 1970.
76 Wilson, *Dawn*, op. cit., p 95; Adams, *The Australians*, op. cit., p.130.
87 Wilson, *Dawn*, op. cit., p 230.
78 Hardy Wilson, 'Cultural War', 11 May 1947, Q701/W, Mitchell Library.
79 William Lobatt Payne and John William Fletcher, *Report of the Board of Inquiry Appointed to Inquire into the Land and Land Industries of the Northern Territory of Australia*, Canberra, 1937.
80 ibid., pp 71, 72.
81 ibid., p 72.

Chapter Twelve

1 F W Eggleston, *Economic Record*, vol 111, no 5, November 1927. For discussion of settlement and population debates see, Stuart Macintyre, *The Oxford History of Australia: Volume 4: 1901-1942: The Succeeding Age*, Melbourne, 1986, ch 9, 'Australia Unlimited?'; Marilyn Lake, *The Limits of Hope: Soldier Settlement in Victoria, 1915-1938*, Melbourne, 1987; Michael Roe, *Australia, Britain and Migration: 1915-1940: A Study of Desperate Hopes*, Cambridge, 1995. For a fascinating discussion on central Australia see Tom Griffiths, *Hunters and Collectors: The Antiquarian Imagination in Australia*, Melbourne, 1996, chp 8, 'Journeys to the Centre'. For a rich account of spatial history and its nineteenth century applications see Paul Carter, *The Road to Botany Bay: An Essay in Spatial History*, London, 1988.
2 K H Bailey, 'Public Opinion and Population Problems', in F W Eggleston *et al.*, (eds), *The Peopling of Australia: Further Studies*, Pacific Relations Series , no 4, Melbourne, 1933, p 72.
3 Professor Edward East, *Mankind at the Crossroads* [1923], New York, 1977, p 84.
4 ibid., p 85.
5 'Geography. Chair at University. Dr Griffith Taylor Appointed', *Sydney Morning Herald*, 30 July 1920. See also Griffith Taylor, 'A Million Farms. A Criticism', *Sydney Morning Herald*, 27 August 1921; ' White Australia. Rainfall and Settlement', *Sydney Morning Herald*, 9 November 1921; 'Our Foreign Neighbours', *Australian Teacher*, November 1923; 'Problems of Tropical Settlement', *Sydney Morning Herald*, 14 August 1924. For a full

account of Taylor's views on Australian settlement see J M Powell, *Griffith Taylor and 'Australia Unlimited'*, Brisbane, 1993.

6   'The Jeremiad of the Prophet Taylor' (editorial), *Bulletin*, 4 May 1922.

7   'Black and White', (editorial), *Sydney Morning Herald*, 4 April, 1925; J W Gregory, *The Menace of Colour: A Study of the Difficulties due to the Association of White & Coloured Races*, London, 1924.

8   Griffith Taylor, 'White Australia: Rainfall and Settlement', *Sydney Morning Herald*, 9 November 1921.

9   Randolph Bedford, *Explorations in Civilisation*, Sydney, 1914.

10   Randolph Bedford, *Nought to Thirty -Three*, Sydney, 1944, p 337.

11   Arthur Adams, *The Australians: A Novel*, London, 1920, p 154.

12   Ella Shohat, 'Gender and Culture of Empire: Towards a Feminist Ethnography of the Cinema', *Quarterly Review of Film & Video*, vol 13, pp 45-84, 1991.

13   Edgeworth David, 'A Wilderness. Australia's Arid Centre', *Sydney Morning Herald*, 13 August 1924; 'II. A Wilderness: True View of Central Australia', *Sydney Morning Herald*, 14 August 1924. See also 'Problems of Tropical Settlement', (editorial), *Sydney Morning Herald*, 14 August 1924.

14   Roger Benjamin, 'The Oriental Mirage' in Roger Benjamin (curator and ed.) *Orientalism: Delacroix to Klee*, Sydney, 1997, pp 7-31.

15   Shohat, 'Gender and Culture of Empire', op. cit.

16   'Arid Australia' (letters to the editor), *Sydney Morning Herald*, 28 May 1924 to 14 July 1924. See also R T Baker, 'Central Australia. A Barren Desert?', *Sydney Morning Herald*, 10 May 1924; 'Olaf', 'A Dust Storm', *Sydney Morning Herald*, 24 May 1924; A Middleton, 'Not Arid. Central Australia', *Sydney Morning Herald*, 31 May 1924; 'Drover', 'Arid Australia. Another Story', *Sydney Morning Herald*, 7 June 1924. For a comprehensive review of the geography of central Australia see C T Madigan, 'A Review of the Arid Regions of Australia and their Economic Potentialities', F J A Brogan (ed.), *Report of the Twenty-Third Meeting of the Australian and New Zealand Association for the Advancement of Science*, Wellington, 1937.

17   'Central Australia', (editorial), *Sydney Morning Herald*, 5 May 1924.

18   Griffith Taylor 'Central Australia' (letter to the editor), *Sydney Morning Herald*, 6 May 1924. See also 'Arid Australia', (letter to the editor), *Sydney Morning Herald*, 2 June 1924 where Taylor presented a controversial map showing areas suitable for settlement. See also *Sydney Morning Herald*, 25 June 1924.

19   'Australian. Future Settlement. Great Arid Area', *Sydney Morning Herald*, 12 May 1924.

20   'Not Arid. Central Australia', op. cit.

21   'Idle Territories', *Sydney Morning Herald*, 21 May 1924. For Major-General William L'Estrange Eames and the Northern Australian White Settlement Association see Bede Nairn and Geoffrey Serle (eds), *Australian Dictionary of Biography: Volume 8: 1891-1939*, Carlton, 1981, pp 399-400.

22   Major-General William L'Estrange Eames, 'Pioneering Difficulties', (letter to the editor), *Sydney Morning Herald*, 22 May 1924. See also 'Arid Australia', (letter to the editor), *Sydney Morning Herald*, 28 May 1924.

23   A G Stephens, 'Fertile Australia', (letter to the editor), *Sydney Morning Herald*, 13 June 1924. For biographical information on A G Stephens see John Ritchie (general ed.), *Australian Dictionary of Biography, vol 12: 1891-1839*, Melbourne, 1990.

24   John Kirkwood, 'Arid Australia', (letter to the editor), *Sydney Morning Herald*, 3 July 1924.

25   'Brisbane's First Century', (editorial), *Daily Telegraph*, 9 August 1924.

26   'Devils, Saharas, and Man's Advance', (editorial), *Sun*, 12 May 1924.

27   Vilhjamur Stefansson, 'Central Australia. Stefansson's Views', *Sydney Morning Herald*, 12 August 1924. For an excellent coverage of the debate see J M Powell, 'Taylor, Stefansson and

the Arid Centre: An Historical Encounter of 'Environmentalism' and 'Possibilism'", *Journal of the Royal Australian Historical Society,* vol 66, 1980.

28 'Central Australia. Stefansson's Opinion. Discussed in Parliament', *Sydney Morning Herald,* 31 July 1924.

29 'Mr Nelson. Dreadful Experience. Details of Rescue', *Sydney Morning Herald,* 3 November 1925; 'Mr Nelson. Three Days in the Bush', *Sydney Morning Herald,* 6 November 1925.

30 See the entry for Thomas Griffith Taylor (1880-1863) in John Ritchie (ed.), *Australian Dictionary of Biography, vol 12: 1891-1939,* Carlton, 1990, p 187.

31 'Australia Unlimited', 'Men, Money and Markets' in F K Crowley, *Modern Australia in Documents: 1901-1939,* Melbourne, 1973, pp 359-360, 400-402. See also G Taylor, 'Group Settlement in Western Australia' in Eggleston et al, *Peopling of Australia,* op. cit.

32 Senator James Guthrie, 'Why I Favour a White Australia', *Stead's Review,* 15 January 1925. For bibliographical information on Senator Guthrie see Bede Nairn and Geoffrey Serle (eds), *Australian Dictionary of Biography, vol 9: 1891-1939,* Melbourne, 1983.

33 'Australia Unlimited', op. cit.

34 Eggleston *et al, Peopling of Australia,* op. cit., p 28.

35 W G K Duncan, 'The Immigration Problem' in W G K Duncan and C V Janes (eds), *The Future of Immigration into Australia and New Zealand,* Sydney, 1937.

36 A G B Fisher, 'Present Large-Scale Migration Policy', ibid.

37 S M Wadham, 'Australia's Absorptive Capacity: The Primary Industries', ibid.

38 Professor J B Brigden, 'Australian Immigration Policy: Absorbing Capacity and Capital Requirements — 35,000 People and £10,000,000 Annually', *Stead's Review,* 1 December 1925.

39 'Introduction' in P D Phillips and G L Wood (eds), *The Peopling of Australia,* Melbourne, 1928.

40 P D Phillips, 'Introduction', ibid.

41 Guthrie, 'Why I Favour a White Australia', op. cit.

42 Millions Club of New South Wales, *Memorandum and Articles of Association,* Sydney, 1913; *Millions Club of New South Wales: What It Is, What It Means, What it Has Done, What It Stands For,* Sydney, 1914; C P Conigrave, 'Looking Back Over the Years', *Millions Magazine,* April 1937, pp 4-9, 37.

43 Phillips, 'Introduction', op. cit., p 28.

44 ibid., p 37.

45 Sydney Upton, 'Settlement in Northern Australia', *United Empire, Journal of the Royal Empire Society,* London, vol 25, September 1934.

46 Eleanor Dark, *The Timeless Land,* London, 1941; Xavier Herbert, *Capricornia: A Novel,* London, 1939.

47 L Dudley Stamp, 'The Future of Tropical Australia', *Nature,* 26 January 1935.

48 W Wynne Williams, 'Northern Australia. The Bogey of the Empty Spaces', *Australian Quarterly,* vol 9, no 1, 1937.

49 'Our Paramount Problem', *Sydney Morning Herald,* 25 December 1935 , 2 January 1936, 6 April 1936, 13 June 1936.

50 Edward Masey, 'Vast Open Spaces: A Study of the Population Problem', *Publicist,* August 1936.

51 Francis Ratcliffe, *Flying Fox and Drifting Sand: The Adventures of a Biologist in Australia,* London, 1938.

52 Francis Ratcliffe, *Soil Drift in the Arid Pastoral Areas of South Australia,* Melbourne, 1936; *Further Observations on Soil Erosion and Drift with Special Reference to South-Western Queensland,* Melbourne, 1937.

53 Masey, 'Vast Open Spaces', op. cit.

54 For biography see Bede Nairn and Geoffrey Serle (eds), *Australian Dictionary of Biography: Volume 9: 1891-1939*, Melbourne, 1983, p 426.
55 'A Plan to Fill Lake Eyre', *Sun*, 8 December 1936.
56 Ion Idriess, *The Great Boomerang*, Sydney, 1941, p 235.
57 ibid., p 247.
58 C H Wickens, 'Australian Population: Its Nature and Growth', in Phillips and Wood, *The Peopling of Australia*, op. cit.
59 E T McPhee, 'The Urbanisation of the Australian Population', in Phillips and Wood, *The Peopling of Australia*, op. cit.
60 Alfred Viscount Northcliffe, *My Journey Round the World (16 July 1921-26 February 1922)*, London, 1923, p 302; 'Lord Northcliffe on Australian Immigration', *Millions Magazine*, 1 October 1921; Sir Leo Chiozza Money, *The Peril of the White*, London, 1925; Fleetwood Chidell, *Australia-White or Yellow?*, London, 1926, pp 156, 157.
61 McPhee, 'The Urbanisation of the Australian Population', op. cit.
62 W D Forsyth, *The Myth of Open Spaces: Australian, British and World Trends in Population and Migration*, Melbourne, 1942.

Chapter Thirteen

1 Walter LaFeber, *The Clash: U.S.-Japanese Relations Throughout History*, New York, 1997, pp 113-14 .
2 Lothrop Stoddard, *The Rising Tide of Color against White World Supremacy*, New York, 1921.
3 Charles H Pearson, *National Life and Character: A Forecast*, London, 1893, and London, 1913.
4 Stoddard, *The Rising Tide of Color*, op. cit., p 29.
5 ibid., pp 5-6.
6 'The Yellow Peril' (editorial), *Daily Telegraph*, 27 August 1904.
7 Homer Lea, *The Valor of Ignorance*, New York, 1909, p 74; *The Day of the Saxon*, London, 1912, p 101. See also Eugene Anschel, *Homer Lea, Sun Yat-Sen, and the Chinese Revolution*, New York, 1984, pp 1-11.
8 Lea, *The Valor of Ignorance*, ibid., p 205.
9 F Scott Fitzgerald, *The Great Gatsby*, first published 1925, Pennsylvannia, 1974, p 13.
10 Stoddard, *The Rising Tide of Color*, op. cit., p 12.
11 ibid., p 12.
12 Richard Arthur, *Stock and Station Journal*, 29 November 1912; newspaper cuttings, Richard Arthur papers, MS 302, Mitchell Library.
13 Stoddard, *The Rising Tide of Color*, op. cit., p 13.
14 ibid., p 9.
15 ibid., p 305.
16 M C Witham, 'Prejudice, Attitude and Belief: Aspects of Australian Perceptions of Japan, 1919 to 1939', BA Hons thesis, University of New South Wales, 1987, p 76. For biographical information on Sir Joseph Carruthers see Bede Nairn and Geoffrey Serle (general eds), *Australian Dictionary of Biography, vol 7: 1891-1939*, Melbourne, 1979.
17 Cited in Ross Laurie , '"Not a Matter of Taste but a Healthy Racial Instinct". Race Relations in Australia in the 1920s: Racial Ideology and the Popular Press', MA thesis, Griffith University, 1989, p 45.
18 Professor K H Bailey, 'Public Opinion and Population Problems', in F W Eggleston *et al* (eds), *The Peopling of Australia: Further Studies*, Pacific Relations Series, no 4, Melbourne, 1933, p 72.

Notes to pages 171-176

19 *Bulletin*, 8 October 1930, as cited in Whitham, 'Prejudice, Attitude and Belief', op. cit., p 63.

20 Captain W H Thring, 'Notes on the Racial Aspect of the Pacific Problem', Piesse Papers, National Library of Australia, Canberra, 882/5/271-4.

21 ibid.

22 ibid. For biographical data on E L Piesse see Geoffrey Serle (general ed.), *Australian Dictionary of Biography, vol 11, 1891-1939*, Melbourne, 1988, and Neville Meaney, *Fears and Phobias: E L Piesse and the Problem of Japan: 1909-39*, Canberra, 1996.

23 'The Population Problem', *Morpeth Review*, no 1, 1927. Lothrop Stoddard, *The Revolt Against Civilisation: The Menace of the Under Man*, New York, 1923.

24 Basil Joseph Mathews, *The Clash of Colour: A Study in the Problem of Race* [1924], Port Washington, 1973.

25 ibid., p 20.

26 ibid., p 31.

27 Lea, *The Valor of Ignorance*, op. cit., p 59.

28 Alfred Deakin, *Temple and Tomb*, London, 1893, p 135.

29 C Spurgeon Medhurst, 'The Chinese Puzzle', *Pacific*, 12 February 1925.

30 Richard Arthur, (letter to ed), *North Sydney News*, 22 May 1906; 'The Japanese Welcome', *Bulletin*, 24 May 1906.

31 Walter Kirton, 'A Jap School for Spies', *Lone Hand*, 1 September 1908.

32 Henry P Frei, *Japan's Southward Advance and Australia from the Sixteenth Century to World War II*, Honolulu, 1990, p 88.

33 ibid.

34 Whitham, 'Prejudice, Attitude and Belief', op. cit., p 86.

35 E L Piesse, 'Japanese Espionage in Australia in its relation to Japanese Policy', MS 882/9/218, Piesse Papers, National Library of Australia.

36 Ellsworth Huntington, *West of the Pacific ... Illustrated*, New York, 1925, p 326.

37 Piesse, 'Japanese Espionage in Australia', op. cit.

38 E George Marks, *Watch The Pacific! Defenceless Australia*, Sydney, 1924, p 12.

39 E George Marks, *Pacific Peril*, Sydney (Australian ed.), 1933, p 26.

40 M P Shiel, *The Yellow Danger*, London, 1898. For other popular stories of this time featuring sinister Orientals see Robert W Chambers, *The Maker of Moons*, first published 1896, Freeport, 1969; Allen Upward, *The Yellow Hand*, London, 1904; Thomas Burke, *Limehouse Nights*, first published 1916, New York, 1974; cited in Chris Steinbrunner, Otto Penzler, Marvin Lachman and Charles Shibuk (eds), *Encyclopedia of Mystery and Detection*, New York, 1976, pp 54 and 302.

41 *The Yellow Danger*, op. cit., pp 10, 11, 13, 16 and 123.

42 Roland Daniel, *Wu Fang: An Adventure of the Secret Service*, London, 1929; *The Yellow Devil: Another Adventure of Wu Fang*, London, 1932; *Ruby of a Thousand Dreams: Another Adventure of Wu Fang*, London, 1933; *Wu Fang's Revenge*, London, 1934; *The Son of Wu Fang*, London, 1935; *Return of Wu Fang*, London, 1937, cited in Steinbrunner et al, *Encyclopedia of Mystery and Detection*, op. cit., p 302.

43 Eugene Thomas, *The Dancing Dead*, New York, 1933; *Shadow of Chu-Sheng* , New York, 1933; *Yellow Magic*, New York, 1934; cited in Steinbrunner et al, *Encyclopedia of Mystery and Detection*, p 304.

44 Steinbrunner et al, *Encyclopedia of Mystery and Detection*, op. cit., pp 303 and 305.

45 Frank D McSherry Jr, 'The Shadow of Ying Ko', *Rohmer Review*, no 16, 1976.

46 Frank Maxwell Grant, 'The Invincible Shiwan Khan', *The Shadow*, 1 March, 1940, as cited in ibid.

47 Earl Derr Biggers, *Charlie Chan, The House Without a Key: from the Saturday Evening Post* [1925], Indianapolis, 1977. The films included such well known titles as *Charlie Chan Carries On* (1931), *Charlie Chan's Courage* (1934), *Charlie Chan at the Opera* (1936) and

Charlie Chan on Broadway (1937). See also Steimbrunner *et al*, *Encyclopedia of Mystery and Detection*, op. cit., pp 71-7; William F Wu, *The Yellow Peril: Chinese Americans in American Fiction 1850-1940*, Hamden, 1982, pp 174-182.

48 Steimbrunner et al, *Encyclopedia of Mystery and Detection*, op. cit., p 71.
49 Harvey Cherok and Martha Torge (eds), *Quotations from Charlie Chan*, New York, 1968, p 6.
50 Wu, *The Yellow Peril*, op. cit., pp 164-173; Steinbrunner et al, *Encyclopedia of Mystery and Detection*, op. cit., pp 160-1. See also James Donald, 'How English Is It? Popular Literature and National Culture', *New Formations*, no 6, Winter 1988.
51 Sax Rohmer, 'The Birth of Dr Fu Manchu', *Daily Sketch*, 24 May 1934, cited in *Rohmer Review*, vol 17, 1977.
52 Bradford M Day, *Sax Rohmer: A Bibliography*, Denver, 1963.
53 Steinbrunner et al, *Encyclopedia of Mystery and Detection*, op. cit., p 161.
54 Jean-Claude Romer, 'Fu-Manchu a l'ecran', *Midi/Minuit Fantastique*, no 14, June 1966.
55 *Pacific*, 7 August 1924.
56 Bram Dijkstra, *Evil Sisters: The Threat of Female Sexuality in Twentieth Century Culture*, New York, 1996, pp 269-274.
57 Sax Rohmer, *President Fu Manchu*, New York, 1936, p 86; *The Bride of Fu Manchu*, London, 1933, p 250.
58 Cyril Pearl, *Morrison of Peking*, Sydney, 1967, p 213.
59 Sax Rohmer, *The Bride of Fu Manchu*, London, 1933, p 76.
60 Sir Francis Galton, *Hereditary Genius: An Inquiry into Laws and Consequences*, London, 1869.
61 'The Japanese Welcome', op. cit.
62 J MacMillan Brown, 'East and West. Japan and the White Race', *Sydney Morning Herald*, 28 June 1913.
63 Sax Rohmer, *President Fu Manchu*, New York, 1936, p 279.
64 Sax Rohmer, *Emperor Fu Manchu*, London, 1959, p 221. For earlier Australian comments on the 'mystic brain' of the Chinese see H E Pratten, *Through Orient to Occident*, Sydney, c1912, pp 26-30.
65 Rohmer, *The Bride of Fu Manchu*, op. cit., p 97.
66 Rohmer, *President Fu Manchu*, op. cit., p 86.
67 Rohmer, *The Bride of Fu Manchu*, op. cit., p 245.
68 ibid., p 188.

Chapter Fourteen

1   Lothrop Stoddard, *The Rising Tide of Color Against White World Supremacy*, Westport, 1920.
2   ibid., p 120.
3   ibid., p 117.
4   Madison Grant, *The Passing of the Great Race or The Racial Basis of European History*, New York, 1916, p 67.
5   ibid., p 81.
6   ibid., p 70.
7   George Meudell, *The Pleasant Career of a Spendthrift and his Later Reflections*, Melbourne, 1939, p 140.
8   ibid., pp 157-8.
9   ibid., pp 6 and 140.
10 Stoddard, *The Rising Tide of Color*, op. cit., p 164.

11 ibid, see ch 9, 'The Shattering of White Solidarity'.
12 ibid., p 164. See also Daniel Pick, *Faces of Degeneration: A European Disorder, c1848-c1918*, Cambridge, 1989, pp 189-203. For further references to nineteenth century British texts on the decadent city see Gail Ching-Liang Low, *White Skins/Black Masks: Representation and Colonialism*, London, 1996, p 168.
13 Robert E Park, 'Race Relations and Certain Frontiers', in E B Reuter (ed.), *Race and Culture Contacts*, New York, 1934, pp 82-83.
14 Mervyn Skipper, 'The Racial Tragedy of Java', *Lone Hand*, 1 October 1910.
15 William Z Ripley, *The Races of Europe: A Sociological Study*, London, 1899, p 570.
16 'The Miscegenation Spectre', *Bulletin*, 30 January 1919.
17 'A Capital in the Tropics', *Bulletin*, 22 May 1919.
18 Edward Byron Reuter, *The Mulatto in the United States including a Study of the Role of Mixed-Blood Races throughout the World*, Boston, 1918, p 31.
19 E L Piesse, 'White Australia', *Round Table*, vol 11, March 1921. For a discussion of the role of white women in maintenance of racial difference see Ann L Stoler, 'Making Empire Respectable: The Politics of Race and Sexual Morality in 20th-Century Colonial Cultures', *American Ethnologist*, vol 16, no 4, 1989; 'Rethinking Colonial Categories: European Communities and the Boundaries of Rule', *Comparative Studies in Society and History*, vol 13, no 1, 1989.
20 Gertrude F Moberley, *Experiences of a 'Dinki Di' R R C Nurse*, Sydney, 1933, p 51.
21 ibid., pp 54, 102.
22 ibid., p.102.
23 ibid., pp 102, 107.
24 M M Kaye, *The Sun in the Morning: My Early Years in India and England*, New York, 1990, pp 194-5, cited in Dane Kennedy, *The Magic Mountains: Hill Stations and the British Raj*, Berkley, 1996, pp 141-2.
25 Dorothy Fry , Letters to J A B Fry 1919-1923, Fry Family Papers, 1861-1923, MS 1159/5, Mitchell Library, Sydney.
26 ibid., 16 March 1919.
27 ibid., 23 April 1919.
28 ibid., 16 March 1919.
29 ibid., 1 April 1919.
30 ibid., 23 April 1919.
31 ibid., 2 March 1921.
32 ibid., 20 October 1920.
33 ibid., 4 June 1919.
34 ibid., 1 April 1919.
35 ibid., 5 September 1921.
36 ibid.
37 ibid.
38 Mary Gaunt, *A Woman in China*, London, 1914; *A Broken Journey. Wanderings from the Hoang-Ho to the Island of Sanghalien and the Upper Reaches of the Amur River*, London, 1919. For biographical details see Bede Nairn and Geoffrey Serle (general eds), *Australian Dictionary of Biography: Volume 8: 1891-1939*, Carlton, 1981, pp 632-3. For an illuminating account of Mary Gaunt and other Australian women travellers see Ros Pesman, *Duty Free: Australian Women Abroad*, Melbourne, 1996, pp 67-8.
39 Gaunt, *A Broken Journey*, op. cit., p 17. See also Ros Pesman, David Walker and Richard White, (eds), *The Oxford Book of Australian Travel Writing*, Melbourne, 1996.
40 ibid., p.18.
41 Janet Mitchell, *Spoils of Opportunity: An Autobiography*, New York, 1939, pp 60, 61, 73 and 74.

42 ibid., p 67-68.

43 Edward Duyker and Coralie Younger, *Molly and the Rajah: Race, Romance and the Raj*, Burwood, 1991, pp 15-26.

44 *Melbourne Punch*, cited in ibid.

45 Duyker and Younger, *Molly and the Rajah*, op. cit., pp 116-117. Another intriguing case of an elite inter-racial union occurred between Ella Strom who later married Percy Grainger and Iyemasa Tokugawa, later Prince Tokugawa, heir of the famous Shogun family. The couple met in London, where they reportedly had a child. Ella Strom followed Tokugawa to Australia in 1926 when he was appointed Japanese Consul-General in Sydney. See Malcolm Gillies and David Pear, *The All-Round Man: Selected Letters of Percy Grainger 1914-1961*, Oxford, 1994, p 88 and p xxi.

46 For a short account of Arthur Upfield's contribution to detective fiction see Chris Steinbrunner, Otto Penzler, Marvin Lachman and Charles Shibuk (eds), *Encyclopedia of Mystery and Detection*, New York, 1976, p 396. See also Jessica Hawke, *Follow My Dust! A Biography of Arthur Upfield*, Melbourne, 1957.

47 Louise Jordan Miln, *In a Shantung Garden*, London, 1924; *The Soul of China*, London, 1925; *It Happened in Peking*, London, 1926; *In a Yün-nan Courtyard*, London, 1927; *Red Lily and Chinese Jade*, London, 1928; *Rice*, London, 1930; *The Vintage of Yon-Yee*, London, 1931; *Pêng Wee's Harvest*, London, 1933; James Miln of Toronto [Louise Jordan Miln], *The Feast of Lanterns*, London, 1920; *Flutes of Shanghai*, London, 1928; *By Soochow Waters*, London, 1929; *A Chinese Triangle*, London, 1932.

48 Miln, *The Vintage of Yon-Yee*, op. cit., p 262.

49 Hebert Spencer, letter to Kentaro Kaneko, 1892, cited in "The Mingling of Races: A Search for Truth — II', *Stead's Review*, 17 September 1922.

50 A L Pullar, *Celestalia. A Fantasy. A D 1975*, Sydney, 1933, pp 104-5.

51 William F Wu, *The Yellow Peril: Chinese Americans in American Fiction 1850-1940*, Hamden, 1982, p 69; Jeanette Dailey, 'Sweet Burning Incense', *Overland Monthly*, vol 77, January-February 1921, cited by Wu, *The Yellow Peril*, op. cit., pp 59-60, 217.

52 John Luther Long, 'Madame Butterfly' [1898] in *Madame Butterfly, Purple Eyes, etc.*, The American Short Story Series, vol 25., New York, 1968. For Australian performances of *Madame Butterfly* see Alison Gyger, *Opera for the Antipodes: Opera in Australia 1881-1939*, Sydney, 1990. For contemporary reviews see '"Mme Butterfly": A Song of Love and Death: Music of Changeful Charm', *Sydney Morning Herald*, 28 March 1910; 'Madam Butterfly', *Sydney Mail*, 30 March 1910; *Bulletin*, 31 March 1910; '"Madam Butterfly": Grand Opera in English', *Argus*, 1 August 1910; 'Grand Opera in English: Miss Amy Castle's Triumph', *Argus*, 3 August 1910.

53 Richard A Oehling, 'The Yellow Menace: Asian Images in American Film' in Randall M Miller (ed.), *The Kalaidoscope Lens: How Hollywood Views Ethnic Groups*, Englewood, NJ, 1995, pp 188-9; Dick Stromgren, 'The Chinese Syndrome: the Evolving Image of Chinese and Chinese-Americans in Hollywood Films', in Paul Loukides and Linda K Fuller (eds), *Beyond the Stars: Stock Characters in American Popular Film*, Bowling Green, 1990, vol 1, p 66.

54 Allen L Woll and Randall M Miller, *Ethnic and Racial Images in American Film and Television. Historical Essays and Bibliography*, New York, 1987, p 190. D W Griffith was best known for his film *Birth of a Nation*, 1915.

55 Oehlung, 'The Yellow Menace', op. cit., pp 194-5.

56 Stromgen, 'The Chinese Syndrome', op. cit., pp 63, 190.

57 'Lafcadio Hearn and his Japanese Wife', *Stead's Review*, 23 July 1921.

58 'A Mingling of Races: A Search for Truth', *Stead's Review*, 20 August 1921; 'The Mingling of Races: A Search for Truth — II', op. cit.

59 Sir Sydney Olivier, 'White Capital and Coloured Labour', *Stead's Review*, 17 September 1922.
60 J Currie Elles, 'British Traditions: Australian Decadence [Being a lecture delivered before the British Empire League in Australia, on Friday, October 12th, 1906, the Hon. Bruce Smith Esq., K C., M P., in the Chair]', *Journal of the Institute of Bankers of New South Wales*, vol 15, part 10, 1906, p 378.
61 ibid., p 382.
62 ibid.
63 ibid., pp 383-385.
64 J MacMillan Brown, 'The Pacific. American Asiatic Institute. Problems of the Future', *Sydney Morning Herald*, 31 May 1913.
65 Gillies and Pear, *The All-Round Man*, op. cit., pp 5-6.
66 Percy Grainger to Ellen Bull, October 23, 1941, ibid., p 184.
67 ibid., fn p 182. The article by Stoddard that Grainger carried was Lothrop Stoddard, 'Racial Realities in Europe', *Saturday Evening Post*, 22 March 1924.
68 Percy Grainger to Ellen Bull, October 23, 1941, op. cit., pp 182-5. For further comment on Grainger's views on art, music and Asia see Alison Broinowski, *The Yellow Lady*, Melbourne, 1992, pp 47-9.
69 J Lyng, *Non-Britishers in Australia: Influence on Population and Progress*, Melbourne, 1927, pp 1-5, 9-12, 23-4.
70 Griffith Taylor, 'Birth-Rate and Race Mixture', (letter to editor), *Sydney Morning Herald*, 11 July 1923; Rupert V Markham, 'The 'Varsity School of Geography. A Valuable Institution', *Evening News*, 24 February 1923.
71 'Marriage with Asiatics. Professor asks "Why Not?" Striking Lecture', *Daily Telegraph*, 20 June 1923; 'The Human Race. White Australia Aspect. The Mongolians. An Advanced Type', *Sydney Morning Herald*, 21 June 1923. For Griffith Taylor's views on Australian Aborigines see also 'Our Own Aboriginals', *Sydney Morning Herald*, 1 March 1924 ; 'Young Aboriginals', (letter to the editor), *Sydney Morning Herald*, 30 October 1924; *Environment, Race, and Migration: Fundamentals of Human Distribution: With Special Sections on Racial Classification; and Settlement in Canada and Australia*, Toronto, 1937, pp 91-95.
72 'Will somebody tell him?', *Daily Telegraph*, 25 June 1923.
73 'To Smear Australia Yellow', *Sun*, 22 June 1923.
74 'The Man of the Week: Counsel for the Yellow Streak', *Smith's Weekly*, 14 July 1923.
75 'Our Girls marrying Orientals. Professor's View. Students Protest', *Evening News*, 22 September 1923.
76 Griffith Taylor, *Environment and Race*, London, 1927, p 218.
77 Griffith Taylor, *Environment, Race, and Migration*, op. cit., p 409.
78 ibid., p 465.
79 ibid., pp 465-467.
80 ibid., p 466.

Chapter Fifteen

1 'The Smile and the Map', *Bulletin*, 27 March 1919.
2 ibid.
3 'Where Australia Fails. Trade with India and the East', *Commerce*, 1 November 1919.
4 ibid.
5 Sandra Tweedie, *Trading Partners: Australia and Asia 1790-1993*, Sydney, 1994, pp.75-76.
6 '"West Australian", Our Nearest White Neighbours. Some Salient Facts about Western Australia', *Sluyter's Monthly*, vol 3, October 1922.

7   Dorothy Fry , Letter to J A B Fry, 30 November 1921, Letters to J A B Fry 1919-1923, Fry Family Papers, 1861-1923, Mitchell Library, MSS 1159/5.
8   'Trade with the East', *West Australian*, 12 April 1922.
9   Tweedie, *Trading Partners*, op. cit., pp.78-79.
10 ibid., p.79.
11 ibid.
12 'Modern China. Wonderful Progress. Unlimited Possibilities of Trade. Mr Little's Mission', *Sydney Morning Herald*, 23 April 1921.
13 'Awakening China. New Trade Outlook. Australia's Commissioner', *Daily Telegraph*, 23 April 1921.
14 'Modern China', op. cit.
15 'Trade with the East. Labor Council Opposes Mission', *Age*, 23 April 1921.
16 'Trade with the East. Mr Sheaf in Sydney. Comprehensive Scheme', *Sydney Morning Herald*, 15 May 1922.
17 Tweedie, *Trading Partners*, op. cit., pp 81-2.
18 ibid., pp 82-3.
19 ibid.
20 'Trade with the East. Mr Sheaf in Sydney', op. cit. See also 'Trade with the East. Commissioner in Launceston. A Man of Experience. Exporters' Opportunity', *Launceston Examiner*, 27 April 1922.
21 Tweedie, *Trading Partners*, op. cit., p 80. See also M Ruth Megaw, 'White Diplomacy and Yellow Gold: The Appointment of Australia's First Governmental Representative in China', *Journal of the Royal Australian Historical Society*, vol 62, no 1, 1976.
22 Senator Thomas Bakhap, 'Report on Trade between the Commonwealth and China. For the Honorable A S Rodgers, Minister for Trade and Customs', *Parliamentary Paper No 62*, vol 2, Melbourne, 1922.
23 Hilary L Rubinstein, 'Bakhap, Thomas Jerome Kingston (1866-1923)', in 'Australia's Senators: Biographical Dictionary of the Australian Senate', manuscript in preparation, The Senate, Canberra. I would like to thank Ann Millar, Director of Research, Procedure Office, The Senate, and Hilary Rubinstein for making this biographical entry available to me. For recent claims that Bakhap was of Asian descent see, 'Chinese in White Australia 1901-1950' in James Jupp, (ed.), *The Australian People: An Encyclopedia of the Nation, its People and their Origins*, North Ryde, 1988 and Eric Rolls, *Citizens: Continuing the Epic Story of China's Centuries Old Relationship with Australia ... the Sequel to the Sojourners*, St Lucia, 1996.
24 'Death of Senator Bakhap', *Hansard: Parliamentary Debates, House of Representatives*, 20 August 1923.
25 Bakhap, 'Report on Trade', op. cit.
26 Tweedie, *Trading Partners*, op. cit., p 81.
27 'Items of Interest. Mr Sheaf's Report on Australian Trade with the East', *Inter-Ocean*, vol 6, 1925.
28 'Bakhap, 'Report on Trade', op. cit.
29 ibid.
30 ibid.
31 E T Sheaf, 'The Eastern Fish Trade', *Inter-Ocean*, vol 5, April, 1924.
32 Bakhap, 'Report on Trade', op. cit.; Tweedie, *Trading Partners*, op. cit., p 80.
33 Bakhap, 'Report on Trade', op. cit.
34 'Obituary. Senator T J K Bakhap End of a Useful Public Career', *Mercury* (Hobart), 20 August 1923.
35 'Overseas Trade. Opening Up New Markets. Government's Efforts', *Commerce*, 1 July 1922.
36 Tweedie, *Trading Partners*, op. cit., p 65.

37 Edward S Little, 'Shipping', *Bulletin No 16*, Trade Commissioner Service: China, Bureau of Foreign and Domestic Commerce, Commonwealth of Australia, no date, Australian Archives, Series A457/1, Canberra.

38 E S Little, 'Work of the Australian Trade Commissioner in China', copy of document presented to Senator Bakhap, no date, Australian Archives, ibid.

39 Edward S Little, 'Jams', *Bulletin No 3*, Trade Commissioner Service: China, Bureau of Foreign and Domestic Commerce, Commonwealth of Australia, no date, Australian Archives, ibid.

40 ibid.

41 'Trade with China. Direct Shipments Urged', *Commerce*, 2 April 1923.

42 'Trade with the East', *Commerce*, 1 October 1924.

43 Sheaf, 'The Eastern Fish Trade', op. cit.

44 Newspaper cutting, 13 November 1923, Australian Archives, Commerce-East General, Series B323/1/5, Canberra.

45 Mrs T R Bowman, President of the National Council of Women to Secretary, Board of Trade, ibid.

46 Australian Trade Commissioner Service in China, 'Comment of Public Press in China on Mr E S Little's Case', Australian Archives, Series 1009/9/214, Canberra.

47 'Trade Commissioner in the East', *Hansard: Parliamentary Debates, House of Representatives*, 24 July 1923.

48 Tweedie, *Trading Partners*, op. cit., p 80.

49 'Trade Commissioner in the East', op. cit. See also *Age*, 23 May 1923.

50 E T Sheaf to Universal Products Co., 16 September 1924, Australian Archives, Series A597, A1924/10129, Canberra. See also E T Sheaf, 'The Fruit Markets of the East', *Inter-Ocean*, vol 6, 1925.

51 Sheaf, 'The Fruit Markets of the East', op. cit.

52 Tweedie, *Trading Partners*, op. cit., p 80.

53 Sheaf, 'The Fruit Markets of the East', op. cit.

54 'Trade in the East. Mr Sheaf's Appointment Terminated', *Commerce*, January 1925.

55 Tweedie, *Trading Partners*, op. cit., p 85.

56 'Trade in the East. Mr Sheaf's Appointment Terminated', op. cit.

57 E T Sheaf to Stirling Taylor, Director, Commercial and Industrial Bureau of the Board of Trade, 17 February 1925, Australian Archives, Series A458, I 510/2, Canberra.

58 'Australia's Trade. Britain Best Customer. Opportunities in the East', *Commerce*, 7 March 1925.

59 'Our Trade with the East. Export Products, Freights and Marketing Conditions', *Commerce*, 1 October 1930.

60 Herbert Gepp, *Report on Trade between Australia and the Far East*, Canberra, 1932; A C V Melbourne, *Report on Australian Intercourse with Japan and China*, Brisbane, 1932. For a contemporary survey of Australia's overseas trade position see Nancy Windett, *Australia as Producer and Trader 1920-1932*, London, 1933. For a lucid overview of Australia's relationship with Asia see Jack Shepherd, *Australia's Interests and Policies in the Far East*, New York, 1939.

61 Grep, *Report on Trade*, op. cit., p 63.

62 ibid.

63 Melbourne, *Report on Australian Intercourse with Japan and China*, op. cit., p 76.

64 A C V Melbourne to J D Story, 16 February 1932, A C V Melbourne Papers on Foreign Policy, Reel 1, National Library of Australia, Canberra.

65 A C V Melbourne to J A Lyons, 18 July 1932, ibid.

66 J G Latham, *The Australian Eastern Mission, 1934*, Canberra, 1934; Ruth Megaw, 'The Australian Goodwill Mission to the Far East in 1934: Its Significance in the Evolution of

Australian Foreign Policy', *Journal of the Royal Australian Historical Society*, vol 59, part 4, 1973.

67 Tweedie, *Trading Partners*, op. cit., p 108.

68 For comments on the question of Australian Trade Representatives see A C V Melbourne to Dr Earle Page, 2 September 1932; A C V Melbourne, 'Trade Commissioners and their Work', manuscript, A C V Melbourne Papers on Foreign Policy, op. cit.

69 'Trade with the East: Objection to Official Commissioners', *Commerce*, 1 November 1932.

70 'Trade Commissioners to the East: Chamber's Policy Stated by President at Farewell Gathering', *Commerce*, 5 August 1935.

71 A C V Melbourne Papers on Foreign Policy, op. cit.

72 A C V Melbourne to Dr Earle Page, 4 March 1935; K Murai to Dr Melbourne, 2 March 1935, ibid. For further commentary on A C V Melbourne see Geoffrey Bolton, 'A C V Melbourne: Prophet Without Honour', in Stuart Macintyre and Julian Thomas (eds), *The Discovery of Australian History, 1890-1939*, Melbourne, 1995. Bolton discusses Melbourne's Asian interests but is inclined to see him as a lone figure, when at this time there was a small, though broadening intellectual community with an interest in Asia.

73 *Daily Telegraph*, 21 December 1940; other material in Longford Lloyd Papers, MS 2887, National Library of Australia, Canberra.

74 'Overseas Trade Commissioners. Appointments to Java, China and Japan', *Commerce*, 5 July 1935.

75 Tweedie, *Trading Partners*, op. cit., pp 90, 108.

76 Marjory Collard O'Dea, *Ian Clunies Ross: A Biography*, Melbourne, 1997.

77 Eleanor Hinder to her mother, 29 November 1935, Eleanor M Hinder Papers, MSS 770/1/2, Mitchell Library, Sydney.

78 'Trade with Japan', *Commerce*, 5 May 1935, p 104.

79 Tweedie, *Trading Partners*, op. cit., p.241.

80 'Japan's Trade with the Pacific: Mr Katsuji Debuchi Writes of Australia and New Zealand', *Commerce*, 5 March 1936. For bibliographic information on Peter Russo see W J Draper (ed.), *Who's Who in Australia*, 25th Edition, Melbourne, 1985, p 745.

81 'Reciprocal Courtesies with Japan. Australian Business Delegation may leave Australia in September', *Commerce*, 5 June 1935.

82 'Australian Exhibition in Japan. Japanese Commercial Leaders Comment on Exhibits', *Commerce*, 5 December 1935.

83 'Trade with Japan', *Commerce*, 5 May 1936.

84 'Japanese Goodwill Volume', *Commerce*.

85 *Japan, Australia and New Zealand*, Osaka, 1935.

86 For an analysis of the Trade Diversion Policy see R D Westmore, 'Japan and the Trade Diversion Policy, *Australian Quarterly*, vol 9, no 1, 1937; D C S Sissons, 'Manchester v Japan: The Imperial Background of the Australian Trade Diversion Dispute with Japan, 1936', *Australian Outlook*, vol 30, no 3, 1976; John B O'Brien, 'Empire *v.* National Interests in Australian-British Relations during the 1930s', *Historical Studies*, vol 22, no 89, 1987; Kosmas Tsokhas, 'The Wool Industry and the 1936 Trade Diversion Dispute between Australia and Japan', *Australian Historical Studies*, vol 23, no 93, 1989; A T Ross, 'Australian Overseas Trade and National Development Policy 1932-1939: A Story of Colonial Larrikins or Australian Statesmen?', *Australian Journal of Politics and History*, vol 36, no 2, 1990.

Chapter Sixteen

1   Hubert Howe Bancroft, *The New Pacific*, [1900], New York, 1912.
2   ibid., p 8.
3   Theodore Roosevelt, 'The Panama Canal' in H Morse Stephens and Herbert E Bolton, *The Pacific Ocean in History: Papers and Addresses Presented at the Panama-Pacific Historical Congress Held at San Francisco, Berkeley and Palo Alto, California July 19-23, 1915*, New York, 1917. For Australia's disputatious involvement in the related Panama-Pacific Exposition see R Megaw, 'Prickly Pear and the Panama-Pacific Exposition: An Incident in Commonwealth Relations', *Royal Australian Historical Society*, vol 55, no 2, 1969.
4   Archibald R Colquhoun, *The Mastery of the Pacific*, New York, 1902, Preface.
5   Frank Fox, *The Struggle for the Pacific*, London, 1912.
6   J Macmillan Brown, 'The Pacific. American Asiatic Institute. Problems of the Pacific,' *Sydney Morning Herald*, 31 May 1913. For the objectives of the Asiatic Institute see Asiatic Institute, *Asiatic Institute Book*, New York, 1914.
7   For commentaries on the commercial impact of the Japanese in Australia see Herbert Easton, to Ernest E Carleton, 16 August 1916, British Immigration League of Australia Papers, Mitchell Library, MS 302, Box 2. For assessment of power changes in the Pacific see Nicholas Roosevelt, *The Restless Pacific*, New York, 1928.
8   James Murdoch, *Australia Must Prepare. Japan, China, India: A Comparison and Some Contrasts. An Inaugural Lecture*, Sydney, 1919.
9   Hubert Foster, Department of Defence to Mr Barff, University of Sydney, 5 May 1917, University of Sydney Archives, G3/13 File no 8290.
10 James Murdoch to E L Piesse, 5 May 1919, Piesse Papers, National Library of Australia, Canberra, File 882/5/23.
11 Murdoch, *Australia Must Prepare*, op. cit.; see also D Dalgleish, 'Japanese at Fort Street', *The Fortian*, 1964; Rory Mungoven, 'Mr Miniechi Miyata: Japanese Teacher at Fort Street', unpublished research notes, 1987.
12 M W MacCallum, 'The Late Professor James Murdoch', *Hermes*, May 1922.
13 'Teeming Millions', *The Pacific*, 12 October 1923. See also, F K., 'Understanding Asia', *The Pacific*, 27 November 1924.
14 A L Sadler, 'Civilization of East and West', *The Pacific*, 26 Jan 1924.
15 'The Editor's Page: The Bridge of Understanding', *The Pacific*, 1 February, 1924; C H Vernon, 'Pacific Peace', *The Pacific*, 1 May 1924; C B S, 'If Japan and America Fought!', *The Pacific*, 29 May, 1924.
16 *Sluyter's Monthly East Indian Magazine*, May 1920 until February 1923; *Inter-Ocean: A Netherlands East Indies Magazine Devoted to Malaysia and Australia*, March 1923 until June 1932; *The Java Gazette*, 1932 until 1939.
17 Articles include: H D Newby, 'Australia's Plans for the Future. Trade and Commercial Expansion and the Growth of Great Industries', *Sluyter's Monthly*, Vol 3, April 1922; 'Australia's Position in the Pacific. Some Aspects of the Changing Commercial Position', *Sluyter's Monthly*, vol 3, November 1922; 'Australia in the World's Markets: The Outlook', *Inter-Ocean*, vol 5, March 1924; E T Sheaf, 'The Eastern Fish Trade' *Inter-Ocean*, vol 5, April 1924; 'Mr Sheaf's Report on Australian Trade in the East, ibid., vol 6, February 1925;
18 Edward P Bailey, 'Australia and Its Great Possibilities', *Pan Pacific Progress*, March 1926.
19 For David Starr Jordan's Australian associations see Hazel Rowley, *Christina Stead: A Biography*, Melbourne, 1993, pp 22-3.
20 Yasuke Tsurumi, 'Japan and America', *Stead's Review*, 1 September 1926; for John Brailsford see *Who's Who in New Zealand and the Western Pacific*, Wellington, 1932, p.108.
21 Griffith Taylor, 'Our Foreign Neighbours', *Australian Teacher*, November 1923.

22 Griffith Taylor, 'By Orient Ways', a 9-part series in the *Sun*, commencing 26 October 1920, MSS1003/4/242, National Library of Australia, Canberra. See also Griffith Taylor, *Journeyman Taylor*, London, 1958.

23 'Resolutions and Recommendations of the First Pan-Pacific Science Conference called by the Pan-Pacific Union and Held in Honolulu in August, 1920', *Journal of the Pan-Pacific Research Institution*, vol 1, January, 1926.

24 Gerald Lightfoot (ed.), *Proceedings of the Pan-Pacific Science Congress, Australia, 1923: Melbourne Meeting: 13th to 22nd August, 1923: Sydney Meeting: 23rd August to 3rd September. Held under the auspices of The Australian National Research Council and through the generosity of The Commonwealth and State Governments*, Melbourne, 1923.

25 Ellsworth Huntington, *West of the Pacific*, New York, 1925.

26 *Proceedings of the Pan-Pacific Science Congress, Australia, 1923*, op. cit.

27 Griffith Taylor, in an 11-part series in the *Sydney Morning Herald* including 'The Far East: We Cross the Line', 11 December 1926; 'The Far East: To the Philippine Islands', 15 December 1926; 'The Far East: Hong Kong', 18 December 1926; 'The Far East: A Japanese Evening', 22 December 1926; 'The Far East: Nikko and its Shrines', 25 December 1926; 'The Far East: A Day at the Congress', 29 December 1926; 'Through the Far East: Kiushiu and its Volcanoes', 5 January 1927; 'The Far East: Mount Fuji and its Lakes', 11 January 1927; 'The Far East: Pekin-Its Palaces and Poor', 15 January 1927; 'Through the Far East: The Japanese People', 8 February 1927. He also published four other articles in the *Sydney Morning Herald*: 'China: Shanghai and its Environs', 5 March 1927; 'China: Among the Hakka Tribes, 12 February 1927; 'China: Is She Awakening?', 29 January 1927; 'China: Is She Awakening?', 1 February 1927.

28 Taylor, 'A Japanese Evening', *Sydney Morning Herald*.

29 'Overseas Delegates to the Third Pan-Pacific Science Congress, Japan, 1926, *Journal of the Pan-Pacific Research Institution*, vol 1, January 1926; Pacific Science Association, *Proceedings of the Fourth Pacific Science Congress, Java, May-June 1929*, Batavia-Bandoeng, 1930, vols.1-4; Commonwealth of Australia, *Report of the International Pacific Health Conference*, Melbourne, 1927. Pacific Science Conferences continued until the 1970s.

30 Janet Mitchell, *Spoils of Opportunity: An Autobiography*, New York, 1939, p 61. See also Nicholas Brown, 'Australian Intellectuals and the Image of Asia, 1920-1960', in David Walker (ed.), 'Australian Perceptions of Asia', *Australian Cultural History*, no 9, 1990.

31 Lawrence T Woods, 'Regional Diplomacy and the Institute of Pacific Relations', *Journal of Developing Societies*, vol 8, no 2, 1992; John N Thomas, *The Institute of Pacific Relations: Asian Scholars and American Politics*, Seattle, 1974 ; Paul F Hooper, 'A Brief History of the Institute of Pacific Relations' in Paul F Hooper (ed.), *Rediscovering the IPR: Proceedings of the First International Research Conference on the Institute of Pacific Relations*, Manoa, 1994; Patricia Neils, 'Henry Luce's Investigation of the Alleged Communist Conspiracy in the IPR', in Paul F Hooper (ed.), ibid; Tomoko Akami, 'The Liberal Dilemma: Internationalism and the Institute of Pacific Relations in the USA, Australia and Japan, 1919-1942', PhD thesis, Australian National University, Canberra, 1995. See also William L Holland, 'Source Materials on the Institute of Pacific Relations: Bibliographical Note', *Pacific Affairs*, vol 58, no 1, 1985.

32 Meredith Atkinson, 'The Washington Conference: II. Australia's Position', *Nineteenth Century and After*, vol 19-20, no 538, 1921. For a survey of the Washington Conference see Michael Graham Fry, 'The Pacific Dominions and the Washington Conference, 1921-22', *Diplomacy and Statecraft*, vol 4, no 3, 1993.

33 C Hartley Grattan, 'Australia and the Pacific', *Foreign Affairs*, October 1928.

34 Herbert Croly, 'The Human Potential in Pacific Politics' in J B Condliffe (ed.) *Problems of the Pacific: Proceedings of the Second Conference of the Institute of Pacific Relations, Honolulu, Hawaii, July 15 to 29, 1927* [1928], New York, 1969; Frank Moorhouse, *Grand Days*, London, 1993. For Persia Crawford Campbell see Barbara Sicherman and Carol Hurd Green (eds),

Notable American Women: The Modern Period; A Biographical Dictionary, Cambridge, Mass., 1980, p.133; Heather Radi (ed.), *200 Australian Women: A Redress Anthology*, Sydney, 1988; Obituary, *New York Times*, 3 March 1974.

35 J Merle Davis, *Notes from a Pacific Circuit*, Honululu, 1927. J Merle Davis resigned from his position as Federal Secretary of the IPR in 1930, see J Merle Davis to F W Eggleston, 30 July 1930, Sir Frederic Eggleston Papers, MSS 423, National Library of Australia, Canberra, item 423/14/50.

36 Davis, *Notes*, op. cit., p 14.

37 ibid., pp 10-14.

38 Masao Miyoshi, *As We Saw Them: The First Japanese Embassy to the United States*, New York, 1994.

39 ibid., pp 15-35.

40 Taylor, *Journeyman Taylor*, op. cit., p 187. See also 'Pacific Relations. Institute's Work. Secretary in Sydney', *Sydney Morning Herald*, 26 July 1926.

41 Persia Crawford Campbell, *Chinese Coolie Immigration to Countries Within the British Empire*, London, 1923.

42 Taylor, *Journeyman Taylor*, op. cit., p 41.

43 ibid., pp 42-3.

44 'In the Pacific. Solving the Problems. Conference Held', *Courier Mail*, 19 July 1926; 'Pacific Relations. Institute's Work. Secretary in Sydney', op. cit.; 'Position in the Pacific. Institute to Improve Relations. Conditions in China and Japan', *Age*, 30 July 1926; 'Peace in the Pacific. A Better Understanding. Japan and the White Australia Policy', *Argus*, 30 July 1926.

45 Davis, *Notes*, op. cit., pp 42-3; see also 'Problems of the East. Expansion and War. Basis of Reciprocity Needed', *Argus*, 2 August 1926.

46 Davis, *Notes*, op. cit., pp 44-5.

47 ibid.

48 Institute of Pacific Relations, *History, Organization, Proceedings, Discussions and Addresses. Honolulu Session. June 30-July 14, 1925*, New York, 1969. For H Duncan Hall see Brian H Fletcher, 'H Duncan Hall and the British Commonwealth of Nations', David Walker and Michael Bennett (eds), 'Intellect and Emotion', *Australian Cultural History*, no 16, 1997/8.

49 Mitchell, *Spoils of Opportunity*, op. cit., pp.60-75. Mitchell gave five broadcasts for the ABC on Manchuria in 1933, see Jacqui Murray, 'Japan: the national news story that was not told', *Australian Studies in Journalism*, no 3, 1994.

50 Condliffe, *Problems of the Pacific*, op. cit. For Eggleston see Warren G Osmond, *Frederic Eggleston: An Intellectual in Australian Politics*, Sydney, 1985. For the quotation see Frederic Eggleston, 'The Viewpoint of Australia on Pacific Affairs', *Institute of Pacific Relations. News Bulletin*, August, 1927.

51 Condliffe, *Problems of the Pacific*, op. cit.; for Condliffe's role in the IPR see John B Condliffe, *Reminiscences of the Institute of Pacific Relations*, Vancouver, 1981.

52 E L Piesse, 'Book Review', *Economic Record*, vol 4, no 7, 1928.

53 J B Condliffe (ed.), *Problems of the Pacific 1929. Proceedings of the Third Conference of the Institute of Pacific Relations, Nara and Kyoto, Japan, October 23 to November 9, 1929*, [1929], New York, 1969.

54 Ian Clunies Ross to his mother, 30 October 1930, Clunies Ross Papers, National Library of Australia, Canberra, MSS 7485. For Clunies Ross see Ian Clunies Ross, *Memoirs & Papers: With Some Fragments of Autobiography*, Melbourne, 1961; A I Clunies Ross, 'Ian Clunies Ross', *Records of the Australian Academy of Science*, vol 3, no 3/4, 1977 and Marjory Collard O'Dea, *Ian Clunies Ross: A Biography*, Melbourne, 1997. For Georgina Sweet see John Ritchie (ed.), *Australian Dictionary of Biography, vol 12:1891-1939*, Melbourne, 1990, pp.140-150; see also Georgina Sweet, 'Women of the Pacific Move Towards Understanding', *The Austral-Asiatic Bulletin*, February-March 1938.

55 Frederic Eggleston, 'Book Review', *Economic Record*, May 1931.
56 Frederic Eggleston, 'Australia's View of Pacific Problems', *Pacific Affairs*, vol 111, no 1, January 1930.
57 Bruno Lasker and W L Holland (eds), *Problems of the Pacific 1931. Proceedings of the Fourth Conference of the Institute of Pacific Relations, Hangchow and Shanghai, China, October 21 to November 2* [1931], New York, 1969. For the Manchurian Crisis see Sandra Wilson, 'The Manchurian Crisis and Moderate Japanese Intellectuals: The Japan Council of the Institute of Pacific Relations', *Modern Asian Studies*, vol 26, no 3, 1992.
58 *Spoils of Opportunity*, op. cit., pp 135-53.
59 Inazo Nitobe, *Bushido: The Soul of Japan*, Rutland,1905; Janet Mitchell, *Tempest in Paradise*, London, 1935.
60 *History, Organization, Proceedings, Discussions and Addresses. Honolulu Session. June 30-July 14, 1925*, op. cit.; *Problems of the Pacific, 1927*, op. cit.; Bruno Lasker and W L Holland (eds), *Problems of the Pacific 1931*, op. cit.; Bruno Lasker and W L Holland (eds), *Problems of the Pacific 1933. Economic Conflict and Control. Proceedings of the Fifth Conference of the Institute of Pacific Relations, Banff, Canada, 14 August-26 August, 1933*, Chicago, 1934; W L Holland and Kate L Mitchell (eds), *Problems of the Pacific 1936. Aims and Results of Social and Economic Policies in Pacific Countries. Proceedings of the Sixth Conference of the Institute of Pacific Relations, Yosemite National Park, California, 15-29 August 1936*, Chicago, 1937; Kate Mitchell and W L Holland (eds), *Problems of the Pacific 1939. Proceedings of the Study Meeting of the Institute of Pacific Relations, Virginia Beach, Virginia, November 18-December 2, 1939*, New York, 1940.
61 J G Latham, *The Australian Eastern Mission, 1934. Report of the Right Honorable J G Latham, Leader of the Mission*, Canberra, 1934. See also Ruth Megaw, 'The Australian Goodwill Mission to the Far East in 1934: Its Significance in the Evolution of Australian Foreign Policy', *Journal of the Royal Australian Historical Society*, vol 59, part 4, 1973.
62 Eric Rolls, *Citizens: Continuing the Epic Story of China's Centuries Old Relationship with Australia ... the Sequel to the Sojourners*, St Lucia, 1996, p 453-4.
63 After the Goodwill Mission, F M Cutlack visited Manchuria. His *Sydney Morning Herald* articles on Manchuria were published as *The Manchurian Arena: An Australian View of the Far Eastern Conflict*, Sydney, 1934.
64 Ian Clunies Ross, 'Factors Influencing the Development of Australia's Trade with Japan', in Ian Clunies Ross (ed.), *Australia and the Far East: Diplomatic and Trade Relations*, Sydney, 1936. See also I Clunies Ross, 'Australian Representation in Japan', *Australian Quarterly*, vol 6, no 2, 1934.
65 Peter Russo, Tokyo University of Commerce to Mr J P Bainbridge, Registrar, University of Melbourne, September 1934, Sir John Latham Papers, National Library of Australia, MSS 1009/58/62.
66 Peter Russo to D C S Sissons, 3 August 1976, Russo Papers, National Library of Australia, Canberra, MSS 8202, no 2, series 6.
67 Megow, 'The Australian Goodwill Mission', op. cit.
68 A C V Melbourne, 'A Foreign Policy for Australia', in Hector Dinning and J G Holmes (eds), *Australian Foreign Policy 1934*, Melbourne, 1935.
69 A C V Melbourne, *Report on Australian Intercourse with Japan and China*, Brisbane, 1932.
70 A C V Melbourne, *Report on a Visit to the Universities of China and Japan*, Brisbane, 1936.
71 O'Dea, *Ian Clunies Ross*, op. cit.
72 Clunies Ross, *Australia and the Far East: Diplomatic and Trade Relations*, op. cit. See also Hazel King, *At Mid Century: A Short History of the N.S.W Branch of the Australian Institute of International Affairs 1924-1980*, Sydney, 1982.
73 Clunies Ross, 'Factors Influencing the Development of Australia's Trade with Japan', op. cit.

74 The Americans used their Boxer indemnity to finance a scholarship program for Chinese students to study in the US. Richard Arthur may have had this scheme in mind when he recommended in 1910 that the Federal Government should encourage Chinese students to study at Sydney or Melbourne University. Richard Arthur to George Ernest Morrison, 12 December 1917, George Ernest Morrison Papers, MSS 312, vol 96, Mitchell Library, Sydney.

75 Department of Overseas Trade [Great Britain], *Report of the British Economic Mission to the Far East, 1930-31*, London, 1931. For a reappraisal of economic relations between America and China see Peter Schran, 'The Minor Significance of Commercial Relations between the United States and China, 1850-1931', in Ernest R May and John K Fairbank (eds), *America's China Trade in Historical Perspective: The Chinese and American Performance*, Cambridge, Mass., 1986.

76 Clunies Ross, 'Factors Influencing the Development of Australia's Trade with Japan', op. cit.

77 Nancy Windett, *Australia as Producer and Trader, 1920-1932*, London, 1933, Foreword.

78 'A Brief History of the Institute of Pacific Relations', op. cit.

79 J Lossing Buck, *Land Utilization in China*, London, 1937; S M Wadham, G L Wood, *Land Utilization in Australia*, Melbourne, 1939; P D Phillips and G L Wood (eds), *The Peopling of Australia*, Melbourne, 1928; G L Wood, *The Pacific Basin*, Oxford, 1930; P D Phillips and G L Wood (eds), *The Peopling of Australia, Further Studies*, Melbourne, 1933.

80 F W Eggleston, 'Book Review', *Economic Record*, vol 6, November 1930.

81 Jacqui Murray, 'Japan: The National News Story that was not Told', op. cit.; K S Inglis, *This is the ABC: The Australian Broadcasting Commission 1932-1983*, Melbourne, 1983, p 61.

82 Eleanor Tupper and George E McReynolds, *Japan in American Public Opinion*, New York, 1938; Walter Lippmann, *Public Opinion*, London 1922 and *The Phantom Public. A Sequel to 'Public Opinion'*, New York, 1930. For developments in media and communications in Australia see Graeme Osborne, Glen Lewis, *Communication Traditions in 20th Century Australia*, Melbourne, 1995.

83 E A Ferguson, T P Fry, J G Holmes and A Murray Smith, 'Australian Foreign Policy-Formation and Expression of Australian Opinion' in Australian Institute of International Affairs, *British Commonwealth Relations Conference, 1938, Australian Supplementary Papers*, Series D, no 2, Sydney, 1938.

84 A G Pearson, 'The Australian Press and Japan' in W Macmahon Ball (ed.), *Press, Radio and World Affairs: Australia's Outlook*, Melbourne, 1938.

85 Topper and McReynolds, *Japan in American Public Opinion*, op. cit.

86 Jack Shepherd, *Australia's Interests and Policies in the Far East*, [1939], New York, 1940.

87 ibid., p.199.

88 R G Menzies, Address at the Town Hall, Sydney, 15 May 1939 cited in *Australia's Interests and Policies in the Far East*, ibid, pp.199-200.

89 Sir Robert Garran, 'A School of Oriental Studies', *Austral-Asiatic Bulletin*, vol 2, no 6, 1939. See also Sir Robert Garran, 'Australia and the Pacific' *Australian National Review*, 1 July 1939.

90 E L Piesse, 'Australia and Imperial Defence'; I Clunies Ross, 'Some Aspects of Japanese Colonization'; A L Sadler, 'Japanese Architecture', *Austral-Asiatic Bulletin*, vol 1, no 1, 1937.

91 Yusuke Tsurumi, 'Japan Speaks to Australia', *Austral-Asiatic Bulletin*, vol 1, no 4, 1937.

Chapter Seventeen

1 H E Pratten, *Through Orient to Occident*, Sydney, c1912, p 61.

2 William Macmahon Ball, *Possible Peace*, Melbourne, 1936, p115.

Bibliography

Books first published before 1939

Adams, Arthur, *The Australians: A Novel*, London, 1920.

Alcock, Sir Rutherford, *Art and Art Industries in Japan*, London, 1878.

Allen, R M, *Mesopotamia and India: A Continuation of 'Letters from a Young Queenslander'*, Brisbane, 1916.

Anon, *The Battle of Mordialloc, or How We Lost Australia*, Melbourne, 1888.

——, *Land of The Rising Sun*, Adelaide, 1893.

——, *Japan, Australia and New Zealand*, Osaka, 1935.

Australian Institute of International Affairs, *British Commonwealth Relations Conference, 1938, Australian Supplementary Papers*, Series D, No 2, Sydney, 1938.

Australasian Medical Congress: Transactions of the Ninth Session held in Sydney, New South Wales. September, 1911, vol 1, Sydney, 1913.

Australasian Medical Congress, 'Tropical Australia': Transactions of the Eleventh Session, Brisbane, 21-28 August 1920, Brisbane 1921.

Backhouse, Edmund and J O P Bland, *Annals and Memoirs of the Court of Peking*, Boston, 1914.

Ball, W Macmahon, *Possible Peace*, Melbourne, 1936.

——, (ed.), *Press, Radio and World Affairs: Australia's Outlook*, Melbourne, 1938.

Bancroft, Hubert Howe, *The New Pacific*, [1900], New York, 1912.

Barker, Lady, *Travelling About over New and Old Ground*, London, 1872.

Bedford, Randolph, *Explorations in Civilisation*, Sydney, 1914.

Bell, Colonel Geo. W, *The Little Giants of The East or Our New Allies*, Sydney, 1905.

——, *The Empire of Business! Or How to People Australia*, Sydney, 1906.

Bland J O P, and E Backhouse, *China under the Empress Dowager*, London, 1910.

Black, John R, *Young Japan. Yokohama and Edo. A Narrative on the Settlement and the City From the Signing of the Treaties in 1858, to the Close of the Year 1879 with a glance at the Progress of Japan during a period of twenty-one Years*, 2 vols, Yokohama, 1881.

Boucault, Sir James Penn, *Letters to My Boys: An Australian Judge and Ex-Premier on His Travels in Europe*, London, 1906.

Braddon, Sir Edward, *Thirty Years of Shikar*, London, 1895.

Brogan, F J A (ed.), *Report of the Twenty-Third Meeting of the Australian and New Zealand Association for the Advancement of Science*, Wellington, 1937.

Brown, Lindon, *Letters from an Australian Abroad*, Parramatta, 1910.

Bryce, Viscount James, *Modern Democracies*, 2 vols, London, 1921.

Butterworth, Arthur R, *The Immigration of Coloured Races into British Colonies*, London, 1898.

Burnett, Frances Hodgson, *The Secret Garden* [1911], New York, 1987.

Burston, G W and H R Stokes, *Round About the World on Bicycles*, Melbourne, 1890.

Campbell, Persia Crawford, *Chinese Coolie Immigration to Countries Within the British Empire*, London, 1923.

[Chesney, Lt-Col Sir George Tomkyns], Anon, *The Battle of Dorking: Reminiscences of a Volunteer*, Melbourne, 1871.

Chidell, Fleetwood, *Australia-White or Yellow?*, London, 1926.

Childers, Erskine, *The Riddle of The Sands* [1903]. Annapolis, 1991.

Cilento, Raphael, *The White Man in the Tropics: With Especial Reference to Australia and its Dependencies*, Brisbane, 1925.

Coghlan, T A, *Labour and Industry in Australia: From the First Settlement in 1788 to the Establishment of the Commonwealth in 1901*, vol 3, London, 1918.

Cole, E W, *A White Australia Impossible*, Melbourne, no date.

Colquhoun, Archibald R, *The Mastery of the Pacific*, New York, 1902

Commonwealth Bureau of Census and Statistics, *Official Year Book of the Commonwealth of Australia*, Melbourne, 1911.

——, *Official Year Book of the Commonwealth of Australia, containing authoritative statistics for the period 1901-1917*, no 11, Melbourne, 1918.

Commonwealth of Australia, *Report of the International Pacific Health Conference*, Melbourne, 1927.

Condliffe, J B (ed.), *Problems of the Pacific: Proceedings of the Second Conference of the Institute of Pacific Relations, Honolulu, Hawaii, July 15 to 29, 1927* [1928], New York, 1969.

——, *Problems of the Pacific 1929. Proceedings of the Third Conference of the Institute of Pacific Relations, Nara and Kyoto, Japan, October 23 to November 9, 1929*, [1929], New York, 1969.

Coote, Walter, *Wanderings South and East*, London, 1882.

Crabapple, J, *The War of 1908 for the Supremacy of the Pacific*, London 1908.

Curzon, George F, *Problems of the Far East*, (revised ed.), New York, 1896.

Cutlack, F M, *The Manchurian Arena: An Australian View of the Far Eastern Conflict*, Sydney, 1934.

Daniel, Roland, *Wu Fang: An Adventure of the Secret Service*, London, 1929.

——, *The Yellow Devil: Another Adventure of Wu Fang*, London, 1932.

——, *Ruby of a Thousand Dreams: Another Adventure of Wu Fang*, London, 1933.

Davis, J Merle, *Notes from a Pacific Circuit*, Honululu, 1927.

Deakin, Alfred, *Temple and Tomb in India*, Melbourne, 1893.

——, *Irrigated India: An Australian View of India and Ceylon, Their Irrigation and Agriculture*, London, 1893.

Department of Overseas Trade, [Great Britain], *Report of the British Economic Mission to the Far East, 1930-31*, London, 1931.

Dilke, Sir Charles, *Problems of Greater Britain*, London, 1890.

Dinning, Hector and J G Holmes (eds), *Australian Foreign Policy 1934*, Melbourne, 1935.

Dodds, Leonard V, *Modern Sunlight*, London, 1930.

Duncan, W G K and C V Janes (eds), *The Future of Immigration into Australia and New Zealand*, Sydney, 1937.

East, Edward, *Mankind at the Crossroads*, [1923], New York, 1977.

Edwards, G [G E Pendray], *The Earth Tube*, New York 1909.

Fischer, T B, *A Month in India: The Collected Writings of T B Fischer*, Melbourne, 1914.

Fitchett, W H, *Deeds That Won the Empire*, Melbourne, 1897.

——, *The Tale of the Great Mutiny*, New York, 1901.

Fitzpatrick, Ernest Hugh, *The Coming Conflict of Nations, or, the Japanese-American War*, Springfield, 1909.

Fox, Frank, *The Struggle for the Pacific*, London, 1912.

Fraser, John Foster, *Australia: The Making of a Nation*, London, 1910.

Gaunt, Mary, *A Woman in China*, London, 1914.

——, *A Broken Journey. Wanderings from the Hoang-Ho to the Island of Sanghalien and the Upper Reaches of the Amur River*, London, 1919.

Gepp, Herbert, *Report on Trade between Australia and the Far East*, Canberra, 1932.

Gibson, Frank, *Charles Conder: His Life and Works*, New York, 1914.

Grant, Madison *The Passing of The Great Race or The Racial Basis of European History*, New York, 1916.

Gregory, J W, *The Menace of Colour: A Study of the Difficulties due to the Association of White & Coloured Races*, London, 1925.

Guthrie, T A, *The Seizure of the Channel Tunnel*, London, 1882.

Hales, A G, *The Little Blue Pigeon*, London, 1904.

Hall, Mary, *A Woman in the Antipodes and in the Far East*, London, 1914.

Herbert, Xavier, *Capricornia. A Novel*, Sydney, 1938.

Hingston, James, *The Australian Abroad on Branches From Main Routes Round the World*, [London, 1880, 2 vols.], Melbourne, 1885.

Holland, W L and Kate L Mitchell (eds), *Problems of the Pacific 1936. Aims and Results of Social and Economic Policies in Pacific Countries. Proceedings of the Sixth Conference of the Institute of Pacific Relations, Yosemite National Park, California, 15-29 August 1936*, Chicago, 1937.

Hopkins, Frances, *Reaping The Whirlwind: An Australian Patriotic Drama for Australian People*, Sydney, 1909.

Huntington, Ellsworth, *Civilization and Climate*, New Haven, 1915.

——, *West of the Pacific*, New York, 1925.

Inglis, James, *Our Australian Cousins*, London, 1880.

——, *How a Great Firm Grew: The Story of the Tea Trade*, Sydney, 1901.

——, *Tent Life in Tigerland and Sport and Work on the Nepaul Frontier*, Sydney, 1888.

Institute of Pacific Relations, *History, Organization, Proceedings, Discussions and Addresses. Honolulu Session. June 30-July 14, 1925*, New York, 1969.

Jerome, Helen, *Japan of Today*, Sydney, 1904.

Johnson, James, *The Influence of Tropical Climates on European Constitutions, including an Essay on Indigestion, or the Morbid Sensibility of the Stomach and Bowels*, London, 1836.

Jose, A W, *The Growth of Empire: A Handbook to the History of Greater Britain*, Sydney, 1897.

Kidd, Benjamin, *The Control of the Tropics*, New York, 1898.

Kipling, A W, *The New Dominion*, London, 1908.

Kipling, Rudyard, *Letters from the East*, [1889], New York, c1890.

Kirmess, C H, *The Australian Crisis*, Melbourne, 1909.

Lasker, Bruno and W L Holland (eds), *Problems of the Pacific 1931. Proceedings of the Fourth Conference of the Institute of Pacific Relations, Hangchow and Shanghai, China, October 21 to November 2* [1931], New York, 1969.

——, *Problems of the Pacific 1933. Economic Conflict and Control. Proceedings of the Fifth Conference of the Institute of Pacific Relations, Banff, Canada, 14 August-26 August, 1933*, Chicago, 1934.

Latham, J G, *The Australian Eastern Mission, 1934. Report of the Right Honorable J G Latham, Leader of the Mission*, Canberra, 1934.

Lea, Homer, *The Valor of Ignorance*, New York, 1909.

——, *The Day of the Saxon*, New York, 1912.

Le Queux, William, *The Great War in England in 1897*, London, 1894.

——, *England's Peril*, London, 1899.

——, *The Invasion of 1910*, London, 1905.

——, *Spies of the Kaiser: Plotting the Downfall of England*, [1909], London, 1996.

Lightfoot, Gerald (ed.), *Proceedings of the Pan-Pacific Science Congress, Australia, 1923: Melbourne Meeting: 13th to 22nd August, 1923: Sydney Meeting: 23rd August to 3rd September. Held under the auspices of The Australian National Research Council and through the generosity of The Commonwealth and State Governments*, Melbourne, 1923.

Lloyd, Ross, *William Lane and the Australian Labor Movement*, Sydney, 1936.

Loti, Pierre, [Viaud, Louis Marie Julien], *Madame Chrysanthème*, [1887], New York, 1910.

Lyng, J, *Non-Britishers in Australia: Influence on Population and Progress*, Melbourne, 1927.

MacFarlane, Charles, *Japan: An Account, Geographical and Historical, From The Earliest Period At Which The Islands Composing This Empire were known to Europeans Down to The Present Time and The Expedition Fitted Out in The United States, etc*, Hartford 1856.

Mackay, Kenneth, *The Yellow Wave: A Romance of the Asiatic Invasion of Australia*, London, 1895.

Manson, Marsden, *The Yellow Peril in Action. A Possible Chapter in History*, San Francisco, 1907.

Marks, E George, *Watch The Pacific! Defenceless Australia*, Sydney, 1924.

Martin, Sir James Ranald, *Influence of Tropical Climates in Producing the Acute Endemic Diseases of Europeans*, [London, 1860], second ed., London, 1861.

Mathews, Basil Joseph, *The Clash of Colour: A Study in the Problem of Race*, [1924] Port Washington, 1973.

Matthews, Franklin, *Back To Hampton Roads: Cruise of the U.S Atlantic Fleet from San Francisco to Hampton Roads July 7, 1908-February 22, 1909*, New York, 1909.

Melbourne, A C V, *Report on Australian Intercourse with Japan and China*, Brisbane, 1932.

——, *Report on a Visit to the Universities of China and Japan*, Brisbane, 1936.

Meudall, George, *The Pleasant Career of a Spendthrift and His Later Reflections*, Melbourne, 1939.

Miles, H Chalmers, *Life in India and Scenes in the Mutiny being a Lecture delivered to the X.C Officers and Men of the Royal Artillery and Royal Engineers in the Gymnasium Shed, Royal Artillery Park, Halifax, on Friday Afternoon, April 27th 1860*, Halifax, 1860.

Miller, John [William Lane], *The Working Man's Paradise: An Australian Labour Novel*, Sydney, [1892], 1948.

Millions Club of New South Wales, *Memorandum and Articles of Association*, Sydney, 1913.

——, *Millions Club of New South Wales: What It Is, What It Means, What it Has Done, What It Stands For*, Sydney, 1914.

Miln, James of Toronto [Louise Jordan Miln], *The Feast of Lanterns*, London, 1920.

——, *Flutes of Shanghai*, London, 1928.

——, *By Soochow Waters*, London, 1929.

——, *A Chinese Triangle*, London, 1932.

Miln, Louise Jordan, *In a Shantung Garden*, London, 1924.

——, *The Vintage of Yon-Yee*, London, 1931.

Mitchell, Kate and W L Holland (eds), *Problems of the Pacific 1939. Proceedings of the Study Meeting of the Institute of Pacific Relations, Virginia Beach, Virginia, November 18-December 2, 1939*, New York, 1940.

Mitchell, Janet, *Tempest in Paradise*, London, 1935.

——, *Spoils of Opportunity: An Autobiography*, New York, 1939.

Moberley, Gertrude F, *Experiences of a 'Dinki Di' R R C Nurse*, Sydney, 1933.

Money, Sir Leo Chiozza, *The Peril of the White*, London, 1925.

Moore, Sir William, *A Manual of Family Medicine and Hygiene for India*, 7th ed., London, 1903.

Morrison, George E, *An Australian in China*, London, 1895.

Müller, Max, *India. What Can it Teach Us?* [Leipzig, 1884], (Indian ed.), Calcutta, 1934.

Murdoch, Walter, *Alfred Deakin: A Sketch*, London, 1923.

[Murdoch, James], A.M, *From Australia and Japan*, London, 1892.

——, *Ayame-san, A Japanese Romance of the 23rd Year of Meiji (1890)*, Yokohama, 1892.

Murdoch, James, *Australia Must Prepare. Japan, China, India: A Comparison and Some Contrasts. An Inaugural Lecture*, Sydney, 1919.

——, *A History of Japan*, vol 1, New York, 1964.

——, *A History of Japan*, 3 vols, New York, 1996.

Muskett, Philip, *The Illustrated Australian Medical Guide*, Sydney, no date.

Neame, L E, *The Asiatic Danger in the Colonies*, London, 1907.

Nitobe, Inazo, *Bushido: The Soul of Japan*, Rutland, 1905.

Northcliffe, Alfred Viscount, *My Journey Round the World (16 July 1921- 26 February 1922)*, London, 1923.
Northern Territory Acceptance Act 1910, reprinted as at 31 December 1983, Canberra, 1984.
Offin, T W, *How The Germans Took London*, London, 1900.
Oliver, W R B (ed.), *Report of the Sixteenth Meeting of Australasian Association for the Advancement of Science, Wellington Meeting, January 1923*, Wellington, New Zealand, 1924.
O'Neill, Rev George, *Life of the Reverend Julian Edmond Tenison Woods (1832-1889)*, Sydney, 1929.
Orwell, George, *Burmese Days*,[1934], New York, 1962.
Pacific Science Association, *Proceedings of the Fourth Pacific Science Congress, Java, May-June 1929*, Batavia-Bandoeng, 1930.
Palmer, J H, *The Invasion of New York or How Hawaii was Annexed*, New York, 1897.
Parabellum [Grautoff, Ferdinand H.], *Banzai !*, New York, 1908.
Payne, William Lobatt and John William Fletcher, *Report of the Board of Inquiry Appointed to Inquire into the Land and Land Industries of the Northern Territory of Australia*, Canberra, 1937.
Peacock, E R, *Little Japan against Mighty Russia being a Popular Statement of the Far Eastern Question*, Melbourne, 1904.
Pearson, C H, *National Life and Character: A Forecast*, London, 1893.
Pettit, Charles, *The Woman Who Commanded 500,000,000 Men*, New York, 1929.
Phillips, P D and G L Wood (eds), *The Peopling of Australia*, Melbourne, 1928.
——, *The Peopling of Australia, Further Studies*, Melbourne, 1933.
Piddington, Marion, *Tell Them! or, The Second Stage of Mothercraft: A Handbook for the Sex Training of the Child*, Sydney 1926.
Playford, Thomas, *Notes of Travel in India, China and Japan*, Adelaide, 1907.
Post, Melville Davisson, *The Gilded Chair*, New York, 1911.
Praed, Mrs Rosa Campbell, *Madame Izàn: A Tourist Story*, London, 1899.
Pratt, Ambrose, *The Big Five*, London, 1910.
[——], K'ung ,Yuan Ku'suh, *The Judgement of the Orient. Some Reflections on the Great War made by the Chinese Student & Traveller K'ung Yuan Ku'suh*, New York, 1916.
——, *Magical Malaya*, Melbourne, 1931.
Pratten, H.E, *Asiatic Impressions*, Sydney, 1908.
——, *Through Orient to Occident*, Sydney, c1912.
Price, A Grenfell, *White Settlers in the Tropics*, New York, 1939.
Pullar, A L [Featherstone, Dr F R.], *Celestalia. A Fantasy. AD 1975*, Sydney, 1933.
Ratcliffe, Francis, *Soil Drift in the Arid Pastoral Areas of South Australia*, Melbourne, 1936.
——, *Further Observations on Soil Erosion and Drift with Special Reference to South-Western Queensland*, Melbourne, 1937.
——, *Flying Fox and Drifting Sand: the Adventures of a Biologist in Australia*, London, 1938.
Report of The Proceedings at The Banquet to Col. Geo. W Bell (US Consul at Sydney), Sydney, 1896.
Reuter, Edward Byron, *The Mulatto in the United States including a Study of the Role of Mixed-Blood Races throughout the World*, Boston, 1918.
——, (ed.), *Race and Culture Contacts*, New York, 1934.
Ripley, William Z, *The Races of Europe*, London, 1899.
Rohmer, Sax [Ward, Arthur Sarsfield], *Tales of Chinatown* [London, 1916], London, 1971.
——, *President Fu Manchu*, New York, 1936.
——, *The Bride of Fu Manchu*, London, 1933.
——, *The Hand of Fu Manchu; The return of Dr Fu Manchu; The Yellow Claw; Dope: 4 Complete Classics*, Secaucus, NJ.

Rollier, Dr A, [*La Cure de Soleil*, Paris, 1914] translated as *Heliotherapy*, London, 1923.

Roosevelt, Nicholas, *The Restless Pacific*, New York, 1928.

Rosa, Samuel Albert, *The Invasion of Australia*, Sydney, 1920.

Ross, Ian Clunies (ed.), *Australia and the Far East: Diplomatic and Trade Relations*, Sydney, 1935.

Rothenstein, John, *The Life and Death of Conder*, London, 1938.

[Roydhouse, T R], Rata, *The Coloured Conquest*, Sydney, 1903.

Ruskin, John, *Crown of Wild Olive*, London, 1866.

Saleeby, C W, *Sunlight and Health*, New York, 1924.

Shepherd, Jack, *Australia's Interests and Policies in the Far East*, [1939] New York, 1940.

Shiel, M P, *The Yellow Danger*, London, 1898; New York, 1899.

Sladen, Douglas, *The Japs at Home. Fifth Edition: To Which are added for the First Time Some Bits of China*, London, 1895.

——, *Twenty Years of My Life*, London, 1914.

——, *Queer Things about Japan*, Fourth Edition, to which is added: 'Life of the late Emperor of Japan', London, 1913.

——, *My Long Life*, London, 1939.

Sowden, William, *Children of the Rising Sun: Commercial and Political Japan*, Adelaide, 1897.

Stebbing, William, *Charles Henry Pearson, Fellow of Oriel and Education Minister of Victoria, Memorials by Himself, His Wife and His Friends*, London, 1900.

Stefansson, Vilhjalmur, *The Northward Course of Empire*, New York, 1922.

Stephens, H Morse and Herbert E Bolton, *The Pacific Ocean in History: Papers and Addresses Presented at the Panama-Pacific Historical Congress Held at San Francisco, Berkeley and Palo Alto, California July 19-23, 1915*, New York, 1917.

Stoddard, Lothrop, *The Rising Tide of Color against White World Supremacy*, New York, 1921.

——, *The Revolt Against Civilisation: The Menace of the Under Man*, New York, 1923.

Stopes, Marie, *Married Love*, London, 1918.

Sydney International Exhibition, *Official Catalogue of Exhibits, Japanese Court*, Sydney, 1879.

Sydney International Exhibition, *Official Awards Sydney International Exhibition, 1879*, Sydney, 1879.

Taylor, Griffith, *Environment and Race: A Study of the Evolution, Migration, Settlement and Status of the Races of Man*, London, 1927.

——, *Environment, Race, and Migration: Fundamentals of Human Distribution: With Special Sections on Racial Classification; and Settlement in Canada and Australia*, Toronto, 1937

Thomas, Eugene, *The Dancing Dead*, New York, 1933.

——, *Shadow of Chu-Sheng*, New York, 1933.

Tracy, Louis, *The Final War*, London, 1896.

Wadham, S M and Wood, G L, *Land Utilization in Australia*, Melbourne, 1939.

[Wakefield, Edward Gibbon], 'Australasia', *Sketch of a Proposal for Colonizing Australasia, &c., &c., &c.*, London, 1829.

Walker, W H, [George Rankin], *The Invasion*, Sydney, 1877.

Weber, Adna Ferrin, *The Growth of Cities in the Nineteenth Century: A Study in Statistics*, New York, 1899.

Wells, H G, *War in the Air*, London, 1907.

Wilson, Hardy, *The Dawn of a New Civilisation*, London, 1929.

Windett, Nancy, *Australia as Producer and Trader, 1920-1932*, London, 1933.

Wolter, Robert, *A Short and Truthful History of the Taking of California and Oregon by the Chinese in the Year AD 1899*, San Francisco, 1882.

Wood, G L, *The Pacific Basin*, Oxford, 1930.

Woodruff, Major Charles E, *The Effects of Tropical Light on White Men*, New York, 1905.

Book published after 1939

Allen, Judith A, *Sex & Secrets: Crimes involving Australian Women since 1880*, Melbourne, 1990.

Anderson, Stuart, *Race and Rapprochement: Anglo-Saxonism and Anglo-American Relations, 1894-1904*, Rutherford, c1981.

Andrews, E M, *Australia and China: The Ambiguous Relationship*, Melbourne, 1985.

Anon, *Mathew Phipps Shiel (1865-1947)*, Cleveland, 1979.

Aslin, Elizabeth, *The Aesthetic Movement: Prelude to Art Nouveau*, London, 1969.

Atkinson, Anne, (compiler), *The Bicentennial Dictionary of Western Australians, vol V*, Nedlands, 1988.

Barker, Francis, Peter Hulme, Margaret Iverson and Diana Loxley (eds), *Europe and its Others*, Colchester, 1985.

Barrett, John, *Falling In: Australians and 'Boy Conscription' 1911-1915*, Sydney, 1979.

Bassett, Marnie, *The Hentys: An Australian Colonial Tapestry*, [London, 1954], Melbourne, 1962.

Bederman, Gail, *Manliness & Civilization: A Cultural History of Gender and Race in the United States, 1880-1917*, Chicago, 1995.

Bedford, Randolph, *Nought to Thirty -Three*, Sydney, 1944.

Benjamin, Roger (Curator and ed.), *Orientalism: Delacroix to Klee*, Sydney, 1997.

Bernal, Martin, *Black Athena: The Afroasiatic Roots of Classical Civilization. Vol 1. The Fabrication of Ancient Greece 1785-1985*, London, 1987.

Bertrand, Ina (ed.), *Cinema in Australia: A Documentary History*, Kensington, 1989.

Bleiler, E F (ed.), *Science Fiction Writers. Critical Studies of the Major Authors from the Early Nineteenth Century to the present Day*, New York, 1982.

——, *Science Fiction: The Early Years*, Kent, 1990.

Brantlinger, Patrick, *Rule of Darkness: British Literature and Imperialism, 1830-1914*, Ithaca, 1988.

Brawley, Sean, *The White Peril: Foreign Relations and Asian Immigration to Australasia and North America 1919-78*, Sydney, 1995.

Broinowski, Alison, *The Yellow Lady: Australian Impressions of Asia*, Melbourne, 1992.

Buruma, Ian, *The Missionary and the Libertine: Love and War in East and West*, London, 1996.

Carter, Paul, *The Road to Botany Bay: An Essay in Spatial History*, London, 1988.

Charles-Roux, Edmonde, *Chanel: Her life, Her World-and the Woman Behind the Legend She Herself Created*, New York, 1975.

Chaudhuri, Sashi, *English Historical Writings on the Indian Mutiny, 1857-1859*, Calcutta, 1979.

Chesler, Ellen, *Woman of Valor: Margaret Sanger and the Birth Control Movement in America*, New York, 1992.

Cilento, Raphael, *Triumph in the Tropics: An Historical Sketch of Queensland*, Brisbane, 1959.

Clark, I F, *Tale of the Future: From the Beginning to the Present Day* (3rd ed.), London, 1978.

——, *Voices Prophesying War*: *Future Wars 1763-3749*, (2nd ed.) Oxford, 1992.

Condliffe, J B, *Reminiscences of the Institute of Pacific Relations*, Vancouver, 1981.

Crowley, F K, *Modern Australia in Documents: 1901-1939*, Melbourne, 1973.

——, (ed.), *A Documentary History of Australia*, vol 2, Sydney, 1980.

Dark, Eleanor, *The Timeless Land*, London, 1941.

Day, Bradford M, *Sax Rohmer: A Bibliography*, Denver, 1963.

D'Cruz, J V, *The Asian Image In Australia: Episodes in Australian History*, Melbourne, 1973.

De Lepervanche, Marie M, *Indians in a White Australia: An Account of Race, Class and Indian Immigration to Eastern Australia*, Sydney, 1984.

Dever, Maryanne (ed.), *Australia and Asia: Cultural Transactions*, Honolulu, 1997.

Dijkstra, Bram, *Idols of Perversity: Fantasies of Feminine Evil in Fin-de-Siècle Culture*, New York, 1986.

——, *Evil Sisters: the Threat of Female Sexuality in Twentieth Century Culture*, New York, 1998.

Dixon, Robert, *Writing the Colonial Adventure: Race, Gender and Nation in Anglo-Australian Popular Fiction, 1875-1914*, Cambridge, 1995.

Donald, James and Ali Rattansi (eds), *'Race', Culture and Difference*, London, 1992.

Draper, W J (ed.), *Who's Who in Australia*, 25th Edition, Melbourne, 1985.

Duyker, Edward and Corale Younger, *Molly and the Rajah: Race, Romance and the Raj*, Burwood, 1991.

Dyer, Richard, *White*, London, 1997.

Evans, Raymond, Kay Saunders and Kathryn Cronin (eds), *Exclusion, Exploitation and Extermination: Race Relations in Colonial Queensland*, Sydney, 1975.

Fitzhardinge, L F, *William Morris Hughes: A Political Biography*, Sydney, 1964.

Fitzpatrick, Peter, *Pioneer Players: The Lives of Louis and Hilda Esson*, Cambridge, 1995.

Forsyth, W D, *The Myth of Open Spaces: Australian, British and World Trends in Population and Migration*, Melbourne, 1942.

Frei, Henry P, *Japan's Southward Advance and Australia*, Carlton, 1991.

Fussell, Paul, *Abroad: British Literary Traveling between the Wars*, New York, 1980.

Gabay, Al, *The Mystic Life of Alfred Deakin*, Cambridge, 1992.

Geist, Christopher D and Jack Nachbar (eds), *The Popular Culture Reader*, Bowling Green, 1983.

Gerster, Robin (ed.), *Hotel Asia: An Anthology of Australian Literary Travelling to the 'East'*, Melbourne, 1995.

Gillies, Malcolm and David Pear, *The All-Round Man: Selected Letters of Percy Grainger 1914-1961*, Oxford, 1994.

Gilmour, David, *Curzon*, London, 1994.

Griffiths, Tom, *Hunters and Collectors: The Antiquarian Imagination in Australia*, Melbourne, 1996.

Grimshaw, Patricia, Marilyn Lake, Anne McGrath and Marian Quartly, *Creating a Nation*, Ringwood, 1994.

Goldberg, S L and F B Smith (eds.), *Australian Cultural History*, Melbourne, 1988.

Goodman, David, *Gold Seeking: Victoria and California in the 1850s*, St Leonards, 1994.

Gordon, Linda, *Woman's Body, Woman's Right: A Social History of Birth Control in America*, New York, 1977.

Hamilton, David Mike, *'The Tools of My Trade': The Annotated Books in Jack London's Library*, Seattle, 1986.

Hart, Robert A, *The Great White Fleet: Its Voyage around the World, 1907-1909*, Boston, 1965.

Hawkins, F, *Critical Years in Immigration: Canada and Australia Compared*, Sydney, 1989.

Hibbert, Christopher, *The Great Mutiny: India, 1857*, New York, 1978.

Hicks, Neville, *'This Sin and Scandal': Australia's Population Debate 1891-1911*, Canberra, 1978.

Hooper, Paul F (ed.), *Rediscovering the IPR: Proceedings of the First International Research Conference on the Institute of Pacific Relations*, Manoa, 1994.

Howell, G, *In Vogue*, Harmondsworth, 1973.

Hseu, Immanuel Chung-yueh, *The Rise of Modern China*, New York, 1990.

Hudson, Wayne and Geoffrey Bolton, *Creating Australia: Changing Australian History*, Sydney, 1997.

Ileto, Reynaldo C, and Rodney Sullivan, *Discovering Australasia: Essays on Philippine-Australian Interactions*, Townsville, 1993.

Inglis, K S, *This is the ABC: The Australian Broadcasting Commission 1932-1983*, Melbourne, 1983.

Irving, Robert (ed.), *The History and Design of the Australian House*, Melbourne, 1985.

Ives, Colta Fella,*The Great Wave: The Influence of Japanese Woodcuts on French Prints*, New York, 1974.

James, Edward T, *Notable American Women: A Bibliographical Dictionary*, vol 1, Cambridge (Mass), 1971.

Jeffreys, Sheila (ed.), *The Sexuality Debates*, New York, 1987.

Jones, Timothy, *The Chinese in the Northern Territory* (revised ed), Darwin, 1997.

Julian, Phillip, *The Orientalists: European Painters of Eastern Scenes*, Oxford, 1977.

Jupp, James (ed.), *The Australian People: An Encyclopedia of the Nation, its People and their Origins*, North Ryde, 1988.

Kennedy, Dane, *The Magic Mountains: Hill Stations and the British Raj*, Berkley, 1996.

Kennedy, Victor and Nettie Palmer, *Bernard O'Dowd*, Melbourne, 1954.

King, Hazel, *At Mid Century: A Short History of the NSW Branch of the Australian Institute of International Affairs 1924-1980*, Sydney, 1982.

Kingston, Beverley (ed.), *The World Moves Slowly: A Documentary History of Australian Woman*, Melbourne, 1977.

Labor, Earle, Robert C Leitz III,and I Milo Shepherd (eds), *The Letters of Jack London, Volume 2: 1906-1912*, Stanford, 1988.

LaFeber, Walter, *The Clash: US-Japanese Relations Throughout History*, New York, 1997.

Lake, Marilyn, *The Limits of Hope: Soldier Settlement in Victoria, 1915-1938*, Melbourne, 1987.

La Nauze, J A, *Alfred Deakin: A Biography*, Melbourne, 1965.

Lancaster, Clay, *The Japanese Influence in America*, New York, 1963.

Lane, Terence and Jessie Serle, *Australians at Home: A Documentary History of Australian Domestic Interiors from 1788 to 1914*, Melbourne, 1990.

Lee, Colonel J E, *Duntroon: The Royal Military College of Australia 1911-1946*, Canberra, 1952.

Levi, Werner, *Australia's Outlook on Asia*, Sydney, 1958.

Lo, Hui-Min (ed.), *The Correspondence of G E Morrison, vol I 1895-1912*, Cambridge, 1976.

London Feminist History Group, *The Sexual Dynamics of History: Men's Power, Women's Resistance*, London, 1983.

Low, Gail Ching-Liang, *White Skins/Black Masks: Representation and Colonialism*, London, 1996.

Lyons, Martyn and Lucy Taksa, *Australian Readers Remember: An Oral History of Reading*, Melbourne, 1992.

Mcleod, Roy and Milton Lewis (eds), *Disease, Medicine and Empire*, London, 1988.

MacDonald, Robert H, *The Language of Empire: Myths and Metaphors of Popular Imperialism, 1880-1918*, Manchester, 1994.

Macintyre, Stuart and Julian Thomas (eds), *The Discovery of Australian History, 1890-1939*, Melbourne, 1995.

Macintyre, Stuart,*The Oxford History of Australia: Volume 4: 1901-1942: The Succeeding Age*, Melbourne, 1986.

Magarey, Susan, Sue Rowley and Susan Sheridan (eds), *Debutante Nation: Feminism Contests the 1890s*, Sydney, 1993.

Markus, Andrew, *Fear and Hatred: Purifying Australia and California 1850-1901*, Sydney, 1979.

Martin R, Koda H, *Orientalism: Visions of the East in Western Dress*, New York, 1994.

May, Ernest R and John K Fairbank (eds), *America's China Trade in Historical Perspective: The Chinese and American Performance*, Cambridge, Mass, 1986.

Meaney, Neville, *The Search For Security in the Pacific, 1901-1914*, Sydney, 1976.

——, *Fears and Phobias: E L Piesse and the Problem of Japan: 1909-39*, Canberra, 1996.

Meech, Julia, and Gabriel P Weisberg, *Japonisme Comes to America: The Japanese Impact on the Graphic Arts 1876-1925*, New York, 1990.

Miyoshi, Masao, *As We Saw Them: The First Japanese Embassy to the United States*, New York, 1994.

Money, John and Herman Musaph, *Handbook of Sexology*, Amsterdam, 1977.

Moore-Gilbert, B J, *Kipling and Orientalism*, New York, 1986.

Moorhouse, Frank, *Grand Days*, Sydney, 1993.

Morse, A Reynolds, *The Works of M P Shiel. A Study in Bibliography*, Los Angeles, 1948.

Nairn, Bede (general ed.), *Australian Dictionary of Biography, vol 6 : 1851-1890*, Melbourne, 1976.

Nairn, Bede and Geoffrey Serle (general eds), *Australian Dictionary of Biography, vol 7: 1891-1939*, Melbourne, 1979.

——, *Australian Dictionary of Biography, vol 8: 1891-1939*, Melbourne, 1981.

Nish, Ian H, *The Anglo-Japanese Alliance: The Diplomacy of Two Island Empires: 1894-1907*, London [1966], 1985.

O'Dea, Marjory Collard, *Ian Clunies Ross: A Biography*, Melbourne, 1997.

Osborne, Graeme and Glen Lewis, *Communication Traditions in 20th Century Australia*, Melbourne, 1995.

Osmond, Warren G, *Frederic Eggleston: An Intellectual in Australian Politics*, Sydney, 1985.

Palfreeman, A C, *The Administration of the White Australia Policy*, Melbourne, 1967.

Pearl, Cyril, *Morrison of Peking*, [1967], Melbourne, 1970.

Pesman, Ros, David Walker and Richard White (eds), *The Oxford Book of Australian Travel Writing*, Melbourne, 1996.

Pesman, Ros, *Duty Free: Australian Women Abroad*, Melbourne, 1996.

Phillips, Walter, *James Jefferis: A Prophet of Federation*, Melbourne, 1993.

Pick, Daniel, *Faces of Degeneration: A European Disorder, c1848-c1918*, Cambridge, 1989.

——, *War Machine: The Rationalisation of Slaughter in the Modern Age*, New Haven, 1993.

Pike Douglas (general ed.), *Australian Dictionary of Biography, vol 1: 1788-1850*, Melbourne, 1966.

——, *Australian Dictionary of Biography*, Melbourne, 1968.

——, *Australian Dictionary of Biography, vol 5, 1851-1890*, Melbourne, 1974

Porter, Hal, *The Watcher on The Cast-Iron Balcony*, London, 1963.

Powell, J H M, *Griffith Taylor and 'Australia Unlimited'*, Brisbane, 1993.

Price, Charles A, *The Great White Walls are Built: Restrictive Immigration to North America and Australasia, 1836-1888*, Canberra, 1974.

Radi, Heather (ed.), *200 Australian Women: A Redress Anthology*, Sydney, 1988.

Read, Brian, *Aubrey Beardsley*, New York, 1967.

Reckner, James R, *Teddy Roosevelt's Great White Fleet*, Annapolis, 1988.

Ritchie, John, (ed.), *Australian Dictionary of Biography, vol 12: 1891-1939*, Melbourne, 1990.

Ritchie, John, *Lachlan Macquarie: A Biography*, Melbourne, 1986.

——, (ed.), *Australian Dictionary of Biography, vol 12: 1891-1939*, Melbourne, 1990.

Rivett, Eleanor, *Memory Plays A Tune, Being Recollections of India 1907-1947*, Melbourne, no date.

Roe, Jill, *Beyond Belief: Theosophy in Australia, 1879-1939*, Sydney, 1986.

Roe, Michael, *Nine Australian Progressives: Vitalism in Bourgeois Social Thought 1890-1960*, Brisbane, 1984 .

——, *Australia, Britain and Migration: 1915-1940: A Study of Desperate Hopes*, Cambridge, 1995.

Rohmer, Sax, *Emperor Fu Manchu*, London, 1959.

Rolls, Eric, *Sojourners: The Epic Story of China's Centuries-old Relationship with Australia: Flowers and the Wide sea*, St Lucia, 1992.

——, *Citizens: Continuing the Epic Story of China's Centuries-old Relationship with Australia ... the Sequel to the Sojourners*, St Lucia, 1996.

Ross, Ian Clunies, *Memoirs & Papers: With Some Fragments of Autobiography*, Melbourne, 1961.

Rowley, Hazel, *Christina Stead: A Biography*, Melbourne, 1993.

Rutledge, Helen (ed.), *A Season in India: Letters of Ruby Madden: Experiences of an Australian Girl at a Great Coronation, Durbar, Delhi, 1903*, Sydney, 1976.

Rydon, Joan, *A Bibliographical Register of the Commonwealth Parliament 1901-1972*, Canberra, 1975.

Salsbury Stephen and Kay Sweeney, *Sydney Stockbrokers: Biographies of Members of the Sydney Stock Exchange 1871 to 1987*, Sydney, 1992.

Sandmeyer, Elmer Clarence, *The Anti-Chinese Movement in California*, Urbana, 1991.

Saunders, Kay and Raymond Evans (eds), *Gender Relations in Australia: Domination and Negotiation*, Sydney, 1992.

Seagrave, Sterling, *Dragon Lady: The Life and Legend of the Last Empress of China*, [1992], New York, 1993.

Serle, Geoffrey, *The Golden Age: A History of the Colony of Victoria, 1851-1861*, Melbourne, 1963.

——, (general ed.), *Australian Dictionary of Biography, vol 11: 1891-1939*, Melbourne, 1988.

Sharpe, Jenny, *Allegories of Empire: The Figure of Woman in the Colonial Text*, Minneapolis, 1993.

Shiel, M P, *Science Life and Literature*, London, 1950.

Shirley, Graham and Brian Adams, *Australian Cinema: The First Eighty Years*, revised edition, Sydney, 1982.

Souter, Gavin, *A Peculiar People: the Australians in Paraguay*, Sydney, 1968.

——, *Lion and Kangaroo: The Initiation of Australia 1901-1919*, Sydney, 1976.

Spearritt Peter and David Walker (eds), *Australian Popular Culture*, Sydney, 1979.

Spencer, Charles R, *The Aesthetic Movement 1869-1890*, London, 1973.

Stefansson, Vilhjalmur, *Discovery, the Autobiography of Vilhjalmur Stefansson*, New York, 1964.

Steinbrunner, Chris, Otto Penzler, Marvin Lachnan and Charles Shibuk (eds), *Encyclopedia of Mystery and Detection*, New York, 1976.

Steven, Margaret, *Merchant Campbell 1769-1846: A Study of Colonial Trade*, Melbourne, 1965.

Stevens, Maryanne (ed.), *The Orientalists: Delacroix to Matisse*, London, 1984

Stewart, Ken (ed.), *The 1890s: Australian Literature and Literary Culture*, St Lucia, 1996.

Storry, J D, *Japan and the Decline of the West in Asia, 1894-1943*, New York, 1979.

Sturgis, Mathew, *Passionate Attributes: The English Decadence of the 1890s*, London, 1995.

Swanson, Vern G, *Alma-Tadema: The Painter of the Victorian Vision of the Ancient World*, New York, 1977.

Szyliowicz, Irene L, *Pierre Loti and the Oriental Woman*, New York, 1988.

Taylor, Griffith, *Australia: A Study of Warm Environments and their Effect on British Settlement*, London, 1940.

——, *Journeyman Taylor*, London, 1958.

The Library Society, State Library of New South Wales, *Asian Influences on Australian Literature: Proceedings of a Symposium*, Sydney, 1988.

Theweleit, Klaus, *Male Fantasies, Vol 1, Women, Floods, Bodies, History*, translated by Stephen Coney, Erica Carter and Chris Turner, Minneapolis, 1987.

Thomas, John N, *The Institute of Pacific Relations: Asian Scholars and American Politics*, Seattle, 1974.

Thompson, Richard Austin, *The Yellow Peril 1890-1924*, New York, 1978.

Tregenza, John, *Professor of Democracy: The Life of Charles Henry Pearson, 1830-1894. Oxford Don and Australian Radical*, London, 1968.

Trevor-Roper, Hugh, *The Hermit of Peking: The Hidden Life of Sir Edmund Backhouse*, London, 1976.

Tweedie, Sandra, *Trading Partners: Australia & Asia 1870-1993*, Sydney, 1994.

Walker, David, *Dream and Disillusion: A Search for Australian Cultural Identity*, Canberra, 1976.

——, (ed) 'Australian Perceptions of Asia', *Australian Cultural History*, vol 9,1990.

Walker, David and Michael Bennett (eds), 'Intellect and Emotion', *Australian Cultural History*, no 16, 1997/8.

Weeks, Jeffrey, *Sex, Politics and Society: The Regulation of Sexuality Since 1800*, 2nd edition, London, 1989.

Weisberg, Gabriel P, Phillip Dennis Cate, Gerald Needham, Martin Edelberg and William R Johnson (eds), *Japonisme: Japanese Influence on French Art 1854-1910*, Cleveland, 1975.

Weisberg, Gabriel P, *Art Nouveau Bing: Paris Style 1900*, New York, 1986.

Widener, Alice, *Gustave Le Bon: The Man and His Works*, Indianapolis, 1979.

Wilde, William H, Joy Hooton and Barry Andrews (eds), *The Oxford Companion to Australian Literature*, Melbourne (2nd ed.), 1994.

Williams, Harold S, *Tales of the Foreign Settlements in Japan*, Rutland, 1972.

Wu, William F, *The Yellow Peril: Chinese Americans in American Fiction 1850-1940*, Hamden, 1982.

Yarwood, A T, *Asian Migration to Australia. The Background to Exclusion 1896-1923*, Melbourne, 1967.

——, *Walers: Australian Horses Abroad*, Melbourne, 1989.

Yokoyama, Toshio, *Japan in the Victorian Mind*, Houndmills, 1987.

Articles and book chapters published before 1939

A B, 'Colonel Geo W Bell (United States Consul)', *Cosmos Magazine*, 31 December 1895.

Acton, William, 'The Functions and Disorders of the Reproductive Organs' [London, 1875] in Jeffreys, Sheila (ed), *The Sexuality Debates*, New York, 1987.

Adams, Arthur, 'The Day the Big Shells Came', *Call*, February 1909.

Adams, Francis, 'Daylight and Dark. White or Yellow: Which Is to Go? What the Chinese Can teach Us', *Boomerang*, 1 February 1888.

Aldridge, Evelyn, 'The Deliverer', *Lone Hand*, 1 July 1910.

Anon, 'The Problem of Australian Sea -Defence', *Review of Reviews*, 20 January 1902.

——, 'The Admirals on Australian Sea -Defence', *Review of Reviews*, 20 February 1902.

Arthur, Richard Dr, 'Australia for the Anglo-Indian', Letter to the Editor, *Madras Times*, 13 May 1907.

——, 'Immigration-The Salvation of Australia', *Commonwealth*, 30 June 1906.

——, 'The Colonisation of Tropical Australia', *Transactions of the 8th Session, Australasian Medical Congress*, Melbourne, October 1908, vol 2.

——, 'A Stone in Empire Building', *Morning Post*, 6 October 1908.

——, 'The Empire for Britons', *Sydney Morning Herald*, 15 January 1910.

Ashmead Bartlett, E, 'Some Famous Men I Have Met', *Town and Country Journal*, 9 January 1918.

Atkinson, Meredith, 'The Washington Conference. II Australia's Position', *Nineteenth Century and After*, vol 19-20, no 538, 1921

Bailey, K H, 'Public Opinion and Population Problems', in F W Eggleston *et al* (eds), *The Peopling of Australia: Further Studies*, Pacific Relations Series, No 4, Melbourne, 1933.

Baker, R T, 'Central Australia. A Barren Desert?', *Sydney Morning Herald*, 10 May 1924.

Bakhap, Senator Thomas, 'Report on Trade between the Commonwealth and China. For the Honorable A S Rogers, Minister for Trade and Customs', *Parliamentary Paper No 62*, vol 2, Melbourne, 1922.

Barrett, Sir James, 'Can Tropical Australia be Peopled by a White Race?', *The Margin*, vol 1, no 1, 1925.

Bayliss, Sir William M, 'Introduction', in C W Saleeby, *Sunlight and Health*, New York, 1924.

Beadnell, Mrs Ellen, 'A Holiday in Japan', *Town and Country Journal*, 9 August 1911.

Bedford, Randolph, 'White, Yellow and Brown', *Lone Hand*, 1 July 1911.

——, 'The Enameller's Shop. The Face of Quong Sue Duk', *Pacific*, 17 August 1923.

Brigden, J B, 'Australian Immigration Policy: Absorbing Capacity and Capital Requirements- 35,000 People and £10,000,000 Annually', *Stead's Review*, 1 December 1925.

Bright, Mrs Charles, 'Mr James Inglis', *Cosmos Magazine*, vol 2, no 6, 29 February 1896.

Brooke, J H, 'Impressions of Japan', *Argus*, 22 August to 28 October, 1867.

Brown, J Macmillan, 'The Pacific. American Asiatic Institute. Problems of the Future', *Sydney Morning Herald*, 31 May 1913.

Cilento, R W, 'Australia's Problems in the Tropics', Report of the Twenty First Meeting of the Australian and New Zealand Association for the Advancement of Science', Sydney, 1932.

Clunies Ross, Ian, 'Factors Influencing the Development of Australia's Trade with Japan', in Clunies Ross, Ian (ed.), *Australia and the Far East: Diplomatic and Trade Relations*, Sydney, 1936.

——, 'Australian Representation in Japan', *Australian Quarterly*, vol 6, no 2, 1934.

——, 'Factors Influencing the Development of Australia's Trade with Japan', in Ross, Ian Clunies (ed.), *Australia and the Far East: Diplomatic and Trade Relations*, Sydney, 1936.

——, 'Some Aspects of Japanese Colonization', *Austral-Asiatic Bulletin*, vol 1, no 1, 1937.

Coghlan, T A, 'The Exclusion of the Chinese', in T A Coghlan, *Labour and Industry in Australia: From the First Settlement in 1788 to the Establishment of the Commonwealth in 1901*, Chapter 3, vol 3, London, 1918.

Croll, R H, 'Kipling in Australia', *Australian National Review*, 1 November 1937.

Croly, Herbert, 'The Human Potential in Pacific Politics' in Condliffe, J B (ed.) *Problems of the Pacific: Proceedings of the Second Conference of the Institute of Pacific Relations, Honolulu, Hawaii, July 15 to 29, 1927* [1928], New York, 1969.

David, Edgeworth, 'A Wilderness. Australia's Arid Centre', *Sydney Morning Herald*, 13 August 1924.

——, 'II. A Wilderness. True View of Central Australia', *Sydney Morning Herald*, 14 August 1924.

Duncan, W G K, 'The Immigration Problem' in W G K Duncan and C V Janes (eds), *The Future of Immigration into Australia and New Zealand*, Sydney, 1937.

Dyer, E J, 'Australia and the Asian-Pacific: An Address delivered in Melbourne Town Hall on October 21, 1895', Melbourne, 1895.

Edmond, James, 'The Australian Fleet', *Living Age*, 12 August 1911.

Eggleston, Frederic 'The Viewpoint of Australia on Pacific Affairs', *Institute of Pacific Relations, News Bulletin*, August, 1927.

——, [Review] *Economic Record*, vol 111, no 5, November 1927.

——, 'Australia's View of Pacific Problems', *Pacific Affairs*, vol 111, no 1, January 1930.

Eitel, Rev Dr E J, 'China and the Far Eastern Question', in *Papers Read Before the Royal Geographical Society of Australasia*, Fourteenth session, 1900-1, South Australian Branch.

Elles, J Currie, 'British Traditions: Australian Decadence [Being a lecture delivered before the British Empire League in Australia, on Friday, October 12th, 1906, the Hon. Bruce Smith Esq, K C, M P, in the Chair]', *Journal of the Institute of Bankers of New South Wales*, vol 15, part 10, 1906.

——, 'The Influence of Commerce on Civilisation', *Journal of The Institute of Bankers of NSW*, 30 April 1908.
Esson, Louis, 'From The Oldest World', *Lone Hand*, 1 May 1908.
——, 'Colombo', *Lone Hand*, 1 June 1908.
——, 'Swadeshi and other Imperial Troubles', *Lone Hand*, 1 July 1908.
——, 'The Decay of the Delhis', *Lone Hand*, 1 July 1908.
——, 'Japan's Jiu-Jitsu Diplomacy', *Lone Hand*, 1 August 1908.
——, 'The Golden Temple of the Sikhs', *Lone Hand*, 1 September 1908.
——, 'Japan the Gamester', *Lone Hand*, 1 September 1908.
——, 'Benares', *Lone Hand*, 1 October 1908.
——, 'Japanese Imperialism', *Lone Hand*, 1 October 1908.
——, 'The Awakening of the Dragon', *Lone Hand*, 2 November 1908.
——, 'Celestial Politics', *Lone Hand*, 1 December 1908.
Fisher, A G, 'Present Large-Scale Migration Policy' in W G K Duncan and C V Janes (eds), *The Future of Immigration into Australia and New Zealand*, Sydney, 1937.
Fitchett, W H, 'The Problem of Australian Sea -Defence', *Review of Reviews*, 20 December 1901.
Garran, Sir Robert, 'A School of Oriental Studies', *Austral-Asiatic Bulletin*, vol 2, no 6, 1939.
——, 'Australia and the Pacific' *Australian National Review*, 1 July 1939.
Gepp, Sir Herbert, 'Australia's Great Backyard', *Living Age*, vol 354, August 1938.
Girard, Louis E, 'The Genius of an Empire', *Pacific*, 18 September 1924.
'Globe Trotter', 'White Australia', *Daily Mail*, 4 September 1920.
Grattan, C Hartley, 'Australia and the Pacific', *Foreign Affairs*, October 1928.
Griffis, W E, 'Reviews of Books' *American Historical Review*, vol 9, no 4, 1903.
——, 'Introduction', Inazo Nitobe, *Bushido: The Soul of Japan*, Rutland, 1905.
Guthrie, Senator James, 'Why I Favour a White Australia', *Stead's Review*, January 1925.
J S [James Smith], 'The Japanese Exhibits and Japanese Art', *Argus*, 5 March 1881.
Jefferis, Rev James, 'Australia's Mission and Opportunity', *Centennial Magazine*, vol 1, August 1888-July 1889.
Kirmess, C H, 'The Commonwealth Crisis', *Lone Hand*, 1 October 1908 to 1 April 1909.
Kirton, Walter, 'A Jap School for Spies', *Lone Hand*, 1 September 1908.
Lamington, Lord, 'A Cheerful View of Queensland', *Review of Reviews*, 20 May 1902.
Lewin, Evans, 'Northern Australia: A Local World-Problem', *Atlantic Monthly*, vol 137, April 1926.
Lorelle, 'Battle of the Warbush', *Californian*, 2 October 1880.
Lusk, Hugh H ,'A Visit of the Fleet to Australia', *Harper's Weekly*, 11 July 1908.
MacCallum, M W, 'The Late Professor James Murdoch', *Hermes*, May 1922.
McPhee, E T, 'The Urbanisation of the Australian Population' in P D Phillips and G L Wood (eds), *The Peopling of Australia*, Melbourne, 1928.
Madden, W, 'Trade With The East. The Proposed Japanese Treaty', *Argus*, 22 October 1895.
Madigan, C T, 'A Review of the Arid Regions of Australia and their Economic Potentialities', Brogan, F J A (ed.), *Report of the Twenty-Third Meeting of the Australian and New Zealand Association for the Advancement of Science*, Wellington, 1937.
Markham, Rupert V,'The 'Varsity School of Geography. A Valuable Institution', *Evening News*, 24 February 1923.
Masey, Edward, 'Vast Open Spaces: A Study of the Population Problem', *Publicist*, August 1936.
Medhurst, C Spurgeon, 'The Chinese Puzzle', *Pacific*, 12 February 1925.
Melbourne, A C V, 'A Foreign Policy for Australia', in Hector Dinning and J G Holmes (eds), *Australian Foreign Policy 1934*, Melbourne, 1935.

Middleton, A, 'Not Arid. Central Australia', *Sydney Morning Herald*, 31 May 1924.

Morton, P K, 'Trade with the East', *Argus*, 22 October 1895.

Newby, H D, 'Australia's Plans for the Future. Trade and Commercial Expansion and the Growth of Great Industries', *Sluyter's Monthly*, vol 3, April 1922.

——, 'Australia's Bid for Trade. The Problem of Production, Marketing and Transport. A Hopeful Outlook', *Sluyter's Monthly*, vol 3, July 1922.

——, 'Australia's Position in the Pacific. Some Aspects of the Changing Commercial Position', *Sluyter's Monthly*, vol 3, November 1922.

——, 'Australia in the World's Markets: The Outlook', *Inter-Ocean*, vol 5, March 1924.

Nicol, Alex M, 'How to People the Commonwealth: A Dream and a Reality', *Australia To-Day*, 1 December 1909.

Nicoll, William, 'The Condition of Life in Tropical Australia', *Journal of Hygiene*, vol 16, December 1917.

O'Connor, T P, 'Is Australia Menaced?', *Sydney Morning Herald*, 6 July 1905.

Olivier, Sir Sydney, 'White Capital and Coloured Labour', *Stead's Review*, 17 September 1922.

Osborne, W A, 'Problem of Tropical Colonisation. From a Physiological Standpoint', *Argus*, 10 April 1909.

Park, Robert E, 'Race Relations and Certain Frontiers', in E B Reuter (ed.), *Race and Culture Contacts*, New York, 1934.

Palm, Dr Theobald Adrian, 'The Geographical Distribution and Aetiology of Rickets', *Practitioner*, October and November, 1890.

Parsons, J Langdon, 'The Northern Territory of South Australia: A Brief Historical Account: Pastoral and Mineral Resources', *Royal Geographical Society of Australasia*, Adelaide, 1901.

Pearson, A G, 'The Australian Press and Japan' in W Macmahon Ball (ed.), *Press, Radio and World Affairs: Australia's Outlook*, Melbourne, 1938.

Piesse, E L, 'White Australia', *Round Table*, vol XI, March 1921.

[Piesse, E L], 'Japanese Immigration into Australia: History of the Immigration Restrictions Act', *Stead's Review*, 1 August 1925.

——, 'Australia and Imperial Defence', *Austral-Asiatic Bulletin*, vol 1, no 1, 1937.

Plummer, John, 'Australian Notes on Japanese Topics', *Japan Daily Mail*, 3 April 1895, 18 April 1895.

——, 'Japanese Topics in Australia', *Japan Daily Mail*, 26 April 1895.

——, 'Australia and Japan', *Japan Daily Mail*, 27 June 1895.

——, 'Japanese Topics in Australia', *Japan Daily Mail*, 9 August 1895.

——, 'Australia and Japan', *Japan Daily Mail*, 29 August 1895, 23 September 1895, 17 January 1896, 10 February 1897, 2 March 1896, 3 April 1895, 6 May 1896, 16 May 1896, 16 July 1896, 25 November 1896, 15 December 1896.

Priestley, Professor H, 'Physiological Aspects of White Settlement in Tropical Australia', *Australian Geographer*, vol 1, part 2, November 1929.

Quinn, Roderic, 'Australia: A Nation', *Australia To-Day*, 1 November 1910.

Roosevelt, Theodore, 'National Life and Character', *The Sewanee Review*, May 1894.

Russell, F A A, 'Australian Problems: Australia and the East', *Sydney Morning Herald*, 25 July 1905.

Ruth, Rev T E, 'Will Australia remain British?', *Millions Magazine*, 15 August 1924.

Sadler, A L, 'Civilization of East and West', *Pacific*, 26 Jan 1924.

——, 'Japanese Architecture', *Austral-Asiatic Bulletin*, vol 1, no 1, 1937.

Scholfield, Guy H, 'The White Peril in Australasia', *Nineteenth Century and After*, vol 58, 1905.

Sheaf, E T, 'The Eastern Fish Trade', *Inter-Ocean*, vol 5, April 1924.

——, 'Mr Sheaf's Report on Australian Trade in the East, *Inter-Ocean*, vol 6, February 1925.

'Sketcher' [William Lane], 'Daylight and Dark. Sunday Night in a Chinese Gambling Hell', *Boomerang*, 14 January 1888.

——, 'Daylight and Dark. Opium Smoking in Brisbane', *Boomerang*, 21 January 1888.

——, 'Daylight and Dark. The Fascinations of Fan-Tan', *Boomerang*, 28 January 1888.

——, 'Daylight and Dark. How the Chinese Live in Queensland', *Boomerang,* 4 February 1888.

——, 'The Case for the Anti-Chinese', *Boomerang*, 11 February 1888.

——, 'White or Yellow? A Story of the Race-War of 1908', *Boomerang*, 18 February 1888 to 5 May 1888.

Skipper, Mervyn ,'The Racial Tragedy of Java', *Lone Hand*, 1 October 1910.

Stamp, L Dudley, 'The Future of Tropical Australia', *Nature*, 26 January, 1935.

Stead, W T, 'Topic of the Month. The Crime against China and Ourselves', *Review of Reviews*, 15 December 1895.

Stefansson, Vilhjamur, 'Central Australia. Stefansson's Views', *Sydney Morning Herald*, 12 August 1924.

Sternberg, Freda, 'White Women in the Australian Tropics', *Living Age*, vol 325, April 1925.

Stoddard, Lothrop, 'Racial Realities in Europe', *Saturday Evening Post*, 22 March 1924.

Strong, Professor H A, 'A Memoir and Portrait', *Charles H Pearson: Reviews and Critical Essays*, London, 1896.

Suttor, J B, 'Report on the Trade of Japan for the Year 1904', *Bulletin no 2*, Intelligence Department, New South Wales, Sydney, 1905.

——, 'Report on Java and the Dutch East Indies', *Bulletin no 26*, Intelligence Department, New South Wales, Sydney, 1908.

——, 'Report on the Trade of Japan, 1907', *Bulletin no 28*, Immigration and Tourist Bureau, New South Wales, Sydney, 1908.

——, 'Report on the Trade of The Dutch East Indies, 1910', *Bulletin no 49*, Immigration and Tourist Bureau, New South Wales, Sydney, 1911.

——, 'Report on the Trade of Japan, 1910', *Bulletin no 47*, Immigration and Tourist Bureau, New South Wales, Sydney, 1911.

Sweet, Georgina, 'Women of the Pacific Move Towards Understanding', *The Austral-Asiatic Bulletin*, February-March 1938.

Taylor, Gordon, 'Group Settlement in Western Australia' in F W Eggleston *et al* (eds), *The Peopling of Australia: Further Studies*, Pacific Relations Series, No 4, Melbourne, 1933.

Taylor, Griffith, 'Geographical Factors Controlling the Settlement of Tropical Australia', *Queensland Geographical Journal*, vol 32-33, 1916-1918.

——, 'The Climate Factors Influencing Settlement in Australia' in Commonwealth Bureau of Census and Statistics, *Official Year Book of the Commonwealth of Australia, containing authoritative statistics for the period 1901-1917*, no 11, Melbourne, 1918.

——, 'Peoples of the Pacific. Stumblings of a New Tongue. Wet-Bulb Meter of Human Energy', *Sun*, 26 October 1920.

——, ' Surabaya, a Stageland City. Bromo, the Fire-God of Java. Wonderful Sea of Sand', *Sun*, 28 October 1920.

——, 'White Australia: Rainfall and Settlement', *Sydney Morning Herald*, 9 November 1921.

——, 'A Million Farms. A Criticism', *Sydney Morning Herald*, 27 August 1921.

——, ' White Australia. Rainfall and Settlement', *Sydney Morning Herald*, 9 November 1921.

——, 'Tropical Problems. Climate, Health and Settlement', *Argus*, 14 October 1922.

——, 'Birth-Rate and Race Mixture' (letter to editor), *Sydney Morning Herald*, 11 July 1923.

——, 'Our Tropical Spaces', *Forum*, 7 November, 1923.

——, 'Our Foreign Neighbours', *Australian Teacher*, November 1923

——, 'Geography and National Problems' in W R B Oliver (ed.), *Report of the Sixteenth Meeting of Australasian Association for the Advancement of Science, Wellington Meeting, January 1923*, Wellington, New Zealand, 1924.

——, 'Central Australia' (letter to the editor), *Sydney Morning Herald*, 6 May 1924.

——, 'Arid Australia' (letter to the editor), *Sydney Morning Herald*, 2 June 1924.

——, 'Problems of Tropical Settlement', *Sydney Morning Herald*, 14 August 1924.
——, 'The Far East:We Cross the Line', *Sydney Morning Herald*, 11 December 1926.
——, 'The Far East: To the Philippine Islands', *Sydney Morning Herald*, 15 December 1926.
——, 'The Far East: Hong Kong', *Sydney Morning Herald*, 18 December 1926.
——, 'The Far East: A Japanese Evening', *Sydney Morning Herald*, 22 December 1926.
——, 'The Far East: Nikko and its Shrines', *Sydney Morning Herald*, 25 December 1926.
——, 'The Far East: A Day at the Congress', *Sydney Morning Herald*, 29 December 1926.
——, 'Through the Far East: Kiushiu and its Volcanoes', *Sydney Morning Herald*, 5 January 1927.
——, 'The Australian Tropics', *News Bulletin, Institute of Pacific Relations*, January 1927.
——, 'The Far East: Mount Fuji and its Lakes', *Sydney Morning Herald*, 11 January 1927.
——, 'The Far East: Pekin-Its Palaces and Poor', *Sydney Morning Herald*, 15 January 1927.
——, 'Through the Far East: The Japanese People', *Sydney Morning Herald*, 8 February 1927.
——, 'China: Shanghai and its Environs', *Sydney Morning Herald*, 5 March 1927.
——, 'China: Among the Hakka Tribes, *Sydney Morning Herald*, 12 February 1927.
——, 'China: Is She Awakening?', *Sydney Morning Herald*, 29 January 1927.
——, 'China: Is She Awakening?', *Sydney Morning Herald*, 1 February 1927.
——, 'Tropical Settlement by the White Race in Australia' in Griffith Taylor, *Environment and Race: A Study of the Evolution, Migration, Settlement and Status of the Races of Man*, London, 1927.
——, 'Australia's Future Population', *Morpeth Review*, no 4, June 1928.
Tenison-Woods, Rev J E, 'Notes of Travel', *Sydney Morning Herald*, 15 June 1887.
Theodore, E G, 'White Settlement in the Australian Tropics. Can White People Live There?', *Stead's Review*, 11 March 1925.
Tsurumi, Yasuke, 'Japan and America', *Stead's Review*, 1 September 1926.
——, 'Japan Speaks to Australia', *Austral-Asiatic Bulletin*, vol 1, no 4, 1937.
Upton, Sydney, 'Settlement in Northern Australia', *United Empire, Journal of the Royal Empire Society*, London, vol 25, September 1934.
'Veronica', 'Guarding Our Northern Gate, *Lone Hand*, 2 August 1909.
Waddell, Rev R, 'The Influence of Climate on Character. The Case for New Zealand', *Review of Reviews*, 15 August 1899.
Wadham, S M, 'Australia's Absorptive Capacity-The Primary Industries' in W G K Duncan and C V Janes (eds), *The Future of Immigration into Australia and New Zealand*, Sydney, 1937.
Want, J H, 'To Japan and Back' (6 parts), *Town and Country Journal*, 3 August 1889 to 27 September 1889.
Wickens, C H, 'Australian Population: Its Nature and Growth', in P D Phillips and G L Wood (eds), *The Peopling of Australia*, Melbourne, 1928.
Williams, W Wynne, 'Northern Australia. The Bogey of the Empty Spaces', *Australian Quarterly*, vol 9, no 1, 1937.
Wood, G L, 'The Settlement of Northern Australia', *Economic Record*, vol 11, no 2, May 1926.

Articles and chapters in books published after 1939

Allen, Judith, '"Our Deeply Degraded Sex" and "The animal in man": Rose Scott, Feminism and Sexuality 1890-1925', *Australian Feminist Studies*, nos. 7 & 8, 1988.
Anderson, Warwick, 'The Trespass Speaks: White Masculinity and Colonial Breakdown', *The American Historical Review*, vol 102, no 5, 1997.
——, 'Geography, Race and Nation: Remapping "Tropical" Australia, 1890-1930', *Historical Records of Australian Science*, vol 11, no 4, 1997.

'Asian Immigrants to Western Australia 1829-1901' in Anne Atkinson (compiler), *The Bicentennial Dictionary of Western Australians, vol 5*, Nedlands, 1988.

Bacchi, Carol and Alison Mackinnon, 'Sex, Resistance and Power: Sex Reform in South Australia', *Australian Historical Studies*, vol 23, no 90, 1988.

Bolton, Geoffrey, 'A C V Melbourne: Prophet Without Honour', in Stuart Macintyre and Julian Thomas (eds), *The Discovery of Australian History, 1890-1939*, Melbourne, 1995.

Boothe, Clare, 'The Valor of Homer Lea', Introduction, in Homer Lea, *The Day of the Saxon*, New York, 1942.

Brown, Nicholas, 'Australian Intellectuals and the Image of Asia, 1920-1960', in David Walker (ed.), *Australian Perceptions of Asia, Australian Cultural History*, no 9, 1990.

Collins, Darryl, 'Asian Art in Australia. One Hundred and Fifty Years of Exhibitions. Connoisseurs and Collections', *Art in Australia*, vol 30, no 3, Autumn 1993.

Cronin, Kathryn, 'On a Fast Boat to Queensland: the Chinese Influx onto Queensland's Goldfields' in Evans, Raymond, Kay Saunders and Kathryn Cronin (eds), *Exclusion, Exploitation and Extermination: Race Relations in Colonial Queensland*, Sydney, 1975.

Cross, J, 'Wilton Hack and Japanese Immigration into North Australia', *Proceedings Geographical Society of Australasia (South Australia Branch)*, 1959-60.

D'Cruz, J V , 'White Australia and the Indian Mutiny', in J V D'Cruz, *The Asian Image In Australia: Episodes in Australian History*, Melbourne, 1973, ch 1.

Donald, James, 'How English Is It? Popular Literature and National Culture', *New Formations*, no 6, Winter 1988.

Firth, Stewart and Jeanette Hoorn, 'From Empire Day to Cracker Night', in Peter Spearritt and David Walker (eds), *Australian Popular Culture*, Sydney, 1979.

Fletcher, Brian H, 'H Duncan Hall and the British Commonwealth of Nations', David Walker and Michael Bennett (eds), *Intellect and Emotion, Australian Cultural History*, no 16, 1997/8.

French, David, 'Spy Fever in Britain, 1900-1915', *Historical Journal*, vol 21, no 2, 1978.

Fry, Michael Graham, 'The Pacific Dominions and the Washington Conference, 1921-22', *Diplomacy and Statecraft*, vol 4, no 3, 1993.

Holland, William L, 'Source Materials on the Institute of Pacific Relations: Bibliographical Note', *Pacific Affairs*, vol 58, no 1, 1985.

Hoppenstand, Gary, 'Yellow Devil Doctors and Opium dens: A Survey of the Yellow Peril Stereotypes in Mass Media Entertainment', in Christopher D Geist and Jack Nachbar (eds) *The Popular Culture Reader*, Bowling Green, 1983.

Inoue, Tadakatsu, 'Pioneering in Australian Direct Trade: The Life of Fusajiro Kanematsu, 1845-1913', *Kobe Economic and Business Review*, 22nd Annual Report, The Research Institute for Economics and Business Administration, Kobe University, 1976.

Kingston, Beverley, 'The Taste of India', in David Walker (ed.), 'Australian Perceptions of Asia', *Australian Cultural History*, vol 9,1990.

Koga, Kurando, 'Origin of Kanematsu Organization in Australia', *Kanematsu Geppo*, Commemorative Number, 15 August 1959, translated by Akira Ocdaira.

Kupperman, Karen Ordahl, 'Fear of Hot Climates in the Anglo-American Colonial Experience', *William and Mary Quarterly*, vol 41, April 1984.

Livingstone, David N, 'Human Acclimatization: Perspectives on a Contested field of Inquiry in Science, Medicine and Geography', *History of Science*, no 25, 1987.

Mackay, Mary, 'Objects, Stereotypes and Cultural Exchange' in Maryanne Dever (ed.), *Australia and Asia: Cultural Transactions*, Honolulu, 1997.

Mathews, Jill Julius, 'Building the Body Beautiful', *Australian Feminist Studies*, no 5, 1986.

Meaney, Neville, ' The "Yellow Peril": Invasion Scare Novels and Australian Political Culture' in Ken Stewart (ed.), *The 1890s: Australian Literature and Literary Culture*, St Lucia, 1996.

Megaw, Ruth, 'Prickly Pear and the Panama-Pacific Exposition: An Incident in Commonwealth Relations', *Journal of the Royal Australian Historical Society*, vol 55, no 2, 1969.

——, 'Australia and the Great White Fleet 1908', *Journal of the Royal Australian Historical Society*, vol 56 Pt 2, 1970.

——, 'The Australian Goodwill Mission to the Far East in 1934: Its Significance in the Evolution of Australian Foreign Policy', *Journal of the Royal Australian Historical Society*, vol 59, part 4, 1973.

——, 'White Diplomacy and Yellow Gold: The Appointment of Australia's First Governmental Representative in China', *Journal of the Royal Australian Historical Society*, vol 62, no 1, 1976.

Menzies, Jackie, 'Never the twain shall meet ... Australian artists and the Orient', *Art in Australia*, vol 31, no 4, 1994.

Mills, Carol, 'The Bookstall Novel: an Australian Paperback Revolution', in David Walker and Martyn Lyons (eds), *Books, Readers, Reading*, Australian Cultural History, no 11, 1992.

Murray, Jacqui, 'Japan: the national news story that was not told', *Australian Studies in Journalism*, no 3, 1994.

O'Brien, John B, 'Empire *v* National Interests in Australian-British Relations during the 1930s', *Historical Studies*, vol 22, no 89, 1987.

Oehling, Richard A, 'The Yellow Menace: Asian Images in American Film' in Randall M Miller (ed.), *The Kalaidoscope Lens: How Hollywood Views Ethnic Groups*, Englewood, NJ, 1995.

Peers, Juliet, 'The Tribe of Mary Jane Hicks: Imaging Women through the Mount Rennie Rape Case 1886', in David Walker, Stephen Garton and Julia Horne (eds), *Crimes and Trials*, Australian Cultural History, no 12, 1993.

Powell, J M, 'Taylor, Stefansson and the Arid Centre: An Historical Encounter of 'Environmentalism' and 'Possibilism'', *Journal of the Royal Australian Historical Society*, vol 66, December 1980.

Ross, A T, 'Australian Overseas Trade and National Development Policy 1932-1939: A Story of Colonial Larrikins or Australian Statesmen?, *Australian Journal of Politics and History*, vol 36, no 2, 1990.

Schran, Peter, 'The Minor Significance of Commercial Relations between the United States and China, 1850-1931', in Ernest R May and John K Fairbank (eds), *America's China Trade in Historical Perspective: The Chinese and American Performance*, Cambridge, Mass, 1986.

Serle, Jessie, 'Asian and Pacific Influences in Australian Domestic Interiors, 1788-1914', *Fabrications*, vol 4, June 1993.

Shohat, Ella, 'Gender and Culture of Empire: Toward a Feminist Ethnography of the Cinema', *Quarterly Review of Film & Video*, vol 13, 1991.

Sissons, D C S, 'Early Australian Contacts with Japan', *Hemisphere*, vol 16, no 4, April 1972.

——, ' Manchester v Japan: The Imperial Background of the Australian Trade Diversion Dispute with Japan, 1936', *Australian Outlook*, vol 30, no 3, 1976.

Stafford, David A T, 'Spies and Gentlemen: Birth of the British Spy Novel, 1893-1914', *Victorian Studies*, vol 24, no 4, 1981.

Stoler, Ann L, 'Making Empire Respectable: the Politics of Race and Sexual Morality in 20th-century Colonial Cultures', *American Ethnologist*, vol 16, no 4, 1989.

——, 'Rethinking Colonial Categories: European Communities and the Boundaries of Rule', *Comparative Studies in Society and History*, vol 13, no 1, 1989.

Trotter, David, 'Introduction', in Erskine Childers, *The Riddle of the Sands* [1903], Oxford, 1995.

Tsokhas, Kosmas, 'The Wool Industry and the 1936 Trade Diversion Dispute between Australia and Japan', *Australian Historical Studies*, vol 23, no 93, 1989.

Walker, David, 'Continence for a Nation: Seminal Loss and National Vigour', *Labour History*, May 1985.

——, 'Modern Nerves/ Nervous Moderns', in S L Goldberg and F B Smith (eds), *Australian Cultural History*, Melbourne, 1988.

——, 'Invasion Literature: The Yellow Wave: Moulding the Popular Imagination', *Asian Influences on Australian Literature: Proceedings of a Symposium,* Library Society, State Library of New South Wales, Sydney, 1988.

——, 'Introduction: Australian Modern: Modernism and its Enemies', *Journal of Australian Studies,* no 32, 1993.

——, 'Climate, Civilization and Character in Australia, 1880-1940', in David Walker and Michael Bennett (eds), *Intellect and Emotion, Australian Cultural History*, no 16, 1997.

——, 'Australia as Asia' in Wayne Hudson and Geoffrey Bolton (eds), *Creating Australia: Changing Australian History*, Sydney, 1997.

Wang, Sing-wu, 'Diplomatic Relations between China and Australia prior to the establishment of the Chinese Consulate in Melbourne in 1909', *Chinese Culture*, vol x, no 2, June 1969.

Waterhouse, Richard, 'The Beginning of Hegemony or a Confluence of Interests: the Australian-American Relationship, 1788-1908', *Australasian Journal of American Studies*, vol 9, no 2, 1990.

Wilson, Sandra, 'The Manchurian Crisis and Moderate Japanese Intellectuals: The Japan Council of the Institute of Pacific Relations', *Modern Asian Studies*, vol 26, no 3, 1992.

Woods, Lawrence T , 'Regional Diplomacy and the Institute of Pacific Relations', *Journal of Developing Societies*, vol VIII, no 2, 1992.

Woolcock, Helen R, '"Our Salubrious Climate": Attitudes to Health in Colonial Queensland', in Roy Mcleod and Milton Lewis (eds), *Disease, Medicine and Empire*, London, 1988.

Manuscripts and archival holdings

Australia and Japan Newspaper Cuttings 1895-1898, vol 56, Mitchell Library, Sydney.

Australian Archives, Series A457/1, Canberra.

——, Commerce-East General, Series B323/1/5, Canberra.

——, Series 1009/9/214, Canberra.

——, Series A597, A1924/10129, Canberra.

——, Series A458, I 510/2, Canberra.

Bedford, Randolph, 'White Australia, or The Empty North', unpublished manuscript, Australian Archives, Canberra.

British Immigration League of Australia, MSS 302, Mitchell Library, Sydney.

Charles S Sperry Papers, 1862-1912, Box 13: World Cruise Correspondence, Manuscript Division, Library of Congress, Washington DC, USA.

Eleanor M Hinder Papers, MSS 770, Mitchell Library, Sydney.

E C Stedman Collection, Special Collection, Butler Library, Columbia University Libraries, Columbia University, New York, NY, USA.

Fry Family Papers, 1861-1923, MSS 1159, Mitchell Library, Sydney.

General Records of the Department of State, Despatches From US Consuls in Melbourne, Australia, RG84, no 306, Microfilm T1&2, US National Archives, College Park, MD, USA.

George Ernest Morrison Papers, MSS 312, Mitchell Library, Sydney.

Griffith Taylor Papers, MSS1003, National Library of Australia, Canberra.

Griffiths, Peter, 'The Influences of Cultural Diffusion upon the Australian House', unpublished research essay, Deakin University, 1996.

Ian Clunies Ross Papers, MSS 7485, National Library of Australia, Canberra.

James Inglis Papers, MSS6239, Mitchell Library, Sydney.

Letter-books 1876-77, File PRG 456/19, South Australian Archives, Adelaide.

Longfield Lloyd Papers, MSS2887, National Library of Australia, Canberra.

Melbourne, A C V, Papers on Foreign Policy, National Library of Australia, Canberra, Mfm G 14442-14446.

Mungoven, Rory, 'The Imperial Chinese Commissioners', unpublished research notes, September 1987.

——, 'James Murdoch: Professor of Japanese', unpublished research notes, September 1987.

——, 'Mr Miniechi Miyata: Japanese Teacher at Fort Street', unpublished research notes, 1987.

Piesse Papers, MSS 882, National Library of Australia.

Richard Arthur Papers, MSS 473, Mitchell Library, Sydney.

Records of Foreign Service Posts, Consular Posts, Sydney, Australia, National Archives and Record Administration, College Park, MD, USA.

Rubinstein, Hilary L, 'Bakhap, Thomas Jerome Kingston (1866-1923)', in 'Australia's Senators: Biographical Dictionary of the Australian Senate', manuscript in preparation, The Senate, Canberra.

Russo Papers, MSS 8202, National Library of Australia, Canberra.

Sir Frederic Eggleston Papers, MSS 423, National Library of Australia, Canberra.

Sir John Latham Papers, MSS 1009, National Library of Australia.

Sissons, D C S, 'Australian-Japanese Relations: The First Phase 1859-91', unpublished paper, School of Pacific Studies, Australian National University, 1980.

Smith, Jo, 'The Girl of The Never Never; an original drama in four acts', unpublished script, c1912, Northern Territory Library.

State Department Records of the Cruise of the Atlantic Fleet to the Pacific, General Records of the State Department (RG 59), Numerical and Minor File, 1906-1910, microfilm # M862, National Archives and Record Administration, College Park, MD, USA.

University of Sydney Archives, G3/13 File no 8290.

Unpublished Catalogue, 'Japanese objects acquired by the museum prior to 1900', Powerhouse Museum, Sydney.

Wilson, Hardy, 'Cultural War', unpublished manuscript, 11 May 1947, Q701/W Mitchell Library, Sydney.

Wilton Hack, 'Sketch of My Life: For the Instruction and Amusement of my Beloved Children', unpublished manuscript, 30 July 1907, PRG 456/59, South Australian Archives, Adelaide.

Theses

Akami, Tomoko, 'The Liberal Dilemma: Internationalism and the Institute of Pacific Relations in the USA, Australia and Japan, 1919-1942', PhD thesis, Australian National University, Canberra, 1995.

Battersby, Paul, 'No Peripheral Concern: The International Political Implications of Australian Tin Mining Investment in Thailand, 1903 to the 1950s', PhD thesis, James Cook University, 1996.

Burnett, Genevieve, 'Fertile Fields: A History of the International Birth Control Movement c1870-1970', PhD thesis, University of New South Wales, Sydney, 1999.

Fitzmaurice, Bradley, 'Red Parasols Over an Antipodean Italy: A Study of the *Lone Hand* and the People Who Made It', MA thesis, University of New South Wales, 1986.

Johnson, Michael R, ' "Complementarity and Conflict": Australian and Japanese Relations in the Nineteenth Century', BA (Hons) thesis, University of New South Wales, October 1981.

Laurie, Ross, '"Not a Matter of Taste but a Healthy Racial Instinct". Race Relations in Australia in the 1920s: Racial Ideology and the Popular Press', MA thesis, Griffith University, 1989.

Sissons, D C S, 'Attitudes to Japan and Defence 1890-1923', 3 vol, MA thesis, University of Melbourne, 1956.

Stuart, Lurline, 'James Smith: his influence on the development of literary culture in colonial Melbourne', PhD thesis, Monash University, 1983.

Takeda, I, 'Australia-Japan Relations in the Era of the Anglo-Japanese Alliance, 1896-1911, PhD thesis, University of Sydney, 1984.

Todd, Jonathan, 'Conceptualisation of the Body in Australia, c1880-c1925', BA (Hons) thesis, University of New South Wales, 1991

Wang, Sing-wu, 'The Organization of Chinese Emigration, 1848-1888 with Special Reference to Chinese Emigration to Australia', MA, Australian National University, 1969.

Walsh, Glen, 'John Bligh Suttor and the New South Wales Commercial Agency in the East', BA (Hons) thesis, University of Sydney, 1979.

Witham, M C, 'Prejudice, Attitude and Belief: Aspects of Australian Perceptions of Japan, 1919 to 1939', BA (Hons) thesis, University of New South Wales, 1987.

Films

Longford, Raymond (director), J Barr and C A Jeffries (script writers), *Australia Calls*, Sydney, 1913.

Mamoulian, Rouben (director), Salka Viertel and S N Behrman (scriptwriters), *Queen Christina*, Los Angeles, 1933.

Electronic databases

Pesman, Ros, David Walker and Richard White (eds), compiled by Terri McCormack, *Annotated Bibliography of Australian Overseas Travel Writing, 1830 to 1970*, Canberra, 1996.

Index

UQP Australian Studies